Semantics

Second Edition

John I. Saeed

Blackwell
Publishing

350 Main Street, Malden, MA 02148-5018, USA
108 Cowley Road, Oxford OX4 1JF, UK
550 Swanston Street, Carlton South, Melbourne, Victoria 3053, Australia
Kurfürstendamm 57, 10707 Berlin, Germany

First edition published 1997
Second edition published 2003 by Blackwell Publishing Ltd

Library of Congress Cataloging-in-Publication Data

Saeed, John I.
  Semantics / by John I. Saeed.—2nd ed.
    p. cm. — (Introducing linguistics ; 2)
  Includes bibliographical references and index.
    ISBN 0-631-22692-3 (hardcover : alk. paper) — ISBN 0-631-22693-1 (pbk. : alk. paper)
    1. Semantics. I. Title. II. Series.
  P325 .S2 2003
  401′.43—dc21

                                                      2002007791

A catalogue record for this title is available from the British Library.

Set in 10.5/12pt Plantin
by Graphicraft Limited, Hong Kong
Printed and bound in the United Kingdom
by MPG Books Ltd, Bodmin, Cornwall

For further information on
Blackwell Publishing, visit our website:
http://www.blackwellpublishing.com

Semantics

Introducing Linguistics

This outstanding series is an indispensable resource for students and teachers – a concise and engaging introduction to the central subjects of contemporary linguistics. Presupposing no prior knowledge on the part of the reader, each volume sets out the fundamental skills and knowledge of the field, and so provides the ideal educational platform for further study in linguistics.

1. Andrew Spencer   *Phonology*
2. John I. Saeed   *Semantics*, Second Edition
3. Barbara Johnstone   *Discourse Analysis*
4. Andrew Carnie   *Syntax*

To Joan and Alexander

Contents

Figures and Tables

Figures

Table

Preface

This is an introduction to semantics for readers new to the subject. The aim of the book is not to propose a new theory of semantics, nor to promote any single current approach but to give the reader access to some of the central ideas in the field and an introduction to some of its most important writers. Semantics, however, is a very broad and diverse field and keeping the book to a manageable size has involved a fairly firm selection of topics. Inevitably this selection will not please everyone but I hope readers will be able to gain a feel for what doing semantics is like, and gain the background to proceed to more advanced and specialized material in the primary literature.

The book assumes no knowledge of semantics but does assume a general idea of what linguistics is, and some familiarity with its traditional division into fields like phonetics, phonology, morphology, syntax, etc. Thus it would be useful if the reader had already looked at a general introduction to linguistics.

The book is organized into eleven chapters, which are grouped into three main sections. Part I, **Preliminaries**, consists of the first two chapters and is concerned with the place of semantics within linguistics and its relations with the disciplines of philosophy and psychology, which share some of the same interests. Part II, **Semantic Description**, is the main part of the book and introduces central topics in the analysis of word and sentence meaning. Part III, **Theoretical Approaches**, reviews three important semantic theories: componential theory, formal semantics and cognitive semantics.

Each chapter includes a set of exercises to allow the reader to explore the issues raised, and suggestions for further reading. These will be a small selection of works which provide accessible investigations of the chapter's topics. In the text there are a large number of references to the semantics literature. These will frequently be works which are too specialized to attempt before the reader completes this book, but are given so that any particular interests may be followed up.

Examples from different languages are given in the transcription of the original source, and are commented on only when it is germane to the discussion. A list of symbols and abbreviations used in this text is given in the Abbreviations and Symbols list on pp. xix–xx.

I have used this book as a text in my courses in the Centre for Language and Communication Studies, Trinity College Dublin. I would like to thank my students for their responses and comments which have been invaluable in getting the text into its present form. I am indebted to Philip Jaggar, Mark Keane, James Levine and Feargal Murphy, who read the entire manuscript and made many suggestions, which improved the book and saved me from my worst mistakes. I am also grateful to those who commented on particular sections, discussed specific language data, and provided me with source materials, in particular Abdullahi Dirir Hersi, Jim Jackson, Jeffrey Kallen, Ruth Kempson, Patricia Maguire, Cathal O Háinle, Sarah Smyth, Tony Veale and Sheila Watts. I am also indebted to two anonymous reviewers of a preliminary draft who made detailed and very helpful suggestions. None of the above is of course responsible for how the book turned out in the end; that is entirely my responsibility. The first draft of the book was written while I was enjoying the academic hospitality of the Department of African Languages and Cultures of the School of Oriental and African Studies, University of London. I would like to thank the members of that department, in particular Dick Hayward and Philip Jaggar, for making my time there so enjoyable and profitable. That visit was supported by the Trinity College Dublin Arts and Social Sciences Benefactions Fund. I would like to acknowledge the encouragement and support of my colleagues in CLCS who make the Centre such a stimulating and enjoyable environment for research and teaching. In particular, I would like to thank its Director, David Little, for technical and administrative support in writing this book and John Duggan for help with all things computing.

For this second edition I would like to thank all of the colleagues, readers and users of this book who sent me their comments. I would like to thank in particular Barbara Abbott, Martin Emms, Tim Fernando, Jeffrey Kallen, Tadaharu Tanomura, Ib Ulbaek and Carl Vogel. I would also like to thank the anonymous reviewers who commented on the proposed revisions. I have made changes throughout the book that I hope will improve it but time and space constraints have meant that I have not been able to reflect all of the valuable comments I received. Finally I owe my greatest debts to Joan for her patience and support and to Alexander for getting me away from it all.

The extract from the screenplay of *Interiors* in chapter 7 is used by kind permission, © 1977 United Artists Corporation. All rights reserved.

J.I.S.

Abbreviations and Symbols

ACC	accusative case
ADJ	adjective
ADV	adverb
AG	agent
AP	adjectival phrase
ART	article
CLASS	classifier
DECL	declarative
DET	determiner
ERG	ergative
f	feminine gender
FUT	future tense
GEN	genitive case
IMP	imperative
IMPERF	imperfective aspect
IMPERS	impersonal
IN	instrument
INDIC	indicative mood
LO	location
m	masculine gender
N	noun
NOMIN	nominative case

NP	noun phrase
P	preposition
PA	patient
PAST	past tense
PERF	perfective aspect
pl	plural
PP	prepositional phrase
PRES	present tense
Q	interrogative
RE	recipient
S	sentence
sg	singular
SO	source
SUBJUN	subjunctive
TH	theme
V	verb
VP	verb phrase
1	first person
2	second person
3	third person
⋆	ungrammatical
?	semantically odd
[ ]	boundaries of a syntactic constituent
[$_{NP}$]	method of labelling a syntactic constituent, here an NP

Logical symbols:

$\neg$	not
$\wedge$	and
$\vee$	or
$\rightarrow$	if . . . then
$\vee_e$	exclusive or
$\equiv$	if and only if, equivalence
$\exists$	existential quantifier
$\forall$	universal quantifier

Less commonly known language names are introduced with the name of the large language family (phylum) they belong to and an indication of where the language is spoken, e.g. Tiv (Niger-Congo; Nigeria).

Preliminaries

part I

chapter 1

Semantics in Linguistics

1.1 Introduction

Semantics is the study of meaning communicated through language. This book is an introduction to the theory and practice of semantics in modern linguistics. Although this is not an introduction to any single theory, we begin with a basic assumption: that a person's linguistic abilities are based on knowledge that they have. It is this knowledge that we are seeking to investigate. One of the insights of modern linguistics is that speakers of a language have different types of linguistic knowledge, including how to pronounce words, how to construct sentences, and about the meaning of individual words and sentences. To reflect this, linguistic description has different **levels of analysis**. So **phonology** is the study of what sounds a language has and how these sounds combine to form words; **syntax** is the study of how words can be combined into sentences; and **semantics** is the study of the meanings of words and sentences.

The division into levels of analysis seems to make sense intuitively: if you are learning a foreign language you might learn a word from a book, know what it means but not know how to pronounce it. Or you might hear a word, pronounce it perfectly but not know what it means. Then again, you might know the pronunciation and meaning of, say, a noun, but not know how its plural is formed or what its genitive case looks like. In this sense knowing a word unites different kinds of knowledge, and this is just as true of your knowledge of how to construct phrases and sentences.

Since linguistic description is an attempt to reflect a speaker's knowledge, the semanticist is committed to describing semantic knowledge. This knowledge allows English speakers to know, for example, that both the following sentences describe the same situation:

1.1   In the spine, the thoracic vertebrae are above the lumbar vertebrae.

1.2   In the spine, the lumbar vertebrae are below the thoracic vertebrae.

that 1.3 and 1.4 below **contradict** each other:

1.3   Addis Ababa is the capital of Ethiopia.

1.4   Addis Ababa is not the capital of Ethiopia.

that 1.5 below has several possible meanings, i.e. is **ambiguous**:

1.5   She gave her the slip.

that 1.6 below **entails** 1.7:

1.6   Henry murdered his bank manager.

1.7   Henry's bank manager is dead.

We will look at these types of semantic knowledge in more detail a little later on; for now we can take **entailment** to mean a relationship between sentences so that if a sentence *A* entails a sentence *B*, then if we know *A* we automatically know *B*. Or alternatively, it should be impossible, at the same time, to assert *A* and deny *B*. Knowing the effect of inserting the word *not*, or about the relationships between *above* and *below*, and *murder* and *dead*, are aspects of an English speaker's semantic knowledge, and thus should be part of a semantic description of English.

As our original definition of semantics suggests, it is a very broad field of inquiry, and we find scholars writing on very different topics and using quite different methods, though sharing the general aim of describing semantic knowledge. As a result semantics is the most diverse field within linguistics. In addition, semanticists have to have at least a nodding acquaintance with other disciplines, like philosophy and psychology, which also investigate the creation and transmission of meaning. Some of the questions raised in these neighbouring disciplines have important effects on the way linguists do semantics. In chapter 2 we discuss some of these questions, but we begin in this chapter by looking at the basic tasks involved in establishing semantics as a branch of linguistics.

1.2 Semantics and Semiotics

So we see our basic task in semantics as showing how people communicate meanings with pieces of language. Note, though, that this is only part of a larger enterprise of investigating how people understand meaning. Linguistic meaning is a special subset of the more general human ability to use signs, as we can see from the examples below:

1.8   Those vultures mean there's a dead animal up ahead.

1.9   His high temperature may mean he has a virus.

1.10   The red flag means it's dangerous to swim.

1.11   Those stripes on his uniform mean that he is a sergeant.

The verb *mean* is being put to several uses here, including inferences based on cause and effect, and on knowledge about the arbitrary symbols used in public signs. These uses reflect the all-pervasive human habit of identifying and creating signs: of making one thing stand for another. This process of creating and interpreting symbols, sometimes called **signification**, is far wider than language. Scholars like Ferdinand de Saussure (1974) have stressed that the study of linguistic meaning is a part of this general study of the use of sign systems, and this general study is called **semiotics**.[1] Semioticians investigate the types of relationship that may hold between a sign and the object it represents, or, in de Saussure's terminology, between a **signifier** and its **signified**. One basic distinction, due to C. S. Peirce, is between **icon**, **index** and **symbol**. An icon is where there is a similarity between a sign and what it represents, as for example between a portrait and its real-life subject, or a diagram of an engine and the real engine. An index is where the sign is closely associated with its signified, often in a causal relationship; thus smoke is an index of fire. Finally, a symbol is where there is only a conventional link between the sign and its signified, as in the use of insignia to denote military ranks, or perhaps the way that mourning is symbolized by the wearing of black clothes in some cultures, and white clothes in others. In this classification, words would seem to be examples of verbal symbols.[2]

In our discussion of semantics we will leave this more comprehensive level of investigation and concentrate on linguistic meaning. The historical development between language and other symbolic systems is an open question: what seems clear is that language represents man's most sophisticated use of signs.

1.3 Three Challenges in Doing Semantics

Analysing a speaker's semantic knowledge is an exciting and challenging task, as we hope to show in this book. We can get some idea of how challenging by adopting a simple but intuitively attractive theory of semantics which we can call the **definitions theory**. This theory would simply state that to give the meaning of linguistic expressions we should establish definitions of the meanings of words. We could then assume that when a speaker combines words to form sentences according to the grammatical rules of her[3] language, the word definitions are combined to form phrase and then sentence definitions, giving us the meanings of sentences. Let us investigate putting this approach into practice.

As soon as we begin our task of attaching definitions to words, we will be faced with a number of challenges. Three in particular prove very tricky for our theory. The first is the problem of **circularity**. How can we state the meaning of a word, except in other words, either in the same or a different language? This is a problem that faces dictionary writers: if you look up a word like *ferret* in a monolingual English dictionary, you might find a definition like 'Domesticated albino variety of the polecat, *Mustela putorius*, bred for hunting rabbits, rats, etc.' To understand this, you have to understand the words in the definition. According to our aims for semantics, we have to describe the meanings of these words too, beginning with *domesticated*. The definition for this might be 'of animals, tame, living with human beings'. Since this definition is also in words, we have to give the meaning, for example, of *tame*. And so on. If the definitions of word meaning are given in words, the process might never end. The question is: can we ever step outside language in order to describe it, or are we forever involved in circular definitions?

A second problem we will meet is how to make sure that our definitions of a word's meaning are exact. If we ask where the meanings of words exist, the answer must be: in the minds of native speakers of the language. Thus meaning is a kind of knowledge. This raises several questions; for example: is there a difference between this kind of knowledge and other kinds of knowledge that people have? In particular: can we make a distinction between **linguistic knowledge** (about the meaning of words) and **encyclopaedic knowledge** (about the way the world is)? For example, if I believe that a whale is a fish, and you believe that it is a mammal, do our words have different meanings when we both use the noun *whale*? Presumably you still understand me when I say *I dreamt that I was swallowed by a whale*.

There is another aspect to this problem: what should we do if we find that speakers of a language differ in their understanding of what a word means? Whose knowledge should we pick as our 'meaning'? We might avoid the decision by picking just one speaker and limiting our semantic description to an **idiolect**, the technical term for an individual's language. Another strategy to resolve differences might be to identify experts and use their knowledge, but as we shall see, moving away from ordinary speakers to use a scientific definition for words has the danger of making semantics equivalent to all of science. It also ignores the fact that most of us seem to understand each other talking about, say, animals, without any training in zoology. This is a point we will come back to in chapter 2.

A third type of challenge facing us comes from looking at what particular utterances mean in context. For example: if someone says to you *Marvellous weather you have here in Ireland*, you might interpret it differently on a cloudless sunny day than when the rain is pouring down. Similarly *He's dying* might mean one thing when said of a terminally ill patient, and another as a comment watching a stand-up comedian failing to get laughs. Or again: *It's getting late* if said to a friend at a party might be used to mean *Let's leave*. The problem here is that if features of context are part of an utterance's meaning then how can we include them in our definitions? For a start, the number of possible situations, and therefore of interpretations, is enormous if not infinite. It doesn't seem likely that we could fit all the relevant information into our definitions.

These three issues: circularity; the question of whether linguistic knowledge is different from general knowledge; and the problem of the contribution of context to meaning, show that our definitions theory is too simple to do the job we want. Semantic analysis must be more complicated than attaching definitions to linguistic expressions. As we shall see in the rest of this book, semanticists have proposed a number of strategies for improving on this initial position. In the next section we discuss some initial ideas that will enable us to follow these strategies.

1.4 Meeting the Challenges

In most current linguistic theories, semantic analysis is as important a part of the linguist's job as, say, phonological analysis. Theories differ on details of the relationship between semantics and other levels of analysis like syntax and morphology, but all seem to agree that linguistic analysis is incomplete without semantics. We need, it seems, to establish a semantic component in our theories. We have to ask: how can we meet the three challenges outlined in the last section? Clearly we have to replace a simple theory of definitions with a theory that successfully solves these problems.

One of the aims of this book is to show how various theories have sought to provide solutions to these problems and we will return to them in detail over subsequent chapters. For now we will simply mention possible strategies which we will see fleshed out later. To cope with the problem of circularity, one solution is to design a semantic **metalanguage** with which to describe the semantic units and rules of all languages. We use metalanguage here with its usual meaning in linguistics: the tool of description. So in a grammar of Arabic written in French, Arabic is the *object language* and

French the *metalanguage*. An ideal metalanguage would be neutral with respect to any natural languages, i.e. would not be unconsciously biased towards English, French, etc. Moreover it should satisfy scientific criteria of clarity, economy, consistency, etc. We will see various proposals for such a metalanguage, for example to represent word meanings and the semantic relations between words, in chapters 9 and 10. We will also meet claims that such a metalanguage is unattainable and that the best policy is to use ordinary language to describe meaning.

For some linguists, though, translation into even a perfect metalanguage would not be a satisfactory semantic description. Such a line of reasoning goes like this: if words are symbols, they have to relate to something; otherwise what are they symbols of? In this view, to give the semantics of words we have to ground them in something non-linguistic. In chapter 2 we will review the debate about whether the things that words signify are real objects in the world or thoughts.

Setting up a metalanguage might help too with the problem of relating semantic and encyclopaedic knowledge, since designing meaning representations, for example for words, involves arguing about which elements of knowledge should be included. To return to our earlier example of *whale*: we assume that English speakers can use this word because they know what it means. The knowledge a speaker has of the meaning of words is often compared to a mental **lexicon** or dictionary. Yet if we open a real dictionary at the entry for *whale*, the definition is likely to begin 'large marine mammal . . .'. To rephrase our earlier question: does it follow that someone who doesn't know that whales are mammals fails to understand the meaning of the word *whale*? What if the speaker knows that it is a large animal that lives in the sea, but is hazy after that? The real issue is the amount of knowledge that it is necessary to know in order to use a word. We shall see aspects of this debate, which is really part of the general psychological debate about the representation of concepts and categories, in chapters 2, 3 and 7.

In tackling the third problem, of context, one traditional solution has been to assume a split in an expression's meaning between the local contextual effects and a context-free element of meaning, which we might call **conventional** or **literal** meaning. We could perhaps try to limit our definitions to the literal part of meaning and deal with contextual features separately. As we shall see in chapter 3, though, it turns out to be no easy task to isolate the meaning of a word from any possible context. We discuss some aspects of this idea of literal meaning in 1.6.3 below. The other side of such an approach is to investigate the role of contextual information in communication, and try to establish theories of how speakers amalgamate knowledge of context with linguistic knowledge. As we shall see in chapter 7, it seems that speakers and hearers cooperate in using various types of contextual information. Investigating this leads us to a view of the listener's role which is quite different from the simple, but common, analogy of decoding a coded message. We shall see that listeners have a very active role, using what has been said, together with background knowledge, to make inferences about what the speaker meant. The study of these processes and the role in them of context is often assigned to a special area of study called **pragmatics**. We discuss the relationship between semantics and pragmatics in 1.6.4 below. We shall see instances of the role of context in meaning throughout this book and this will give us the opportunity to review the division of labour between semantics and this newer field of pragmatics.[4]

Each of these strategies will be investigated in later chapters of this book: the creation of semantic metalanguages, the modelling of conceptual knowledge, the theory of literal language, and factoring out context into pragmatics. Meanwhile in the next section we look at how semantics might fit into a model of language.

1.5   Semantics in a Model of Grammar

1.5.1   Introduction

As has been suggested already, for many linguists the aim of doing semantics is to set up a component of the grammar which will parallel other components like syntax or phonology. Linguists like to draw flowchart-style diagrams of grammatical models, and in many of them there is a box labelled 'semantics', as in figure 1.1:

Figure 1.1   Components of grammar

Before we go on, it might be worthwhile to consider whether it is justified to view semantics as a component equal and parallel to, say, syntax.

We saw earlier that linguists identify different levels of analysis. Another way of describing this is to say that linguistic knowledge forms distinct **modules**, or is **modularized**. As a result, many linguistic theories are themselves modularized, having something like our boxes in figure 1.1. Our question, though, remains: what kind of module is semantics? The answer varies from theory to theory. The real problem is, of course, that units at all linguistic levels serve as part of the general enterprise: to communicate meaning. This means that in at least one sense, meaning is a product of all linguistic levels. Changing one phoneme for another, one verb ending for another, or one word order for another will produce differences of meaning. This view leads some writers to believe that meaning cannot be identified as a separate level, autonomous from the study of other levels of grammar. A strong version of this view is associated with the theory known as **cognitive grammar,** advocated by linguists such as Ronald Langacker (e.g. Langacker 1987);[5] see, for example, this claim from a recent collection of articles:

1.12   the various autonomy theses and dichotomies proposed in the lin-
        guistic literature have to be abandoned: a strict separation of syn-
        tax, morphology and lexicon is untenable; furthermore it is
        impossible to separate linguistic knowledge from extra-linguistic
        knowledge.   (Rudzka-Ostyn 1993: 2)

As we shall see in the course of this book, however, many other linguists
do see some utility in maintaining both types of distinction referred to
above: between linguistic and non-linguistic knowledge; and within linguistic
knowledge, identifying distinct modules for knowledge about pronunciation,
grammar and meaning.

1.5.2   Word meaning and sentence meaning

If an independent component of semantics is identified, one central issue is
the relationship between word meaning and sentence meaning. Knowing a
language, especially one's native language, involves knowing thousands of
words. As mentioned earlier, we can call the mental store of these words a
lexicon, making an overt parallel with the lists of words and meanings
published as dictionaries. We can imagine the mental lexicon as a large but
finite body of knowledge, part of which must be semantic. This lexicon is
not completely static because we are continually learning and forgetting
words. It is clear, though, that at any one time we hold a large amount of
semantic knowledge in memory.
   Phrases and sentences also have meaning, of course, but an important difference between word meaning on the one hand, and phrase and sentence
meaning on the other, concerns **productivity**. It is always possible to create
new words, but this is a relatively infrequent occurrence. On the other hand,
speakers regularly create sentences that they have never used or heard before,
confident that their audience will understand them. Noam Chomsky in particular has commented on the creativity of sentence formation (for example
Chomsky 1965: 7–9). It is one of generative grammar's most important
insights that a relatively small number of combinatory rules may allow speakers
to use a finite set of words to create a very large, perhaps infinite, number
of sentences. To allow this the rules for sentence formation must be **recursive**,
allowing repetitive embedding or coordination of syntactic categories. To
give a simple example, a compositional rule like 1.13 below, where elements
in parentheses are optional and the asterisk means the optional group is
repeatable, will allow potentially limitless expansions of S, as in 1.14:

1.13   S → [$_S$ S (and S)*]

1.14   a.   [$_S$ S and S]
        b.   [$_S$ S and S and S]]
        c.   [$_S$ S and S and S and S] etc.

The idea is that you can always add another clause to a sentence, or, as 1.15 and 1.16 below show, another nominal within a nominal:

1.15   NP → [$_{NP}$ NP (and NP)*]

1.16   a. I bought [$_{NP}$ a book]
        b. I bought [$_{NP}$ [$_{NP}$ a book] and [$_{NP}$ a magazine]]
        c. I bought [$_{NP}$ [$_{NP}$ a book] and [$_{NP}$ a magazine] and [$_{NP}$ some pens]] etc.

See Lyons (1968: 221–2) for discussion of such recursive rules in syntax.

This insight has implications for semantic description. Clearly, if a speaker can make up novel sentences and these sentences are understood, then they obey the semantic rules of the language. So the meanings of sentences cannot be listed in a lexicon like the meanings of words: they must be created by rules of combination too. Semanticists often describe this by saying that sentence meaning is **compositional**. This term means that the meaning of an expression is determined by the meaning of its component parts and the way in which they are combined.

This brings us back to our question of levels. We see that meaning is in two places, so to speak, in a model of grammar: a more stable body of word meanings in the lexicon, and the limitless composed meanings of sentences. How can we connect semantic information in the lexicon with the compositional meaning of sentences? It seems reasonable to conclude that semantic rules have to be compositional too and in some sense 'in step' with grammatical rules. The relationship is portrayed differently in different theories of language. In the evolving forms of Noam Chomsky's generative grammar (e.g. Chomsky 1965, 1988) syntactic rules operate independently of semantic rules but the two types are brought together at a level of Logical Form. In many other theories semantic rules and grammatical rules are inextricably bound together, so each combination of words in a language has to permissible under both. Such an approach is typical of functional approaches like Halliday's Functional Grammar (1994), and Role and Reference Grammar (Van Valin and LaPolla 1997), as well as variants of generative grammar like Head-Driven Phrase Structure Grammar (Sag and Wasow 1999).[6]

1.6   Some Important Assumptions

At this point we can introduce some basic ideas that are assumed in many semantic theories and that will come in useful in our subsequent discussion. In most cases the descriptions of these ideas will be simple and a little on the vague side: we will try to firm them up in subsequent chapters.

Figure 1.2   Reference and sense in the vocabulary

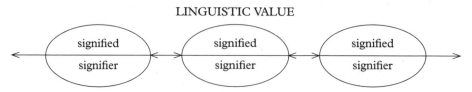

LINGUISTIC VALUE

1.6.1   Reference and sense

One important point made by the linguist Ferdinand de Saussure (1974), whose ideas have been so influential in the development of modern linguistics, is that the meaning of linguistic expressions derives from two sources: the language they are part of and the world they describe. Words stand in a relationship to the world, or our mental classification of it: they allow us to identify parts of the world, and make statements about them. Thus if a speaker says _He saw Paul_ or _She bought a dog_, the underlined nominals identify, pick out, or **refer** to specific entities in the world. However words also derive their value from their position within the language system. The relationship by which language hooks onto the world is usually called **reference.** The semantic links between elements within the vocabulary system are an aspect of their **sense**,[7] or meaning.

Ferdinand de Saussure (1974: 115) used the diagram in figure 1.2 to show this patterning. Each oval is a word, having its own capacity for reference, but each is also linked to other words in the same language, like a cell in a network. His discussion of this point is excellent and we cannot really do it justice here, except to recommend the reader to the original. His well-known examples include a comparison of English _sheep_ and French _mouton_. In some cases they can be used to refer in a similar way but their meaning differs because they are in different systems and therefore have different ranges: in English there is an extra term _mutton_, used for meat, while the French word can be used for both the animal and the meat. Thus, the meaning of a word derives both from what it can be used to refer to and from the way its semantic scope is defined by related words. So the meaning of _chair_ in English is partly defined by the existence of other words like _stool_. Similarly, the scope of _red_ is defined by the other terms in the colour system: _brown, orange, yellow_, etc. The same point can be made of grammatical systems: de Saussure pointed out that plural doesn't 'mean' the same in French, where it is opposed to singular, as it does in Sanskrit or Arabic, languages which, in addition to singular, have **dual** forms, for exactly two entities. In the French system, plural is 'two or more'; in the other systems, 'three or more'.

1.6.2   Utterances, sentences and propositions

These three terms are used to describe different levels of language. The most concrete is **utterance**: an utterance is created by speaking (or writing) a piece of language. If I say *Ontogeny recapitulates phylogeny*, this is one utterance. If another person in the same room also says *Ontogeny recapitulates phylogeny*, then we would be dealing with two utterances.

Sentences, on the other hand, are abstract grammatical elements obtained from utterances. Sentences are abstract because if a third and fourth person in the room also say *Ontogeny recapitulates phylogeny* with the same intonation, we will want to say that we have met four utterances of the same sentence. In other words, sentences are abstracted, or generalized, from actual language use. One example of this abstraction is direct quotation. If someone reports *He said 'Ontogeny recapitulates phylogeny'*, she is unlikely to mimic the original speaker exactly. Usually the reporter will use her normal voice and thus filter out certain types of information: the difference in pitch levels between men, women and children; perhaps some accent differences due to regional or social variation; and certainly those phonetic details which identify individual speakers. Speakers seem to recognize that at the level of the sentence these kinds of information are not important, and so discard them. So we can look at sentences from the point of view of the speaker, where they are abstract elements to be made real by uttering them; or from the hearer's point of view, where they are abstract elements reached by filtering out certain kinds of information from utterances.

One further step of abstraction is possible for special purposes: to identify **propositions**. In trying to establish rules of valid deduction, logicians discovered that certain elements of grammatical information in sentences were irrelevant; for example, the difference between active and passive sentences:

1.17   Caesar invaded Gaul.

1.18   Gaul was invaded by Caesar.

From a logician's perspective, these sentences are equivalent, for whenever 1.17 is true, so is 1.18. Thus the grammatical differences between them will never be significant in a chain of reasoning and can be ignored. Other irrelevant information (for these purposes) includes what we will in chapter 7 call **information structure**, i.e. the difference between the following sentences:

1.19   It was Gaul that Caesar invaded.

1.20   It was Caesar that invaded Gaul.

1.21   What Caesar invaded was Gaul.

1.22   The one who invaded Gaul was Caesar.

These sentences seem to share a description of the same state of affairs. Once again, if one is true all are true, and if one is false then all are false.

To capture this fact, logicians identify a common proposition. Such a proposition can be represented in various special ways to avoid confusion with the various sentences which represent it, e.g. by using capitals:

1.23   CAESAR INVADED GAUL.

Thus the proposition underlying the sentence *The war ended* might be written:

1.24   THE WAR ENDED.

Logicians commonly use formulae for propositions in which the verb is viewed as a function, and its subject and any objects as arguments of the function. Such formulae often delete verb endings, articles and other grammatical elements, so that corresponding to 1.23 and 1.24 we would get 1.25 and 1.26 below:

1.25   invade (Caesar, Gaul)

1.26   end (war)

Some semanticists have borrowed from logicians both this notion of proposition and the use of logical formulae. We will see various applications of such formulae in later chapters.[8] As we shall see, some linguists employ this notion of proposition in their semantic analysis, often to identify a description of an event or situation which might be a shared element in different sentences. So, for example, the statement *Joan made the sorbet*, the question *Did Joan make the sorbet?*, and the command: *Joan, make the sorbet!* might be seen to share a propositional element: JOAN MAKE THE SORBET. In this view, these different sentences allow the speaker to do different things with the same proposition: to assert it as a past event; to question it; or to request someone to bring it about.

Propositions, then, can be a way of capturing part of the meaning of sentences. They are more abstract than sentences because, as we saw in examples 1.17–22 above, the same proposition can be represented by several different statements. Moreover in non-statements like questions, orders, etc. they cannot be the complete meaning since such sentences include an indication of the speaker's attitude to the proposition. We will come back to the linguistic marking of such attitudes in chapter 8.

To sum up: **utterances** are real pieces of speech. By filtering out certain types of (especially phonetic) information we can get to abstract grammatical elements, **sentences**. By going on to filter out certain types of grammatical information, we can get to **propositions**, which are descriptions of states of affairs and which some writers see as a basic element of sentence meaning. We will get some idea of the different uses to which these terms are put in the remainder of this book.[9]

1.6.3 Literal and non-literal meaning

This distinction is assumed in many semantics texts but attempting to define it soon leads us into some difficult and theory-laden decisions. The basic distinction seems a common-sense one: distinguishing between instances where the speaker speaks in a neutral, factually accurate way, and instances where the speaker deliberately describes something in untrue or impossible terms in order to achieve special effects. Thus if one afternoon you were feeling the effects of missing lunch, you might speak literally as in 1.27, or non-literally as in 1.28–30:

1.27   I'm hungry.

1.28   I'm starving.

1.29   I could eat a horse.

1.30   My stomach thinks my throat's cut.

Non-literal uses of language are traditionally called **figurative** and are described by a host of rhetorical terms including **metaphor, irony, metonymy, synecdoche, hyperbole** and **litotes**. We will meet examples of these terms later on. On closer examination, though, it proves difficult to draw a firm line between literal and non-literal uses of language. For one thing, one of the ways languages change over time is by speakers shifting the meanings of words to fit new conditions. One such shift is by metaphorical extension, where some new idea is depicted in terms of something more familiar. For a while the new expression's metaphorical nature remains clear, as for example in the expressions *glass ceiling* for promotional barriers to women, or *surfing* the internet. Slightly older coinings might include *mouse* for the computer keyboard extension, or expressions like *toy boy*, or *junk bonds*. After a while such expressions become fossilized and their metaphorical quality is no longer apparent to speakers. It is doubtful, for example, whether anyone taking advantage of the commuter air service between London and Brussels or between New York and Washington thinks of looms or sewing machines when they talk of catching a *shuttle*. The vocabulary of a language is littered with fossilized metaphors such as these, and this continuing process makes it difficult to decide the point at which the use of a word is literal rather than figurative. Facts such as these have led some linguists, notably George Lakoff (Lakoff and Johnson 1980; Lakoff 1987), to claim that there is no principled distinction between literal and metaphorical uses of language. Such scholars see metaphor as an integral part of human categorization: a basic way of organizing our thoughts about the world. Lakoff and Johnson identify clusterings of metaphoric uses, giving them labels such as 'Time is money' to explain clusters such as 1.31 (Lakoff and Johnson 1980: 7):

1.31   You're **wasting** my time.
         This gadget will **save** you hours.
         I don't have the time to **give** you.
         How do you **spend** your time these days?
         That flat tire **cost** me an hour.
         I've **invested** a lot of time in her.

Their claim is that whole semantic fields are systematically organized around central metaphors such as these, and that their use is not just an isolated stylistic effect: that we think, culturally, of time as a commodity.

  Clearly, if sentences like *How do you spend your time these days?* are identified as metaphorical, then it will prove difficult to find any uses of language that are literal. Many linguists, however, would deny that this use of *spend* is metaphorical. The position adopted by many semanticists is that this is an example of a faded or dead metaphor. The idea is that metaphors fade over time, and become part of normal literal language, much as we described for *shuttle* above. In this approach, there *is* a valid distinction between literal and non-literal language. In what we can call the **literal language theory**, metaphors and other non-literal uses of language require a different processing strategy than literal language. One view is that hearers recognize non-literal uses as semantically odd, i.e. factually nonsensical like 'eating a horse' in 1.29 earlier, but then are motivated to give them some interpretation by an assumption that speakers generally are trying to make sense. The hearer then makes inferences in order to make sense out of a non-literal utterance. Clearly some figurative expressions like *eat a horse* are quite conventionalized (i.e. well on their way to being 'dead') and do not require much working out. Other examples of non-literal language might require a little more interpretative effort, as when a reader gets to this exchange in Sean O'Faolain's novel *And Again?* (1972: 82):

1.32   'Of course,' my host said with a sigh, 'the truth is he didn't get
          on with the wife.'
          'Really?'
          'She flew her kite a bit too often. All Dublin knew it.'

In the literal language theory, the reader's task here is firstly to reject the literal interpretation, that the husband had a phobia about kite flying, and then to work out what kind of behaviour is being referred to so obliquely here.

  We discuss hearers' assumptions about speakers' intentions in chapter 7, when we also investigate the inferences hearers routinely make to interpret utterances. In chapter 11 we discuss arguments from writers in **cognitive semantics**, like Lakoff (1987), that the literal language theory is mistaken in viewing metaphor as something extra to, and different from, ordinary literal language.

1.6.4 Semantics and pragmatics

A similarly difficult distinction is between **semantics** and **pragmatics**. These terms denote related and complementary fields of study, both concerning the transmission of meaning through language. Drawing the line between the two fields is difficult and controversial but as a preliminary we can turn to an early use of the term **pragmatics** in Charles Morris's division of semiotics:

1.33   syntax: the formal relation of signs to each other;
         semantics: the relations of signs to the objects to which the
                          signs are applicable;
         pragmatics: the relation of signs to interpreters.
                                          (adapted from Morris 1938, 1955)

Narrowing signs to *linguistic* signs, this would give us a view of pragmatics as the study of the speaker/hearer's interpretation of language, as suggested by Rudolph Carnap (1942: 9, cited in Morris 1955: 218) below:

1.34   If in an investigation explicit reference is made to the speaker, or,
         to put it in more general terms, to the user of a language, then we
         assign it to the field of pragmatics. (Whether in this case reference
         to designata is made or not makes no difference for this classifica-
         tion.) If we abstract from the user of the language and analyze only
         the expressions and their designata, we are in the field of seman-
         tics. And if, finally, we abstract from the designata also and analyze
         only the relations between the expressions, we are in (logical) syn-
         tax. The whole science of language, consisting of the three parts
         mentioned, is called semiotic.

We might interpret this, rather crudely, as:

1.35   meaning described in relation to speakers = pragmatics
            and hearers
         meaning abstracted away from users   = semantics.

   Let's investigate what this might mean, using a simple example. A speaker can utter the same sentence to a listener, e.g. *The place is closing*, and mean to use it as a simple statement, or as a warning to hurry and get that last purchase (if they're in a department store) or drink (if in a bar). It could also be an invitation or command to leave. In fact we can imagine a whole series of uses for this simple sentence, depending on the speaker's wishes and the situation the participants find themselves in. Some semanticists would claim that there is some element of meaning common to all of these uses and that this common, non-situation-specific meaning is what semantics is concerned with. On the other hand, the range of uses a sentence can be put to, depending on context, would be the object of study for pragmatics.

One way of talking about this is to distinguish between **sentence meaning** and **speaker meaning**. This suggests that words and sentences have a meaning independently of any particular use, which meaning is then incorporated by a speaker into the particular meaning she wants to convey at any one time. In this view semantics is concerned with sentence meaning and pragmatics with speaker meaning. We can see how this distinction might be used when we consider the use of pronouns, which as we mentioned earlier are very dependent on contextual support. For example if someone says to a listener *Is he awake?* we would say that the listener has to understand two things, amongst others, to get the meaning: the first is that in English sentence meaning *he* means something like 'male entity referred to by the speaker, not the speaker and not the person spoken to', and the second is how to work out who right now the speaker is referring to by *he*. In this view knowing the first is part of semantic knowledge and working out the second is a task for one's pragmatic competence.

The advantage of such a distinction is that it might free the semanticist from having to include all kinds of knowledge in semantics. It would be the role of pragmaticists to investigate the interaction between purely linguistic knowledge and general or encyclopaedic knowledge: an issue we touched on earlier. As we shall see in chapter 7, in order to understand utterances, hearers seem to use both types of knowledge, along with knowledge about the context of the utterance and common-sense reasoning, guesses etc. A semantics/pragmatics division enables semanticists to concentrate on just the linguistic element in utterance comprehension. Pragmatics would then be the field which studies how hearers fill out the semantic structure with contextual information (for example, work out who the speaker is referring to by pronouns etc.) and make inferences which go beyond the meaning of what was said to them (for example that *I'm tired* might mean *Let's go home*).

The semantics/pragmatics distinction seems then to be a useful one. The problems with it emerge when we get down to detail: precisely which phenomena are semantic and which pragmatic? As discussed in chapters 3 and 7, much of meaning seems to depend on context: it is often difficult, for example, to identify a meaning for a word that does not depend on the context of its use. Our strategy in this book will be not to try too hard to draw a line along this putative semantics/pragmatics divide. Some theorists are sceptical of the distinction (e.g. George Lakoff 1987, Langacker 1987, 1991), while others accept it but draw the line in different places. The reader is referred to discussions in Levinson (1983) and Mey (2001) for detail. What will become clear as we proceed is that it is very difficult to shake context out of language and that the structure of sentences minutely reveals that they are designed by their speakers to be uttered in specific contexts and with desired effects. Chapter 7 is largely devoted to providing examples of these contextual aspects of meaning.

1.7 Summary

In this chapter we have taken a brief look at the task of establishing semantics as a branch of linguistics. We identified three challenges to doing this: circularity, context and the status of linguistic knowledge. We will see examples of these problems and proposed solutions as we proceed through this book. We noted that establishing a semantics component in linguistic theory involves deciding how to relate word meaning and sentence meaning. Finally, we introduced some background ideas that are assumed in many semantic theories and which we will examine in more detail in subsequent chapters: reference and sense; utterance, sentence and proposition; literal and nonliteral meaning; and semantics and pragmatics. We turn to reference and sense in the next chapter.

FURTHER READING

A concise general history of linguistics is Robins (1990) and the influence of the ideas of de Saussure on modern linguistics is described in Lepschy (1982). Matthews (1993) describes American linguistics from Bloomfield to Chomsky. Two very detailed surveys of semantics, which include the topics mentioned in this chapter and others we will cover later, are Lyons (1977) and Allan (1986). These both consist of two volumes and are very useful as works of reference. An introduction to the areas covered by pragmatics is given by Mey (2001).

EXERCISES

1.1 We made the claim that meaning is **compositional**, that is, that the meaning of complex linguistic expressions is built up from the meaning of their constituent parts. However there are a number of areas where compositionality is restricted and one of these is compound words. Below is a list of English compound nouns. One very common pattern is for the second element to identify the type of thing the compound is, while the first is some kind of qualifier. So a *teacup* is a kind of cup out of which tea may be drunk. Divide the list below into two types: one where the meaning is predictable from the meaning of the two parts and a second type where the meaning is not predictable in this way. For the first type, which show a certain compositionality, how would you characterize the type of qualification made by the first part of the compound? Check your explanations against a dictionary's entries.

blackmail	foxhound	leisure centre	software
boyfriend	greenhouse	mouse mat	sunstroke
businessman	half-sister	redhead	taste bud
daydream	hotdog	six-pack	textbook
deadlock	houseboat	sky-scraper	spin-doctor
flight deck	housewife	softball	windsock

1.2   We raised the issue of a speaker's **linguistic** and **encyclopaedic knowledge**. Most English speakers will have encountered the words below, which we partly define below by their part of speech and some indication of context of use. Try to give an exact definition of their meanings, as if you were writing your own dictionary:

yew   (noun: a tree)
copper   (noun: a metal)
vodka   (noun: a drink)
hay   (noun: farming product)

How would you distinguish between the following pairs, using your original definitions as a basis?

yew/oak   copper/bronze   vodka/gin   hay/straw

When you have done this exercise, you may like to compare your definitions against a dictionary.

1.3   We used the term **reference** for the use of nominals (noun phrases and names) and pronouns to identify or pick out individuals in the world. For each of the following, imagine the sentence being spoken in an average kind of situation. Discuss which elements would be used to **refer** in your situation.

a.   This schedule is crazy.
b.   She enjoyed herself at the party.
c.   There's a policeman looking at your car.
d.   The script calls for a short fat guy.
e.   You asked for a ham sandwich; this is a ham sandwich.

1.4   Discuss the use of **figurative** language in the following extracts from (a) *The Economist* magazine and (b) *The New Scientist* magazine:

a.   The recent verdict of *Fortune* magazine was that AT&T is 'dying', and who could disagree? The telecoms giant's sales are falling, predators are snapping at its heels, and the ambitions of its boss, Michael Armstrong, lie in expensive rubble around him. Even Golden Boy, the statue that decorates the firm's New Jersey headquarters, is up for sale: the company is seeking more modest accommodation elsewhere. If it really is dying, however, nobody seems to have told AT&T. The company thinks itself in ruddy health.[10]

b. But why should cells want to detect light? The most obvious answer is that they are talking to one another, says Albrecht-Buehler. Cells in embryos might signal with photons so that they know how and where to fit into the developing body. And now he wants to learn their language. He envisages doctors telling cells what they want them to do in words they understand. You might tell cancer cells to stop growing or encourage cells near wounds to start again. 'We may learn to compose our own messages in the language of cells to compel them to carry out specialized tasks that they've never performed.'[11]

NOTES

1　For an accessible introduction to semiotics, see Sebeok (1994). A more advanced discussion is in Eco (1976).

2　There are, however, iconic elements to language, as for example the use of **onomatopoeia**, or sound symbolism, as in the English words *tick-tock, cuckoo, ratatat* and *sizzle*. Some writers claim that iconicity is a much more extensive feature of language than this; see Haiman (1985) for example.

3　To avoid cumbersome devices like 's/he', we will when discussing simple conversations use 'he' and 'she' at random.

4　For introductions to pragmatics see Levinson (1983) and Mey (2001).

5　We look at semantics within this Cognitive Grammar approach in chapter 11.

6　As mentioned earlier, in Cognitive Grammar (Langacker 1987, 1996), discussed later in chapter 11, no distinction is made between semantic and grammatical rules.

7　This distinction between sense and reference is a translation of Frege's distinction between *Sinn* and *Bedeutung*; see Frege (1980), especially the section 'On Sense and Reference' (originally published in 1892). We discuss these notions further in chapter 2.

8　See Allwood et al. (1977) for details of translating from English sentences into such logical formulae. We will look at this strategy again in chapter 10.

9　For simplicity this section has concentrated on the relationship between propositions and the utterance of full sentences. In fact, as we can see from examples 1 and 2 below, in the right context propositions can be communicated by less than full sentences:

1   What's the longest river in the world?

2   a.   The Nile is the longest river in the world.
    b.   The Nile is.
    c.   The Nile.

It seems reasonable to say that in the context of the question in 1 above, each of 2a–c can communicate the proposition THE NILE IS THE LONGEST RIVER IN THE WORLD, even though only 2a is a full sentence; 2b is a reduced or elliptical sentence, while 2c is of course just a noun phrase. This is another example of the possible indirectness of the relationship between utterances, sentences and propositions: a proposition can be communicated by the utterance of various grammatical units, one of which is a sentence. See Lyons (1981: 195ff.) for discussion of this point. We assume here that grammatical units like sentence (S), noun phrase (NP), verb phrase (VP) etc. are defined and specified at the level of syntax.

10 From *The Economist*, 23 February–1 March 2002: 69.
11 From *The New Scientist*, 23 February 2002: 33.

chapter 2

Meaning, Thought and Reality

2.1 Introduction

In this chapter we look at the basic question of how it is that we can use language to describe the world. How is it possible, for example, that by uttering strings of sounds I can convey information to a listener about what is happening in a scene, say, outside my window? Clearly all languages allow speakers to describe, or as we might say model, aspects of what they perceive. We routinely pick out, for example, individuals or locations, as in:

2.1   I saw **Nelson Mandela** on television last night.

2.2   We've just flown back from **Paris**.

where *Nelson Mandela* and *Paris* are names allowing us to do this. In semantics this action of picking out or identifying with words is often called **referring** or **denoting**. Thus one can use the word *Paris* to **refer** to or **denote** the city. The entity referred to, in this case the city, is usually called the **referent** (or more awkwardly, the **denotatum**). Some writers, like John Lyons (1977: 396–409), separate the terms **refer** and **denote**. For these writers **denote** is used for the relationship between a linguistic expression and the world, while **refer** is used for the action of a speaker in picking out entities in the world. We will adopt this usage, so that if I say *A sparrow flew into the room*, I am using the two noun phrases *a sparrow* and *the room* to refer to things in the world, while the nouns *sparrow* and *room* denote certain classes of items. In other words, referring is what speakers do, while denoting is a property of words. Another difference which follows from these definitions is that denotation is a stable relationship in a language which is not dependent on any one use of a word. Reference, on the other hand, is a moment-by-moment relationship: what entity somebody refers to by using the word *sparrow* depends on the context.

As we shall see, there are different views of how semanticists should approach this ability to talk about the world. Two of these are particularly important in current semantic theories: we can call them the **referential** (or **denotational**) approach and the **representational** approach. For semanticists adopting the first approach this action of putting words into relationship with the world *is* meaning, so that to provide a semantic description for a language we need to show how the expressions of the language can 'hook onto' the world.

Thus theories of meaning can be called **referential** (or **denotational**) when their basic premise is that we can give the meaning of words and sentences by showing how they relate to situations. Nouns, for example, are meaningful because they denote entities in the world and sentences because they denote situations and events.[1] In this approach, the difference in meaning between the sentences:

2.3   There is a casino in Grafton Street.

2.4   There isn't a casino in Grafton Street.

arises from the fact that the two sentences describe different situations. If we assume the sentences were spoken at the same time about the same street, then they can be said to be incompatible, i.e. one of them is a false description of the situation.

For semanticists adopting the second approach our ability to talk about the world depends on our mental models of it. In this view a language represents a theory about reality: about the types of things and situations in the world. Thus, as we shall see in later chapters, a speaker can choose to view the same situation in different ways. Example 2.5 below shows us that in English we can view the same situation either as an activity (2.5a) or as a state (2.5b):

2.5   a.   Joan is sleeping.
       b.   Joan is asleep.

Such decisions are influenced by each language's conventional ways of viewing situations. We can compare the three ways of saying that someone has a cold in 2.6–8 below:

2.6   English
       You have a cold.

2.7   Somali
       Hargab baa   ku   haya.
       a.cold FOCUS you has
       'A cold has you.' i.e. 'You have a cold.'

2.8   Irish
       Tá slaghdán ort.
       is   a.cold   on.you
       'A cold is on you.' i.e. 'You have a cold.'

In English and Somali, 2.6 and 2.7, we see the situation viewed as **possession**: in English the person possesses the disease; in Somali the disease possesses the person. In Irish, 2.8, the situation is viewed as **location**: the person is the location for the disease. We shall look at such differences in later chapters. The point here is that different conceptualizations influence the description of the real-world situations. Theories of meaning can be called **representational** when their emphasis is on the way that our reports about reality are influenced by the conceptual structures conventionalized in our language.

We can see these two approaches as focusing on different aspects of the same process: talking about the world. In referential theories, meaning derives from language being attached to, or grounded in, reality. In representational approaches meaning derives from language being a reflection of our conceptual structures. This difference of approach will surface throughout this book and we outline a specific referential theory in chapter 10, and versions of representational theories in chapters 9 and 11. These two approaches are influenced by ideas from philosophy and psychology and in this chapter we review some of the most important of these. We begin, however, with language: by looking at the different ways linguistic expressions can be used to refer. We then go on to ask whether reference is indeed all of meaning and examine arguments that reference relies on conceptual knowledge. Here we review some basic theories about concepts from the philosophical and psychological literature. Finally we discuss how these ideas from philosophy and psychology have influenced the ways that semanticists view the task of describing meaning.

2.2 Reference

2.2.1 Types of reference

We can begin our discussion by looking briefly at some major differences in the ways that words may be used to refer. For the introductory purposes of this chapter we will for the most part confine our discussion to the referential possibilities of names and noun phrases, which together we can call **nominals**, since the nominal is the linguistic unit which most clearly reveals this function of language. Later, in chapter 10, we look at a more fully fledged theory of denotation and discuss the denotations of other linguistic elements like verbs and sentences. In this section we discuss some basic distinctions in reference.

Referring and non-referring expressions   We can apply this distinction in two ways. Firstly there are linguistic expressions which can never be used to refer, for example the words *so, very, maybe, if, not, all.* These words do of course contribute meaning to the sentences they occur in and thus help sentences denote, but they do not themselves identify entities in the world. We will say that these are intrinsically non-referring items. By contrast, when someone says the noun *cat* in a sentence like *That cat looks vicious*, the noun is a referring expression since it is being used to identify an entity. So nouns are potentially referring expressions.

The second use of the distinction *referring*/*non-referring* concerns potentially referring elements like nouns: it distinguishes between instances when speakers use them to refer and instances when they do not. For example, the indefinite noun phrase *a cholecystectomy* is a referring expression in the following sentence:

2.9   They performed a cholecystectomy this morning.

where the speaker is referring to an individual operation, but not in:

2.10   A cholecystectomy is a serious procedure.

where the nominal has a generic interpretation. Some sentences can be ambiguous between a referring and a non-referring reading, as is well known to film writers. Our hero, on the trail of a missing woman, is the recipient of leers, or offers, when he tells a barman *I'm looking for a woman.* We know, but the barman doesn't, that our hero won't be satisfied by the non-referring reading.

Constant versus variable reference   One difference among referring expressions becomes clear when we look at how they are used across a range of different utterances. Some expressions will have the same referent across a range of utterances, e.g. *the Eiffel Tower* or *the Pacific Ocean*. Others have their reference totally dependent on context, for example the items in bold below, where to identify the referents we need to know who is speaking to whom, etc.:

2.11   **I** wrote to **you**

2.12   **She** put **it** in **my office**.

Expressions like *the Pacific Ocean* are sometimes described as having **constant reference**, while expressions like *I, you, she,* etc. are said to have **variable reference**. To identify who is being referred to by pronouns like *she, I, you,* etc. we obviously need to know a lot about the context in which these words were uttered. We look at such context-dependent elements in chapter 7, where we will use the term **deixis**, a term from Greek meaning roughly 'pointing', as a label for words whose denotational capability so obviously needs contextual support.

In fact, though, our examples so far turn out to be the extreme cases. As we shall see in chapter 7, most acts of referring rely on some contextual information: for example, to identify the referent of the nominal *the President of the United States* we need to know when it was uttered.

Referents and extensions   So far we have been looking at referential differences between expressions. We can also make useful distinctions among the things referred to by expressions. We use the term **referent** of an expression for the thing picked out by uttering the expression in a particular context; so the referent of *the capital of Nigeria* would be, since 1991, the city of Abuja. Similarly, the referent of *a toad* in *I've just stepped on a toad* would be the unfortunate animal on the bottom of my shoe.

The term **extension** of an expression is the set of things which could possibly be the referent of that expression. So the extension of the word *toad* is the set of all toads. As mentioned earlier, in the terminology of Lyons (1977), the relationship between an expression and its extension is called **denotation**.

As we mentioned, names and noun phrases, which together we can call nominals, are the paradigmatic case of linguistic elements used to refer. In the next sections we outline some of the main ways that nominals are used to refer. The referential uses of different nominals has, of course, been an important area of investigation in the philosophy of language and there is a large literature on names, common nouns, definite nominals, etc. We won't attempt to cover the philosophical arguments in detail here: we will just touch on some major aspects of nominal reference.[2]

2.2.2   Names

The simplest case of nominals which have reference might seem to be names. Names after all are labels for people, places, etc. and often seem to have little other meaning. It does not seem reasonable to ask what the meaning of *Karl Marx* is, other than helping us to talk about an individual.

Of course, context is important in the use of names: names are definite in that they carry the speaker's assumption that her audience can identify the referent. So if someone says to you:

2.13   He looks just like Eddie Murphy.

the speaker is assuming you can identify the American comedian.

But even granting the speaker's calculation of such knowledge, how do names work? This, like most issues in semantics, turns out to be not quite as simple a question as it seems and we might briefly look at a couple of suggestions from the philosophical literature.

One important approach can be termed the **description theory**, associated in various forms with Russell (1967), Frege (1980) and Searle (1958). Here a name is taken as a label or shorthand for knowledge about the referent, or in the terminology of philosophers, for one or more definite descriptions. So for *Christopher Marlowe*, for example, we might have such descriptions as *The writer of the play Dr Faustus* or *The Elizabethan playwright murdered in a Deptford tavern*. In this theory understanding a name and identifying the referent are both dependent on associating the name with the right description.

Another, very interesting, explanation is the **causal theory** espoused by Devitt and Sterelny (1987), and based on the ideas of Kripke (1980) and Donnellan (1972). This theory is based on the idea that names are socially inherited, or borrowed. At some original point, or points, a name is given, let us say to a person, perhaps in a formal ceremony. People actually present at this begin to use this name and thereafter, depending on the fate of the named person and this original group, the name may be passed on to other people. In the case of a person who achieves prominence, the name might be used by thousands or millions of people who have never met or seen the named person, or know very much about him. So the users of the name form a kind of chain back to an original naming or **grounding**. This is a very simplified sketch of this theory: for example, Devitt and Sterelny (1987: 61ff.) argue that in some cases a name does not get attached by a single grounding. It may arise from a period of repeated uses. Sometimes there are competing names and one wins out; or mistakes may be made and subsequently fixed by public practice. The great advantage of this causal theory is that it recognizes that speakers may use names with very little knowledge of the referent. It is easy to think of examples of historical figures whose names we might bandy about impressively, but, sadly for our education, about whom we might be hard pressed to say anything factual.

So where the causal theory stresses the role of social knowledge in the use of names, the description theory emphasizes the role of identifying knowledge. See Devitt and Sterelny (1987) for a detailed discussion of these proposals. The importance of this debate is that the treatment chosen for names can be extended to other nominals like **natural kinds**, a term in the philosophy of language for nouns referring to classes which occur in nature, like *giraffe* or *gold* (see S. Schwartz 1979, 1980; Churchland 1985). We will look at this proposal later in this chapter.

2.2.3 Nouns and noun phrases

Nouns and noun phrases (NPs) can be used to refer: indefinite and definite NPs can operate like names to pick out an individual, e.g.

2.14   a. I spoke to *a woman* about the noise.
        b. I spoke to *the woman* about the noise.

where of course the difference between the nominals hangs on whether the woman to whom the speaker refers is known to the listener and/or has been identified earlier in the conversation.

Definite noun phrases can also form definite descriptions where the referent is whoever or whatever fits the description, as in:

2.15   She has a crush on *the captain of the hockey team.*

An account of reference has to deal with cases where there is no referent to fit the definite description, as in Bertrand Russell's famous example:

2.16   *The King of France* is bald.

or where the referent is not real, for example *the man in the iron mask* or *the wizard of Oz.* We look at the problematic status of such sentences in chapter 4, when we discuss the semantic notion, **presupposition**.

NPs can also be used to refer to groups of individuals, either **distributively** where we focus on the individual members of the group, as in 2.17, or **collectively**, when we focus on the aggregate, as in 2.18:

2.17   *The people in the lift* avoided each other's eyes.

2.18   *The people in the lift* proved too heavy for the lift motor.

As well as individuals and groups of individuals, nominals can of course denote substances, actions and abstract ideas, e.g.

2.19   Who can afford *coffee?*

2.20   *Sleeping* is his hobby.

2.21   She has a passion for *justice.*

We will see some attempts to set up semantic classes of nominals to reflect such differences in chapter 9.

Some nominals are trickier in their denotational behaviour: for example the nominal *no student* in 2.22 below:

2.22   No student enjoyed the lecture.

where *no student* does not of course denote an individual who enjoyed the lecture. The meaning of this sentence can be paraphrased as in 2.23a, or, in a logical framework we will investigate in chapter 10, as in 2.23b:

2.23   a. Of the students, not one enjoyed the lecture.
        b. For each student *x*, *x* did not enjoy the lecture.

This complex denotational behaviour is characteristic of **quantifiers**: a class of words that in English includes *each, all, every, some, none, no.* These allow a speaker, among other things, the flexibility to predicate something of a whole class of entities, or of some subpart, for example:

2.24   *Every Frenchman* would recognize his face.

2.25   *Some Frenchmen* voted for him twice.

2.26   *A few Frenchmen* voted for him.

Speakers can combine quantifiers with negative words to produce some subtle effects; for example, the sentence:

2.27   Every American doesn't drink coffee.

which has an interpretation which is not 'The class of Americans does not drink coffee' but rather 'Not every American drinks coffee.' We will look at some proposals for describing the use of quantifiers in chapter 10. Having taken this brief look at the referential properties of nominals, in the next section we take up the more general issue of the role of reference in a theory of meaning.

2.3   Reference as a Theory of Meaning

As we observed earlier, perhaps the simplest theory of meaning is to claim that semantics *is* reference, i.e. that to give the meaning of a word one shows what it denotes. In its simplest form this theory would claim that reference picks out elements in the real world. As described by Ruth Kempson (1977: 13), such an approach might claim the following:

2.28   proper names   denote   individuals
        common names   denote   sets of individuals
        verbs   "   actions
        adjectives   "   properties of individuals
        adverbs   "   properties of actions

As she points out, there are a number of problems with this simplest version as a theory of semantics. Firstly, it seems to predict that many words have no meaning, for as we mentioned earlier, it is very difficult to find a real-world referent for words like *so, not, very, but, of.* A second problem is that many nominal expressions used by speakers do not have a referent that exists or has ever existed, as the elements in bold in 2.29–31 below:

2.29   In the painting **a unicorn** is ignoring a maiden.

2.30   **World War Three** might be about to start.

2.31   **Father Christmas** might not visit you this year.

We would have to make the rather odd claim that expressions like *unicorn*, *World War Three* and *Father Christmas* are meaningless if meaning is taken to be a relation between words and items in the real world. If a speaker using these expressions is not referring to anything in reality, and such reference *is* meaning, how do sentences 2.29–31 have meaning? Since they clearly do, it seems that we must have a more sophisticated theory of meaning.

A further problem is that even when we are talking about things in the real world, there is not always a one-to-one correspondence between a linguistic expression and the item we want to identify. To take a simple example, we can refer to the same individual in different ways, as in:

2.32   Then in 1981 Anwar El Sadat was assassinated.

2.33   Then in 1981 the President of Egypt was assassinated.

In 2.32 and 2.33 the same individual is referred to by a **name**, Anwar El Sadat, and by a **definite description**, the President of Egypt. These two expressions would share the same referent but we probably want to say they have different meanings. If so, there is more to meaning than reference. One might object that names do not really have any meaning. This is often so in English, where we commonly use names derived from other languages like Hebrew, Greek etc., but is not necessarily true of other cultures. Still, even if we allow this objection, the phenomenon is not restricted to names. You might refer to the woman who lives next door to you by various descriptions like *my neighbour*, *Pat's mother*, *Michael's wife*, *the Head of Science at St Helen's School*, etc. It seems clear that while these expressions might all refer to the same individual, they differ in meaning. Indeed it is possible to know that some nominal expressions refer to an individual but be ignorant of others that do. We might understand expressions like *the President of the United States* and *the Commander-in-chief of the United States Armed Forces* but not know that they both refer to the same man. This has traditionally been an issue in the philosophical literature where we can find similar but more complicated examples: the logician Gottlob Frege (1980) pointed out that a speaker might understand the expressions *the morning star* and *the evening star* and use them to refer to two apparently different celestial bodies without knowing that they both refer to sightings of Venus. For such a speaker, Frege noted, the following sentence would not be a tautology:

2.34   The morning star is the evening star.

and might have a very different meaning from the referentially equivalent sentence (but for our hypothetical speaker, much less informative):

2.35   Venus is Venus.

If we can understand and use expressions that do not have a real-world referent, and we can use different expressions to identify the same referent, and even use two expressions without being aware that they share the same referent, then it seems likely that meaning and reference are not exactly the same thing. Or to put it another way; there is more to meaning than reference. How should we characterize this extra dimension? One answer is to follow Frege in distinguishing two aspects of our semantic knowledge of an expression: its **sense** (Frege used the German word *Sinn*) and its **reference** (Frege's *Bedeutung*). In this division, sense is primary in that it allows reference: it is because we understand the expression *the President of Ireland* that we can use it to refer to a particular individual at any given time. Other ways of describing this same person will differ in sense but have the same reference.[3]

   If we follow this line of argument, then our semantic theory is going to be more complicated than the simple referential theory: the meaning of an expression will arise both from its sense and its reference. In the next section, we discuss some suggestions of what this sense element may be like.

2.4   Mental Representations

2.4.1   Introduction

In the last section we concluded that although reference is an important function of language, the evidence suggests that there must be more to meaning than simply denotation. We adopted the convention of calling this extra dimension **sense**.[4] In the rest of this chapter we explore the view that sense places a new level between words and the world: a level of mental representation.[5] Thus, a noun is said to gain its ability to denote because it is associated with something in the speaker/hearer's mind. This gets us out of the problem of insisting everything we talk about exists in reality, but it raises the question of what these mental representations are. One simple and very old idea is that these mental entities are images. Presumably the relationship between the mental representation (the image) and the real-world entity would then be one of resemblance; see Kempson (1977) for discussion. This might conceivably work for expressions like *Paris* or *your mother*; it might also work for imaginary entities like *Batman*. This theory, however, runs into serious problems with common nouns. This is because of the variation in images that different speakers might have of a common noun like *car* or *house*, depending on their experience. One example often cited in the literature is of the word *triangle*: one speaker may have a mental image of an equilateral triangle, another may have a mental image of an isosceles or scalene triangle. It is difficult to conceive of an image which would combine the features shared by all triangles, just as it is difficult to have an image which corresponds to all cars or dogs. This is to ignore the difficulties of what kind of image one might have for words like *animal* or *food*; or worse, *love*, *justice* or *democracy*. So even if images are associated with some words, they cannot be the whole story.

The most usual modification of the image theory is to hypothesize that the sense of some words, while mental, is not visual but a more abstract element: a concept. This has the advantage that we can accept that a concept might be able to contain the non-visual features which make a dog a dog, democracy democracy, etc. We might also feel confident about coming up with a propositional definition of a triangle, something corresponding to 'three-sided polygon, classifiable by its angles or sides'. Another advantage for linguists is that they might be able to pass on some of the labour of describing concepts to psychologists rather than have to do it all themselves. Some concepts might be simple and related to perceptual stimuli – like SUN,[6] WATER, etc. Others will be complex concepts like MARRIAGE or RETIRE-MENT which involve whole theories or cultural complexes.

This seems reasonable enough but the problem for many linguists is that psychologists are still very involved in investigating what concepts might be like. Unless we have a good idea of what a concept is, we are left with rather empty definitions like 'the sense of the word *dog* is the concept DOG'.

It is at this point that different groups of linguists part company. Some, like Kempson in the quotation below (1977: 16–17) have seemed sceptical of psychologists' success and do not see much point in basing a theory of meaning on reference, if reference is based on concepts:

2.36   What is involved in this claim that a word has as its meaning a 'convenient capsule of thought' [Edward Sapir's definition of mean-ing]? If this is a retraction from an image theory of meaning, as it is, then it is a retraction from a specific, false claim to one that is entirely untestable and hence vacuous. It does no more than substitute for the problem term *meaning* the equally opaque term *concept*.

Kempson makes this point as part of an argument for a denotational seman-tics and in favour of modelling sense in a formal, rather than psychological way. Linguists who favour a representational approach have gone on to set up models of concepts to form the basis of semantics, throwing linguistic light onto a traditional line of research in cognitive psychology. There are a number of proposals for conceptual structure in the semantics literature; we shall look at some details of these later, especially in chapters 9 and 11. For now we can follow this representation line of enquiry and briefly examine some basic approaches from the psychological literature to the task of describing concepts.

2.4.2 Concepts

If we adopt the hypothesis that the meaning of, say, a noun, is a combination of its denotation and a conceptual element, then from the point of view of a linguist, two basic questions about the conceptual element are:

1. What form can we assign to concepts?
2. How do children acquire them, along with their linguistic labels?

We can look at some answers to these questions. In our discussion we will concentrate on concepts that correspond to a single word, i.e. that are **lexicalized**. Of course not all concepts are like this: some concepts are described by phrases, as in the underlined concept in 2.37 below:

2.37   On the shopping channel, I saw <u>a tool for compacting dead leaves into garden statuary</u>.

We can speculate that the reason why some concepts are lexicalized and others not is **utility**. If we refer to something enough it will become lexicalized. Possibly somebody once said something like 2.38 below:

2.38   We're designing a device for cooking food by microwaves.

describing something that for a while was given the two-word label *microwave oven*, but is now usually called just a *microwave*. Presumably if every home ends up having a tool to turn leaves into statues, a name for it will be invented and catch on. We see this process happening all the time, of course, as new concepts are invented and new words or new senses of old words given to them. An example of such a new word is *phreaking*, now to be found in print with its colloquial meaning 'gaining unauthorized access into telecommunications systems, for example to avoid paying telephone call charges'. Someone who does this is, naturally, a *phreaker*. For the rest of this chapter we deal only with such lexicalized concepts.

When we talk of children acquiring concepts we have to recognize that their concepts may differ from the concepts of adults. Work in developmental psychology has shown that children may operate with concepts that are quite different: students of child language describe children both **underextending** concepts, as when for a child *dog* can only be used for their pet, not the one next door; and **overextending** concepts, where a child uses *daddy* for every male adult, or *cat* for cats, rabbits and other pets. Or the concepts may be just different, reflecting the fact that items in a child's world may have different salience than for an adult. See Mervis (1987), Keil (1989) and Markman (1989) for discussion of the relationship between child and adult categorization.

2.4.3 Necessary and sufficient conditions

One traditional approach to describing concepts is to define them by using sets of **necessary and sufficient conditions**. This approach comes from thinking about concepts as follows. If we have a concept like WOMAN, it must contain the information necessary to decide when something in the world is a woman or not. How can this information be organized? Perhaps as a set of characteristics or attributes, i.e.

2.39 x is a woman if and only if L.

where L is a list of attributes, like:

2.40 x is human;
         x is adult;
         x is female, etc.

One can see these attributes as conditions: if something must have them to be a woman, then they can be called necessary conditions. In addition, if we can find the right set, so that just that set is enough to define a woman, then they can be called sufficient conditions, i.e. we have identified the right amount of information for the concept.

So this theory views concepts as lists of bits of knowledge: the necessary and sufficient conditions for something to be an example of that concept. One major problem with this approach has been that it seems to assume that if speakers share the same concept they will agree on the necessary and sufficient conditions: if something has them, it is an X; if not, not. But it has proved difficult to set these up even for nouns which identify concrete and natural kinds like *dog* or *cat*. Let us take as an example the noun *zebra*. We might agree on some attributes:

2.41   is an animal,
         has four legs,
         is striped,
         is a herbivore, etc.

The problem we face though is: which of these is necessary? The first obviously; but the rest are more problematic. If we find in a herd of zebra one that is pure white or black, we might still want to call it a zebra. Or if by some birth defect, a three-legged zebra comes into the world, it would still be a zebra. Similarly, if a single zebra got bored with a grass diet and

started to include a few insects, would it cease to be a zebra? These, you
might think, are rather whimsical questions, perhaps problems for philosophers rather than linguists, and indeed this zebra example is just a version
of Saul Kripke's example about tigers (Kripke 1980: 119–21), or Putnam's
fantasy about cats (Putnam 1962). If we suddenly discovered that cats had
always been automata rather than animals, would the meaning of the word
cat be different? Questions such as these have important consequences for
our ideas about concepts: if we cannot establish a mutual definition of a
concept, how can we use its linguistic label?

Another argument against necessary and sufficient conditions as the basis
for linguistic concepts is Putnam's (1975) observations about ignorance.
Speakers often use words to refer knowing very little, and sometimes nothing, about the identifying characteristics of the referent. Putnam's examples
include the tree names *beech* and *elm*: like Putnam, many English speakers
cannot distinguish between these two trees yet use the words regularly. Such
a speaker would presumably be understood, and be speaking truthfully, if
she said:

2.42   In the 1970s Dutch elm disease killed a huge number of British elms.

Perhaps, as Putnam suggests, we rely on a belief that somewhere there are
experts who do have such knowledge and can tell the difference between
different species of tree. In any case it seems, as with other natural kind
terms like *gold* or *platinum*, we can use the words without knowing very
much about the referent. It seems unlikely then that a word is referring to
a concept composed of a set of necessary and sufficient conditions, or what
amounts to the same thing, a **definition**.

This is reminiscent of our earlier discussion of the use of names. There
we saw that one of the advantages claimed for the causal theory of names
over the description theory is that it allows for speaker ignorance: we can
use a name for a person or place knowing little or nothing about the referent. This parallel is overtly recognized by writers such as Putnam (1975)
and Kripke (1980), who have proposed that the causal theory be extended
to natural kind terms. The idea is that natural kind terms, like names, are
originally fixed by contact with examples of the kind. Thereafter, speakers
may receive or borrow the word without being exposed to the real thing, or
knowing very much about its characteristics. As we have seen, philosophers
like to use examples of metals like gold or silver. Any inability to identify
correctly or define the substance silver does not prevent one from using
the word *silver*. We assume that someone once had the ability or need to
recognize the individual metal and that somewhere there are experts who
can identify it empirically. The latter is Putnam's 'division of labour' in
a speech community: between 'expert' and 'folk' uses of a term. Only the
expert or scientific uses of a word would ever be rigorous enough to support
necessary and sufficient conditions, but speakers happily go on using the
word.

2.4.4 Prototypes

Because of problems with necessary and sufficient conditions, or definitions, several more sophisticated theories of concepts have been proposed.
One influential proposal is due to Eleanor Rosch and her co-workers (e.g.
Rosch 1973b, 1975, Rosch and Mervis 1975, Rosch et al. 1976), who have
suggested the notion of **prototypes**. This is a model of concepts which
views them as structured so that there are central or typical members of a
category, such as BIRD or FURNITURE, but then a shading off into less typical
or peripheral members. So *chair* is a more central member of the category
FURNITURE than *lamp*, for example. Or *sparrow* a more typical member of the
category BIRD than *penguin*. This approach seems to have been supported by
Rosch's experimental evidence: speakers tend to agree more readily on typical members than on less typical members; they come to mind more quickly,
etc. Another result of this and similar work (e.g. Labov 1973) is that the
boundaries between concepts can seem to speakers uncertain, or 'fuzzy',
rather than clearly defined.

This approach allows for borderline uncertainty: an item in the world
might bear some resemblance to two different prototypes. Here we might
recall our hypothetical example in chapter 1 of an English speaker being
able to use the word *whale* yet being unsure about whether a whale is a
mammal or fish. In the prototype theory of concepts, this might be explained by the fact that whales are not typical of the category MAMMAL,
being far from the central prototype. At the same time, whales resemble
prototypical fish in some characteristic features: they live underwater in the
oceans, have fins, etc.

There are a number of interpretations of these typicality effects in the
psychology literature: some researchers, for example, have argued that the
central prototype is an abstraction. This abstraction might be a set of **characteristic features**, to which we compare real items; see Smith and Medin
(1981) for discussion. These characteristic features of BIRD might describe
a kind of average bird, small, perhaps, with wings, feathers, the ability to fly,
etc. but of no particular species. Other researchers have proposed that we
organize our categories by **exemplars**, memories of actual typical birds, say
sparrows, pigeons and hawks, and we compute the likelihood of something
we meet being a bird on the basis of comparison with these memories of
real birds. An overview of this area of investigation is given by Medin and
Ross (1992).

There is another approach to typicality effects from within linguistics,
which is interesting because of the light it sheds on the relationship between
linguistic knowledge and encyclopaedic knowledge, a topic we discussed in
chapter 1. Charles Fillmore (1982b) and George Lakoff (1987) both make
similar claims that speakers have folk theories about the world, based on
their experience and rooted in their culture. These theories are called **frames**
by Fillmore and **idealized cognitive models** (ICMs) by Lakoff.[7] They are
not scientific theories or logically consistent definitions, but collections of

cultural views. Fillmore gives an example of how these folk theories might work by using the word *bachelor*. It is clear that some bachelors are more prototypical than others, with the Pope, for example, being far from prototypical. Fillmore, and Lakoff in his discussion of the same point (1987: 68–71), suggests that there is a division of our knowledge about the word *bachelor*: part is a **dictionary**-type definition (perhaps simply 'an unmarried man') and part is an **encyclopaedia**-type entry of cultural knowledge about bachelorhood and marriage – the frame or ICM. The first we can call linguistic or semantic knowledge and the second real-world or general knowledge. Their point is we only apply the word *bachelor* within a typical marriage ICM: a monogamous union between eligible people, typically involving romantic love, etc. It is this idealized model, a form of general knowledge, which governs our use of the word *bachelor* and restrains us from applying it to celibate priests, or people living in isolation like Robinson Crusoe on his island or Tarzan living among apes in the jungle. In this view then using a word involves combining semantic knowledge and encyclopaedic knowledge, and this interaction may result in typicality effects.

Prototype theory,[8] frames and ICMs are just a few of the large number of proposals for conceptual structure. We will look at some suggestions from the specifically linguistics literature in later chapters.

2.4.5   Relations between concepts

One important issue that our discussion has bypassed so far is the **relational** nature of conceptual knowledge. We will see in chapter 3 that words are in a network of semantic links with other words and it is reasonable to assume that conceptual structures are similarly linked. Thus if all you know about *peccary* is that it is a kind of wild pig and of *pecorino* that it is a kind of Italian cheese, then your knowledge of these concepts 'inherits' knowledge you have about pigs and cheese. This has implications for our earlier discussion of how much knowledge a speaker has to have in order to use a word. It suggests that the crucial element is not the amount of knowledge but its integration into existing knowledge. Thus, knowing that a peccary is a kind of pig, together with what you know about pigs, is perhaps enough to begin to understand the meaning of sentences containing the word, and thereby to start to gain extra knowledge about the concept.

Such relations between concepts have been used to motivate models of **conceptual hierarchies** in the cognitive psychology literature. A model based on defining attributes was proposed by Collins and Quillian (1969). In this model, concepts are represented by nodes in a network, to which attributes can be attached and between which there are links. One such link is **inclusion** so that a subordinate node inherits attributes from a superordinate node. An example of such a network is in figure 2.1. Here we can see that CANARY inherits the attributes of BIRD and ANIMAL and thus inherits the attributes *breathes, eats, has skin, has wings, can fly, has*

Figure 2.1   Conceptual networks

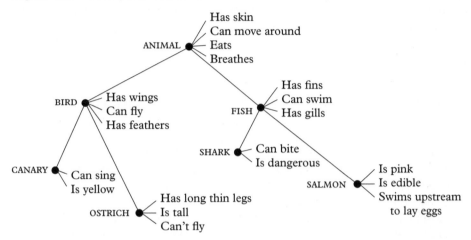

Source: Collins and Quillian (1969: 241)

feathers. We can see too that the Collins and Quillian model has the ability to block inheritance, so that for example OSTRICH does not inherit *can fly* from BIRD.

If the attributes in this model are taken to be the equivalent of the necessary and sufficient conditions we discussed earlier then it suffers from the disadvantages of that approach. Proponents of prototype theory, for example Rosch et al. (1976), have also investigated conceptual hierarchies and have proposed that such hierarchies contain three levels of generality: a superordinate level, a basic level, and a subordinate level. The idea is that the levels differ in their balance between informativeness and usefulness. If we take one of Rosch et al.'s (1976) examples, that of furniture, the superordinate level is FURNITURE, which has relatively few characteristic features; the basic level would include concepts like CHAIR, which has more features, and the subordinate level would include concepts like ARMCHAIR, DINING CHAIR, etc. which have still more features and are thus more specific again. The basic level is identified as cognitively important: it is the level that is most used in everyday life; it is acquired first by children; in experiments it is the level at which adults spontaneously name objects; such objects are recognized more quickly in tests, and so on.

This model has proved to be very robust in the psychological literature, though the simple picture we have presented here needs some modifications. It seems that the relationship between the basic level and the intermediate term might vary somewhat from domain to domain: man-made categories like FURNITURE differ somewhat from natural kind terms, and the relationship may vary depending on the person's experience of the categories. So a person's expert knowledge of a domain might influence the relationship between the basic and subordinate levels. See for example Tanaka and Taylor

(1991) for a study suggesting that experts on dogs and birds might have a different, richer structure at subordinate levels for these categories from the average person.

2.4.6 Acquiring concepts

Our second basic issue was: how do we acquire concepts? One simple and intuitively satisfying theory is that we do it by **ostensive definition**. This is the idea that children (and adults) acquire concepts by being directed to examples in the world. So if you are walking with a child and you see a dog, you say *That's a dog* or *Look at the doggie!* and the child begins to acquire the concept DOG, which is filled out by subsequent experience of dogs.

This common-sense picture cannot be the whole story, however. The philosopher W. V. O. Quine has pointed out that ostension (defining by example) is usually couched in language. Quine's famous example is of walking with someone whose language you do not know, who, when a rabbit runs past, says *Gavagai*. You do not know whether it is a warning or an instruction, or what the content might be: 'They are a menace', 'They are good to eat', 'Wow, that scared me', etc. To understand that you are being given a name you need to know something about the language that the ostension takes place in. So in English, a sentence frame like '*It's a*' tells you this. Similarly, you cannot even tell what is being pointed to without some linguistic support: is it the whole rabbit, its tail, or the way it is running? The point is that even ostensive definition depends on prior knowledge of some word meanings. Where, we may ask, do these come from? Are we forced to admit that we may be born with certain basic concepts innately within us? See J. A. Fodor (1975, 1980, 1981b) and Samet and Flanagan (1989) for discussion of these ideas. Once again, we will not try to deal with these issues in detail here; we can merely point out that the acquisition of concepts must be a more complicated process than simple ostension.

Our discussion in this section has focused on the relationship between words and concepts; in the next section we discuss the relationship between words and thinking in general.

2.5 Words, Concepts and Thinking

In our discussion so far, we have assumed a straightforward association between words and concepts: that is, that a speaker has a store of lexicalized concepts which is of course smaller than the larger set that she is capable of thinking about or talking about, using phrases or sentences. There are, though, a number of positions that can be taken on the issue of the relationship between these lexicalized concepts and general thinking and reasoning. In this section we discuss two opposing views: the first, **linguistic relativity**, is that lexicalized concepts impose restrictions on possible ways of thinking;

the second, the **language of thought** hypothesis, maintains that thinking and speaking, while obviously related, involve distinct levels of representation. There are strong and weak versions of both of these positions, but we will for clarity outline fairly strong versions.

2.5.1 Linguistic relativity

The notion of **linguistic relativity**, associated with Edward Sapir and Benjamin Lee Whorf, is an idea that has spread far outside the fields of anthropology and linguistics where it began. One reason perhaps is that it provides an explanation for a common experience when dealing with different languages. Writers translating between languages have often remarked on the lack of fit between words in two languages. For example, colour words might not have exactly the same range: does French *pourpre* describe the same range as English *purple*?[9] Similarly, while the English verbs for putting on clothes (*put on*, *don* etc.) make no distinction about the part of the body the clothing goes on, other languages like Japanese (as discussed by E. V. Clark 1983) and Korean (Choi and Bowerman 1992) have separate verbs for putting clothes on various parts of the body. It seems obvious too that words for social institutions and customs will vary between cultures. There is no easy translation in English for the Somali verb *maddooyeyso*, except the approximation: 'to play the children's game called *maddooyamaddooyo*, where an object is hidden in the hand and a special kind of rhyme is recited'.

The fact that language mirrors cultural differences became an important issue in the school of American anthropological linguistics which followed the work of the distinguished anthropologist Franz Boas. In one line of thought this idea of language as a mirror of culture developed into a much stronger idea: that people's thoughts are *determined* by the categories available to them in their language. We can follow this line of development, starting with the following famous quotation where we find Boas suggesting that different languages, reflecting their speakers' cultural practices, might embody different conceptual classifications of the world:

2.43   As an example of the manner in which terms that we express by independent words are grouped together under one concept, the Dakota language may be selected. The terms *naxta'ka* TO KICK, *paxta'ka* TO BIND IN BUNDLES, *yaxta'ka* TO BITE, *ic'a'xtaka* TO BE NEAR TO, *boxta'ka* TO POUND, are all derived from the common element *xtaka* TO GRIP, which holds them together, while we use distinct words for expressing the various ideas.

It seems fairly evident that the selection of such simple terms must to a certain extent depend upon the chief interests of a people; and where it is necessary to distinguish a certain phenomenon in many aspects, which in the life of the people each play an entirely independent role, many independent words may develop, while in other cases modifications of a single term may suffice.

Thus it happens that each language, from the point of view of
another language, may be arbitrary in its classifications; that what
appears as a single simple idea in one language may be characterized
by a series of distinct phonetic groups in another.   (Boas 1966: 22)

Boas observed that the effect of this was largely unconscious because the
use of language is largely an automatic process which we do not normally
pause to reflect on.

These observations open the debate in this literature about the relationship between language, culture and thought. To what extent does the particular language we speak determine the way that we think about the world?
Perhaps Boas's most famous student is the anthropologist and linguist Edward
Sapir; in the following quotation, we see him proposing the view that the
particular language we speak conditions our conceptualization of the world:

2.44   Language is a guide to 'social reality' . . . Human beings do not live
         in the objective world alone, nor alone in the world of social activity
         as ordinarily understood, but are very much at the mercy of the
         particular language which has become the medium of expression for
         their society . . . the 'real world' is to a large extent unconsciously
         built up on the language habits of the group. No two languages are
         ever sufficiently similar to be considered as representing the same
         social reality. The worlds in which different societies live are distinct
         worlds, not merely the same world with different labels attached . . .

         We see and hear and otherwise experience very largely as we do
         because the language habits of our community predispose certain
         choices of interpretation . . . From this standpoint we may think of
         language as the *symbolic guide* to culture.   (Sapir 1949b: 162)

It seems fair to say that Sapir had a stronger view of the determining role
of language than Boas. Stronger still are the views of Benjamin Lee Whorf,
a linguist well known for his work on native American languages, especially
the Uto-Aztecan languages of the south-west United States and Mexico.
Whorf strengthened this idea of the link between language and thought
into the notion he called **linguistic relativity**. Its basic premise is that the
way we think about the world is determined by our cultural and linguistic
background:

2.45   We cut nature up, organize it into concepts, and ascribe significances
         as we do, largely because we are parties to an agreement to organ-
         ize it in this way – an agreement that holds through our speech
         community and is codified in the patterns of our language. The
         agreement is, of course, an implicit and unstated one, BUT ITS
         TERMS ARE ABSOLUTELY OBLIGATORY; we cannot talk at
         all except by subscribing to the organization and classification of
         data which the agreement decrees.   (Whorf 1956: 213–14)

Whorf's observation is not restricted to word meaning; indeed, he believed that meanings derived from grammatical systems (e.g. notions of number and space in nouns, or aspect and tense in verbs)[10] were even stronger determinants of thought. The idea is that speakers can reflect on word meanings but grammatical systems are largely unavailable to conscious reflection.

If this view is correct then our own language predisposes us to see both reality and other languages through its own filter. This would have serious implications for the prospects of a universal semantic theory. It might mean that we could always, with some difficulty and inexactitude, translate from one language to another. But if speaking different languages means that we think in different ways, how could we ever step outside our own language to set up a neutral metalanguage which does not privilege any particular language or language family? Such metalanguages are, of course, the basis for theories in other areas of linguistics like syntax or phonology.

2.5.2   The language of thought hypothesis

The idea of linguistic relativity is rejected by many linguists and researchers in **cognitive science**, the interdisciplinary study of intelligence which draws on cognitive psychology, computer science and linguistics. A typical response is to dismiss as a fallacy such a strict identification of thought and language. We can identify two main types of argument used to support this view. The first is that there is evidence of thinking without language; and the second is that linguistic analysis has shown us that language underspecifies meaning. We can look briefly at these two types of argument. A succinct presentation of the first type of argument is given by Pinker (1994: 59ff.), who presents various kinds of evidence that thinking and language are not the same thing. He gives examples of evidence of thought processes, such as remembering and reasoning, which have been identified in psychological studies of human babies and of primates, both providing examples of creatures without language. He also recounts the various reports of artists and scientists who claim that their creativity sometimes derives from ideas which are non-linguistic images. There is also evidence from psychological experiments of visual thinking: subjects seem able to manipulate images mentally, rotating them, scanning them, zooming in and out, etc., exhibiting a variety of mental processes which do not seem to involve language. Finally Pinker casts doubt on the various attempts in psychological experiments to suggest that people from different linguistic communities perform reasoning or other cognitive tasks in any very different ways.[11]

Such evidence for mental processes not involving language is often used to argue that cognitive processes do not employ a spoken language like English or Arabic but make use of a separate computational system in the mind: a **language of thought**. For a philosophical defence of this position see for example J. A. Fodor (1975). Stillings et al. (1995) provide a range of evidence from psychological experiments to support the same view. The basic idea is that memory and processes such as reasoning seem to make use of a kind of propositional representation that does not have the surface syntax of a spoken language like English.

Turning to the second type of argument – that language underspecifies meaning – some indirect support for this position emerges from the characteristic view of the communication of meaning that has emerged from research in semantics and pragmatics, as we shall see in the course of this book. It has become clear that meaning is richer than language at both ends, so to speak, of the communication process. Speakers compress their thoughts, and often imply rather than state explicitly what they mean, while hearers fill out their own version of the intended meaning from the language presented to them. This idea, that language underspecifies meaning and has to be enriched by hearers, would seem to fit naturally with the idea that speakers are putting their thoughts into language, i.e. translating into the spoken language, rather than simply voicing their thoughts directly. This does not of course provide direct evidence for this view: we could equally imagine English speakers thinking in English and still compressing their thoughts when speaking, on some grounds of economy and social cooperation.

Nonetheless these different types of argument are often taken, especially in cognitive science, to support the view that we think in a language of thought, sometimes called **Mentalese**. When we want to speak, we translate from Mentalese into our spoken language, be it Mohawk or Russian. One natural extension of this view is the proposal that everybody's Mentalese is roughly the same; that is, that the language of thought is universal. Thus we arrive at a position diametrically opposed to linguistic relativity: human beings have essentially the same cognitive architecture and mental processes, even though they speak different languages.[12]

2.5.3 Thought and reality

If we leave this question of the relation between words and thinking for the time being, we might ask whether semanticists must also consider questions of the relationship between thought and reality. We can ask: must we as aspiring semanticists adopt for ourselves a position on traditional questions of **ontology**, the branch of philosophy that deals with the nature of being and the structure of reality, and **epistemology**, the branch of philosophy concerned with the nature of knowledge? For example, do we believe that reality exists independently of the workings of human minds? If not, we are adherents of **idealism**. If we do believe in an independent reality, can we perceive the world as it really is? One response is to say yes. We might assert that knowledge of reality is attainable and comes from correctly conceptualizing and categorizing the world. We could call this position **objectivism**. On the other hand, we might believe that we can never perceive the world as it really is: that reality is only graspable through the conceptual filters derived from our biological and cultural evolution. We could explain the fact that we successfully interact with reality (run away from lions, shrink from fire, etc.) because of a notion of ecological viability. Crudely: that those with very inefficient conceptual systems (not afraid of lions or fire) died out and weren't our ancestors. We could call this position **mental constructivism**: we can't get to a God's eye view of reality because of the way we are made. These are, of course, very crude characterizations of difficult philosophical issues. By now any philosophers chancing on this text will have thrown it into the back of their own fire. But the relevance of these issues to semantics is that, as we shall see in later chapters, different theories of semantics often presuppose different answers to these very basic questions.

Still, for the linguist keen to describe the semantics of Swahili or English these are a heavy set of issues to deal with before getting on with the job, especially when added to the complex issues of conceptual representation that we discussed a little earlier. One understandable response is to decide that only language is the proper object of study for linguists and issues of mental representations and the existence of reality are best left to psychologists and philosophers. See for example the following comment by Charles Hockett:

2.46　　We can leave to philosophers the argument whether the abstract relationships themselves have any sort of existence in the world outside of speech. Whatever they may decide, it is clear that the 'meaning' of a word like *and* or *the* . . . is a very different thing from the meaning of a word like *morning* or *sunbeam*.　(Hockett 1958: 263)

and we can see a similar sentiment in John Lyons's (1968) discussion of semantics:

2.47　　the view that semantics is, or ought to be, an empirical science, which as far as possible avoids commitment with respect to such philosophical and psychological disputes as the distinction of 'body' and 'mind' and the status of 'concepts'. This view will be accepted in the discussion of semantics given in this chapter. It should be stressed, however, that the methodological renunciation of 'mentalism' does not imply the acceptance of 'mechanism', as some linguists have suggested . . . The position that should be maintained by the linguist is one that is neutral with respect to 'mentalism' and 'mechanism'; a position that is consistent with both and implies neither.　(1968: 408)

Thus some linguists have decided to leave the philosophical high ground to other disciplines, to put aside discussion of the reality of the world, and the nature of our mental representations of it, and to concentrate instead on the meaning relations between expressions within a language, or to try to compare meanings across languages. As we will see, this turning inward

towards language, a position we could call **linguistic solipsism**,[13] leads to
an interest in describing semantic relations like **ambiguity, synonymy,
contradiction, antonymy**, etc., which we will look at in chapter 3. The
decision is that it is more the task of linguists to describe, for example, how
the meaning of the word *dog* is related to the words *animal* or *bitch*, than to
discuss what the mental concept of DOG might look like, or how this relates
to the real dogs running around in the world.

2.6 Summary

In this chapter we have seen that, though it seems true that through language
we can identify or refer to real world entities, it is difficult to use reference
as the whole of a theory of meaning. We have seen that our semantic
knowledge seems to include both **reference** and **sense**. We have seen that
there are two different approaches to our ability to talk about the world: a
denotational approach which emphasizes the links between language and
external reality; and a **representational** approach which emphasizes the
link between language and conceptual structure. Each approach has to
answer certain key questions. For example, how do denotational approaches
cope with our ability to talk about imaginary or hypothetical entities? Of
representational approaches we might ask: do we need to establish a theory
of conceptual structure in order to describe meaning? In this chapter we
have seen some aspects of such a task.

These issues of the relationship between language, thought and reality
have typically led linguists to adopt one of three positions:

1 to leave these issues to philosophers and psychologists and decide
   that linguists should concentrate on **sense relations** within a
   language, or between languages;
2 to decide that meaning *is* essentially denotation and try to develop
   a theory to cope with the various types of reference we looked at
   earlier in 2.4, including the ability to talk about imagined situations;
3 to decide that meaning *does* rely on a theory of conceptual structure
   and go on to try to determine the nature of linguistic concepts.

We will see examples of each of these approaches in this book. The first
is characteristic of traditional semantics and especially of lexical semantics,
with its concentration on semantic relations like ambiguity, synonymy, and
so on. We turn to these topics in chapter 3. The second approach, beefing
up denotational theories to cope with the referential characteristics of different linguistic categories and the problems of mental entities, is characteristic
of **formal semantics**, as we will describe in chapter 10. The third approach
is characteristic of much recent work, as in Jackendoff's (1990) **conceptual
semantics**, described in chapter 9, or **cognitive semantics**, which we turn
to in chapter 11. Before we look in detail at these theories, in part II of this

book we identify key areas of semantic description that any theory must come to terms with.

FURTHER READING

Devitt and Sterelny (1987) is an accessible overview of philosophical approaches to reference. Martin (1987) discusses the topics in this chapter as part of a general introduction to the philosophy of language. For an accessible introduction to Frege's distinction between sense and reference and its place in his philosophy see Kenny (1995). Stillings et al. (1995) review the issue of mental representations from the perspective of **cognitive science**, the name used for an interdisciplinary approach to mental representations and processes, drawing on research in cognitive psychology, computer science, philosophy of mind and linguistics. Taylor (1989) is a comprehensive discussion of the implications of prototype theory for linguistics. Medin and Ross (1992) and Eysenck and Keane (2000) give introductions to cognitive psychology which include accessible discussions of the nature of concepts. An interesting collection of papers on the linguistic relativity hypothesis is Gumperz and Levinson (1996), which has useful introductory sections.

EXERCISES

2.1   Imagine the sentences below being spoken. Decide for each of the nominal expressions in bold, whether the speaker would be using the nominal to **refer**.

   a.   We waited for twelve hours at **Nairobi Airport**.
   b.   They had **no food**.
   c.   Edward opened the cupboard and **a pair of shoes** fell out.
   d.   Henry is going to make **a cake**.
   e.   Doris passed through the office like **a whirlwind**.
   f.   He was run over by **a bus** in Donnybrook.
   g.   What we need is **an army of volunteers**.

2.2   Try to devise alternative descriptions for the **referents** of the nominals in bold below:

   a.   The Senator paid a visit to **the Ukrainian capital**.
   b.   **The British Prime Minister** refused to comment.
   c.   They arrived on **Christmas Day**.
   d.   Craig took a bus to **Washington DC**.
   e.   He had reached the summit of **the tallest mountain in the world**.

2.3   We discussed the **description theory of names**. We saw that this theory views the use of names as based on knowledge about the name bearer. Test this theory with the names below. For each name you recognize decide on two different descriptive sentences based on what you know about the individual.

    a.   Karl Marx
    b.   Alexander Graham Bell
    c.   Confucius
    d.   James Joyce
    e.   Alexander the Great
    f.   Indira Gandhi

Discuss too how a **causal theory** might explain your knowledge of these names. You might also discuss whether you think that some combination of these theories might be possible.

2.4   We discussed the traditional proposal that a concept can be defined by a set of **necessary and sufficient conditions**, where the right set of attributes might define a concept exactly. If words are labels for concepts these attributes might also define word meaning. Lehrer (1974) discusses the definitions of words associated with cooking. Some of her examples are in the two groups below. For each word try to establish sets of attributes that would distinguish it from its companions in the group.

    a.   cake   biscuit   bread   roll   bun   cracker
    b.   boil   fry   broil   sauté   simmer   grill   roast.

2.5   We discussed the **prototype** theory of concepts. Assume that each of the following is a label for a concept and suggest a list of **characteristic features** for the concept's prototype. Discuss some actual examples of members of the category and grade them for typicality, as we graded *sparrow* and *penguin* as examples of BIRD.

    a.   VEHICLE
    b.   HOME
    c.   WORK
    d.   MOTHER
    e.   SCIENCE

2.6   Using paraphrases, describe what is odd about the following exchanges:

> 1 A: No American came in here today.
>   B: What did he say?
>
> 2 A: This sandwich is better than nothing.
>   B: You're right. Nothing is worse than that sandwich.
>
> 3 A: Everybody doesn't know that.
>   B: Well then, let's tell everybody.

NOTES

1 In chapter 10, Formal Semantics, we outline a Fregean-style denotational semantics, where nouns denote entities, predicates denote sets of entities, and sentences denote a truth value, a true or false match with a situation.

2 For accessible introductions to the topics of naming and reference in the philosophical literature, see Devitt and Sterelny (1987) and Macnamara (1982).

3 See the articles in Frege (1980) for discussion.

4 In cognitive psychology and formal semantics a term **intension** is used for a similar notion. In this usage the intension of a concept or a word is the set of criteria for identifying the concept together with the properties which relate it to other concepts.

5 Note that this implies that the sense of a word is a conceptual representation in an individual's mind. This is somewhat different from Frege's emphasis on sense as a means of determining reference that is objective, public and independent of any one individual mind. See Kenny (1995) for a brief discussion and Dummett (1981) for a detailed exposition.

6 Since in this section we will be talking about words, concepts and things in the world, and the relation between them, we will adopt a typographical convention to help us keep them apart: words will be in italics (*dog*); concepts in small capitals (DOG) and things in the world in plain type (dog).

7 These proposals are similar to a number of suggestions within cognitive science for representing knowledge: an example is Minsky's (1977) frames. See Stillings et al. (1995) for an overview of such proposals. The idea that concepts are based on knowledge and theories about the world has been discussed in psychology by several writers, for example Murphy and Medin (1985) and Keil (1987).

8 See Taylor (1989) for a detailed discussion of prototype theory and a suggestion that this structure is not limited to word meaning but is characteristic of all linguistic categories, even in syntax and phonology.

9 We discuss the comparison of colour words in different languages in 3.7 later.

10 We will discuss these notions of tense, aspect etc. in later chapters.

11 Such a study is Kay and Kempton's (1984) experiment comparing speakers of English and Tarahumara (an Uto-Aztecan language of Mexico) and their abilities to sort and compare coloured chips in colour ranges where the two languages differ.

12 This view also fits in well with the influential hypothesis of the **modularity of mind**: that is, that there are separate and self-contained faculties of mind, of

which language is one. In this view, these faculties function independently from one another and from general cognition; they are dedicated to only one kind of input (e.g. language; facial recognition); and they are not under conscious control. See J. A. Fodor (1983) for discussion.

13 Here we are borrowing and adapting Putnam's (1975) term **methodological solipsism**, as discussed in J. A. Fodor (1981a). Putnam applies the term to psychological research: here we use the term **linguistic solipsism** to describe a decision to focus on language-internal issues, ignoring the connections to thought and/or to the world.

Semantic Description

part II

chapter 3

Word Meaning

3.1 Introduction

In this chapter we turn to the study of word meaning, or **lexical semantics**.[1] The traditional descriptive aims of lexical semantics have been: (a) to represent the meaning of each word in the language; and (b) to show how the meanings of words in a language are interrelated. These aims are closely related because, as we mentioned in chapter 1, the meaning of a word is defined in part by its relations with other words in the language. We can follow structuralist thought and recognize that as well as being in a relationship with other words in the same sentence, a word is also in a relationship with other, related but absent words.[2] To take a very simple example, if someone says to you:

3.1   I saw my mother just now.

you know, without any further information, that the speaker saw a woman. As we will see, there are a couple of ways of viewing this: one is to say that this knowledge follows from the relationship between the uttered word *mother* and the related, but unspoken word *woman*, representing links in the vocabulary. Another approach is to claim that the word *mother* contains a semantic element WOMAN[3] as part of its meaning.

Whatever our particular decision about this case, it is easy to show that lexical relations are central to the way speakers and hearers construct meaning.[4] One example comes from looking at the different kinds of conclusions that speakers may draw from an utterance. See, for example, the following sentences, where English speakers would probably agree that each of the b sentences below follows automatically from its a partner (where we assume as usual that repeated nominals have the same reference), whereas the c sentence, while it might be a reasonable inference in context, does not follow in this automatic way:

3.2   a.   My bank manager has just been murdered.
        b.   My bank manager is dead.
        c.   My bank will be getting a new manager.

3.3   a.   Rob has failed his statistics exam.
        b.   Rob hasn't passed his statistics exam.
        c.   Rob can't bank on a glittering career as a statistician.

3.4   a.   This bicycle belongs to Sinead.
        b.   Sinead owns this bicycle.
        c.   Sinead rides a bicycle.

The relationship between the a and b sentences in (3.2–4) was called **entailment** in chapter 1, and we look at it in more detail in chapter 4. For now we can say that the relationship is such that if we believe the a sentence, then we are automatically committed to the b sentence. On the other hand, we can easily imagine situations where we believe the a sentence but can deny the associated c sentence. As we shall see in chapters 4 and 7, this is a sign that the inference from a to c is of a different kind from the entailment relationship between a and b. This entailment relationship is important here because in these examples it is a reflection of our lexical knowledge: the entailments in these sentences can be seen to follow from the semantic relations between *murder* and *dead*, *fail* and *pass*, and *belong* and *own*.

As we shall see, there are many different types of relationship that can hold between words, and investigating these has been the pursuit of poets, philosophers, writers of laws and others for centuries. The study of word meanings, especially the changes that seem to take place over time, are also the concern of philology, and of lexicology. As a consequence of these different interests in word meaning there has evolved a large number of terms describing differences and similarities of word meaning. In this chapter we begin by discussing the basic task of identifying words as units, and then examine some of the problems involved in pinning down their meanings. We then look at some typical semantic relations between words, and examine the network-like structure that these relations give to our mental lexicon. Finally we discuss the search for lexical universals. The topics in this chapter act as a background to chapter 9, where we discuss some specific theoretical approaches to word meaning.

3.2   Words and Grammatical Categories

It is clear that grammatical categories like noun, preposition etc., though defined in modern linguistics at the level of syntax and morphology, do reflect semantic differences: different categories of words must be given different semantic descriptions. To take a few examples: names, common nouns, pronouns and what we might call **logical words** (see below and chapter 4) all show different characteristics of reference and sense:

3.5   a.   names   e.g. Fred Flintstone
      b.   common nouns   e.g. dog, banana, tarantula
      c.   pronouns   e.g. I, you, we, them
      d.   logical words   e.g. not, and, or, all, any

Looking at these types of words, we can say that they operate in different ways: some types may be used to refer (e.g. names), others may not (e.g. logical words); some can only be interpreted in particular contexts (e.g. pronouns), others are very consistent in meaning across a whole range of contexts (e.g. logical words); and so on. It seems too that semantic links will tend to hold between members of the same group rather than across groups, so that semantic relations between common nouns like *man, woman, animal* etc. are clearer than between any noun and words like *and, or, not,* and vice versa.

Note too that this is only a selection of categories: we will have to account for others like verbs, adjectives, adverbs, prepositions etc. Having said this, we deal mainly with nouns and verbs in this chapter; the reader should bear in mind that this is not the whole story.

3.3   Words and Lexical Items

We will follow general linguistic tradition and assume that we must have a list of all the words in a language, together with idiosyncratic information about them; and call this body of information, a **dictionary** or **lexicon**. Our interest in semantics is with **lexemes** or **semantic words**, and, as we shall see, there are a number of ways of listing these in a lexicon. But first we should examine this unit **word**. Words can be identified at the level of writing, where we are familiar with them being separated by white space, where we can call them **orthographic words**. They can also be identified at the levels of phonology, where they are strings of sounds which may show internal structuring which does not occur outside the word, and syntax, where the same semantic word can be represented by several grammatically distinct variants. Thus *walks, walking, walked* in 3.6 below are three different **grammatical** words:

3.6   a.   He walks like a duck.
       b.   He's walking like a duck.
       c.   He walked like a duck.

However, for semantics we will want to say these are instances of the same lexeme, the verb **walk**. We can then say that our three grammatical words share the meaning of the lexeme. This abstraction from grammatical words to semantic words is already familiar to us from published dictionaries, where lexicographers use abstract entries like **go**, **sleep**, **walk**, etc. for purposes of explaining word meaning, and we don't really worry too much what grammatical status the reference form has. In Samuel Johnson's *A Dictionary of the English Language*, for example, the infinitive is used as the entry form, or **lemma**, for verbs, giving us entries like *to walk, to sleep*, etc. (Johnson 1983), but now most of us are used to dictionaries and we accept an abstract dictionary form to identify a semantic word.

Our discussion so far has assumed an ability to identify words. This doesn't seem too enormous an assumption in ordinary life, but there are a number of well-known problems in trying to identify the word as a well-defined linguistic unit. One traditional problem was how to combine the various levels of application of word, mentioned above, to an overall definition: what is a word? As Edward Sapir noted, it is no good simply using a semantic definition as a basis, since across languages speakers package meaning into words in very different ways:

3.7   Our first impulse, no doubt, would have been to define the word as
       the symbolic, linguistic counterpart of a single concept. We now
       know that such a definition is impossible. In truth it is impossible
       to define the word from a functional standpoint at all, for the word
       may be anything from the expression of a single concept – concrete
       or abstract or purely relational (as in *of* or *by* or *and*) – to the
       expression of a complete thought (as in Latin *dico* 'I say' or, with
       greater elaborateness of form, as in a Nootka verb form denoting
       'I have been accustomed to eat twenty round objects [e.g. apples]
       while engaged in [doing so and so]'). In the latter case the word
       becomes identical with the sentence. The word is merely a form,
       a definitely molded entity that takes in as much or as little of the
       conceptual material of the whole thought as the genius of the lan-
       guage cares to allow.   (Sapir 1949a: 32)

Why then bother attempting to find a universal definition? The problem is that in very many languages, words do seem to have some psychological reality for speakers, a fact also noted by Sapir from his work on native American languages:

3.8   Linguistic experience, both as expressed in standardized, written form and as tested in daily usage, indicates overwhelmingly that there is not, as a rule, the slightest difficulty in bringing the word to consciousness as a psychological reality. No more convincing test could be desired than this, that the naive Indian, quite unaccustomed to the concept of the written word, has nevertheless no serious difficulty in dictating a text to a linguistic student word by word; he tends, of course, to run his words together as in actual speech, but if he is called to a halt and is made to understand what is desired, he can readily isolate the words as such, repeating them as units. He regularly refuses, on the other hand, to isolate the radical or grammatical element, on the ground that it 'makes no sense.' (Sapir 1949a: 33–4)

One answer is to switch from a semantic definition to a grammatical one, such as Leonard Bloomfield's famous definition:

3.9   A word, then, is a free form which does not consist entirely of (two or more) lesser free forms; in brief, a word is a *minimum free form*.
        Since only free forms can be isolated in actual speech, the word, as the minimum of free form, plays a very important part in our attitude towards language. For the purposes of ordinary life, the word is the smallest unit of speech.   (Bloomfield 1984: 178)

This distributional definition identifies words as independent elements, which show their independence by being able to occur in isolation, i.e. to form one-word utterances. This actually works quite well for most cases, but leaves elements like *a*, *the*, and *my* in a grey area. Speakers seem to feel that these are words, and write them separately, as in *a car*, *my car* etc., but they don't occur as one-word utterances, and so are not words by this definition. Bloomfield was, of course, aware of such problem cases:

3.10   None of these criteria can be strictly applied: many forms lie on the border-line between bound forms and words, or between words and phrases; it is impossible to make a rigid distinction between forms that may and forms that may not be spoken in absolute position.[5]   (Bloomfield 1984: 181)

There have been other suggestions for how to define words grammatically: Lyons (1968), for example, discusses another distributional definition, this time based on the extent to which morphemes stick together. The idea is that the attachments between elements within a word will be firmer than will the attachments between words themselves. This is shown by numbering the morphemes as in 3.11, and then attempting to rearrange them as in 3.12:

3.11   Internal cohesion (Lyons 1968: 202–4)
        the$_1$ + boy$_2$ + s$_3$ + walk$_4$ + ed$_5$ + slow$_6$ + ly$_7$ + up$_8$ + the$_9$ + hill$_{10}$

3.12   a.   slow$_6$ + ly$_7$ + the$_1$ + boy$_2$ + s$_3$ + walk$_4$ + ed$_5$ + up$_8$ + the$_9$ + hill$_{10}$
        b.   up$_8$ + the$_9$ + hill$_{10}$ + slow$_6$ + ly$_7$ + walk$_4$ + ed$_5$ + the$_1$ + boy$_2$ + s$_3$
        c.   *s$_3$ + boy$_2$ + the$_1$
        d.   *ed$_5$ + walk$_4$

This works well for distinguishing between the words *walked* and *slowly*, but as we can see also leaves *the* as a problem case. It behaves more like a bound morpheme than an independent word: we can no more say *boys the* than we can say just *the* in isolation.

We can leave the debate at this point: that words seem to be identifiable at the level of grammar, but that there will be, as Bloomfield said, border-line cases. As we said earlier, the usual approach in semantics is to try to associate phonological and grammatical words with semantic words or lexemes. Earlier we saw an example of three grammatical words represent-ing one semantic word. The inverse is possible: several lexemes can be represented by one phonological and grammatical word. We can see an example of this by looking at the word *foot* in the following sentences:

3.13   a.   He scored with his left **foot**.
        b.   They made camp at the **foot** of the mountain.
        c.   I ate a **foot**-long hot-dog.

Each of these uses has a different meaning and we can reflect this by identifying three lexemes in 3.13. Another way of describing this is to say that we have three **senses** of the word *foot*. We could represent this by numbering the senses:

3.14   **foot**^{1}:   part of the leg below the ankle;
        foot^2:   base or bottom of something;
        foot^3:   unit of length, one-third of a yard.

Once we have established our lexemes, the lexicon will be a listing of them with a representation of:

    1   the lexeme's pronunciation;
    2   its grammatical status;
    3   its meaning;
    4   its meaning relations with other lexemes.[6]

Traditionally, each entry has to have any information that cannot be pre-dicted by general rules. This means that different types of information will have to be included: about unpredictable pronunciation; about any exceptional morphological behaviour; about what syntactic category the item is, etc. and, of course, the semantic information that has to be there: the meaning of the lexeme, and the semantic relations it enters into with other lexemes in the language.

One point that emerges quite quickly from such a listing of lexemes is that some share a number of the properties we are interested in. For example the three lexemes in 3.13 all share the same pronunciation ([fʊt]), and the same syntactic category (noun). Dictionary writers economize by grouping senses and listing the shared properties just once at the head of the group, e.g.

3.15   **foot** [fʊt] noun. **1.** part of the leg below the ankle. **2.** base or bottom of something. **3.** unit of length, one-third of a yard.

This group is often called a **lexical entry**. Thus a lexical entry may contain several lexemes or senses. The principles for grouping lexemes into lexical entries vary somewhat. Usually the lexicographer tries to group words that, as well as sharing phonological and grammatical properties, make some sense as a semantic grouping, either by having some common elements of meaning, or by being historically related. We will look at how this is done in section 3.5 below when we discuss the semantic relations of **homonymy** and **polysemy**. Other questions arise when the same phonological word belongs to several grammatical categories, e.g. the verb *heat*, as in *We've got to heat the soup*, and the related noun *heat*, as in *This heat is oppressive*. Should these belong in the same entry? Many dictionaries do this, sometimes listing all the nominal senses before the verbal senses, or vice versa. Readers can check their favourite dictionary to see the solution adopted for this example.

There are traditional problems associated with the mapping between lexemes and words at other levels, which we might mention but not investigate in any detail here. One example, which we have already mentioned, is the existence of multi-word units, like **phrasal verbs**, for example: *throw up* and *look after*; or the more complicated *put up with*. We can take as another example **idioms** like *kick the bucket, spill the beans*, etc. Phrasal verbs and idioms are both cases where a string of words can correspond to a single semantic unit.

3.4 Problems with Pinning Down Word Meaning

As every speaker knows if asked the meaning of a particular word, word meaning is slippery. Different native speakers might feel they know the meaning of a word, but then come up with somewhat different definitions. Other words they might have only the vaguest feel for and have to use a dictionary to check. Some of this difficulty arises from the influence of context on word meaning, as discussed by Firth (1957), Halliday (1966) and Lyons (1963). Usually it is easier to define a word if you are given the phrase or sentence it occurs in. These contextual effects seem to pull word meanings in two opposite directions. The first, restricting influence is the tendency for words to occur together repeatedly, called **collocation**. Halliday (1966), for example, compares the collocation patterns of two adjectives *strong* and *powerful*, which might seem to have similar meanings. Though we can use both for some items, e.g. *strong arguments* and *powerful arguments*, elsewhere there are collocation effects. For example, we talk of *strong tea* rather than *powerful tea*; but a *powerful car* rather than a *strong car*. Similarly *blond* collocates with *hair* and *addle* with *eggs*. As Gruber (1965) notes, names for groups act like this: we say a *herd of cattle*, but a *pack of dogs*.

These collocations can undergo a fossilization process until they become fixed expressions. We talk of *hot and cold running water* rather than *cold and hot running water*; and say *They're husband and wife*, rather than *wife and husband*. Such fixed expressions are common with food: *salt and vinegar, fish and chips, curry and rice, bangers and mash, franks and beans*, etc.[7] A similar type of fossilization results in the creation of **idioms**, expressions where the individual words have ceased to have independent meanings. In expressions like *kith and kin* or *spick and span*, not many English speakers would be able to assign a meaning here to *kith* or *span*.

Contextual effects can also pull word meanings in the other direction, towards creativity and semantic shift. In different contexts, for example, a noun like *run* can have somewhat different meanings, as in 3.16 below:

3.16   a. I go for a run every morning.
        b. The tail-end batsmen added a single run before lunch.
        c. The ball-player hit a home run.
        d. We took the new car for a run.
        e. He built a new run for his chickens.
        f. There's been a run on the dollar.
        g. The bears are here for the salmon run.

The problem is how to view the relationship between these instances of *run* above. Are these seven different senses of the word *run*? Or are they examples of the same sense influenced by different contexts? That is, is there some sketchy common meaning that is plastic enough to be made to fit the different context provoked by other words like *batsmen, chickens* and *the dollar*? The answer might not be simple: some instances, for example 3.16b and c, or perhaps, a, b and c, seem more closely related than others. Some writers have described this distinction in terms of **ambiguity** and **vagueness**. The proposal is that if each of the meanings of *run* in 3.16 is a different sense, then *run* is seven ways ambiguous; but if 3.16a–g share the same sense, then *run* is merely vague between these different uses. The basic idea is that in examples of vagueness the context can add information that is not specified in the sense, but in examples of ambiguity the context will cause one of the senses to be selected. The problem, of course, is to decide, for any given example, whether one is dealing with ambiguity or vagueness. Several tests have been proposed, but they are difficult to apply. The main reason for this is once again context. Ambiguity is usually more potential than real since in any given context one of the readings is likely to fit the context and be automatically selected by the participants; they may not even be aware of readings that they would naturally prefer in other contexts. This means that we have to employ some ingenuity in applying ambiguity tests: usually they involve inventing a sentence and a context where both readings could be available. We can briefly examine some of the tests that have been proposed.

One test proposed by Kempson (1977) relies on the use of abbreviatory forms like *do so, do so too, so do*. These are short forms used to avoid repeating a verb phrase, e.g.

3.17　　a.　Charlie hates mayonnaise and **so does** Mary.
　　　　b.　He took a form and Sean **did too**.

Such expressions are understandable because there is a convention of **identity** between them and the preceding verb phrase: thus we know that in 3.17a Mary hates mayonnaise and in 3.17b Sean took a form. Kempson's test relies on this identity: if the preceding verb phrase has more than one sense, then whichever sense is selected in this first full verb phrase must be kept the same in the following *do so* clause. For example, 3.18a below has the two interpretations in 3.18b and 3.18c:

3.18　　a.　Duffy discovered a mole.
　　　　b.　Duffy discovered a small burrowing mammal.
　　　　c.　Duffy discovered a long dormant spy.

This relies, of course, on the two meanings of *mole*, and is therefore a case of **lexical ambiguity**. If we add a *do so* clause as in 3.18d:

　　　　d.　Duffy discovered a mole, and so did Clark.

whichever sense is selected in the first clause has to be repeated in the second, i.e. it is not possible for the first clause to have the *mammal* interpretation and the second the *spy* interpretation, or vice versa. By contrast, where a word is vague, the unspecified aspects of meaning are invisible to this *do so* identity. Basically, they are not part of the meaning and therefore are not available for the identity check. We can compare this with the word *publicist* which can be used to mean either a male or female, as 3.19 below shows:

3.19   a.   He's our publicist.
         b.   She's our publicist.

Is *publicist* then ambiguous? In a sentence like 3.20 below:

3.20   They hired a publicist and so did we.

it is quite possible for the publicist in the first clause to be male and in the second, female. Thus this test seems to show that *publicist* is unspecified, or 'vague', for gender. We can see that vagueness allows different specifications in *do so* clauses, but the different senses of an ambiguous word cannot be chosen.

    This *do so* identity test seems to work, but, as mentioned earlier, its use relies on being able to construct examples where the same sentence has two meanings. In our *run* examples earlier, the different instances of *run* occur in different contexts and it is difficult to think of an example of a single sentence which could have two interpretations of *run*, say the cricket interpretation and the financial one.

    Other tests for ambiguity rely on one sense being in a network of relations with certain other lexemes and another sense being in a different network. So, for example, the *run* of 3.16a above, might be in relation of near synonymy to another noun like *jog*, while *run* in 3.16e might be in a similar relation to nouns like *pen, enclosure*, etc. Thus while the b sentences below are fine, the c versions are bizarre:

3.21   a.   I go for a run every morning.
         b.   I go for a jog every morning.
         c.   ?I go for an enclosure every morning.

3.22   a.   He built a new run for his chickens.
         b.   He built a new enclosure for his chickens.
         c.   ?He built a new jog for his chickens.

This **sense relations test** suggests that *run* is ambiguous between the 3.16a and 3.16e readings.

    There are a number of other tests for ambiguity, many of which are difficult to apply and few of which are uncontroversially successful; see Cruse (1986: 49–83) for a discussion of these tests. It seems likely that whatever intuitions and arguments we come up with to distinguish between contextual colouring and different sense, the process will not be an exact one. We'll see a similar problem in the next section, when we discuss **homonymy** and **polysemy**, where lexicographers have to adopt procedures for distinguishing related senses of the same lexical entry from different lexical entries.

    In the next section we describe and exemplify some of the semantic relations which can hold between lexical items.

3.5 Lexical Relations

There are a number of different types of lexical relation, as we shall see. A particular lexeme may be simultaneously in a number of these relations, so that it may be more accurate to think of the lexicon as a **network**, rather than a listing of words as in a published dictionary.

An important organizational principle in the lexicon is the **lexical field**. This is a group of lexemes which belong to a particular activity or area of specialist knowledge, such as the terms in cooking or sailing; or the vocabulary used by doctors, coal miners or mountain climbers. One effect is the use of specialist terms like *phoneme* in linguistics or *gigabyte* in computing. More common, though, is the use of different senses for a word, for example:

3.23   **blanket**[1]   verb.   to cover as with a blanket.

           blanket[2]   verb.   *Sailing.* to block another vessel's wind by sailing close to it on the windward side.

3.24   **ledger**[1]   noun.   *Bookkeeping.* the main book in which a company's financial records are kept.

           ledger[2]   noun.   *Angling.* a trace that holds the bait above the bottom.

Dictionaries recognize the effect of lexical fields by including in lexical entries labels like *Banking, Medicine, Angling* etc., as in our examples above.

One effect of lexical fields is that lexical relations are more common between lexemes in the same field. Thus **peak**[1] 'part of a mountain' is a near synonym of *summit*, while **peak**[2] 'part of a hat' is a near synonym of *visor*. In the examples of lexical relations which follow, the influence of lexical fields will be clear.

3.5.1 Homonymy

Homonyms are unrelated senses of the same phonological word. Some authors distinguish between **homographs**, senses of the same written word, and **homophones**, senses of the same spoken word. Here we will generally just use the term homonym. We can distinguish different types depending on their syntactic behaviour, and spelling, for example:

1   lexemes of the same syntactic category, and with the same spelling: e.g. *lap* 'circuit of a course' and *lap* 'part of body when sitting down'.

2   of the same category, but with different spelling: e.g. the verbs *ring* and *wring*.

3   of different categories, but with the same spelling: e.g. the verb *keep*
    and the noun *keep*;
4   of different categories, and with different spelling: e.g. *not, knot.*

Of course variations in pronunciation mean that not all speakers have the
same set of homonyms. Some English speakers, for example, pronounce the
pairs *click* and *clique*, or *talk* and *torque*, in the same way, making these
homonyms which are spelled differently.

3.5.2   Polysemy

There is a traditional distinction made in lexicology between homonymy
and **polysemy**. Both deal with multiple senses of the same phonological
word, but polysemy is invoked if the senses are judged to be related. This
is an important distinction for lexicographers in the design of their dictionaries, because polysemous senses are listed under the same lexical entry,
while homonymous senses are given separate entries. Lexicographers tend
to use criteria of 'relatedness' to identify polysemy. These criteria include
speakers' intuitions, and what is known about the historical development of
the items. We can take an example of the distinction from the *Collins English
Dictionary* (Treffry 2000: 743) where, as 3.25 below shows, various senses
of *hook* are treated as polysemy and therefore listed under one lexical entry:

3.25   **hook** (hʊk) *n.*   **1.** a piece of material, usually metal, curved or
        bent and used to suspend, catch, hold, or pull something. **2.** short
        for fish-hook. **3.** a trap or snare. **4.** *Chiefly US* something that
        attracts or is intended to be an attraction. **5.** something resembling
        a hook in design or use. **6.a.** a sharp bend or angle in a geological
        formation, esp. a river. **b.** a sharply curved spit of land. **7.** *Boxing.*
        a short swinging blow delivered from the side with the elbow bent.
        8. *Cricket.* a shot in which the ball is hit square on the leg side with
        the bat held horizontally. **9.** *Golf.* a shot that causes the ball to
        swerve sharply from right to left. **10.** *Surfing.* the top of a breaking
        wave, etc.

Two groups of senses of *hooker* on the other hand, as 3.26 below shows, are
treated as unrelated, therefore a case of homonymy, and given two separate
entries:

3.26   **hooker**[1]   ('hʊk2) *n.*   **1.** a commercial fishing boat using hooks
                       and lines instead of nets. **2.** a sailing boat of the west of
                       Ireland formerly used for cargo and now for pleasure
                       sailing and racing.
        hooker[2]   ('hʊk2) *n.*   **1.** a person or thing that hooks. **2.** *US and
                       Canadian slang.* **2a.** a draught of alcoholic drink, esp. of

spirits. **2b**. a prostitute. **3**. *Rugby*. the central forward in the front row of a scrum whose main job is to hook the ball.

Such decisions are not always clear cut. Speakers may differ in their intuitions, and worse, historical fact and speaker intuitions may contradict each other. For example, most English speakers seem to feel that the two words *sole* 'bottom of the foot' and *sole* 'flatfish' are unrelated, and should be given separate lexical entries as a case of homonymy. They are, however, historically derived via French from the same Latin word *solea* 'sandal'. So an argument could be made for polysemy. Since in this case, however, the relationship is really in Latin, and the words entered English from French at different times, dictionaries side with the speakers' intuitions and list them separately. A more recent example is the adjective *gay* with the two meanings 'lively, light-hearted, bright' and 'homosexual'. Although the latter meaning was derived from the former in recent history, for many speakers the two senses are quite distinct, and they may seem like homonyms to some, especially younger, English speakers.

3.5.3 Synonymy

Synonyms are different phonological words which have the same or very similar meanings. Some examples might be the pairs below:

3.27   couch/sofa   boy/lad   lawyer/attorney   toilet/lavatory   large/big

Even these few examples show that true or exact synonyms are very rare. As Palmer (1981) notes, the synonyms often have different distributions along a number of parameters. They may have belonged to different dialects and then become synonyms for speakers familiar with both dialects, like Irish English *press* and British English *cupboard*. Or the words may belong to different **registers**, those styles of language, colloquial, formal, literary, etc. that belong to different situations. Thus *wife* or *spouse* is more formal than *old lady* or *missus*. The synonyms may portray positive or negative attitudes of the speaker: for example *naive* or *gullible* seem more critical than *ingenuous*. Finally, as mentioned earlier, one or other of the synonyms may be collocationally restricted. For example, the sentences below might mean roughly the same thing in some contexts:

3.28   She called out to the young lad.

3.29   She called out to the young boy.

In other contexts, however, the words *lad* and *boy* have different connotations; compare:

3.30   He always was a bit of a lad.

3.31   He always was a bit of a boy.

Or we might compare the synonymous pair 3.32 with the very different pair in 3.33:

3.32   a big house: a large house

3.33   my big sister: my large sister.

As an example of such distributional effects on synonyms, we might take the various words used for the police around the English-speaking world: *police officer, cop, copper,* etc. Some distributional constraints on these words are regional, like Irish English *the guards* (from the Irish *garda*), British English *the old Bill*, or American English *the heat*. Formality is another factor: many of these words are, of course, slang terms used in colloquial contexts instead of more formal terms like *police officer*. Speaker attitude is a further distinguishing factor: some words, like *fuzz, flatfoot, pigs* or *the slime*, reveal negative speaker attitudes, while others like *cop* seem neutral. Finally, as an example of collocation effects, one can find speakers saying *a police car* or *a cop car*, but not very likely are ?*a guards car* or ?*an Old Bill car*.

3.5.4 Opposites (antonymy)

In traditional terminology, **antonyms** are words which are opposite in meaning. It is useful, however, to identify several different types of relationship under a more general label of **opposition**. There are a number of relations which seem to involve words which are at the same time related in meaning yet incompatible or contrasting; we list some of them below.

Simple antonyms
This is a relation between words such that the negative of one implies the positive of the other. The pairs are also sometimes called **complementary pairs** or **binary pairs**. In effect, the words form a two-term classification. Examples would include:

3.34   dead/alive (of e.g. animals)
        pass/fail (a test)
        hit/miss (a target)

So, using these words literally, *dead* implies *not alive* etc., which explains the semantic oddness of sentences like:

3.35   ?My pet python is dead but luckily it's still alive.

Of course speakers can creatively alter these two-term classifications for special effects: we can speak of someone being *half dead*; or we know that in horror films the *undead* are not alive in the normal sense.

Gradable antonyms

This is a relationship between opposites where the positive of one term does not necessarily imply the negative of the other, e.g. *rich/poor, fast/slow, young/old, beautiful/ugly.*[8] This relation is typically associated with adjectives and has two major identifying characteristics: firstly, there are usually intermediate terms so that between the gradable antonyms *hot* and *cold* we can find:

3.36   hot (warm tepid cool) cold

This means, of course, that something may be neither hot nor cold. Secondly, the terms are usually relative, so *a thick pencil* is likely to be thinner than *a thin girl*; and *a late dinosaur fossil* is earlier than *an early Elvis record*. A third characteristic is that in some pairs one term is more basic and common, so for example of the pair *long/short*, it is more natural to ask of something *How long is it?* than *How short is it?* For other pairs there is no such pattern: *How hot is it?* and *How cold is it?* are equally natural depending on context. Other examples of gradable antonyms are: *tall/short, clever/ stupid, near/far, interesting/boring.*

Reverses

The characteristic **reverse** relation is between terms describing movement, where one term describes movement in one direction, →, and the other the same movement in the opposite direction, ←; for example the terms *push* and *pull* on a swing door, which tell you in which direction to apply force. Other such pairs are *come/go, go/return, ascend/descend.* When describing motion the following can be called reverses: (go) *up/down*, (go) *in/out*, (turn) *right/left.*

By extension, the term is also applied to any process which can be reversed: so other reverses are *inflate/deflate, expand/contract, fill/empty* or *knit/unravel.*

Converses

These are terms which describe a relation between two entities from alternate viewpoints, as in the pairs:

3.37   own/belong to
         above/below
         employer/employee

Thus if we are told *Alan owns this book* then we know automatically *This book belongs to Alan.* Or from *Helen is David's employer* we know *David is Helen's employee*. Again, these relations are part of a speaker's semantic knowledge and explain why the two sentences below are **paraphrases**, i.e. can be used to describe the same situation:

3.38   My office is above the library.

3.39   The library is below my office.

Taxonomic sisters
The term antonymy is sometimes used to describe words which are at the same level in a taxonomy. Taxonomies are classification systems; we take as an example the colour adjectives in English, and give a selection below:

3.40   red   orange   yellow   green   blue   purple   brown

We can say that the words *red* and *blue* are sister-members of the same taxonomy and therefore incompatible with each other. Hence one can say:

3.41   His car isn't red, it's blue.

Other taxonomies might include the days of the week: *Sunday, Monday, Tuesday* etc., or any of the taxonomies we use to describe the natural world, like types of dog: *poodle, setter, bulldog* etc. Some taxonomies are **closed**, like days of the week: we can't easily add another day, without changing the whole system. Others are **open**, like the flavours of ice-cream sold in an ice-cream parlour: someone can always come up with a new flavour and extend the taxonomy.

   In the next section we see that taxonomies typically have a hierarchical structure, and thus we will need terms to describe vertical relations, as well as the horizontal 'sisterhood' relation we have described here.

3.5.5 Hyponymy

Hyponymy is a relation of inclusion. A **hyponym** includes the meaning of a more general word, e.g.

3.42   *dog* and *cat* are hyponyms of *animal*
         sister and *mother* are hyponyms of *woman*

The more general term is called the **superordinate** or **hypernym**. Much of the vocabulary is linked by such systems of inclusion, and the resulting semantic networks form the hierarchical taxonomies mentioned above. Some taxonomies reflect the natural world, like 3.43 below, where we only expand a single line of the network:

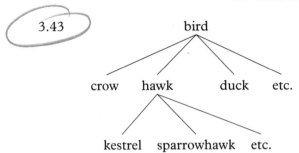

3.43

Here *kestrel* is a hyponym of *hawk*, and *hawk* a hyponym of *bird*. We assume the relationship is transitive so that *kestrel* is a hyponym of *bird*. Other taxonomies reflect classifications of human artefacts, like (3.44) below:

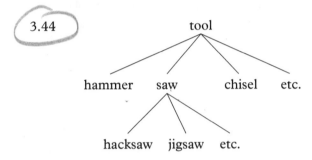

3.44

From such taxonomies we can see both hyponymy and the taxonomic sister-hood described in the last section: hyponymy is a vertical relationship in a taxonomy: so *saw* is a hyponym of *tool* in 3.44; while taxonomic sisters are in a horizontal relationship: so *hacksaw* and *jigsaw* are sisters in this taxonomy with other types of saw. Such classifications are of interest for what they tell us about human culture and mind. Anthropologists and anthropological linguists have studied a range of such folk taxonomies in different languages and cultures, including colour terms (Berlin and Kay 1969; Kay and McDaniel 1978), folk classifications of plants and animals (Berlin et al. 1974; Hunn 1977) and kinship terms (Lounsbury 1964; Tyler 1969; Goodenough 1970). The relationship between such classifications and the vocabulary is discussed by Rosch et al. (1976), Downing (1977) and George Lakoff (1987).

Another lexical relation that seems like a special sub-case of taxonomy is the ADULT–YOUNG relation, as shown in the following examples:

3.45   dog   puppy
        cat   kitten
        cow   calf
        pig   piglet
        duck   duckling
        swan   cygnet

A similar relation holds between MALE–FEMALE pairs:

3.46   dog   bitch
       tom   ?queen
       bull   cow
       hog   sow
       drake   duck
       cob   pen

As we can see, there are some asymmetries in this relation: firstly, the relationship between the MALE–FEMALE terms and the general term for the animal varies: sometimes there is a distinct term, as in *pig–hog–sow* and *swan–cob–pen*; in other examples the male name is general, as in *dog*, while in others it is the female name, e.g. *cow* and *duck*. There may also be gaps: while *tom* or *tomcat* is commonly used for male cats, for some English speakers there doesn't seem to be an equivalent colloquial name for female cats (though others use *queen*, as above).

3.5.6   Meronymy

Meronymy[9] is a term used to describe a part–whole relationship between lexical items. Thus *cover* and *page* are meronyms of *book*. We can identify this relationship by using sentence frames like *X is part of Y*, or *Y has X*, as in *A page is part of a book*, or *A book has pages*. Meronymy reflects hierarchical classifications in the lexicon somewhat like taxonomies: a typical system might be:

3.47

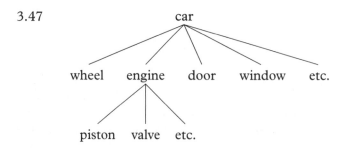

Meronymic hierarchies are less clear-cut and regular than taxonomies. Meronyms vary, for example, in how necessary the part is to the whole. Some are necessary for normal examples, for example *nose* as a meronym of *face*; others are usual but not obligatory, like *collar* as a meronym of *shirt*; still others are optional like *cellar* for *house*.

Meronymy also differs from hyponymy in transitivity. Hyponymy is always transitive, as we saw, but meronymy may or may not be. A transitive example is: *nail* as a meronym of *finger*, and *finger* of *hand*. We can see that *nail* is a meronym of *hand*, for we can say *A hand has nails*. A non-transitive example is: *pane* is a meronym of *window* (*A window has a pane*), and *window* of *room* (*A room has a window*); but *pane* is not a meronym of *room*, for we cannot say *A room has a pane*. Or *hole* is a meronym of *button*, and *button* of *shirt*, but we wouldn't want to say that *hole* is a meronym of *shirt* (*A shirt has holes!*).

One important point is that the networks identified as meronymy are lexical: it is conceptually possible to segment an item in countless ways, but only some divisions are coded in the vocabulary of a language. There are a number of other lexical relations which seem similar to meronymy. In the next sections we briefly list a couple of the most important.

3.5.7 Member–collection

This is a relationship between the word for a unit and the usual word for a collection of the units. Examples include:

3.48
ship	fleet
tree	forest
fish	shoal
book	library
bird	flock
sheep	flock
worshipper	congregation

3.5.8 Portion–mass

This is the relation between a mass noun and the usual unit of measurement or division. For example in 3.49 below the unit, a count noun, is added to the mass noun, making the resulting noun phrase into a count nominal. We discuss this process further in chapter 9.

3.49
drop	of	liquid
grain	of	salt/sand/wheat
sheet	of	paper
lump	of	coal
strand	of	hair

3.6 Derivational Relations

As mentioned earlier, our lexicon should include derived words when their meaning is not predictable. In the creation of real dictionaries this is rather an idealized principle: in practice lexicographers often find it more economical to list many derivatives rather than attempt to define the morphological rules with their various irregularities and exceptions. So while in principle we want to list only unpredictable forms in individual entries, in practice the decision rests on the aims of the lexicon creators.

We can look briefly at just two derivational relations as examples of this type of lexical relation: causative verbs and agentive nouns.

3.6.1 Causative verbs

We can identify a relationship between an adjective describing a state, e.g. *wide* as in *the road is wide*, a verb describing a beginning or change of state, e.g. *widen* as in *The road widened*, and a verb describing the cause of this change of state, e.g. *widen*, as in *The City Council widened the road*. These three semantic choices can be described as a **state, change of state** (or **inchoative**), and **causative**.

This relationship is marked in the English lexicon in a number of different ways. There may be no difference in the shape of the word between all three uses as in: *The gates are **open**; The gates **open** at nine; The porters **open** the gates*. Despite having the same shape, these three words are grammatically distinct: an adjective, an intransitive verb and a transitive verb, respectively. In other cases the inchoative and causative verbs are morphologically derived from the adjective, as in: *The apples are **ripe**; The apples are **ripening**; The sun is **ripening** the apples*.

Often there are gaps in this relation: for example we can say *The soil is **rich*** (state) and *The gardener **enriched** the soil* (causative) but it sounds odd to use an inchoative: *?The soil is **enriching***. For a state adjective like *hungry*, there is no colloquial inchoative or causative: we have to say *get hungry* as in *I'm getting hungry*; or *make hungry* as in *All this talk of food is making me hungry*.

Another element in this relation can be an adjective describing the state which is a result of the process. This **resultative** adjective is usually in the form of a past participle. Thus we find examples like: *closed, broken, tired, lifted*. We can see a full set of these relations in: *hot* (state adjective)–*heat* (inchoative verb)–*heat* (causative verb)–*heated* (resultative adjective).

We have concentrated on derived causatives, but some verbs are inherently causative and not derived from an adjective. The most famous English example of this in the semantics literature is *kill*, which can be analysed as a causative verb 'to cause to die'. So the semantic relationship state–inchoative –causative for this example is: *dead–die–kill*. We can use this example to see something of the way that both derivational and non-derivational lexical relations interact. There are two senses of the adjective *dead*: **dead[1]**: not alive; and **dead[2]**: affected by a loss of sensation. The lexeme **dead[1]** is in a relationship with the causative verb *kill*; while **dead[2]** has a morphologically derived causative verb *deaden*.

3.6.2 Agentive nouns

There are several different types of agentive nouns.[10] One well-known type is derived from verbs and ends in the written forms -er or -or. These nouns have the meaning 'the entity who/which performs the action of the verb'. Some examples are: *skier, walker, murderer, whaler, toaster, commentator, director, sailor, calculator, escalator.* The process of forming nouns in -er is more productive than -or, and is a good candidate for a regular derivational rule. However, dictionary writers tend to list even these forms, for two reasons. The first is that there are some irregularities: for instance, some nouns do not obey the informal rule given above: *footballer*, for example, is not derived from a verb *to football*. In other cases, the nouns may have several senses, some of which are quite far from the associated verb, as in the examples in 3.50 below:

3.50	**lounger**	a piece of furniture for relaxing on
	undertaker	mortician
	muffler	*US*: a car silencer
	creamer	*US*: a jug for cream
	renter	*Slang.* a male prostitute

A second reason for listing these forms in published dictionaries is that even though this process is quite regular, it is not possible to predict for any given verb which of the strategies for agentive nouns will be followed. Thus, one who depends upon you financially is not a **depender* but a *dependant*; and a person who cooks is a *cook* not a *cooker*. To cope with this, one would need a kind of default structure in the lexical entries: a convention that where no alternative agentive noun was listed for a verb, one could assume that an -er form is possible. This kind of convention is sometimes called an **elsewhere condition** in morphology: see Spencer (1991: 109–11) for discussion.

Other agentive nouns which have to be listed in the lexicon are those for which there is no base verb. This may be because of changes in the language, as, for example, the noun *meter* 'instrument for making measurements' which no longer has an associated verb *mete*.[11]

3.7 Lexical Universals

Our discussion so far has concentrated on the lexicon of an individual language. As we mentioned in chapter 2, translating between two languages highlights differences in vocabulary. We discussed there the hypothesis of linguistic relativity, and saw how the basic idea of language reflecting culture can be strengthened into the hypothesis that our thinking reflects our linguistic and cultural patterns. In this strong view of relativism, speakers of different languages may think in significantly different ways. The lexicon is one area of language where differences are readily apparent and this raises the question of whether there are any universals of lexical semantics. We can identify two sides to this question. One is whether there are universals of lexical organization or principles, and the other is whether there are some lexemes that have correspondences in all the languages of the world. The answer to the former seems to be yes: all languages seem to show evidence of the lexical relations discussed in 3.5 earlier, for example. The second question is more difficult and has been the subject of enquiry by a number of scholars. In the next sections we briefly discuss some lines of this enquiry.

3.7.1 Colour terms

One important area of discussion has been the differences in colour terms in languages. While we might readily expect differences for words relating to things in the environment such as animals and plants, or for cultural systems like governance or kinship terms, it might seem surprising that terms for colours should vary. After all, we all share the same physiology. In an important study Berlin and Kay (1969) investigated the fact that languages vary in the number and range of their basic colour terms. Their claim is that though there are various ways of describing colours, including comparison to objects, languages have some lexemes which are basic in the following sense:

3.51 Basic colour terms (Berlin and Kay 1969):
    a. The term is monolexemic, i.e. not built up from the meaning of its parts. So terms like *blue-grey* are not basic.
    b. The term is not a hyponym of any other colour term, i.e. the colour is not a kind of another colour. Thus English *red* is basic, *scarlet* is not.
    c. The term has wide applicability. This excludes terms like English *blonde*.
    d. The term is not a semantic extension of something manifesting that colour. So *turquoise, gold, taupe* and *chestnut* are not basic.

The number of items in this basic set of colour terms seems to vary widely from as few as two to as many as eleven; examples of different systems reported in the literature include the following:

3.52 Basic colour term systems[12]
    Two terms: Dani (Trans-New Guinea; Irin Jaya)
    Three: Tiv (Niger-Congo; Nigeria), Pomo (Hokan; California, USA)
    Four: Ibibio (Niger-Congo; Nigeria), Hanunóo (Austronesian; Mindoro Island, Philippines)
    Five: Tzeltal (Mayan; Mexico), Kung-Etoka (Khoisan; Southern Africa)
    Six: Tamil (Dravidian; India), Mandarin Chinese

Seven: Nez Perce (Penutian; Idaho, USA), Malayalam (Dravidian; India)
Ten/eleven: Lebanese Arabic, English[13]

While this variation might seem to support the notion of linguistic relativity, Berlin and Kay's (1969) study identified a number of underlying similarities which argue for universals in colour term systems. Their point is that rather than finding any possible division of the colour spectrum into basic terms, they were able to pinpoint quite a narrow range of possibilities, with some shared structural features. One claim they make is that within the range of each colour term there is a basic focal colour that speakers agree to be the best prototypical example of the colour. Moreover they claim that this focal colour is the same for the colour term cross-linguistically. The conclusion drawn in this and subsequent studies is that colour naming systems are based on the neurophysiology of the human visual system (Kay and McDaniel 1978). A further claim is that there are only eleven basic categories; and that these form the implicational hierarchy below (where we use capitals, WHITE etc., to show that the terms are not simply English words):

3.53   Basic colour term hierarchy (Berlin and Kay 1969):

$$\begin{Bmatrix} \text{WHITE} \\ \text{BLACK} \end{Bmatrix} < \text{RED} < \begin{Bmatrix} \text{GREEN} \\ \text{YELLOW} \end{Bmatrix} < \text{BLUE} < \text{BROWN} < \begin{Bmatrix} \text{PURPLE} \\ \text{PINK} \\ \text{ORANGE} \\ \text{GREY} \end{Bmatrix}$$

This hierarchy represents the claim that in a relation A < B, if a language has B then it must have A, but not vice versa. As in implicational hierarchies generally, leftward elements are seen as more basic than rightward elements.[14] A second claim of this research is that these terms form eight basic colour term systems, as shown:

3.54   Basic systems

System	Number of terms	Basic colour terms
1	Two	WHITE, BLACK
2	Three	WHITE, BLACK, RED
3	Four	WHITE, BLACK, RED, GREEN
4	Four	WHITE, BLACK, RED, YELLOW
5	Five	WHITE, BLACK, RED, GREEN, YELLOW
6	Six	WHITE, BLACK, RED, GREEN, YELLOW, BLUE
7	Seven	WHITE, BLACK, RED, GREEN, YELLOW, BLUE, BROWN
8	Eight, nine, ten or eleven	WHITE, BLACK, RED, GREEN, YELLOW, BLUE, BROWN, PURPLE +/PINK +/ORANGE +/GREY

Systems 3 and 4 show that either GREEN or YELLOW can be the fourth colour in a four-term system. In system 8, the colour terms PURPLE, PINK, ORANGE and GREY can be added in any order to the basic seven-term system. Berlin and Kay made an extra, historical claim that when languages increase the number of colour terms in their basic system they must pass through the sequence of systems in 3.54. In other words, the types represent a sequence of historical stages through which languages may pass over time (where types 3 and 4 are alternatives).

In her experimentally based studies of Dani (Heider 1971, 1972a, 1972b) the psychologist Eleanor Rosch investigated how speakers of this Papua New Guinea language compared with speakers of American English in dealing with various colour memory tasks. Dani has just two basic colour terms: *mili* for cold, dark colours and *mola* for warm, light colours; while English has eleven. Both groups made similar kinds of errors and her work suggests that there is a common, underlying conception of colour relationships that is due to physiological rather than linguistic constraints. When Dani speakers used their kinship terms to learn a new set of colour names they agreed on the best example of focal points with the English speakers. This seems to be evidence that Dani speakers can distinguish all the focal colour distinctions that English speakers can. When they need to, they can refer to them linguistically by circumlocutions, the colour of mud, sky etc. and they can learn new names for them. The conclusion seems to be that the perception of the colour spectrum is the same for all human beings but that languages lexicalize different ranges of the spectrum for naming. As Berlin and Kay's work shows, the selection is not arbitrary and languages use the same classificatory procedure. Berlin and Kay's work can be interpreted to show that there are universals in colour naming and thus forms a critique of the hypothesis of linguistic relativity.[15]

3.7.2   Core vocabulary

The idea that each language has a core vocabulary of more frequent and basic words is widely used in foreign language teaching and dictionary writing. Morris Swadesh, a student of Edward Sapir, suggested that each language has a core vocabulary that is more resistant to loss or change than other parts of the vocabulary. He proposed that this core vocabulary could be used to trace lexical links between languages to establish family relationships between them. The implication of this approach is that the membership of the core vocabulary will be the same or similar for all languages. Thus comparison of the lists in different languages might show **cognates**, related words descended from a common ancestor language. Swadesh originally proposed a 200-word list which was later narrowed down to the 100-word list below:

3.55 Swadesh's (1972) 100-item basic vocabulary list

1.	I	26.	root	51.	breasts	76.	rain
2.	you	27.	bark	52.	heart	77.	stone
3.	we	28.	skin	53.	liver	78.	sand
4.	this	29.	flesh	54.	drink	79.	earth
5.	that	30.	blood	55.	eat	80.	cloud
6.	who	31.	bone	56.	bite	81.	smoke
7.	what	32.	grease	57.	see	82.	fire
8.	not	33.	egg	58.	hear	83.	ash
9.	all	34.	horn	59.	know	84.	burn
10.	many	35.	tail	60.	sleep	85.	path
11.	one	36.	feather	61.	die	86.	mountain
12.	two	37.	hair	62	kill	87.	red
13.	big	38.	head	63.	swim	88.	green
14.	long	39.	ear	64.	fly	89.	yellow
15.	small	40.	eye	65.	walk	90.	white
16.	woman	41.	nose	66.	come	91.	black
17.	man	42.	mouth	67.	lie	92.	night
18.	person	43.	tooth	68.	sit	93.	hot
19.	fish	44.	tongue	69.	stand	94.	cold
20.	bird	45.	claw	70.	give	95.	full
21.	dog	46.	foot	71.	say	96.	new
22.	louse	47.	knee	72.	sun	97.	good
23.	tree	48.	hand	73.	moon	98.	round
24.	seed	49.	belly	74.	star	99.	dry
25.	leaf	50.	neck	75.	water	100.	name

To give one example, the Cushitic language Somali has for number 12 'two' the word *laba* and for 41 'nose' *san* while the Kenyan Cushitic language Rendille has 12 *lama* and 41 *sam*. Other cognates with consistent phonological alternations in the list will show that these two languages share a large proportion of this list as cognates. Swadesh argued that when more than 90 per cent of the core vocabulary of two languages could be identified as cognates then the languages were closely related. Despite criticisms, this list has been widely used in comparative and historical linguistics.

The identification of semantic equivalences in this list is complicated by semantic shift. Cognates in two languages may drift apart because of historical semantic processes, including narrowing and generalization. Examples in English include *meat*, which has narrowed its meaning from 'food' in earlier forms of the languages, and *starve*, which once had the broader meaning 'die'. The problem for the analyst is deciding how much semantic shift is enough to break the link between cognates. The idea that this basic list will be found in all languages has been contested. Swadesh's related proposal that change in the core vocabulary occurs at a regular rate and therefore can be used to date the splits between related languages has attracted stronger criticism.[16]

3.7.3 Universal lexemes

Another important investigation of universal lexical elements is that undertaken by Anna Wierzbicka and her colleagues (Wierzbicka 1992, 1996;
Goddard and Wierzbicka 1994; Goddard 2001). These scholars have analysed a large range of languages to try to establish a core set of universal
lexemes. One feature of their approach is the avoidance of formal
metalanguages. Instead they rely on what they call 'reductive paraphrase in
natural language'. In other words, they use natural languages as the tool of
their lexical description, much as dictionary writers do. Like dictionary
writers, they rely on a notion of a limited core vocabulary that is not defined
itself but is used to define other lexemes. Another way of putting this is to
say that these writers use a subpart of a natural language as a natural
semantic metalanguage, as described below:

3.56   Natural Semantic Metalanguage (Goddard 2001: 3):
        a 'meaning' of an expression will be regarded as a paraphrase,
        framed in semantically simpler terms than the original expression,
        which is substitutable without change of meaning into all contexts
        in which the original expression can be used . . . The postulate
        implies the existence, in all languages, of a finite set of indefinable
        expressions (words, bound morphemes, phrasemes). The meanings
        of these indefinable expressions, which represent the terminal ele-
        ments of language-internal semantic analysis, are known as 'semantic
        primes'.

A selection of the semantic primes proposed in this literature is given below,
informally arranged into types:

3.57   Universal semantic primes (from Wierzbicka 1996, Goddard 2001):
        Substantives: I, you, someone/person,
                                         something, body
        Determiners: this, the same, other
        Quantifiers: one, two, some, all, many/much
        Evaluators: good, bad
        Descriptors: big, small
        Mental predicates: think, know, want, feel, see, hear
        Speech: say, word, true
        Actions, events, movement: do, happen, move, touch
        Existence and possession: is, have
        Life and death: live, die
        Time: when/time, now, before, after, a
                                         long time, a short time, for
                                         some time, moment

Space:	where/place, here, above, below, far, near, side, inside
'Logical' concepts:	not, maybe, can, because, if
Intensifier, augmentor:	very, more
Taxonomy:	kind (of), part (of)
Similarity:	like

About sixty of these semantic primes have been proposed in this literature. They are reminiscent of Swadesh's notion of core vocabulary but they are established in a different way: by the in-depth lexical analysis of individual languages. The claim made by these scholars is that the semantic primes of all languages coincide. Clearly this is a very strong claim about an admittedly limited number of lexical universals.

3.8 Summary

In this chapter we have looked at some important features of word meaning. We have discussed the difficulties linguists have had coming up with an airtight definition of the unit *word*, although speakers happily talk about them and consider themselves to be talking in them. We have seen the problems involved in divorcing word meaning from contextual effects and we discussed lexical ambiguity and vagueness. We have also looked at several types of lexical relations: homonymy, synonymy, opposites, hyponymy, meronymy, etc.; and seen two examples of derivational relations in the lexicon: causative verbs and agentive nouns. These represent characteristic examples of the networking of the vocabulary that a semantic description must reflect.[17] Finally we discussed some attempts to discover universals of lexical semantics. In chapter 9 we will look at approaches which try to characterize the networking of the lexicon in terms of semantic components.

FURTHER READING

John Lyons's *Semantics* (1977) discusses many of the topics in this chapter at greater length. Cruse (1986) is a useful and detailed discussion of word meaning and lexical relations. Lehrer and Feder (1992) contains applications of the concept of lexical fields to the study of lexical relations, and Evens (1988) is a collection of papers outlining different lines of research in lexical relations. Pustejovsky and Boguraev (1996) and Ravin and Leacock (2000) contain technical discussions of polysemy. George Lakoff (1987) is an enjoyable and stimulating discussion of the relationship between conceptual categories and words. Svensén (1993) is an introduction to the practical issues involved in creating dictionaries. Finally Foley (1997) discusses issues in the relationship between language and culture, including kinship and colour terms.

EXERCISES

3.1 We saw that lexicographers group **lexemes**, or **senses, into lexi-cal entries** by deciding whether they are related or not. If they are related (i.e. **polysemous**) then they are listed in a single lexical entry. If they are not related (i.e. **homonymous**) they are assigned independent entries. Below are groups of senses sharing the same phonological shape; decide for each group how the members should be organized into lexical entries.

    port[1] noun. a harbour.
    port[2] noun. a town with a harbour.
    port[3] noun. the left side of a vessel when facing the prow.
    port[4] noun. a sweet fortified dessert wine (*originally from Oporto in Portugal*).
    port[5] noun. an opening in the side of a ship.
    port[6] noun. a connector in a computer's casing for attaching peripheral devices.

    mould[1] (*US* **mold**) noun. a hollow container to shape material.
    mould[2] (*US* **mold**) noun. a furry growth of fungus. ·
    mould[3] (*US* **mold**) noun. loose earth.

    ear[1] noun. organ of hearing.
    ear[2] noun. the ability to appreciate sound (*an ear for music*).
    ear[3] noun. the seed-bearing head of a cereal plant.

    stay[1] noun. the act of staying in a place.
    stay[2] noun. the suspension or postponement of a judicial sentence.
    stay[3] noun. *Nautical*. a rope or guy supporting a mast.
    stay[4] noun. anything that supports or steadies.
    stay[5] noun. a thin strip of metal, plastic, bone etc. used to stiffen corsets.

When you have done this exercise, you should check your decisions against a dictionary.

3.2 In the chapter we noted that **synonyms** are often differentiated by having different **collocations**. We used the examples of *big/large* and *strong/powerful*. Below is a list of pairs of synonymous adjectives. Try to find a collocation for one adjective that is impossible for the other. One factor you should be aware of is the difference between an **attributive** use of an adjective, when it modifies a noun, e.g. *red* in *a red face*, and a **predicative use** where the adjective follows a verb, e.g. *is red, seemed red, turned red*, etc. Some adjectives can only occur in one of these positions (*the man is unwell*, *the unwell man), others change meaning in the two positions (*the late king, the king is late*), and synonymous adjectives may differ in their ability to occur in these two positions. If you think this is the case for any of the following pairs, note it.

   safe/secure   quick/fast   near/close

   fake/false   sick/ill   expensive/dear

   dangerous/perilous   wealthy/rich

   mad/insane   correct/right

3.3 The sentence in a below could have, in various contexts, several interpretations, including those in b below:

   a. *Powell complained about the new case.*
   b. interpretation 1: Powell complained about the new suitcase.
       interpretation 2: Powell complained about the new police investigation.
       interpretation 3: Powell complained about the new medical patient.

Use the ambiguity tests of *do so* **identity** and of **sense relations** to decide whether the word *case* is **ambiguous** or **vague** among these three interpretations.

3.4 Below is a list of incompatible pairs. Classify each pair into one of the following types of relation: **simple antonyms**, **gradable antonyms**, **reverses**, **converses** or **taxonomic sisters**. Explain the tests you used to decide on your classifications and discuss any shortcomings you encountered in using them.

   temporary/permanent   monarch/subject   advance/retreat
   strong/weak   buyer/seller   boot/sandal
   assemble/dismantle   messy/neat   tea/coffee
   clean/dirty   open/shut   friend/enemy

3.5 Using nouns, provide some examples to show the relationship of **hyponymy**. Use your examples to discuss how many levels of hyponymy a noun might be involved in.

3.6   Try to find examples of the relationship of **hyponymy** with verbs. As in the last exercise, try to establish the number of levels of hyponymy that are involved for any examples you find.

3.7   Give some examples of the relationship of **meronymy**. Discuss the extent to which your examples exhibit **transitivity**.

3.8   Below are some nouns ending in *-er* and *-or*. Using your intuitions about their meanings, discuss their status as **agentive nouns**. In particular, are they derivable by regular rule or would they need to be listed in the lexicon? Check your decisions against a dictionary's entries.

       author, blazer, blinker, choker, crofter, debtor, loner, mentor, reactor, roller

3.9   How would you describe the semantic effect of the suffix *-ist* in the following sets of nouns?

       a.   socialist   b.   artist
            Marxist   scientist
            perfectionist   novelist
            feminist   chemist
            optimist   dentist
            humanist   satirist

      For each example, discuss whether the derived noun could be produced by a general rule.

3.10 For each sentence pair below discuss any meaning relations you identify between the verbs marked in bold:

       1   a.   Freak winds **raised** the water level.
           b.   The water level **rose**.

       2   a.   Fred **sent** the package to Mary.
           b.   Mary **received** the package from Fred.

       3   a.   Ethel **tried** to win the cookery contest.
           b.   Ethel **succeeded** in winning the cookery contest.

       4   a.   She didn't **tie** the knot.
           b.   She **untied** the knot.

> 5 a. Vandals **damaged** the bus stop.
>   b. The women **repaired** the bus stop.
>
> 6 a. Harry **rented** the car.
>   b. Harry **hired** the car.
>
> 7 a. Sheila **showed** Klaus her petunias.
>   b. Klaus **saw** Sheila's petunias.

NOTES

1 In this chapter we talk only of whole word meaning. Strictly speaking, lexical semantics is wider than this, being concerned both with the meaning of **morphemes** and **multi-word units**. Morphemes are the minimal meaningful units which make up words and larger units. So we can identify the word *hateful* as being composed of the two morphemes *hate* and *ful*, each of which have meaning. Some morphemes are words, traditionally called **free morphemes**, like *sleep, cat, father*. Others are **bound morphemes**: parts of word like *un-, re-,* and *pre-* in *unlikely, reanalyse* and *prebook*. These elements exhibit a consistent meaning but do not occur as independent words. For reasons of space, we ignore here the question of the status of bound morphemes in the lexicon. See Spencer (1991) and Carstairs-McCarthy (1992) for very accessible descriptions of morpheme theory. Lexical semanticists must also account for multi-word units: cases where a group of words have a unitary meaning which does not correspond to the compositional meaning of their parts, like the idiomatic phrases: *pass away, give up the ghost, kick the bucket, snuff it, pop one's clogs*, all of which mean *die*. Again, for reasons of space we won't pursue discussion of these multi-word semantic units here; see Cruse (1986) for discussion.

2 Ferdinand de Saussure called the relationship between a word and other accompanying words a **syntagmatic** relation, and the relationship between a word and related but non-occurring words, an **associative** relationship. This latter is also sometimes called a **paradigmatic** relationship. So the meaning of a phrase like *a red coat*, is partly produced by the syntagmatic combination of *red* and *coat*, while *red* is also in a paradigmatic relationship with other words like *blue, yellow*, etc.; and *coat* is in a relationship with words like *jacket*. The idea is that these paradigmatically related words help define the meaning of the spoken words. See de Saussure (1974: 122–34) for discussion.

3 Here we follow the convention of writing postulated semantic elements in small capitals to distinguish them from real words. We discuss the hypothesis that words are composed of such semantic elements in chapter 9.

4 It is also possible to argue that this knowledge is not linguistic at all but knowledge about the world. Such an approach is consistent with the view that there is no distinction between linguistic and factual knowledge: it is all knowledge about the world. See N. L. Wilson (1967) for similar arguments and Katz (1972: 73ff.) for counter-arguments. One of Katz's arguments is that you still

have to have a division amongst knowledge to distinguish what would be the two following facts or beliefs:

   a.   Women are female.
   b.   Women are under fifty feet tall.

We know both a and b from our experience of the world but there is a difference between them. If you meet a fifty-foot woman, you would probably say that you had met a woman, albeit an unusual one. However, if you meet a woman who is not female, there is some doubt: did you meet a woman at all? This difference is evidence for a conceptual/linguistic category of *woman*. See our earlier discussion of concepts and necessary and sufficient conditions in chapter 2.

5   By 'absolute position' here Bloomfield means 'in isolation'.

6   It is often proposed that the ideal lexicon would also include a fifth point: the lexical rules for the creation of new vocabulary, e.g. for just about any adjective X ending in *-al*, you can form a verb meaning 'to cause to become X' by adding *-ize*: *radical* → *radicalize*, → *legal* → *legalize*. However, it is clear that the results of derivational morphology are often semantically unpredictable: e.g. as Allan (1986, vol. 1: 223) points out, this *-ize* morpheme sometimes doesn't have this 'cause to become' meaning, as in *womanize*, 'to chase women'. It seems that some forms formed by derivational processes, including compounding, are predictable in meaning, like *dog food*, *cat food*, *fish food* etc., while others are not, like *fullback* or *night soil*. The latter type will have to be listed in the lexicon. See Allan (1986, vol. 1: 214–56) for discussion.

7   These pairs are called *irreversible binomials* by Cruse (1986: 39), after Malkiel (1959). Cruse discusses their fossilization in terms of increasing degrees of *semantic opacity*, where the constituent elements begin to lose their independent semantic value.

8   Some authors use the term **antonymy** narrowly for just this class we are calling **gradable antonyms**. Cruse (1986), for example, calls this class **antonyms** and uses the cover term **opposites** for all the relations we describe in section 3.5.4.

9   This term should not be confused with **metonymy**. Metonymy, as described in chapter 7, describes a referential strategy where a speaker refers to an entity by naming something associated with it. If, for example, in a mystery novel, one detective at a crime scene says to another: *Two uniforms got here first*, we might take the speaker to be using the expression *two uniforms* to refer to two uniformed police officers. This is an example of metonymy. Note that since a uniform could by extension be seen as part of a police officer, we can recognize some resemblance between metonymy and the part–whole relation **meronymy**. However, we can distinguish them as follows: metonymy is a process used by speakers as part of their practice of referring; meronymy describes a classification scheme evidenced in the vocabulary.

10   We discuss the semantic role of AGENT in chapter 6. As we shall see there, AGENT describes the role of a voluntary initiator of an action, while ACTOR describes an entity which simply performs an action. Since the *-er/-or* nouns are used both for people, e.g. *teacher*, *actor*, and for machines, e.g. *blender*, *refrigerator*, a term like **actor nouns** would be more suitable than **agentive nouns**. Since this latter is well established, though, we continue to use it here.

11   Of course a noun may just coincidentally have the appearance of an agentive noun, and not contain a productive English *-er* or *-or* suffix at all, like *butler*, *porter* or *doctor*, which were borrowed as units already possessing French or Latin agentive endings.

12   The source for these languages' colour systems is Berlin and Kay (1969), except Dani (Heider 1971, 1972a, 1972b). A recent update on this research, which has become the World Color Survey project is Kay et al. (1997).

13   English has ten or eleven items depending on whether *orange* is included as a basic term. More recently. Wierzbicka (1990) has noted that twelve-term systems exist in Russian, which has two terms corresponding to BLUE, and in Hungarian, which has two for RED.

14   See Croft (1990) for discussion of such hierarchies in typological studies.

15   But see Lucy (1992a, 1997) and Sahlins (1976) for debate.

16   This counting of percentages of cognates between languages is known as **lexicostatistics**, while the attempt to date languages by lexical changes is called **glottochronology**. See Swadesh (1972), Anttila (1989) and Trask (1996) for discussion.

17   There are differing views in the literature on how many lexical relations we should identify. For a very full list of relations, see Mel'čuk and Zholkovsky (1988).

chapter 4

Sentence Relations and Truth

4.1 Introduction

In the last chapter we looked at some of the semantic relations which hold between words and at the network effect that this gives to the lexicon. In this chapter we move on to semantic relations that may hold between sentences of a language. As we shall see, sometimes these relations are the result of particular words in the sentences, but in other cases the relations are the result of syntactic structure. As an example of an attempt to represent these relations, we will look at an approach to meaning based on the notion of **truth**, which has grown out of the study of logic. In particular we examine how successful a truth-based approach is in characterizing the semantic relations of **entailment** and **presupposition**. We begin by going back to our early, deceptively simple question: what is meaning?

Many linguists would argue (see for example J. D. Fodor 1983) that there is no answer to this question and that in this it is like the question 'what is a number?' in mathematics; or 'what is grammaticality?' in syntax. The only true answer to such questions, it is argued, are whole theories: so one has to have a syntactic theory to give a substantive answer to the question: 'what is grammaticality?' Otherwise, it is claimed, we are reduced to empty answers like: 'Grammaticality is a property assigned to sentences by a grammar' (J. D. Fodor 1983). One way around this problem is to identify the kinds of phenomena a theory of semantics must cover. As we have seen, generative linguists orient their explanation in terms of a native speaker's competence. In this approach, the question then becomes: what kind of knowledge about the meaning of his or her language does the native speaker have? Answers to this question differ but there is a consensus in the literature that for sentence meaning, a semantic theory should reflect an English speaker's knowledge:[1]

4.1   That a and b below are **synonymous**:
       a.   My brother is a bachelor.
       b.   My brother has never married.

4.2   That a below **entails** b:
       a.   The anarchist assassinated the emperor.
       b.   The emperor is dead.

4.3   That a below **contradicts** b:
       a.   My brother Sebastian has just come from Rome.
       b.   My brother Sebastian has never been to Rome.

4.4   That a below **presupposes** b, as c does d:
       a.   The Mayor of Manchester is a woman.
       b.   There is a Mayor of Manchester.
       c.   I regret eating your sandwich.
       d.   I ate your sandwich.

4.5   That a and b are necessarily true, i.e. **tautologies**:
       a.   Ireland is Ireland.
       b.   Rich people are rich.

4.6   That a and b are necessarily false, i.e. **contradictions**:
       a.   ?He is a murderer but he's never killed anyone.
       b.   ?Now is not now.

We shall be looking at some of these relations in more detail in this chapter but for now we can give a rough characterization of each, as follows:

4.7   A is synonymous with B: A has the same meaning as B.

4.8   A entails B: we know that if A then automatically B.

4.9   A contradicts B: A is inconsistent with B.

4.10   A presupposes B: B is part of the assumed background against which A is said.

4.11   A is a tautology: A is automatically true by virtue of its own meaning, but informationally empty.

4.12   A is a contradiction: A is inconsistent with itself, i.e. asserts and
        denies the same thing.

The problem for semantics is to provide a more rigorous account of these
and similar notions. In the following sections we look at how a notion of
truth might be used to do this.

4.2 Logic and Truth

In this section, we take a brief excursion into the realm of logic. In doing
this we are following a number of writers, like Richard Montague (1974),
who have hypothesized that the tools of logic can help us to represent
sentence meaning. We won't be going very far on this excursion and the
interested reader is referred to an excellent introduction to logic in Allwood
et al. (1977). We will go on to look at logic-based semantics in more detail
ourselves in chapter 10.
    The study of logic, of course, comes down to us from the Classical Greek
world, most famously from Aristotle. The beginnings of logic lie in a search
for the principles of valid argument and inference. A well-known example
is Aristotle's **modus ponens**, a type of argument in three steps, like the
following:

4.13   a.   If Arnd left work early, then he is in the pub.
        b.   Arnd left work early.
        c.   Arnd is in the pub.

If steps a and b (called the premises) are true then step c (the conclusion)
is also guaranteed to be true. Here we follow the tradition of separating the
premises from the conclusion by a horizontal line. Other rules of valid inference include the **modus tollens** exemplified in 4.14 below, the **hypothetical
syllogism** in 4.15 and the **disjunctive syllogism** in 4.16:

4.14   a.   If Arnd has arrived, then he is in the pub.
        b.   Arnd is not in the pub.
        c.   Arnd has not arrived.

4.15   a.   If Arnd is in the pub, then he is drinking beer.
        b.   If Arnd is drinking beer, then he is drinking Guinness.
        c.   If Arnd is in the pub, then he is drinking Guinness.

4.16   a.   Arnd is in the public bar or he is in the lounge.
        b.   Arnd isn't in the public bar.
        c.   Arnd is in the lounge.

A part of this study is a concern for the truth of statements and whether truth is preserved or lost by putting sentences into different patterns. Truth here is taken to mean a correspondence with facts, or, in other words, correct descriptions of states of affairs in the world.[2] For the most part this truth is said to be **empirical** (or **contingent**), because we have to have some access to the facts of the world to know whether a statement is true or not. Thus the truth or otherwise of the sentence:

4.17   My father was the first man to visit Mars.

depends on facts about the speaker's father's life: if her father did go to Mars and was the first man there, then the sentence is true; otherwise it is false. In the same way the empirical truth of 4.18 below:

4.18   The earth revolves around the sun.

depends upon the facts of the universe.

Semanticists call a sentence's being true or false its **truth value**, and call the facts that would have to obtain in reality to make a sentence true or false, its **truth conditions**. A simple example of a linguistic effect on truth value comes from negating a sentence. If we have a sentence like a below in English, adding *not* will reverse its truth value:

4.19   a.   Your car has been stolen.
        b.   Your car has not been stolen.

If a is true then b is false; also if a is false then b is true. To show that this relationship works for any statement, logicians use a schema called **logical form**, where a lower-case letter (**p**, **q**, **r**, etc.) stands for the statement and a special symbol for negation: ¬. So the logical form for 4.19a is 4.20a and for 4.19b is 4.20b:

4.20   a.   **p**
        b.   ¬**p**

The effect of negation on the truth value of a statement can be shown by a truth table, where T represents 'true' and F 'false', as below:

4.21   **p**   ¬**p**

        T   F
        F   T

This table shows that when **p** is true (T), ¬**p** is false (F); when **p** is false (F), ¬**p** is true (T). This is then a succinct way of describing the truth effect of negation.

The truth value of other linguistic elements is studied in logic in the same way. A number of connectives are especially important to logicians because they have a predictable effect on the truth conditions of compound statements. For example, the truth value of a compound formed by using *and* to join two statements is predictable from the truth of the constituent statements. See, for example:

4.22   a.   The house is on fire.
        b.   The fire brigade are on the way.
        c.   The house is on fire and the fire brigade are on the way.

If 4.22a and b above are true, then the compound c is also true. If, however, either of a or b is false then the compound will be false. This can be shown by designing a truth table for *and*, and representing it by a special symbol ∧:

4.23   **p**   **q**   **p ∧ q**

         T   T   T
         T   F   F
         F   T   F
         F   F   F

This table tells us that only when both statements connected by ∧ are true will the compound be true. So 4.22c above will be false if the house is on fire but the fire brigade are not on the way, and also false if the fire brigade are on their way but to a false alarm: the house is not on fire. Most obviously of all, 4.22c is false if there is no fire and no fire brigade on the way.

The study of the truth effects of connectives like ¬ and ∧ is called **propositional logic**, and logicians have studied the truth effects of a number of other connectives, for example those corresponding to the English words *or* and *if. . . then*. We can look briefly at these here and we will come back to them again in chapter 10.

There are two logical connectives which can correspond to English *or*. The first is called **disjunction** (or alternatively **inclusive or**) and is symbolized as ∨, thus giving logical forms like **p ∨ q**. The truth table for this connective is as follows:

4.24   **p**   **q**   **p ∨ q**

         T   T   T
         T   F   T
         F   T   T
         F   F   F

Thus a compound created with ∨ is true if one or both of the constituent sentences is true. This connective corresponds to the use of English *or* in sentences like the following:

4.25   I'll see you today or tomorrow.

Sentence 4.25 is true if either *I'll see you today* or *I'll see you tomorrow* is true, or both. It is only false if both are false.

The second connective which can correspond to English *or* is called **exclusive or**, which we can symbolize as $\vee_e$. This connective has the truth table in 4.26 below:

4.26

p	q	p $\vee_e$ q
T	T	F
T	F	T
F	T	T
F	F	F

From 4.26 we can see that **p** $\vee_e$ **q** is only true if just one of its disjuncts is true. This connective corresponds to the use of English *or* in sentences like 4.27 below:

4.27   You will pay the fine or you will go to jail.

This exclusive *or* seems to have an implicit qualification of 'but not both'. Thus if a judge said sentence 4.27 to a defendant, it would seem very unfair if the defendant paid the fine and then was still sent to jail, as would be consistent with inclusive *or*.

The next connective we will look at here is the **material implication**, symbolized as $\rightarrow$. This connective has the truth table in 4.28:

4.28

p	q	p $\rightarrow$ q
T	T	T
T	F	F
F	T	T
F	F	T

As 4.28 shows, the expression **p** $\rightarrow$ **q** is only false when **p** (the **antecedent**) is true and **q** (the **consequent**) is false. This connective is something like my use of English *if . . . then* if I utter a sentence like 4.29:

4.29   If it rains, then I'll go to the movies.

We can identify the *if*-clause in 4.29 as the antecedent and the *then*-clause as the consequent. This conditional sentence can only be false if it rains and I don't go to the movies, i.e. **p** = T, **q** = F. If it doesn't rain (**p** = F), my conditional claim cannot be invalidated by whatever I do: whether I go to the movies (**q** = T) or not (**q** = F). We can describe this relation by saying that **p** is a **sufficient condition** for **q** (rain will cause me to go) but not a **necessary condition** (other things might make me go; it might snow!).

This relation is a little hard to grasp and the reason is because we intuitively try to match it with our ordinary use of conditional sentences in English. However, conditionals in real languages often have more to them than this truth-conditional connective shows. For example, there is often an assumption of a causal connection between the antecedent clause (the *if*-clause) and the consequent (the *then*-clause), as in 4.30 below:

4.30   If Patricia goes to the party, then Emmet will go too.

A natural implication of sentence 4.30 is that Emmet is going **because** Patricia is. This is partly like our connective → because if Patricia goes to the party but Emmet doesn't (**p** = T, **q** = F) then the conditional sentence 4.30 is false, as the truth table for → suggests. However because of the causal implication, we might feel that if Patricia doesn't go (**p** = F) the conditional 4.30 implies that Emmet won't go. Thus we might feel that if he does go (**q** = T), the claim is invalidated. The logical connective, however, doesn't work like this: as 4.28 shows, if the antecedent is false, the compound is true, whatever the truth value of the consequent.

This truth–conditional relation also seems to miss our intuitions about another ordinary language use of conditional *if . . . then* constructions: **counterfactuals**, where the speaker overtly signals that the antecedent is false, for example:

4.31   If wishes were money, then we'd all be rich.[3]

The lack of fit here with our intuitions can be shown by the sentences in 4.32 below:

4.32   a.   If I were an ostrich, then I would be a bird.
         b.   If I were an ostrich, then I would not be a bird.

Let us interpret each of these conditionals as the **p** → **q** relation: since I am not in fact an ostrich, we might take **p** in 4.32a to be false, and if we follow the reasoning of the conditional then **q** might seem to be true. Thus, by the truth table in 4.28 the sentence 4.32a is true. This seems a reasonable fit with our intuition about 4.32a. The problem is that assuming the same antecedent **p** in 4.32b to be false means that 4.32b also has to be true, according to our truth table 4.28. Even if we accept the less likely 4.32b as true, it is uncomfortable to try and hold both 4.32a and b to be true for the same speaker in the same context. It seems likely that the material implication relation simply doesn't fit our use of counterfactuals. We will not follow this issue any further here; for a discussion of logical implication and ordinary language conditionals, see Lewis (1973) and the overview in Haack (1978). What we can say is that the logical relation of material implication captures some but not all aspects of our use of *if . . . then* in English.

There is one other related connective we might mention here, the **biconditional**, symbolized by ≡ (or alternatively ↔). This connective has the truth table in 4.33 below:

4.33

p	q	p ≡ q
T	T	T
T	F	F
F	T	F
F	F	T

As 4.33 shows, a statement **p** ≡ **q** is true when **p** and **q** have the same truth value. The name 'biconditional' reflects the fact that the **p** ≡ **q** is equivalent to the compound conditional expression (**p** → **q**) ∧ (**q** → **p**), which we can paraphrase as 'if **p** then **q** and if **q** then **p**'. This connective corresponds to the English words *if and only if* as in 4.34:

4.34   We'll leave if and only if we're forced to.

If we reverse the English clause order and identify the condition *if and only if we are forced to* as **p**, and the consequent *We'll leave* as **q**, then we can say that **p** is a **necessary condition** for **q**, i.e. **p** is the only possible cause for **q**. Given this, this connector is a plausible translation of the intended meaning of our earlier example 4.30 with *if . . . then*. In logic this relation '**p** if and only if **q**' is often abbreviated to '**p** iff **q**'.

This has been just a brief look at logical connectives and their English counterparts. As we have mentioned, in logic these connectives are important for the establishment of valid arguments and correct inductive reasoning. Using the symbols we have introduced in this section, we can represent the types of valid inference exemplified earlier in 4.13–16, as follows:

4.35   Modus ponens
         p → **q**
         p
         _____

         q

4.36   Modus tollens
         p → **q**
         ¬**q**
         _____

         ¬**p**

4.37   Hypothetical syllogism
         p → q
         q → r
         ───────
         p → r

4.38   Disjunctive syllogism
         p ∨ q
         ¬p
         ───────
         q

For our current purposes, what we need to hold onto are these ideas from logic: that statements have a truth value; that this truth value depends upon a correspondence to facts, and that different ways of connecting statements have different effects on the truth value of the compounds produced.

4.3   Necessary Truth, *A Priori* Truth and Analyticity

As we have seen, the notion of empirical truth depends on a correlation to states of affairs in reality. Philosophers and logicians have identified another type of truth which seems instead to be a function of linguistic structure. For example, we know that the tautology:

4.39   My father is my father.

is always true (in its literal meaning) without having to refer to the facts of the world, as is a sentence like:

4.40   Either he's still alive or he's dead.

We do not have to check a pulse to find out whether this sentence is true.
   In the same way, contradictions are false simply by virtue of their own meaning, e.g.

4.41   ?She was assassinated last week but fortunately she's still alive.

This second kind of truth has been the focus of much investigation. The question of how it is that we might know a statement to be true without checking the facts of the world has been discussed by many philosophers[4] and various distinctions of truth have been made. For example, we started out by characterizing this type of truth in epistemological terms, i.e. in terms of what the speaker knows (or needs to know before making a judgement about truth). From this perspective, truth that is known before or without experience has traditionally been called **a priori**. This *a priori* truth is contrasted with **a posteriori** truth: truth which, as in our examples 4.17 and 4.18 earlier, can only be known on the basis of empirical testing.

Another related concept is Leibniz's distinction between **necessary** truths, which cannot be denied without forcing a contradiction (for example the arithmetical statement *Two and two make four*), and **contingent** truths, which can be contradicted, depending on the facts (for example the sentence *The dodo is extinct*). If someone unexpectedly found a dodo in a forest on Mauritius, this latter sentence would become false. It is difficult, on the other hand, to imagine circumstances in which *Two and two make four* would unexpectedly become false. This is similar to our *a priori/a posteriori* distinction but comes at truth from another viewpoint: not in terms of what the speaker knows but in terms of what the world is like. We can say that it is hard to think how our sentence about two and two making four could not be true without changing our view of the present facts of the world.[5] From this perspective a sentence like 4.40 is also **necessarily true** and a contradiction like 4.41 is **necessarily false**.

In another, related terminology tautologies like 4.39 are **analytic** while a sentence like *My father is a sailor* is **synthetic**. Analytic statements are those where the truth follows from the meaning relations within the sentence, regardless of any relationship with the world, while a synthetically true statement is true because it accords with the facts of the world.

Thus we have three related distinctions of truth: between *a priori* and *a posteriori*, necessary and contingent, and analytic and synthetic. These notions are closely linked, yet not quite identical. As noted by Kripke (1980), part of their difference comes from the concerns of the analyst: the *a priori/a posteriori* distinction is an epistemological one: it concerns what the speaker knows. Indeed when we use the term *a priori* we are not concerned with how the speaker knows that a statement must be true, except that it is not by experience. The necessary/contingent distinction, on the other hand, is really a metaphysical one, where we are philosophically questioning the nature of reality. We can hypothesize that it is the nature of reality that ensures that a sentence like *Two and two make four* is a necessary truth. Finally, the analytic/synthetic distinction is semantic in orientation. The traditional claim has been that analytic sentences are true because of the meaning of the words within them: for example, the meaning of the predicate might somehow be included in the meaning of the subject: it might not add anything new.[6] This certainly seems to be true of our tautology *My father is my father*.

We can see that the three notions are related because under the kind of definitions we have introduced so far, our example sentence *My father is my father* is an *a priori* truth, it is necessarily true and it is analytic. As we have mentioned, this classification of truth has been the subject of much debate in the philosophical literature and it has been argued by some philosophers, for example Kripke (1980), that the terms do not characterize exactly the same set of statements: for example, that a statement might be a necessary

truth but not an *a priori* truth. To parallel a standard example, a statement
of identity like *Mogadishu is Hamar* is necessarily true because these are
two names for the same city, the capital of Somalia. Clearly, though, it is
possible for a person not to know this and therefore, for this person, our
sentence is not an *a priori* truth. The person might have to ask people or
look it up in a book, making the knowledge *a posteriori*.[7]

This sketch is enough for our present purposes. In our discussion we will
informally use necessary truth and analytic truth as synonymous terms to
describe sentences which are true by virtue of their meaning, and which
therefore are known to be true by a speaker of the language without any
checking of the facts. See Grayling (1982) for further discussion of the
relations of these notions.

We can provide further examples of sentences which are analytic or necessarily true in this sense if we imagine logically minded sports fans looking
forward to the World Cup Final and saying the following:

4.42   a.   Either Germany will win the World Cup or Germany won't
             win the World Cup.
        b.   If Germany are champions and Brazil are runners-up then
             Germany are champions.
        c.   All teams who win are teams.
        d.   If Germany beat Brazil then Brazil lose to Germany.

Sentences like 4.42a–c above have been important in the development of
logic. This is because their truth can be predicted from their logical form.
Take 4.42a for example: if, as before, we replace each clause by an arbitrary
letter, we produce a logical form, e.g.

4.43   Either **p** or not-**p**

This formula will be true for any clause, as long as each clause is the same,
represented above by using the same letter. For example:

4.44   Either we'll make it on time, or we won't make it on time.

Similarly, sentence 4.42b above can be given the logical form:

4.45   If **p** and **q** then **p**

Once again whatever clauses we use for **p** and **q** the formula will be true, e.g.

4.46   If the house is sold and we aren't there, the house is sold.

Sentence 4.42c is also necessarily true because of its logical form, but in this
case the truth behaviour is caused by the presence within the clause of the
quantifier *all*. To find its logical form we have to go inside the clause and
replace the subject and predicate by variables, e.g.

4.47   All X's that Y are X's

Again, this form will be true whatever subject and predicate we insert for X and Y, e.g.:

4.48   All birds that fly are birds.[8]

The study of the truth behaviour of such sentences with quantifiers like *all*, *every*, *each*, *some*, *one* gave rise to a second type of logic usually called **predicate logic**. Once again, good introductions to this logic can be found in Allwood et al. (1977). We will come back to both propositional and predicate logic again in chapter 10.

The important point here is that, as we have seen, there are certain words like the connectors *and*, *or*, *if . . . then*, the negative word *not*, and quantifiers like *all*, *some*, *one*, which influence the truth behaviour of sentences. For this reason these are sometimes called **logical words**. So the sentences 4.42a–c are necessarily true because of the presence of logical words, which means that their truth behaviour is predictable from their logical form.

The truth of sentence 4.42d (*If Germany beat Brazil then Brazil lose to Germany*), however, depends on the meaning of individual words like *beat* and *lose*, and not any logical form we might give the sentence, like 4.49:

4.49   If $G \ X \ B$ then $B \ Y \ G$.

We can see this, because if we replace the verbs with other verbs, we cannot predict that the resulting sentence will also be analytically true, e.g.

4.50   If Germany attack Brazil then Brazil outscore Germany.

This sentence might be true, or not: we cannot tell just from the sentence. It seems that sentence 4.42d is necessarily true because of the semantic relationship in English between the verbs *beat* and *lose*. This kind of necessary truth has not traditionally been a concern of logicians, because its effects cannot easily be reduced to general rules or schemas: it relies on the very varied and individual lexical relations we looked at in chapter 3. Thus such necessarily true sentences can derive from synonymy as in 4.51a below; from simple antonymy as in 4.51b; from converse pairs as in 4.51c; or hyponymy as in 4.51d:[9]

4.51   a.   My bachelor brother is an unmarried man.
        b.   If Elvis is dead then he is not alive.
        c.   If she's his sister then he's her brother.
        d.   A cat is an animal.

So our examples have shown us that sentences can be analytically true because of the behaviour of logical words (connectors, quantifiers) or because of the meaning of individual nouns and verbs. In each case we know that the sentences are true without having to check any facts about the world.

4.4   Entailment

Using this special meaning of 'truth' that we have been looking at, some semanticists have claimed that the meaning relations discussed in section 4.1 can be given a more rigorous definition. The claim is that there are fixed **truth relations** between sentences which hold regardless of the empirical truth of the sentences. We can examine this claim by looking at the semantic relation of **entailment**. Let's take as an example the relationship between sentences 4.52a and b below, where a is said to entail b:

4.52   a.   The anarchist assassinated the emperor.
          b.   The emperor died.

Assuming as usual that the same individual is denoted by *the emperor* here, there are a number of ways of informally describing this relationship. We could say that if somebody tells us 4.52a and we believe it, then we know 4.52b without being told any more. Or we could say that it is impossible for somebody to assert 4.52a but deny b. What such definitions have to try to capture is that entailment is not an inference in the normal sense: we do not have to reason to get from 4.52a to b, we just know it instantaneously because of our knowledge of English. A truth-based definition of entailment might allow us to state the relationship more clearly and would be something like 4.53 below:

4.53   Entailment defined by truth:
          A sentence **p** entails a sentence **q** when the truth of the first (**p**) guarantees the truth of the second (**q**), and the falsity of the second (**q**) guarantees the falsity of the first (**p**).

We can see how this would work for our examples:

4.54   Step 1:   If **p** (The anarchist assassinated the emperor) is true, is **q** (The emperor died) automatically true? Yes.
          Step 2:   If **q** (The emperor died) is false, is **p** (The anarchist assassinated the emperor) also false? Yes.
          Step 3:   Then **p** entails **q**. Note if **p** is false then we can't say anything about **q**; it can be either true or false.

We can try to show this relation in an accessible form if we take the logician's truth tables, seen earlier, and adapt them somewhat. We can continue to use the symbols **p** and **q** for our two sentences, and T and F for true and false, as in normal truth tables, but we will add arrows ($\rightarrow$ and $\leftarrow$) to show the direction of a relation 'when . . . then'. So the first line of 4.55 below is to be read 'When **p** is true, **q** is true', and the last line is to be read 'when **q** is true, **p** can be either true or false'. By taking these liberties with traditional truth tables, we can show the truth relations of entailment in 4.55, a composite truth table:

4.55   Composite truth table for entailment

p		**q**
T	$\rightarrow$	T
F	$\rightarrow$	T or F
F	$\leftarrow$	F
T or F	$\leftarrow$	T

When this set of relations hold between **p** and **q**, **p** entails **q**. From this table we can see that only the truth of the entailing sentence or the falsity of the entailed sentence have consequences for the other sentence. When **p** is false, **q** can be either true or false: if all we were told was that the anarchist didn't assassinate the emperor, we wouldn't know whether the emperor was dead or alive. When **q** is true, **p** can be either true of false: if we just know that the emperor is dead, that doesn't tell us anything about whether the anarchist assassinated him or not.[10]

We have said that an entailment relation is given to us by linguistic structure: we do not have to check any fact in the world to deduce the entailed sentence from the entailing sentence. The source may be lexical or syntactic. In our example above it is clearly lexical: the relationship of entailment between 4.52a and b derives from the lexical relationship between *assassinate* and *die*. In some sense the meaning of *assassinate* contains the meaning of *die*. In chapter 3 we called a similar relationship of meaning **hyponymy**; and indeed hyponymy between lexical items is a regular source for entailment between sentences. For example, the noun *dog* is a hyponym of *animal*, so it follows that sentence 4.56 below entails sentence 4.57:

4.56   I bought a dog today.

4.57   I bought an animal today.

Other sources for entailment are syntactic: for example, active and passive versions of the same sentence will entail one another. Sentence 4.58 below entails 4.59, and vice versa:

4.58   The Etruscans built this tomb.

4.59   This tomb was built by Etruscans.

In fact, the relationship of entailment allows us to define **paraphrase**. Paraphrases, like 4.58 and 4.59, are sentences which have the same set of entailments, or, to put it another way, **mutually entail** each other.

This truth-based definition does seem to capture our basic intuitions about entailment and semanticists have gone on to characterize other semantic relations in terms of truth relations. For example, we could very simply characterize synonymy with the table:

4.60   Composite truth table for synonymy

p		q
T	→	T
F	→	F
T	←	T
F	←	F

This table simply says, of course, that **p** and **q** always have the same truth value, i.e. if **p** describes a situation so will **q**, and vice versa; while if either incorrectly describes a situation so will the other. We can see this is true for examples like:

4.61   Alice owns this book.

4.62   This book belongs to Alice.

where again we observe the convention that it is the same Alice and the same book in the two sentences.[11]

The opposite of this relation of synonymy would be contradiction, with the truth table below:

4.63   Contradiction

p		q
T	→	F
F	→	T
T	←	F
F	←	T

where the simplest examples involve negation, as below:

4.64   Mr Jones stole my car.

4.65   Mr Jones did not steal my car.

but other examples might also include the lexical relation of simple or binary antonymy, as in our earlier examples with *beat/lose to*.

So thus far it seems that recasting semantic relations as truth relations allows us to describe neatly the relations we listed in section 4.1 as being the focus of our investigations. In the next section, however, we look at one of these relations, **presupposition**, which seems to lend itself less well to a truth-based description.

4.5 Presupposition

4.5.1 Introduction

In ordinary language, of course, to presuppose something means to assume it, and the narrower technical use in semantics is related to this. In the following examples the a sentence is said to **presuppose** the b sentence:

4.66   a. He's stopped turning into a werewolf every full moon.
        b. He used to turn into a werewolf every full moon.

4.67   a. Her husband is a fool.
        b. She has a husband.

4.68   a. I don't regret leaving London.
        b. I left London.

4.69   a. The Prime Minister of Malaysia is in Dublin this week.
        b. Malaysia has a prime minister.

4.70   a. I do regret leaving London.
        b. I left London.

Presupposition has been an important topic in semantics: the 1970s in particular saw lively debates in the literature. Books devoted largely to the subject include Kempson (1975), D. Wilson (1975), Boer and Lycan (1976), Gazdar (1979) and Oh and Dinneen (1979); and important papers include J. D. Fodor (1979) and Wilson and Sperber (1979). In retrospect this interest in presupposition can be seen as coinciding with the development of pragmatics as a sub-discipline. The basic idea, mentioned in chapter 1, is that semantics would deal with conventional meaning, those aspects which do not seem to vary too much from context to context, while pragmatics would deal with aspects of individual usage and context-dependent meaning.

The importance of presupposition to the pragmatics debate is that, as we shall see, it seems to lie at the borderline of such a division. In some respects presupposition seems like entailment: a fairly automatic relationship, involving no reasoning, which seems free of contextual effects. In other respects, though, presupposition seems sensitive to facts about the context of utterance. We will look at this sensitivity to context in section 4.5.5.

For now we can begin by identifying two possible types of approach to presupposition, arising from different ways of viewing language.

4.5.2 Two approaches to presupposition

In the first approach, rather in the philosophical tradition, sentences are viewed as external objects: we don't worry too much about the process of producing them, or the individuality of the speaker or writer and their audience. Meaning is seen as an attribute of sentences rather than something constructed by the participants. Semantics then consists of relating a sentence-object to other sentence-objects and to the world. When in the last section we characterized sentence relations in terms of truth relations we adopted this perspective. The second approach views sentences as the utterances of individuals engaged in a communication act. The aim here is about modelling the strategies that speakers and hearers use to communicate with one another. So we might look at communication from the speaker's viewpoint and talk about presupposition as part of the task of packaging an utterance; or adopt the listener's viewpoint and see presupposition as one of a number of inferences that the listener might make on the basis of what the speaker has just said. The first approach is essentially semantic and the second pragmatic.

Let's use 4.71 below and its presupposition 4.72 as an example to show these different views.

4.71   John's brother has just got back from Texas.

4.72   John has a brother.

We can adopt the sentences-as-external-objects approach and try to identify a semantic relationship between these two sentences. One obvious way is to cast this as a truth relation, as we did for entailment and other relations in the last section. To do this we might reason as in 4.73, to set up the partial truth table in 4.74:

4.73   Presupposition as a truth relation.
         Step 1: If **p** (the presupposing sentence) is true then **q** (the presupposed sentence) is true.
         Step 2: If **p** is false, then **q** is still true.
         Step 3: If **q** is true, **p** could be either true or false.

4.74   A first composite truth table for presupposition

p		**q**
T	→	T
F	→	T
T or F	←	T

At the risk of being long-winded, we can work through 4.73. If it is true that John's brother has come back from Texas, it must be true that John has a brother. Similarly, if it is false that John's brother has come back from Texas (if he is still there, for example), the presupposition that John has a brother still survives. Finally, if is true that John has a brother, it doesn't tell us anything about whether he has come back from Texas or not: we just don't know.

So viewing presupposition as a truth relation allows us to set up a truth table like 4.74, and allows us to capture an important difference between entailment and presupposition. If we negate an entailing sentence, then the entailment fails; but negating a presupposing sentence allows the presupposition to survive. Take for example the entailment pair in 4.75:

4.75   a.   I saw my father today.
        b.   I saw someone today.

If we negate 4.75a to form 4.76a then it no longer entails 4.75b, repeated as 4.76b:

4.76   a.   I didn't see my father today.
        b.   I saw someone today.

Now 4.76b no longer automatically follows from the preceding sentence: again it might be true, we just don't know. Compare this with the presupposition pair:

4.77   a.   The mayor of Liverpool is in town.
        b.   There is a mayor of Liverpool.

If we negate 4.77a to form 4.78a the resulting sentence still has the presupposition, shown as 4.78b:

4.78   a.   The mayor of Liverpool isn't in town today.
        b.   There is a mayor of Liverpool.

So negating the presupposing sentence does not affect the presupposition, whereas, as we saw, negating an entailing sentence destroys the entailment. So it seems that viewing presupposition as a truth relation allows us to capture one interesting difference between the behaviour of presupposition and entailment under negation.

By comparison, we can sketch an idea of how an alternative, interactional view of presupposition might work for our original example; *John's brother has just got back from Texas*. This approach views presupposition as one aspect of a speaker's strategy of organizing information for maximum clarity for the listener. Let us say roughly that the speaker wants to inform the listener that a particular individual has returned from Texas. The way she does this will depend on what she estimates about her listener's knowledge. If she thinks he knows John but not his brother, we can see in her use of 4.71 an ordering of the assertions in 4.79–80:

4.79   Assertion 1: John has a brother X.

4.80   Assertion 2: X has come back from Texas.

In our example 4.71 the first assertion is downgraded or backgrounded by being placed in a noun phrase [*John's brother*] while the second assertion is highlighted or foregrounded by being given the main verb. Why foreground one assertion rather than another? The answer must depend on the speaker's intentions and her guesses about the knowledge held by the participants. For example the speaker might judge that the listener knows 4.79 but that 4.80 is new information, and therefore needs to be foregrounded. Here we could speculate that the speaker decides to include the old information 4.79 to help the listener to identify the individual that the new information is about. Note too that a speaker can use 4.71 even if the listener does not know John has a brother. In such a case both assertions are new but the speaker has decided to rank them in a particular order.

4.5.3 Presupposition failure

One phenomenon which has traditionally caused problems for a truth relations approach but may be less problematic in an interactional approach is **presupposition failure**. It has been observed that using a name or a definite description to refer presupposes the existence of the named or described entity:[12] so the a sentences below presuppose the b sentences:

4.81   a.   Ronald is a vegetarian.
          b.   Ronald exists.

4.82   a.   The King of France is bald.
          b.   There is a King of France.

Example 4.82 is, of course, the subject of Bertrand Russell's discussion of the problem (Russell 1905), and is by now one of the most discussed examples in this literature. The problem arises when there exists no referent for the nominal. If there's no Ronald or King of France, i.e. if the b sentences above are false, what is the status of the a sentences? Are they false, or are they in a grey area, neither true nor false? In a truth-based approach, on a grey-area analysis, we need to add a line to our truth table, but what does the line look like?

4.83   A second truth table for presupposition

p		q
T	$\rightarrow$	T
F	$\rightarrow$	T
T or F	$\leftarrow$	T
?(T v F)	$\leftarrow$	F

What this table tries to show is that if **q** is false, the status of **p** is dubious, possibly neither true nor false. This is a problem for truth-based theories, known as a **truth-value gap**. If a statement can be neither true nor false, it opens a nasty can of worms. How many degrees in between are possible? A good deal of the attractive simplicity of the truth-based approach seems in danger of being lost. It is a problem that has generated a number of solutions in the philosophical literature; see McCulloch (1989) for discussion and for a solution in the linguistics literature, J. D. Fodor (1979). Russell's famous solution was to analyse definite descriptions as complex expressions roughly equivalent to 4.84 (adapted from McCulloch 1989: 47):

4.84   The King of France is bald is true if and only if:
a.   at least one thing is the king
b.   at most one thing is the king
c.   whatever is the king is bald.

From 4.84, it follows that sentence 4.82a is false if there is no king of France, and that there is no grey area between true and false, no truth-value gap. The cost, however, is a large discrepancy between the surface language and the semantic representation. Do we really want to say that a name is underlying a cluster of three statements?

For an interactional approach, there is less of a problem. Such an approach would claim that a speaker's use of definite NPs like names and definite descriptions to refer is governed by conventions about the accessibility of the referents to the listener. In some obvious way, I have made a communication error if I say to you:

4.85   Heronymous is bringing us a crate of champagne.

if you don't know any person called Heronymous. Your most likely response would be to ask 'Who's Heronymous?', thus signalling the failure. So we can hypothesize that there is an interactional condition on referring: a speaker's use of a name or definite description to refer usually carries a guarantee that the listener can identify the referent.[13]

So in an interactional approach the issue of presuppositional failure shifts attention from the narrow question of the truth value of statements about nonexistent entities to the more general question of what conventions license a speaker's referring use of definite nominals.

4.5.4 Presupposition triggers

We have seen that the use of a name or definite description gives rise to a presupposition of existence. Other types of presupposition are produced by particular words or constructions, which together are sometimes called **presupposition triggers**. Some of these triggers derive from syntactic structure, for example the cleft construction in 4.86 and the pseudo-cleft in 4.87 share the presupposition in 4.88:

4.86   It was his behaviour with frogs that disgusted me.

4.87   What disgusted me was his behaviour with frogs.

4.88   Something disgusted me.

Other forms of subordinate clauses may produce presuppositions, for example, time adverbial clauses and comparative clauses. In the following sentences, the a sentence has the presupposition in b:

4.89   a. I was riding motorcycles before you learned to walk.
        b. You learned to walk.

4.90   a. He's even more gullible than you are.
        b. You are gullible.

Many presuppositions are produced by the presence of certain words. Many of these **lexical triggers** are verbs. For example, there is a class of verbs like *regret* and *realize* that are called **factive** verbs because they presuppose the truth of their complement clause. Compare sentences 4.91 and 4.92 below: only the sentence with the factive *realize* presupposes 4.93. There is no such presupposition with the non-factive verb *think*.

4.91   Sean realized that Miranda had dandruff.

4.92   Sean thought that Miranda had dandruff.

4.93   Miranda had dandruff.

Similarly compare 4.94–6:

4.94   Sheila regretted eating the banana.

4.95   Sheila considered eating the banana.

4.96   Sheila ate the banana.

Some verbs of judgement produce presuppositions. Compare 4.97–9 below:

4.97   John blamed me for telling her.

4.98   John accused me of telling her.

4.99   I told her.

Once again one verb, *blame*, produces the presupposition in 4.99, while another, *accuse*, does not.

For a final example of lexical triggers, consider change-of-state verbs, like *start, begin, stop*. These verbs have a kind of switch presupposition: the new state is both described and is presupposed not to have held prior to the change; see for example 4.100–1 below, where again the a sentences presuppose the b sentences:

4.100   a. Judy started smoking cigars.
          b. Judy used not to smoke cigars.

4.101   a. Michelle stopped seeing werewolves.
          b. Michelle used to see werewolves.

4.5.5 Presuppositions and context

As mentioned earlier, one problem for a simple truth-based account of presupposition is that often the presuppositional behaviour seems sensitive to context. While a given sentence always produces the same set of entailments, it seems that this is not true of presuppositions. Levinson (1983) gives as an example the type of presupposition usually triggered by time adverbial clauses, e.g. 4.102a presupposing 4.102b below:

4.102   a. She cried before she finished her thesis.
          b. She finished her thesis.

However, if we change the verb, as in 4.103a below, the presupposition 4.103b is no longer produced:

4.103   a. She died before she finished her thesis.
          b. She finished her thesis.

Why is this? It is argued that in 4.103 the presupposition is blocked or cancelled by our general knowledge of the world: quite simply we know that dead people do not normally complete unfinished theses. This characteristic is sometimes known as **defeasibility**, i.e. the cancelling of presuppositions. If presuppositions arise or not depending on the context of knowledge, this suggests that we need an account of them that can make reference to what the participants know, as in an interactional approach, rather than an account limited to formal relations between sentences.

Another example of context sensitivity, pointed out by Strawson (1950), occurs with sentences like 4.104 and 4.105 below:

4.104   It was Harry who Alice loved.

4.105   It was Alice who loved Harry.

These sentences seem to describe the same essential situation of Alice loving Harry; or, to put it another way, we might say that they embody the same proposition. The difference between them is that they belong to different conversational contexts: whether the participants have been discussing Harry or Alice. As Strawson points out, they seem to give rise to different presuppositions, with 4.104 producing 4.106 and 4.105 producing 4.107:

4.106   Alice loved someone.

4.107   Someone loved Harry.

The same phenomenon is found with **intonation** in English, where stressing different parts of the sentence can produce different presuppositions. Using capitals to show the position of this stress, we can produce the presupposition in 4.106 above with 4.108 below, and 4.107 above with 4.109 below:

4.108   Alice loved HARRY.

4.109   ALICE loved Harry.

Such phenomena are discussed by Jackendoff (1972) and Allan (1986) amongst others. So these examples seem to provide another case where presuppositional behaviour is related to context: in this case the context of the discourse.

Another, narrower, contextual feature is traditionally called the **projection problem**, and is discussed in Gazdar (1979), Levinson (1983) and Heim (1992). Sometimes the presupposition produced by a simple clause does not survive when the clause is incorporated into a complex sentence. Levinson (1983: 191ff.) gives the example of conditional clauses. Sentence 4.110a contains the factive verb *regret* and would normally produce the presupposition in 4.110b:

4.110   a.   John will regret doing linguistics.
          b.   John is doing/will do linguistics.

However, in the context of a conditional clause like 4.111 below, the presupposition 4.110b disappears:

4.111   If John does linguistics, he'll regret it.

The context here is the syntactic one provided by the adjoining clause.

So we can see that different levels of context can cause fluctuations in presuppositional behaviour. At the most general level, the context provided by background knowledge; then, the context provided by the topic of conversation; and finally, the narrower linguistic context of the surrounding syntactic structures – all can affect the production of presuppositions. Simply giving a truth table of fixed relations between presupposing and presupposed sentences cannot adequately describe this complicated behaviour. Some more sophisticated account is required which takes account of how what participants know forms a background to the uttering of a sentence.

4.5.6   Pragmatic theories of presupposition

There have been a number of responses in the semantics literature to the features of presupposition we have outlined. Some writers (for example Leech 1981) have divided presuppositions into two types: one, **semantic presupposition**, amenable to a truth-relations approach; another, **pragmatic presupposition**, which requires an interactional description. In contrast, Stalnaker (1974) argued that presupposition is essentially a pragmatic phenomenon: part of the set of assumptions made by participants in a conversation, which he termed the **common ground**. This set of assumptions shifts as new sentences are uttered. In this view a speaker's next sentence builds on this common ground and it is pragmatically odd to assert something which does not fit it. Presumably cases of presuppositional failure like *The king of France is bald* would be explained in terms of the speaker assuming something (*There is a king of France*) that is not in the common ground.

This type of approach can cope with cases where presuppositions are not necessarily already known to the hearer, as when a speaker says *My sister just got married* (with its presupposition *I have a sister*) to someone who didn't know she had a sister. To capture this ability Lewis (1979: 127) proposes a principle of **accommodation**, where: 'if at time *t* something is said that requires presupposition *p* to be acceptable, and if *p* is not presupposed just before *t* then – ceteris paribus – presupposition *p* comes into existence'. In other words, presuppositions can be introduced as new information.[14]

A pragmatic view of presupposition is also proposed by Sperber and Wilson (1995), who argue that presupposition is not an independent phenomenon but one of a series of effects produced when the speaker employs syntactic structure and intonation to show the hearer how the current sentence fits into the previous background. These writers integrate presupposition with other traditional discourse notions like **given** and **new** information, and **focus**. They propose (1995: 215) that that the same principle of relevance to contextual assumptions covers both presupposition and the choice of the different word orders and intonations in 4.112 below:

4.112   a.   It rained on MONDAY.
             b.   On Monday it RAINED.
             c.   On MONDAY it rained.

These sentences belong to different contexts of use in a similar way to our presupposition examples in 4.104–9, that is, the preceding context will naturally lead a speaker to choose one of the sentences in 4.112 over another. In Sperber and Wilson's view a general theory of conversational cooperation will explain all such cases. We will look at further examples of this in chapter 7.

4.6   Summary

In this chapter we have identified a number of semantic relations that hold between sentences: **synonymy, entailment** and **presupposition**; and the sentential qualities of **tautology** and **contradiction**. We have reviewed an approach which characterizes these in terms of truth relations, using a notion of linguistic or analytic **truth**. We have seen that while this approach provides an attractive account of entailment, for example, it fails to account for the full range of presuppositional behaviour, in particular presupposition's sensitivity to contextual features. We contrasted this purely semantic approach with accounts which assume a pragmatic approach: describing presupposition in terms of a speaker's strategies to package her message against her estimate of what her audience knows. We will come back to this idea of processes of packaging information again in chapter 7.

FURTHER READING

A very clear introduction to logic for linguists is given by Allwood et al. (1977). Grayling (1982) contains a very readable discussion of the different notions of truth used in logic and the philosophy of language. Chierchia and McConnell-Ginet (2000) propose a truth-based account of entailment and other sentential relations which is probably best approached after reading chapter 10 below. Levinson (1983) has an accessible discussion of approaches to presupposition, and Allan (1986) has as its basic principle the kind of interactional approach we have discussed in this chapter. Beaver (1997) is a discussion of formal approaches to presupposition.

EXERCISES

4.1 Take three sentences, **p**, **q** and **r** as follows:

    p: The sun is shining.
    q: The day is warm.
    r: The sun is shining and the day is warm.

Let's make the working assumption that we can represent sentence **r** by the logical formula **p** $\wedge$ **q**. Use the truth table for $\wedge$ given in 4.23 in this chapter to show the truth value of **r** in the three situations (S1–3) below:

    S1. **p** is true; **q** is false
    S2. **p** is true; **q** is true
    S3. **p** is false; **q** is true.

4.2 In propositional logic it is assumed that **p** $\wedge$ **q** and **q** $\wedge$ **p** are logically equivalent, i.e. that the order of the elements is irrelevant. Discuss how the following examples show that this is not true for the way that speakers use English *and*.

    a. He woke up and saw on TV that he had won the lottery.
    b. Combine the egg yolks with water in a bowl and whisk the mixture until foamy.
    c. He made two false starts and was disqualified from the race.
    d. Move and I'll shoot!

4.3 Take three sentences, **p**, **q** and **r** as follows:

    p: Peter is drinking.
    q: Aideen is driving home.
    r: It is not the case that Peter is drinking or Aideen is driving home.

Let's make the working assumption that sentence **r** is ambiguous: in one reading the whole sentence is negated; in the other, just the first disjunct is negated. Thus the sentence may be given the two logical forms in a and b below:

    a. $\neg$ (**p** $\vee$ **q**)
    b. $\neg$**p** $\vee$ **q**

Use the truth tables for ¬ given in 4.21 and ∨ in 4.24 in this chapter to show the truth values of a and b above in the three situations (S1–3) below:

S1.   **p** is true; **q** is false
S2.   **p** is true; **q** is true
S3.   **p** is false; **q** is true.

4.4   To begin with, assume a general rule of **disjunction reduction**, by which any phrasal or clausal disjunction is derived from the disjunction of full sentences, i.e. assume that a sentence like *You can say yes or no* is equivalent to *You can say yes or you can say no*. For each of the sentences below, decide whether the use of *or* corresponds to inclusive (∨) or exclusive (∨ₑ) disjunction. Discuss your reasoning. Do any of these sentences have meanings that you feel are not captured by assuming disjunction reduction; or by the truth table characterization of the two logic connectors in 4.24 and 4.26 earlier?

    a.   We spend the afternoons swimming or sunbathing.
    b.   They can resuscitate him or allow him to die.
    c.   If the site is in a particularly sensitive area, or there are safety considerations, we can refuse planning permission.
    d.   You can take this bus or wait till the next one.
    e.   Breffni is a man's name or a woman's name.
    f.   The base camp is five or six days' walk from here.
    g.   He doesn't smoke or drink.
    h.   She suffers from agoraphobia, or fear of open places.
    i.   Stop or I'll shoot!

4.5   Decide which of the following sentences are **analytically true**. Discuss the reasons for your decision.

    a.   The train will either arrive or it won't arrive.
    b.   If it rains, we'll get wet.
    c.   Every doctor is a doctor.
    d.   If Albert killed a deer, then Albert killed an animal.
    e.   Madrid is the capital of Spain.
    f.   Every city has pollution problems.

4.6   Below are some paired sentences. Use the composite truth table for **entailment** given in 4.55 in this chapter to decide whether the a sentence **entails** its b partner. (As usual, assume that repeated nouns, names and pronouns refer to the same entity twice, and that the b sentences are uttered immediately after the a sentences.)

1   a.   Olivia passed her driving test.
      b.   Olivia didn't fail her driving test.

2   a.   Cassidy inherited a farm.
      b.   Cassidy owned a farm.

3   a.   Cassidy inherited a farm.
      b.   Cassidy owns a farm.

4   a.   Arnold poisoned his wife.
      b.   Arnold killed his wife.

5   a.   We brought this champagne.
      b.   This champagne was brought by us.

6   a.   Not everyone will like the show.
      b.   Someone will like the show.

4.7   We noted that factive predicates, like English *realize*, presuppose the truth of their clausal complements, as in *They realized that the dam had burst*. Using your own examples, identify the factive predicates from the following list: *announce, assume, be aware, believe, be fearful, be glad, be sorry, be worried, know, reason, report*.

4.8   Using the different behaviour of entailment and presupposition under negation as a test, decide whether the a sentences below **entail** or **presuppose** their b counterparts. (Again, assume that repeated nouns, names and pronouns refer to the same entity twice, and that the b sentences are uttered immediately after the a sentences.)

1   a.   Dave is angry because Jim crashed the car.
      b.   Jim crashed the car.

2   a.   Zaire is bigger than Alaska.
      b.   Alaska is smaller than Zaire.

3   a.   The minister blames her secretary for leaking the memo to the press.
      b.   The memo was leaked to the press.

4   a.   Everyone passed the examination.
      b.   No-one failed the examination.

5   a.   Mr Singleton has resumed his habit of drinking stout.
      b.   Mr Singleton had a habit of drinking stout.

NOTES

1   In 4.1–4 we assume, as in other examples, that pairs of sentences are uttered by the same speaker, in sequence, and that repeated nominals identify the same individual.

2   We assume here a simple **correspondence** theory of truth; see Grayling (1982) for a discussion of this and other theories of truth.

3   Logicians sometimes distinguish between two types of what we are here calling counterfactuals: **subjunctive conditionals**, which set up a hypothetical situation in the antecedent, as in *If Liverpool were to win the championship, he'd be a happy man*; and **counterfactual conditionals** where the antecedent is implied to be false, as in *If Liverpool had won the championship, he would have been a happy man*. For the rest of this book, we will use the term **counterfactual** as a cover term for both types. See Lewis (1973) and Haack (1978) for discussion.

4   Including, for example, Leibniz (1981), Kant (1993), Quine (1953), Carnap (1956), and Kripke (1980).

5   Another definition of necessary truth uses the notion of **possible worlds**, due originally to Leibniz. Possible worlds in the work of, for example, Lewis (1973, 1986), is a notion used to reflect the way speakers use language to do more than describe the world as it is. Speakers can, for example, hypothesize situations different from reality, as in **counterfactuals** like *If Ireland was a Caribbean island, we'd all be drinking rum*. Such situations that are not asserted as real are called possible worlds, the idea being that the world where Ireland is a Caribbean island is linguistically set up as a possible world, not the actual world. One definition of necessary truth uses this notion as follows: A statement is necessarily true if it is true in all possible worlds. However, since the constraints on setting up hypothetical worlds and their possibilities of difference from the real world are far from easy to ascertain, such a definition needs some work to establish. See Grayling (1982: 43–95) for introductory discussion and Kripke (1971), Lewis (1973) and the papers in Loux (1979) for more detailed discussion. We come back to this idea of possible worlds again in chapters 5 and 10.

6   This idea, often known as **concept containment**, derives from Leibniz. See the papers in Jolley (1995) for discussion.

7   An anonymous reviewer has suggested that an example like *Whales are mammals* brings out the difference between necessary and *a priori* truth. Following Kripke, this sentence is a necessary truth, but it is not an *a priori* truth for our hypothetical speaker who thinks that whales are fish.

8   This assumes that we rule out self-reference to avoid paradoxes. For example, by choosing to instantiate Y as 'are not Xs', we would get the necessarily false statement *All Xs that are not Xs are Xs*.

9   We discuss a formal approach to these lexical relations, **meaning postulates**, in chapter 10.

10 Another, more strictly logical way of describing this entailment relation is to say that **p** entails **q** when an argument that takes **p** as a premise and **q** as a conclusion must be valid, for example the argument:

The anarchist assassinated the emperor.
∴ The emperor died.

is valid.

11 Since this relation is clearly similar to the biconditional connective described earlier, we could give a logical definition of synonymy as in: **p** and **q** are synonymous when the expression $\mathbf{p} \equiv \mathbf{q}$ is always true.

12 Of course not all definite nominals are used to refer: so, for example, the definite NP in bold in the following sentence is traditionally described as being predicative and not referential: *Stuart is **the answer to our prayers***.

13 As we will note later, in chapter 8, Austin (1975) suggested that this condition is a **felicity condition** on the making of statements.

14 See Heim (1983) for a development of this idea of presuppositions as a set of assumptions forming part of the context for a sentence being uttered.

chapter 5

Sentence Semantics 1: Situations

5.1 Introduction

In chapter 3 we discussed aspects of word meaning. In this chapter we investigate some aspects of meaning that belong to the level of the sentence. One aspect is the marking of time, known as **tense**. How this is marked varies from language to language: it might be marked on a verb in languages like English or by special time words as in Chinese, as shown in 5.1a–c below:[1]

5.1   a.   Tā xiànzài yǒu kè
             he now   have classes
             'He now has classes.'
    b.   Tā zuótian yǒu kè
             he yesterday have classes
             'He had classes yesterday.'
    c.   Tā míngtian yǒu kè
             he tomorrow have classes
             'He will have classes tomorrow.'
                      (Tiee 1986: 90)

Here the verb *you* 'has/have' does not change form: the time reference is given by the time words, *xiànzài* 'now', *zuótian* 'yesterday' and *míngtian* 'tomorrow'. We can compare this with the English translations where the verb *have* changes for tense to give the forms, *have*, *had* and *will have*.

However it is marked, the location in time identified by tense belongs not to a single word but to the whole sentence. Take for example the English sentence 5.2 below:

5.2   Hannibal and his armies brought elephants across the Alps.

Though it is the verb *bring* which carries the morphological marker of tense, it seems sensible to say that the whole event described belongs in the past. In this chapter we will look at a number of semantic categories which, like tense, belong at the sentence level and which can be seen as ways that languages allow speakers to construct different views of situations. We begin by looking in section 5.2 at how languages allow speakers to classify situations by using semantic distinctions of **situation type**, **tense** and **aspect**. Then in section 5.3 we look at how systems of **mood** and **evidentiality** allow speakers to adopt differing attitudes towards the factuality of their sentences. Each of these are sentence-level semantic systems which enable speakers to organize descriptions of situations.

5.2 Classifying Situations

5.2.1 Introduction

We can identify three important dimensions to the task of classifying a situation in order to talk about it. These dimensions are **situation type**, **tense** and **aspect**. Situation type, as we shall see in section 5.2.2, is a label for the typology of situations encoded in the semantics of a language. For example, languages commonly allow speakers to describe a situation as static or unchanging for its duration. Such **states** are described in the following examples:

5.3   Robert loves pizza.

5.4   Mary knows the way to San José.

In describing states the speaker gives no information about the internal structure of the state: it just holds for a certain time, unspecified in the above examples. We can contrast this with viewing a situation as involving change, e.g.

5.5   Robert grew very quickly.

5.6   Mary is driving to San José.

These sentences describe **dynamic** situations. They imply that the action has subparts: Robert passed through several sizes and Mary is driving through various places on the way to San José.

This distinction between static and dynamic situations is reflected in the choice of lexical items. In English, for example, adjectives are typically used for states and verbs for dynamic situations. Compare the states in the a examples below with the dynamic situations in the b sentences:

5.7   a.   The pears are ripe.
        b.   The pears ripened.

5.8   a.   The theatre is full.
        b.   The theatre filled up.

This is not an exact correlation, however: as we saw above there are a number of **stative verbs** like _be, have, remain, know, love_ which can be used to describe states, e.g.

5.9   The file **is** in the computer.

5.10   Ann **has** red hair.

5.11   You **know** the answer.

5.12   The amendment **remains** in force.

5.13   Jenny **loves** to ski.

We will say that adjectives and stative verbs are inherently static, i.e. that it is part of their lexical semantics to portray a static situation type.

We have already briefly mentioned the dimension of **tense**. As we will describe in section 5.2.3, many languages have grammatical forms, such as verb endings, which allow a speaker to locate a situation in time relative to the 'now' of the act of speaking or writing. **Aspect** is also a grammatical system relating to time, but here the speaker may choose how to describe the internal temporal nature of a situation. If the situation is in the past, for example, does the speaker portray it as a closed completed event, as in 5.14 below, or as an ongoing process, perhaps unfinished, as in 5.15?

5.14   David wrote a pornographic novel.

5.15   David was writing a pornographic novel.

This is a difference of aspect, usually marked as with tense by grammatical devices. Tense and aspect are discussed together in section 5.2.4 and we discuss the problems of comparing the aspectual systems of different languages in 5.2.5. Finally section 5.2.6 is a brief look at how these dimensions combine to allow speakers to portray different situations.

5.2.2 Verbs and situation types

We saw in the last section that certain lexical categories, in particular verbs, inherently describe different situation types. Some describe states, others are dynamic and describe processes and events. In this section we describe elements of the meaning of verbs which correlate to differences of situation type.

Stative verbs In the last section we saw examples of inherently stative verbs like *be*, *have*, *know* and *love*. These verbs allow the speaker to view a situation as a steady state, with no internal phases or changes. Moreover the speaker does not overtly focus on the beginning or end of the state. Even if the speaker uses a stative in the past, e.g.

5.16   Mary loved to drive sports cars.

no attention is directed to the end of the state. We do not know from 5.16 if or how the state ended: whether Mary's tastes changed, or she herself is no longer around. All we are told is that the relationship described between Mary and sports cars existed for a while. We can contrast this with a sentence like 5.17 below, containing a dynamic verb like *learn*:

5.17   Mary learned to drive sports cars.

Here the speaker is describing a process and focusing on the end-point: at the beginning Mary didn't know how to drive sports cars, and at the end she has learnt. The process has a conclusion.

    Stative verbs display some grammatical differences from dynamic verbs. For example, in English progressive forms can be used of dynamic situations like 5.18a below but not states like 5.18b:

5.18   a. I am learning Swahili.
        b. *I am knowing Swahili.

As noted by Vlach (1981), this is because the progressive aspect, marked by -*ing* above, has connotations of dynamism and change which suits an activity like *learn* but is incompatible with a stative verb like *know*. We discuss the English progressive in sections 5.2.3 and 5.2.5 below.

    Similarly it usually sounds odd to use the imperative with statives; we can compare the following:

5.19   a.   Learn Swahili!
         b.   ?Know Swahili!

Once again, we can speculate that imperatives imply action and dynamism, and are therefore incompatible with stative verbs.

It may be, however, that the distinction between state and dynamic situations is not always as clear-cut. Some verbs may be more strongly stative than others; *remain* for example, patterns like other stative verbs in not taking the progressive, as in 5.20b below, but it does allow the imperative, as in 5.20c:

5.20   a.   The answer remains the same: no!
         b.   *The answer is remaining the same: no!
         c.   Remain at your posts!

It is important too to remember that verbs may have a range of meanings, some of which may be more stative than others. We can contrast the stative and non-stative uses of *have*, for example, by looking at how they interact with the progressive:[2]

5.21   a.   I have a car.
         b.   *I am having a car.
         c.   I am having second thoughts about this.

5.22   a.   She has a sister in New York.
         b.   *She is having a sister in New York.
         c.   She is having a baby.

Dynamic verbs   **Dynamic** verbs can be classified into a number of types, based on the semantic distinctions **durative/punctual** and **telic/atelic** which we will discuss below. These different verb types correlate to different dynamic situation types. One possible distinction within dynamic situation types, for example, is between **events** and **processes**. In events, the speaker views the situation as a whole, e.g.

5.23   The mine blew up.

while in a process, we view, as it were, the internal structure of a dynamic situation, e.g.

5.24   He walked to the shop.

Processes can be subdivided into several types, for example **inchoatives** and **resultatives**. Inchoatives are processes where our attention is directed to the beginning of a new state, or to a change of state, e.g.

5.25   The ice melted.

5.26   My hair turned grey.

Resultatives are processes which are viewed as having a final point of completion: our attention is directed to this end of the process, e.g.

5.27   Ardal baked a cake.

5.28   Joan built a yacht.

One difference between these types concerns interruption. If the action of melting is interrupted in 5.25 or my hair stops turning grey in 5.26, the actions of melting and turning grey can still be true descriptions of what went on. However if Ardal in 5.27 and Joan in 5.28 are interrupted halfway, then it is no longer true to describe them as having baked a cake or built a yacht. In some sense, to use resultatives we have to describe a successful conclusion. In this section we look at two important semantic distinctions in verbs which underlie these different dynamic situation types.

The first distinction is between **durative** and **punctual**: **durative** is applied to verbs which describe a situation or process which lasts for a period of time, while **punctual** describes an event that seems so instantaneous that it involves virtually no time. A typical comparison would be between the punctual 5.29 and the durative 5.30:

5.29   John coughed.

5.30   John slept.

What matters, of course, is not how much time an actual cough takes but that the typical cough is so short that conventionally speakers do not focus on the internal structure of the event.

In Slavic linguistics the equivalent of verbs like _cough_ are called **semelfactive** verbs, after the Latin word _semel_, 'once'. This term is adopted for general use by C. S. Smith (1991), Verkuyl (1993) and other writers. Other semelfactive verbs in English would include _flash_, _shoot_, _knock_, _sneeze_ and _blink_. One interesting fact is that in English a clash between a semelfactive verb and a durative adverbial can trigger an **iterative** interpretation, i.e. where the event is assumed to be repeated for the period described, e.g.

5.31   Fred coughed all night.

5.32   The drunk knocked for ten minutes.

5.33   The cursor flashed until the battery ran down.

In each of these examples the action is interpreted as being iterative: 5.31 is not understood to mean that Fred spent all night uttering a single drawn-out cough!

The second distinction is between **telic** and **atelic**. Telic refers to those processes which are seen as having a natural completion. Compare for example:

5.34   a.   Harry was building a raft. *false*
        b.   Harry was gazing at the sea.

If we interrupt these processes at any point then we can correctly say:

5.35   Harry gazed at the sea.

but we cannot necessarily say:

5.36   Harry built a raft.

As we saw earlier, telic verbs are also sometimes called **resultatives**. Another way of looking at this distinction is to say that *gaze* being atelic can continue indefinitely, while *build* has an implied boundary when the process will be over.

It is important to recognize that although verbs may be inherently telic or atelic, combining them with other elements in a sentence can result in a different aspect for the whole, as below:

5.37   a.   Fred was running. (atelic)
        b.   Fred was running in the London Marathon. (telic)

5.38   a.   Harry was singing songs. (atelic)
        b.   Harry was singing a song. (telic)

This telic/atelic distinction interacts with aspectual distinctions: for example, a combination of either the English perfect or simple past with a telic verb will produce an implication of completion. Thus, as we have seen, both 5.39 and 5.40 entail 5.41:

5.39   Mary painted my portrait.

5.40   Mary has painted my portrait.

5.41   The portrait is finished.

However, the combination of a progressive aspect and a telic verb, as in 5.42 below, does not produce this implication: 5.42 does not entail 5.41 above:

5.42   Mary was painting my portrait.

Comrie (1976) gives examples of derivational processes which can create telic verbs from atelic verbs, e.g. the German pairs in 5.43:

5.43   a.   *essen* 'eat', *aufessen* 'eat up'
         b.   *kämpfen* 'fight', *erkämpfen* 'achieve by fighting'

He contrasts the following sentences:

5.44   a.   die Partisanen haben für die Freiheit ihres Landes gekämpft.
         b.   die Partisanen haben die Freiheit ihres Landes erkämpft.
              'The partisans have fought for the freedom of their country.'
                                                    (Comrie 1976: 46–7)

where 5.44b implies that their fight was successful while 5.44a does not.

5.2.3   A system of situation types

Speakers use their knowledge of these semantic distinctions – stative/ dynamic, durative/punctual, telic/atelic – to draw distinctions of situation type. We have seen that some verbs, like *paint, draw* and *build*, are inherently telic while others like *talk, sleep* and *walk* are atelic. Similarly some verbs are inherently stative, like *know, love* and *resemble*, while others, like *learn, die* and *kill*, are non-stative. We have also seen from examples like 5.37 and 5.38 above that while these distinctions are principally associated with verbs, combining a verb with other elements in a sentence, like object noun phrases and adverbials, can alter the situation type depicted.
   The task for the semanticist is to show how the inherent semantic distinctions carried by verbs, and verb phrases, map into a system of situation types. One influential attempt to do this is Vendler (1967). Below are the four kinds of situations he identified, together with some English verbs and verb phrases exemplifying each type (Vendler 1967: 97–121):

5.45   a.   States
              desire, want, love, hate, know, believe
         b.   Activities (unbounded processes)
              run, walk, swim, push a cart, drive a car
         c.   Accomplishments (bounded processes)
              run a mile, draw a circle, walk to school, paint a picture, grow up, deliver a sermon, recover from illness
         d.   Achievements (point events)
              recognize, find, stop, start, reach the top, win the race, spot someone

C. S. Smith (1991), building on Vendler's system, adds the situation type **semelfactive**, distinguishing it from achievements as follows:

5.46   *Semelfactives* are instantaneous atelic events, e.g. [knock], [cough].
         Achievements are instantaneous changes of states, with an outcome of
         a new state, e.g. [reach the top], [win a race].   (Smith 1991: 28)

She identifies three semantic categories or features: [stative], [telic] and
[duration], with roughly the characteristics we have already described, and
uses these to classify five situation types, as follows (1991: 30):

5.47

Situations	**Static**	**Durative**	**Telic**
States	[+]	[+]	n.a.
Activity	[−]	[+]	[−]
Accomplishment	[−]	[+]	[+]
Semelfactive	[−]	[−]	[−]
Achievement	[−]	[−]	[+]

We can provide examples of each situation type, as follows:

5.48   She hated ice cream.   (State)

5.49   Your cat watched those birds.   (Activity)

5.50   Her boss learned Japanese.   (Accomplishment)

5.51   The gate banged.   (Semelfactive)

5.52   The cease-fire began at noon yesterday.   (Achievement)

It is important to remember that these situation types are interpretations of
real situations. Some real situations may be conventionally associated with
a situation type; for example, it seems unlikely that the event described in
5.53 below would be viewed other than as an accomplishment:

5.53   Sean knitted this sweater.

Other situations are more open, though: 5.54 and 5.55 below might be used
of the same real-world situation, but give two different interpretations of it:
5.54 as an activity and 5.55 as a state:

5.54   Sean was sleeping.

5.55   Sean was asleep.

5.2.4 Tense and aspect

Tense and aspect systems both allow speakers to relate situations to time,
but they offer different slants on time. Tense allows a speaker to locate a

Figure 5.1 Simple tenses

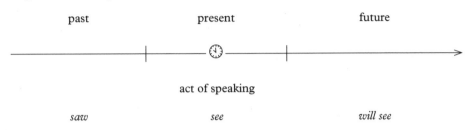

situation relative to some reference point in time, most likely the time of speaking. Sometimes in English this information is given by a temporal adverb; compare the following:

5.56   Yesterday they cut the grass.

5.57   Tomorrow they cut the grass.

Here, because the shape of the verb *cut* does not change, the temporal information is given by the adverbs *yesterday* and *tomorrow*. Usually in English, though, tense is marked on the verb by endings and the use of special **auxiliary verbs**, as in the forms of *speak* below:

5.58   She spoke to me.

5.59   She will speak to me.

5.60   She is speaking to me.

Tense is said to be a **deictic** system, since the reference point for the system is usually the act of speaking. As we shall see in chapter 7, deictic systems are the ways in which a speaker relates references to space and time to the 'here and now' of the utterance. Most grammatical tense systems allow the speaker to describe situations as prior to, concurrent with, or following the act of speaking. So in English, we have the three tenses: past, future and present as in 5.58–60 above. These are basic tenses and we could use a diagram like figure 5.1 to represent them, metaphorically representing time as a line moving left to right, and using the clock symbol for the time of the act of speaking.

More complicated time references are possible. For example, the speaker can locate an event in the past or future and use that event as the reference point for its own past, present and future. To do this in English, complex tenses are used. If a speaker in 1945 said, for example:

5.61   By 1939 my father had seen several arrests.

Figure 5.2   Complex past tense

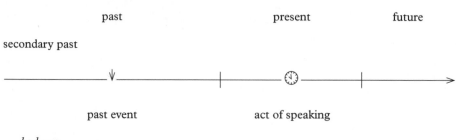

the verb *had seen* is one of these complex tenses, called the **pluperfect**. The year 1939 is in the past of the utterance, of course, but the speaker has made it the anchoring point for its own past. The father's acts of seeing are marked as being in this secondary past, as well as in the past relative to the act of speaking. Again we could represent this in a simple diagram as in figure 5.2.

Complex future tenses like *will have seen* allow a similar creation of a past-of-a-future-event, as in an utterance now of 5.62:

5.62   By 2050 we will have experienced at least two major earthquakes.

Here, of course, the earthquakes are portrayed as in the past relative to 2050, but in the future relative to the act of speaking.

It is difficult to go much further than these brief remarks about tense without discussing aspect. This is because in many languages, including English, aspect and tense interact in subtle ways and are marked on verbs in similar ways, often sharing composite endings. Aspect systems allow speakers to relate situations and time, but instead of fixing situations in time relative to the act of speaking like tense does, aspect allows speakers to view an event in various ways: as complete, or incomplete, as so short as to involve almost no time, as something stretched over a perceptible period, or as something repeated over a period. As Charles Hockett (1958: 237) describes it:

5.63   *Aspects* have to do, not with the location of an event in time, but with its temporal distribution or contour.

We can compare the sentences 5.64 and 5.65 below, for example:

5.64   Ralph was building a fire-escape last week.

5.65   Ralph built a fire-escape last week.

Both sentences describe a situation in the past but they differ: 5.65 views the fire-escape as completed, while 5.64 gives no information about whether the fire-escape ever got finished. The difference arises, of course, because the verb forms are each at a different intersection of the tense and aspect systems of English: *was building* is in a **past progressive** tense/aspect form in 5.64 and *built* is in a **simple past** tense/aspect form in 5.65.

We can look at this interdependence between aspect and tense by outlining some of the main forms in English. Our discussion of each will necessarily be brief and readers are referred to Leech (1971), Quirk et al. (1985) and Binnick (1991) for detailed descriptions.

English progressive forms

5.66 Present progressive   *I am listening*
Past progressive   *I was listening*
Future progressive   *I will be listening*

The progressives describe action as on-going and continuing. As mentioned earlier, progressives are used with dynamic situations rather than states and provide a way of describing processes as being extended through time without any implication of completion. In the past and future progressives can be used to provide a background activity against which another event occurs, e.g.

5.67 She was hiding the money when the doorbell rang.

5.68 She'll be washing the car when you arrive.

Aside from this central use there are a number of subsidiary uses of the progressive, e.g. for intentions or plans in the immediate future, as in 5.69:

5.69 I'm catching the midnight train tonight.

Reference grammars of English like Jespersen (1931) and Quirk et al. (1985) provide comprehensive descriptions of these uses.

English perfect forms

5.70 Present perfect   *I have listened*
Past perfect   *I had listened*
Future perfect   *I will have listened*

The perfect aspect allows a speaker to emphasize the relevance of events in the past to the 'present'. In the simplest case, the present perfect, this 'present' is the time of speaking, what we could call the unmarked anchoring point. This relevance can be of different types: one is to give a 'just now' sense of the immediate past, compare:

5.71 Don't run. The train has left.

5.72 ?Don't run. The train left.

Another interpretation of a sentence like 5.73

5.73   The train has left.

is that the speaker is focusing interest on the consequences now of the event
described, i.e. that the train is no longer here. This sense of 'relevance to
now' is reflected by the fact that the perfect is often used with the adverb
already, which means, of course, 'by now, by then', e.g.

5.74   I've already eaten.

In fact in some dialects of English this adverb can do the same job as the
perfect aspect, thus making it redundant and allowing sentences like:

5.75   I already ate.

   With the past and future perfect the connection, or relevance, relies on
a secondary location in time, an anchoring point in the past or future of the
time of speaking. See for example the past perfect in 5.76:

5.76   The train had left.

Here the anchoring point is in the past relative to the act of speaking and
the verb form links the time prior to the anchoring point with the anchoring
point itself. Though the locations in time are different, the same interpretations are possible as with the present perfect: a sense of immediacy, i.e. a
'just then' sense; or an emphasis on consequences – at that point the train
was no longer there:

5.77   He was too late. The train had left.

The future perfect allows the same interpretations with an anchoring point
in the future:

5.78   The train will have left.

So the perfect aspect is a relative aspect: it allows a speaker to emphasize
the relevance to an anchoring point of an event in its past. This anchoring
point can be the time that the speaker is speaking, or a time she chooses
in the past or future. The economy allowed by such verbal forms as we find
in 5.78 is clear as soon as we try to paraphrase such meanings as 'events in
the past of a future time but in the future of now'.

English simple forms

5.79	Simple present	*I listen*
	Simple past	*I listened*
	Simple future	*I will listen*

These forms are simple tense forms which can be seen as basically neutral with respect to aspect: depending on other elements in the sentence, and on context, they are compatible with a number of aspects. Take for example the simple past form in 5.80:

5.80   I watched the six o'clock news.

This is compatible with a couple of interpretations: referring to one occasion in the past or describing a habitual action. As we will see below, when a simple past like 5.80 refers to a single occasion it portrays the action as completed.

The simple present is more restricted than the past. For most verbs, the use of the simple present to describe present events has largely been supplanted by the use of the present progressive: in an exchange like 5.81:

5.81   a.   What are you doing?
         b.   I'm looking for my ticket.

the present progressive is used where many other languages would use a simple present, e.g. French:

5.82   a.   Que'est-ce que tu fais?
         b.   Je cherche mon billet.

However, the English simple present is used as an ordinary present tense with stative verbs, as in 5.83:

5.83   a.   He knows the answer.
         b.   *He is knowing the answer.

With non-stative verbs the simple present has other uses: it is used for habitual action, as in 5.84; for general or universal statements, as in 5.85, and in some instances for the future, as in 5.86:

5.84   She reads the *Independent*.

5.85   Earthworms belong to the phylum Annelida.

5.86   The ship departs tomorrow at dawn.

These, then, are examples of some basic tense and aspect forms in English. We have concentrated on the intersection of three tenses and three aspects, but we haven't, of course, exhausted the system: as learners of English know, more complex forms like *they will have been listening* are possible. See Quirk et al. (1985) for a more complete listing of the forms.

However, as foreign language learners also know, it is one thing to learn the verbal tense and aspect forms of a language and quite another to learn to use them correctly. One example of difficulty is that there are often restrictions on sequences of tense and aspect within complex sentences: for example, while the a sentence sequences below are possible, the b versions with a complex sentence sound very strange:

5.87   a.   Joan walked out. She has left her bag.
         b.   ?Joan walked out and has left her bag.

5.88   a.   You will get your results next Thursday. Come over for a drink.
         b.   ?When you will get your results next Thursday, come over for a drink.

See Comrie (1985: 102–21) and Binnick (1991: 339ff.) for discussion of sequencing constraints on tense and aspect forms.[3]

Speakers may also employ unusual tenses and aspects in narratives to add freshness to the telling. For example, in many languages, including English, speakers and writers may narrate past events in the present tense, sometimes known as the **historical present**, to give immediacy to a description. See for example the following extract from John le Carré's novel *The Night Manager*:

5.89   Jonathan is in the bedroom of the little flat in Luxor, with the moonlight sloping between the half-closed curtains. Sophie is lying on the bed in her white nightgown, eyes closed and face upward. Some of her drollness has returned. She has drunk a little vodka. So has he. The bottle stands between them.   (1993: 122)

Within the novel this scene is a flashback, situated in time before the main action of the novel, which itself is often described in the past tense. Since the description is in the present, the whole tense/aspect system is shifted, with the present perfect replacing the expected past perfect in, for example, 'She has drunk a little vodka.' See Schiffrin (1981) for a discussion of such effects.

5.2.5 Comparing aspect across languages

Although aspect is a sentential feature, we expect, especially in Indo-European languages, that it will be marked on verbs. Many languages, most famously Slavic languages, have inflectional affixes that give aspectual information, e.g. Russian:

5.90   On čital   pis'mo. (imperfective)
         he read.PAST.IMPERF a letter
         'He was reading a letter.'

5.91   On pročital   pis'mo. (perfective)
         he   read.PAST.PERF a letter
         'He read a letter.'[4]

This perfective/imperfective distinction of aspect is very widespread among
the languages of the world: Dahl (1985) and Bybee (1985) identify it as the
most commonly found and in many senses the most basic distinction. Some
writers view the difference as being one of viewpoint: Comrie (1976) describes perfectivity as viewing a situation externally, from outside, with no
reference to its internal temporal structure, while imperfectivity allows the
viewing of a situation from within, making explicit reference to the internal
temporal structure. C. S. Smith (1991) proposes a similar definition: perfectivity includes the viewing of the beginning and end of a situation, while
imperfectivity focuses on the middle phase, leaving especially the end unspecified. She supports this with examples from Russian, where the oddity
of 5.93 below comes from taking a situation described in 5.92 in the perfective, and therefore ended, and trying to extend it into the present (1991:
302):

5.92   On napisal   pis'mo.
         He wrote.PERF a letter
         'He wrote^{perf} a letter.'

5.93   ?On napisal   pis'mo i   ešče pišet   ego.
         he   wrote.PERF a letter and still writes.IMPERF it
         'He wrote^{perf} the letter and is still writing^{imperf} it.'

However, with a situation described in the imperfective, like 5.94 below, the
end-point is unspecified and is thus compatible with an extension into the
present as in 5.95 (Smith 1991: 304):

5.94   My pisali   pis'mo.
         we wrote.IMPERF a letter
         'We were writing^{imperf} a letter.'

5.95   My pisali   pis'mo i   ešče pišem   ego.
         we wrote.IMPERF a letter and still write.IMPERF it
         'We were writing^{imperf} a letter and are still writing^{imperf} it.'

These definitions allow us to correlate the imperfective/perfective system
with the distinction we saw earlier in English between the simple past and
the past progressive. Returning to our earlier example:

5.96   John was building a fire-escape.

5.97   John built a fire-escape.

we can identify the simple past verb form *built* in 5.97 as an English representative of the **perfective** aspect, with *was building* in 5.96 representing the **imperfective**. As we have seen, the perfective focuses on the end-points of a situation while the imperfective does not, producing a distinction between complete and incomplete action. This helps explain why we can interleave another event into the progressive as in (5.95) but not the simple past in 5.97, as 5.98 and 5.99 below show:

5.98   Ralph was building a fire-escape last week, when Rosemary came to stay.

5.99   Ralph built a fire-escape last week, when Rosemary came to stay.

In 5.98 Rosemary interrupts the building process, while in 5.99 Rosemary's arrival can only be placed outside the closed event, i.e. before or after the building of the fire-escape, perhaps most naturally the latter. Though the added clause is the same in both sentences, we understand different sequences of events: indeed the sequence understood in 5.99 can lead to the implication that Rosemary's arrival was the cause of Ralph building the fire-escape.

We can parallel Smith's examples from Russian with similar examples from English: 5.100 below is odd because the second clause contradicts the perfective nature of the first clause, while 5.101 is fine:

5.100   ?I baked a cake and I'm still baking it.

5.101   I was baking a cake, and I am still baking it.

What this brief comparison of English and Russian disguises is that while we can compare the aspectual systems of different languages, it is very difficult to characterize a typical aspectual system. Firstly, of course, the means of marking aspects differ: Russian, as we saw, uses prefixes on the verb, while English tends to use combinations of verbal endings and auxiliary verbs like *be, have, use to*, e.g.

5.102   a. He read *The Irish Times*.
         b. He has read *The Irish Times*.
         c. He used to read *The Irish Times*.
         d. He was reading *The Irish Times*.

A second and more serious problem in trying to come up with universal aspectual distinctions is that the aspectual systems of different languages tend not to correspond very closely. As we noted, it has been claimed that the aspectual distinction between perfective and imperfective aspects is very widespread: forty-five of the sixty-four languages in Dahl's (1985) worldwide sample possess an aspectual distinction of this type. However, there are numerous differences between uses of these two aspects amongst these languages. For example, the perfective in Arabic is only used with reference to the past, for example:

5.103   Harbat   al-bint min al-madrasa.
          run away.3f.sg.PERF the-girl from the-school
          'The girl ran/has run away from the school.'

In Russian, on the other hand, a perfective can occur with past and non-past tenses: a perfective non-past is understood to refer to the future, for example:

5.104   Ja napišu   pis'mo.
          I write.PERF.NON-PAST a letter
          'I'll write a letter.'
                            (Dahl 1985: 80)

The examples we have seen of tense and aspect have been marked grammatically, for example by verbal affixes and auxiliary verbs. As mentioned earlier, a speaker's characterization of a situation derives from combining a choice from the situation types encoded in the verbal semantics with forms from the grammatical systems of tense and aspect. We end our discussion of aspect by looking briefly at the interaction of situation types and aspect in the next section.

5.2.6 Combining situation type and aspect

We saw in section 5.2.2 that situation type and aspect interact: for example, certain verb forms such as progressives are used with some situation types but not with others. In fact the options for describing situations in any language are constrained by natural combinations of situation type, aspect and tense. Inherent features of a verb's meaning fit in with the meaning of certain tense and aspect forms, but not with others. Speakers know the valid combinations and the semanticist's task is to reflect this knowledge. The difficulty is that the combinations are very language specific. For example, in the last section we saw that the English progressive aspect has features of the cross-linguistic aspect **imperfective**. However, it also has connotations of activity, dynamism and volition. C. S. Smith (1991: 224) gives examples of contrasts between simple and progressive forms which show this:

5.105   a. She blinked her eyes.
          b. She was blinking her eyes.

5.106   a. The ship moved.
          b. The ship was moving.

The observation is that the b sentences have a vividness missing from the a sentences. Additionally, 5.105b has connotations of wilful behaviour missing from 5.105a; and in 5.106b the description of motion is more vivid than in 5.106a because of the progressive's focus on internal successive phases. As we saw earlier, these connotations of dynamism means that the progressive does not combine with stative situation types in English:

5.107   a.   *He was understanding the problem.
            b.   He understood the problem.

5.108   a.   *She was having long legs.
            b.   She had long legs.

However, in French the **imparfait** aspect, which might be seen as a corresponding imperfective,[5] does not have these connotations of dynamism and therefore does occur with statives, as below (Rand: 1993: 39):

5.109   L'air   sentait   le   jasmin.
            the-air smell.IMP-PAST the jasmin
            'The air smelled of jasmin.'

5.110   Je vous entendais   bien.
            I   you   hear.IMP-PAST well
            'I heard you well.'

Part of the semantic description of particular languages then is to reflect which aspectual viewpoints are available on a particular situation type. Thus for English we need to recognize that a speaker can choose to view an accomplishment from a perfective viewpoint, as in 5.111a below, or from an imperfective viewpoint, as in 5.111b:

5.111   a.   Rory painted a seascape.
            b.   Rory was painting a seascape.

Thus the interaction between situation type and aspect is a complex area of semantics, but what seems clear is that in describing a speaker's aspectual choices we must distinguish between three dimensions: real situations, the situation types lexically coded in languages, and ways of viewing these situation types in terms of their internal structure (the choice of whether or not to focus on their beginning, middle and end phases). There are some differences in the terminology applied across these three dimensions. Some writers use **aspect** for both the second and third dimensions: situation type and viewpoint. Others reserve **aspect** for viewpoint and use terms like **modes d'action** or **Aktionsarten** for the situation types, or the real situations, or both. Binnick (1991) picks a very detailed path through the terminology.

5.3 Modality and Evidentiality

5.3.1 Modality

Another important semantic category which operates at the sentence level
is **modality**. Modality is a cover term for devices which allow speakers to
express varying degrees of commitment to, or belief in, a proposition. Let
us take a simple assertion like 5.112:

5.112   Niamh has gone to the airport.

It seems that when being told 5.112, we assume a certain commitment on
behalf of the speaker to its truth. The speaker may be wrong, of course, or
be lying in order to mislead us. Our conversational practice, however, seems
to be built upon an assumption that speakers generally try to tell the truth,
as they know it. If we discover that Niamh hasn't gone to the airport then
our reactions will be very different depending on whether we think the
speaker was simply wrong in her belief, or intentionally misleading us. We
discuss this assumption of truthfulness as part of the more general issue of
conversational conventions in chapter 7. We might take the opposite of the
assertion 5.112 to be the denial 5.113:

5.113   Niamh hasn't gone to the airport.

However, without any further spoken qualification, both 5.112 and its negation 5.113 seem to carry an unspoken guarantee of 'to the best of my
knowledge'.
   Modal systems allow speakers to modulate this guarantee: to signal stronger
and weaker commitment to the factuality of statements. There are a number
of possible linguistic strategies: for example, the sentence can be embedded
under a higher clause with an adjective or adverb of modality, e.g. (where
S represents our sentence):

5.114   a. It is certain that S
          b. It is probable that S
          c. It is likely that S
          d. It is possible that S

Here versions a–d move from strong to weak commitment to S. Another
strategy is to put into the higher clause a verb which describes the extent
of the speaker's belief – what is often called in the philosophical literature
her **propositional attitude**:

5.115   a. I know that S
          b. I believe that S

  c. I think that S
  d. I don't know that S
  e. I doubt that S
  f. I know that not S

In 5.115 we have a gradient from the certainty of the truth of the proposition expressed by S through to the certainty of its falsity.

 A third strategy we find in English is to employ auxiliary verbs: in 5.117 below these mark the variations of commitment towards the assertion in 5.116:

5.116 She has left by now.

5.117 a. She must have left by now.
    b. She might have left by now.
    c. She could have left by now.
    d. She needn't have left by now.
    e. She couldn't have left by now.

Auxiliary verbs in this role are called **modal verbs**.

 These modal verbs have another function. The examples so far have been of **epistemic** modality, so called because the speaker is signalling degrees of knowledge. A second use is to signal **deontic** modality, where the verbs mark the speaker's attitude to social factors of obligation, responsibility and permission. Take for example 5.118 below:

5.118 You can drive this car.

A speaker can use this to mean either of the following:

5.119 It is possible for you to drive this car.

5.120 You have my permission to drive this car.

 The first is another example of epistemic modality; the second is an example of deontic modality. Deontic modals communicate two types of social information: **obligation** as in 5.121 and **permission** as in 5.122:

5.121 a. You must take these books back.
    b. You should take these books back.
    c. You need to take these books back.
    d. You ought to take these books back.

5.122 a. You can leave them there.
    b. You could leave them there.
    c. You might leave them there.

Deontic modals, like epistemic modals, signal a speaker's judgements but while with epistemics the judgement is about the way the real world is, with deontics it is about how people should behave in the world. This means that the use of deontics is tied in with all sorts of social knowledge: the speaker's belief systems about morality and legality; and her estimations of power and authority. The sentences in 5.121 and in 5.122 step down in modal strength. Thus 5.121a is a stronger statement of obligation than 5.121d and while 5.122a, for example, is a bald granting of permission, 5.122c is a weaker and politer version. We can imagine that deciding which of 5.122a–c to use would depend on different judgements by the speaker of her authority over the listener and the degree of formality of their relationship.

Sometimes the relationship between epistemic and deontic modality is more complicated than an ambiguity resolvable in context, like 5.118 earlier. Speakers can use an epistemic modal to imply a deontic interpretation as in 5.123:

5.123   You could have told me you were coming.

Here the possibility of telling is used to imply a missed obligation, turning 5.123 into a reproof.

We have seen that epistemic and deontic modality can be marked by the same means, for example modal verbs, and indeed that some sentences are ambiguous in form between an epistemic and deontic reading. This has led semanticists to ask what they have in common, and to speculate whether one type of modality has developed out of the other. One suggestion is that modality in general allows us to compare the real world with hypothetical versions of it. This approach derives from work on **possible world semantics** by David Lewis (1973, 1986) and others;[6] some of its grammatical implications are discussed by Chung and Timberlake (1985) and Palmer (1986). In this view, epistemic modals allow us to set up hypothetical situations and express different strengths of prediction of their match with the real world. Thus if a speaker says:

5.124   It might be raining in Belfast.

she is setting up a hypothetical situation (rain in Belfast) and predicting a reasonable match with reality. If, on the other hand, she says:

5.125   It must be raining in Belfast.

she is proposing a very strong match between her prediction and reality.

This approach views deontic modality in the same way. Here, though, the speaker is proposing a match between an ideal moral or legal situation and the real world of behaviour. So if a speaker says:

5.126   You should pay for that doughnut.

she is proposing a match between the ideal situation and the real situation;
a match more strongly proposed in 5.127:

5.127   You must pay for that doughnut.

This approach would relate modality to **conditional sentences** like 5.128
and 5.129 below, which also set up hypothetical situations:

5.128   If I were rich, I would be living somewhere hotter.

5.129   You would sleep all day, if we let you.

We can call the *if*-clause in sentences like 5.128–9, the **condition**, and the
other clause, the **consequent**. This view of conditionals as part of the modal
system neatly explains why we also find modal verbs used in consequent
clauses, like *would* in 5.128–9 above, or *should* in the condition clauses below:

5.130   If you should go to Paris, stay near the river.

5.131   Should you meet Christy, there's something I would like you to
           ask him.

This approach to modality is also supported by the existence of languages
that have verb forms which regularly distinguish between events in the real
world and events in future or imaginary worlds. This two-term modal distinction is often called a **realis/irrealis** modality (i.e. a reality/unreality
distinction): for example, Palmer (1986: 47) describes a distinction between
realis and irrealis moods in the Australian language Ngiyambaa:

5.132   a.   yuruŋ-gu ŋidja-ṛa.[7]
                rain-ERG rain-PRES
                'It is raining.' (realis)

           b.   yuruŋ-gu ŋidja-l-aga.
                rain-ERG rain-CM-IRREALIS
                'It might/will rain.' (irrealis)

   In this section we have looked briefly at the semantic system of modality; in the next we look at how modality distinctions are encoded in the
grammar, and in particular we will examine **mood**.

5.3.2   Mood

Thus far we have seen modality distinctions in English being marked by
various means including adverbs and modal verbs. When such distinctions

are marked by verb endings which form distinct conjugations, there is a grammatical tradition of calling these **moods**. Thus the distinction in the Ngiyambaa verb in 5.132 would be described as a distinction between a realis mood and an irrealis mood. In the verbal inflection of the Cushitic language Somali we find in addition to the basic indicative mood in 5.133 a conditional mood, as in 5.134, and a potential mood as in 5.135:

5.133   Wuu sameeyey.
         he   make.PAST
         'He made it.'

5.134   Wuu sameyn   lahaa.
         he   make.INFINITIVE have
         'He would make it, he would have made it.'

5.135   Show   sameyee.
         possibly make.POTENTIAL
         'Maybe he'll make it, it's possible he will make it.'

The indicative in 5.133, which is a *realis* form, and the potential in 5.135 are marked by specific verb endings, while the conditional in 5.134 uses the infinitive with an auxiliary verb 'have', rather like English.[8]

A more familiar example of mood is the subjunctive mood found in many European languages. The label subjunctive is applied somewhat differently in different languages, but we can identify two opposite poles of use, with an area of mixing and overlap between them. One pole is the grammatical one of syntactic subordination, i.e. subjunctive verb forms show that a verb is in a subordinate clause. The other pole is semantic, where the subjunctive marks language-specific types of irrealis mood, and is thus used for wishes, beliefs, exhortations, commands etc. At the syntactic pole, we can cite the example of Somali again where subordinated clause verbs are always differentiated from their main clause equivalents by a combination of tone and endings; compare 5.136 and 5.137 below:

5.136   Lacágta way   kéenaysaa.[9]
         lacág-ta waa-ay kéenaysaa
         'money-the CLASS-she bring.PROGRESSIVE
         'She is bringing the money.'

5.137   ínay lacágta kéenaysó
         ín-ay lacág-ta kéenaysó
         that-she money-the bring.SUBJUNCTIVE
         'that she is bringing the money'

In 5.136 the classifier *waa* identifies a main clause, while in 5.137 the complementizer *in* 'that' identifies a subordinate clause. As is clear, the main clause and subordinate clause forms of the verb *keen* 'bring' have different tonal shapes and different endings.[10]

If such subordinate verb forms are termed 'subjunctive', then this use of the term does not seem to have anything to do with the semantic system of modality. However, in classical Greek and in Latin, the subjunctive describes a verbal form that occurs in both main and subordinate clauses, though with somewhat different applications in each. Palmer (1986: 39–43), citing R. T. Lakoff (1968), gives six meanings of the subjunctive in Latin main clauses: imperative, optative (for wishes), jussive, concessive, potential and deliberative. Each of these can be identified with descriptions of unreal situations, and thus be examples of our semantic pole of unreality. They contrast with the **indicative** mood used for descriptions of factual, or real, situations.

In-between positions are very common, especially in modern European languages. In many languages, the subjunctive is most commonly found in subordinate clauses, but often with some special meaning: often following verbs of wishing and preference, as in the Spanish example 5.138 below (Butt and Benjamin 1994: 246) and the French 5.139; for the future in Spanish 5.140 (Butt and Benjamin 1994: 241); or indirect speech as in German 5.141 (Hammer 1991: 310):

5.138   Quiero   que estudies   más.
         want.INDIC.PRES.1sg that study.SUBJUN.PRES.2sg more
         'I want you to study more.'

5.139   Il vaut   mieux qu'elle   le sache.
         it worth better that+she it know.SUBJUN.PRES.3sg
         'It's better that she know it.'

5.140   Iremos   allí   cuando haga   buen tiempo
         go.INDIC.FUT.1p there when   have.SUBJUN.PRES.3sg good weather
         'We'll go there when the weather's good.'

5.141   Sie sagte sie   schreibe   den Brief.
         she said she   write.SUBJUN.IMPERF.3sg the letter
         'She said she was writing the letter.'

While there seems to be some shared element of modality in these uses, i.e. of non-factuality,[11] the range of use of subjunctives is usually both complex and language specific. Often the choice between indicative and subjunctive moods allows speakers to make subtle semantic distinctions, as for example between the different degrees of possibility marked by the French indicative and subjunctive in 5.142 and 5.143 below (Judge and Healey 1985: 141):

5.142   Je pense   qu'il viendra.
         I think.INDIC.PRES that-he come.INDIC.FUT
         'I think that he'll come.'

5.143   Je doute   qu'il   vienne.
        I   doubt.INDIC.PRES that-he come.SUBJUN.PRES
        'I doubt that he'll come.'

Before we close this section on mood, we should point out that there is another quite distinct use of the term in semantics. This applies to changes in verbal morphology associated with the different social functions or **speech acts** that a speaker may intend. For example, a speaker may intend a sentence as a statement, a question, a command or a wish. Depending on the language, these different functions may be marked by different word orders or special intonation tunes. Some languages mark this information by particular verb forms: for example, some languages have special **optative** verb conjugations to express wishes like the English phrases 'may he get well', 'I hope he gets well', 'if only he would get well', etc. See for example the Nahuatl sentence (Bybee 1985: 171):

5.144   mā choca.   'If only he would weep.'

Such special speech act verbal forms are often called moods: the example above would therefore be in the optative mood, and in some languages this would contrast with an imperative mood (for commands), an interrogative mood (for questions) or a declarative mood (for statements). We will discuss this grammaticalization of speech functions in chapter 8 on speech acts. See Foley and Van Valin (1984) for discussion of the relationship between this use of mood and the epistemic and deontic modality we have been concerned with here.

5.3.3   Evidentiality

Under epistemic modality we looked at ways in which a speaker can mark different attitudes towards the factuality of a proposition. There is a related semantic category **evidentiality** which allows a speaker to communicate her attitude to the source of her information. This is possible in English, of course, by the use of a separate clause or by parenthetic adverbials. Compare the bare assertion in 5.145 with the various evidentially qualified versions in 5.146a–g:

5.145   She was rich.

5.146   a. I saw that she was rich.
        b. I read that she was rich.
        c. She was rich, so they say.
        d. I'm told she was rich.
        e. Apparently she was rich.
        f. She was rich, it seems.
        g. Allegedly, she was rich.

These qualifications allow the speaker to say whether the statement relies on
personal first-hand knowledge, or was acquired from another source; and if
the latter, perhaps to say something of the source.

Some languages routinely mark such information grammatically, by special particles or specific verb forms, so that in these languages evidentiality
is coded in the morphology. A collection of descriptions of such languages
is Chafe and Nichols (1986), which contains articles both on the North and
South American languages where such systems were first described and also
on evidential systems in European and Asian languages. We can take as an
example Makah, a Nootkan language spoken in Washington State, whose
morphology distinguishes several different sources for information (Jacobsen
1986: 10):

5.147   a.   wiki·ċaxaw.   'It's bad weather.'
                                     (seen or experienced directly)
         b.   wiki·ċaxakpi·d.   'It looks like bad weather.'
                                     (inference from physical evidence)
         c.   wiki·ċaxakq̇ad?i.   'It sounds like bad weather.'
                                     (on the evidence of hearing)
         d.   wiki·ċaxakwa·d.   'I'm told there's bad weather.'
                                     (quoting someone else)

From examples like these one can identify the morphological markers of
evidentiality in Makah, a set of suffixes (Jacobsen 1986):

5.148   direct experience: zero marking
         inference from physical evidence: -pi:t
         auditory source: -q̇adi
         quotative: -wa:t

What emerges from these studies of evidential systems are differences
among languages in whether the evidential markers are obligatory in ordinary
speech or an optional resource for speakers. Hardman, for example, reports
that among the Jaqi languages of Peru, Bolivia and Chile the identification
of what she calls 'data source' (i.e. the use of evidentials) is a central part
of knowing how to communicate (1986: 114):

5.149   Accuracy on the part of the speaker is a crucial element in the
         public reputation of individuals; misuse of data-source is some-
         how somewhat less than human, or is insulting to the listener.

Speakers of Jaqi languages, which include Jaqaru, Aymara and Kakwi, have
obligatorily to signal whether the source of information for their statements
is personal experience, or knowledge gained from other individuals by lan-

guage, or comes from the remote past where no witnesses are available, i.e. from myths, history and religion. In other languages the use of evidentials is more voluntary, providing a speaker with creative resources to structure a point of view in a discourse, or perhaps to argue more convincingly. See Chafe (1986) for a description of evidentials in English.

5.4   Summary

In this chapter we looked at aspects of sentence meaning which allow the speaker to classify situations. The category of **situation type**, for example, incorporating semantic distinctions like **static/dynamic**, **durative/punctual** and **telic/atelic**, allows a basic classification of situations into **states**, **activities**, **accomplishments**, etc. The categories of **tense** and **aspect** interact with situation type to allow a speaker to relate a situation to time in two ways: to locate it relative to the act of speaking, and to portray its internal temporal shape. We saw something of how these choices are reflected in grammar. We also saw that the distinctions available to speakers may be very subtle and language specific.

We also looked at the semantic categories of **modality** and **evidentiality**, which allow the speaker to assume various attitudes towards a proposition. **Epistemic** modality reflects various judgements of factuality and **deontic** modality communicates judgements of moral and legal obligation. Both can be seen as implying a comparison between the real world and hypothetical versions of it. **Evidentiality** is a term for the ways in which a speaker qualifies a statement by referring to the source of the information. We saw that in some languages this information is grammaticalized and therefore obligatory, implying that in these communities, calculation of evidence is assumed of speakers by their hearers. We look at the role of similar hearer assumptions, e.g. that the speaker is estimating and updating her audience's state of knowledge, in chapter 7.

FURTHER READING

Comrie's *Aspect* (1976) and *Tense* (1985) are concise monographs, using examples from a range of languages. C. S. Smith (1991) discusses universals of situation type and aspect and gives brief descriptions of the aspectual systems of English, French, Russian, Mandarin Chinese, and Navajo. Palmer (1986) and Bybee and Fleischman (1995) contain discussions of modality systems in various languages. Bybee et al. (1994) contains a large cross-linguistic survey of tense, aspect and modality. The marking of these semantic categories on the English verb can be seen in Leech (1971), and the comprehensive reference grammar Quirk et al. (1985).

EXERCISES

5.1 **Stative verbs** typically cannot occur in the progressive aspect nor as imperatives. Use these two facts as tests to decide which of the following verbs are stative:

> comprise own imitate possess know resemble lack seize last think lose prefer

5.2 As we saw, some verbs can have distinct **stative** and **dynamic** senses. For each of the following verbs, provide two sentences: one with the verb in a stative sense and the other a dynamic sense. You can use the progressive test, as in the last exercise, to distinguish between the senses.

> admire equal appear hold contain reach cost smell

5.3 We noted that adding a **durative** adverb like *all night* or *for three hours* to a **punctual** verb like *cough* results in an **iterative** or repetitive interpretation (i.e. 'again and again'). Thus in *The patient coughed all night* we interpret the activity as a sequence of individual coughs throughout the night. Use this behaviour to identify the punctual verbs amongst the following:

> drive ring tap sigh fly twitch sob float read

5.4 We saw that some verbs may describe **bounded** (**telic**) or **unbounded** (**atelic**) processes, depending on the form of their complements. Thus while *build a bridge* is a bounded process, *build bridges* is an unbounded process. Below is a list of verb phrases. For each one decide whether it is bounded or unbounded, then see if you can change this value by altering the verb's complement.

> dismantle a car   ripen
> swim   direct movies
> rig an election   sink a beer
> put out fires

5.5 In this chapter, we identified a number of English tense/aspect forms, e.g. the past perfect form in *she had realized*. Identify the tense/aspect forms of the italicized verbs below:

> a.   They *founded* a school of medicine.
> b.   A guy *was telling* them a joke.
> c.   Who *decides*?
> d.   They'*ve eaten* a lot of peanuts.

  e. She *will bring* the money.
  f. You're *treating* me like a child.
  g. They *will have reached* the warehouse by now.
  h. I'm *sitting* here.

5.6 Below are paired examples containing **simple present** and **present progressive** verb forms. Explain what semantic differences you detect (if any) between the pairs.

  1 a. My brother works in France.
     b. My brother is working in France.

  2 a. We leave tomorrow.
     b. We're leaving tomorrow.

  3 a. You look good.
     b. You're looking good.

  4 a. She lives near the airport.
     b. She's living near the airport.

  5 a. You eat too much meat.
     b. You're eating too much meat.

  6 a. You always laugh at me.
     b. You're always laughing at me.

5.7 We described the use of **modal verbs** to convey **epistemic modality**. In the following sentences discuss what the modal verbs (in bold) tell us about the speaker's attitude.

  a. This **could** be our bus now.
  b. They **would** be very happy to meet you.
  c. You **must** be the bride's father.
  d. The bus **should** be here soon.
  e. It **might** freeze tonight.
  f. He **will** be home by now.

5.8 Some sentences with modal verbs are ambiguous between an **epistemic** and a **deontic** reading. For each of the sentences below, try to imagine two contexts: one where the sentence might be used with an epistemic reading and the other a deontic reading. Once again modal verbs appear in bold type.

  a. Alcohol **may** not be served to persons under eighteen.
  b. You **can** go home now.
  c. We **could** take the examination early.
  d. You **will** not leave this island.
  e. We **should** be at the hotel by nine.

5.9   One use of the **subjunctive** mood in English is in *that*-clauses which report a suggestion or proposal, as in 1 below. As is shown by 2 below, this use is paralleled by clauses with the modal verb *should*:

1   Subjunctive
   a.   He proposed *that the meeting come to a close.*
   b.   She agreed *that the house be sold.*

2   Modal verb
   a.   He proposed *that the meeting should come to a close.*
   b.   She agreed *that the house should be sold.*

As 1 shows, the form of the subjunctive in English is the base (or bare stem) form of the verb. Decide which of the following verbs may take a subjunctive *that*-clause by constructing example sentences:

beg   remember   command   report   tell   warn   deny   urge insist   decide   demand   request   promise   suggest

5.10 Chafe (1986), discussing **evidentiality** in English, identifies five sources for information. In the following the marker of evidentiality is shown in bold:

1   belief: the information is already held by the speaker, who makes no overt reference to evidence, e.g. *I think that democracy means more than just one person one vote*;

2   induction: the speaker concludes the information from evidence, without specifying the type of evidence, e.g. *The exit must be blocked*;

3   sensory evidence: information from perceptual evidence, e.g. *It smells like they're having a barbecue next door*;

4   hearsay evidence: information acknowledged as being told to the speaker by others, e.g. *They're supposed to be having an affair*;

5   deduction: the speaker uses a hypothesis to predict a fact, e.g. *The snow should melt more quickly near the sea.*

Below are some sentences containing markers of evidentiality. For each sentence identify the marker and say which of these five sources of information you think is involved.

a. Evidently we're no longer welcome here.
b. Electrons should flow through the wire from Fe^{2+} to MnO_{4-}.
c. You look like you need a stiff drink.
d. Apparently he turned up in drag.
e. He sounds a bit unsure of himself.
f. You must be very tired after your journey.
g. The jeweller was the ringleader, allegedly.
h. I suppose that I'd better go to the lecture.

NOTES

1 Transcription as in the original, where tone is marked as follows: ā (macron) = high level tone, ó = rising; o = fall-rise, ò = falling.

2 See Dowty (1979) for a discussion of stativity and English verbs, especially verbs like *sit* and *stand*, which act like statives in many ways but allow progressive forms.

3 See also Ogihara (1989).

4 Note that our translations here are meant to be suggestive: in fact, as my colleague Sarah Smyth has pointed out to me, the contrast between the English past progressive and past simple doesn't exactly capture the Russian distinction between imperfective and perfective. Thus 5.91 can also mean *He read a letter* or *He has read a letter*. The perfective form in 5.92 is more likely to mean *He read a letter (and then threw it away)*, for perfective verbs in Russian suggest continuation of narrative.

5 The French *imparfait* does not of course correspond to the Russian imperfective: for example, the French perfective *Tu as vu ce film?* would be translated into Russian as an imperfective *Ty videl etot fil'm?*.

6 We discuss this notion of possible worlds in chapter 10.

7 In this transcription CM = 'conjugation marker', ERG = ergative case.

8 We have glossed *show* in 5.135 as 'possibly' but in fact it is a sentence-type indicator, or **classifier**, which can only be used with verbs in the potential mood. See Saeed (1993) for more details, and chapter 8, section 8.5, where we discuss these classifiers in Somali and their status as sentence-type markers.

9 The tone markings used here are *á* = high tone, and *a* (i.e. unmarked) = low tone. They are only marked on the first vowel of long vowels, e.g. *ée*.

10 Note that such subordinate clause verbs are finite, showing inflectional marking of person, tense and aspect.

11 Another way of viewing what these uses of the subjunctive have in common comes from the modality of speech acts, to be discussed in chapter 8. This view recognizes a common element of *non-assertion* in these clauses.

chapter 6

Sentence Semantics 2: Participants

6.1 Introduction: Classifying Participants

In the last chapter we looked at aspects of sentence-level semantics: how speakers may choose to characterize situations and express various degrees of commitment to the portrayal. Another set of semantic choices which face a speaker seeking to describe a situation concerns how to portray the roles of any entities involved. Take for example 6.1 below:

6.1   Gina raised the car with a jack.

This sentence identifies three entities, *Gina*, *the car* and *a jack*, related by the action described by the verb *raise*. The sentence portrays these entities in specific roles: Gina is the entity responsible for initiating and carrying out the action, the car is acted upon and has its position changed by the action, and the jack is the means by which Gina is able to cause the action. Such roles have a number of labels in semantics, including participant roles (Allan 1986), deep semantic cases (Fillmore 1968), semantic roles (Givón 1990), thematic relations (Gruber 1976; Jackendoff 1972) and thematic roles (Dowty 1986, 1989, 1991; Jackendoff 1990). Given its wide usage in recent work, we will use the last term here: **thematic roles**.

In this chapter we examine this notion of thematic roles. We begin by sketching the basic picture of these roles that seems to be assumed by much of the syntax and semantics literature. Thus in sections 6.2–6.4 we outline the main contenders for individual types of roles, look at the relationship between thematic roles and grammatical relations, and discuss the idea that verbs must have their thematic role requirements listed in the lexicon. In the second part of the chapter we look more critically at the idea of thematic roles: first, in section 6.5, we review criticisms that have been levelled at the notion. Then in 6.6 we review the job these roles do in linguistic description. In the third and final part of the chapter, section 6.7, we investigate **voice** systems and see how they allow speakers some flexibility in the relationship between thematic roles and grammatical structure: we focus on **passive** voice and **middle** voice.

6.2 Thematic Roles

Each of the writers mentioned above, and others, for example Andrews (1985) and Radford (1988), have proposed lists of thematic roles. From this extensive literature we can extract a list of thematic roles like the following (where the relevant role-bearing nominal is in bold):

AGENT: the initiator of some action, capable of acting with volition, e.g.

6.2   **David** cooked the rashers.

6.3   **The fox** jumped out of the ditch.

PATIENT: the entity undergoing the effect of some action, often undergoing some change in state, e.g.

6.4   Enda cut back **these bushes**.

6.5   The sun melted **the ice**.

THEME: the entity which is moved by an action, or whose location is described, e.g.

6.6   Roberto passed **the ball** wide.

6.7   **The book** is in the library.

EXPERIENCER: the entity which is aware of the action or state described by the predicate but which is not in control of the action or state, e.g.

6.8   **Kevin** felt ill.

6.9   **Mary** saw the smoke.

6.10   **Lorcan** heard the door shut.

BENEFICIARY: the entity for whose benefit the action was performed, e.g.

6.11   Robert filled in the form for **his grandmother**.

6.12   They baked **me** a cake.

INSTRUMENT: the means by which an action is performed or something comes about, e.g.

6.13   She cleaned the wound with **an antiseptic wipe**.

6.14   They signed the treaty with **the same pen**.

LOCATION: the place in which something is situated or takes place, e.g.

6.15   The monster was hiding **under the bed**.

6.16   The band played **in a marquee**.

GOAL: the entity towards which something moves, either literally as in 6.17 or metaphorically as in 6.18:

6.17   Sheila handed her licence **to the policeman**.

6.18   Pat told the joke **to his friends**.

SOURCE: the entity from which something moves, either literally as in 6.19 or metaphorically as in 6.20:

6.19   The plane came back **from Kinshasa**.

6.20   We got the idea **from a French magazine**.

Thus to return to our first example, repeated below:

6.21   Gina raised the car with a jack.

we can describe the thematic roles by calling *Gina* the AGENT of the action, *the car* the THEME, and *the jack* the INSTRUMENT.

There is some variation in the use of these terms: for example Radford (1988) treats PATIENT and THEME as different names for the same role. Here we adopt the distinction that PATIENT is reserved for entities acted upon and changed by the verb's action while THEME describes an entity moved in literal or figurative space by the action of the verb, but constitutionally unchanged. Thus the noun phrase *the rock* would be a PATIENT in 6.22 below but a THEME in 6.23:

6.22   Fred shattered **the rock**.

6.23   Fred threw **the rock**.

A number of tests for identifying thematic roles have been suggested. Jackendoff (1972), for example, provides a test for AGENT: whether the phrases like *deliberately*, *on purpose*, *in order to*, etc. can be added to the sentence. This reflects the fact that an AGENT characteristically displays animacy and volition. The contrast between 6.24 and 6.25 below identifies John as an AGENT in 6.24 but not 6.25:

6.24   **John** took the book from Bill in order to read it.

6.25   ?**John** received the book from Bill in order to read it.

Some writers (e.g. Foley and Van Valin 1984, Jackendoff 1990) have suggested that AGENT is a particular type of a more general thematic role ACTOR, where ACTOR 'expresses the participant which performs, effects, instigates, provoke or controls the situation denoted by the predicate' (Foley and Van Valin 1984: 29). So every AGENT is an ACTOR, but not the other way round: in 6.26 below *the car* is an ACTOR but not AGENT since it presumably is in possession neither of a wish to kill nor to animate:

6.26   **The car** ran over the hedgehog.

Other simple tests suggested by Jackendoff (1990) include predicting that for an ACTOR (X) it will make sense to ask 6.27 below, and for a PATIENT (Y) that it will be able to occur in the frames in 6.28:

6.27   What did X do?

6.28   a.   What happened to Y was . . .
         b.   What X did to Y was . . .

So for example 6.29 below the tests would give 6.30–1, identifying *Robert* as the ACTOR and *the golf club* as PATIENT:

6.29   Robert snapped the golf club in half.

6.30   What Robert did was to snap the golf club in half.

6.31   a.   What happened to the golf club was that Robert snapped it in half.
         b.   What Robert did to the golf club was snap it in half.

Some writers have suggested other thematic roles in addition to those we have discussed. For example a role of PERCEPT is sometimes used for the entity which is perceived or experienced, e.g.

6.32   a.   The general inspected **the troops**.
       b.   Did you hear **that thunder**?
       c.   **That shark** frightened the swimmers.

A role of RECIPIENT is sometimes identified, e.g. by Andrews (1985), as a type of GOAL involved in actions describing changes of possession, e.g.

6.33   a.   He sold **me** this wreck.
       b.   He left his fortune **to the church**.

While these roles, ACTOR, AGENT, PATIENT, EXPERIENCER, THEME, INSTRUMENT etc. may seem intuitively clear, in practice it is sometimes difficult to know which role to assign to a particular noun phrase. For example, in a sentence like 6.34 below *to the lighthouse* is clearly a GOAL, and in 6.35 *him* is a BENEFICIARY, but in 6.36 below is *Margarita* the GOAL/RECIPIENT, or the BENEFICIARY, or both?

6.34   Fergus carried the bag **to the lighthouse**.

6.35   Sylvie bought **him** a sports car.

6.36   **Margarita** received a gift of flowers.

Examples like these raise the difficult question of whether a single entity can fulfil two or more thematic roles at the same time; for example in 6.37 below, are we to say that Mr Wheeler is both AGENT and THEME?

6.37   **Mr Wheeler** jumped off the cliff.

These issues are still under investigation in various theoretical approaches. A central claim of Chomsky's Principles and Parameters theory, for example, is the **Theta-Criterion**, which states that there must be a one-to-one correspondence between noun phrases and thematic roles (see Chomsky 1988; Haegeman 1994). Jackendoff (1972), on the other hand, suggested that one entity might fulfil more than one role. In Jackendoff (1990) the idea that one nominal might fulfil more than one role is elaborated into a theory of tiers of thematic roles: a **thematic tier**, which describes spatial relations, and an **action tier** which describes ACTOR–PATIENT-type relations. His examples include the following (1990: 126–7):

6.38   a.   Sue hit   Fred.
            Theme   Goal   (thematic tier)
            Actor   Patient   (action tier)

       b.   Pete threw   the ball.
            Source   Theme   (thematic tier)
            Actor   Patient   (action tier)

    c. Bill entered   the room.
        Theme   Goal   (thematic tier)
        Actor   (action tier)

    d. Bill received   a letter.
        Goal   Theme   (thematic tier)
                                     (action tier)

Thus *Fred* in 6.38a is simultaneously the GOAL and the PATIENT of the action. The gaps in a tier reflect instances where the nominal has only one thematic role: thus *the room* in 6.38c has no role in the action tier. Presumably these tiers would divide thematic roles into two types, perhaps as follows:

6.39   a. Action tier roles: ACTOR, AGENT, EXPERIENCER, PATIENT, BENEFICIARY, INSTRUMENT.
        b. Thematic tier roles: THEME, GOAL, SOURCE, LOCATION.

To these dimensions of action and space, Jackendoff also proposes a dimension of time, which we will not investigate here. The basic insight is clear: the roles that speakers assign to entities may be more complicated than a single thematic role label. For a detailed discussion of this proposal, see Jackendoff (1990: 125–51).

    Having identified these thematic roles, the next question we might ask is: how are such roles identified in the grammar? For our English examples above, the answer is: by a combination of syntactic structure and the choice of verb. There are typical matchings between participant roles and grammatical relations. As in our original example 6.21, the subject of the sentence often corresponds to the AGENT, the direct object to the THEME, while the INSTRUMENT often occurs as a prepositional phrase. Though this is the typical case, it is not necessarily so: for example, it is possible to omit the AGENT from the sentence and as a result have the INSTRUMENT occupy subject position, e.g.:

6.40   **The jack** raised the car.

We can see the effect of the choice of verb if we try to describe this same situation without either the AGENT or the INSTRUMENT. We cannot simply allow the THEME to occupy subject position as in 6.41; we have to change the verb as in 6.42:

6.41   *The car raised.

6.42   The car rose.

This is because the verb *raise* requires an ACTOR. The verb *rise*, however, describes a change of state without any slot for an ACTOR so that while 6.42 above is fine, 6.43 and 6.44 below are not possible:

6.43   *Gina rose the car.

6.44   *The jack rose the car.

What this simple example shows is that a speaker's choice of participant roles has two aspects: the choice of a verb with its particular requirements for thematic roles, and within the limits set by this, the choice of grammatical relations for the roles. We look at these choices in the rest of this chapter, beginning with the relationship between thematic roles and grammatical relations: first we describe how various thematic roles may occupy subject position, then we look briefly at the selection of thematic roles as part of a verb's lexical semantics. Later we discuss the role of *voice* in allowing speakers to alter prototypical matchings between thematic roles and grammatical relations.

6.3 Grammatical Relations and Thematic Roles

We have seen that while in English there is a tendency for subjects to be AGENTS, direct objects to be PATIENTS and THEMES, and INSTRUMENTS to occur as prepositional phrases, this need not always be the case. There are two basic situations where this is not the case: the first is where roles are simply omitted, and the grammatical relations shift to react to this, as we will discuss in this section; and the second is where the speaker chooses to alter the usual matching between roles and grammatical relations, a choice often marked by an accompanying change of verbal *voice*. We deal with voice later on in section 6.7.

We can begin with a simple example of thematic role omission in 6.45–7 below:

6.45   Ursula broke the ice with a pickaxe.

6.46   The pickaxe broke the ice.

6.47   The ice broke.

This is similar to our example 6.21 earlier: in 6.45 Ursula is the AGENT and subject, the ice is the PATIENT and direct object, and the pickaxe, the INSTRU-MENT, is in a prepositional phrase. In 6.46 the AGENT is omitted and now the INSTRUMENT is subject; and finally in 6.47 with no AGENT or INSTRUMENT expressed, the PATIENT becomes subject. The verb *break*, unlike *raise* earlier, allows all three thematic roles to occupy subject position. Several writers have suggested that this process of different roles occupying the subject position is a hierarchical process, not only in English but across many languages. The observation is that when speakers are constructing a sentence, they tend to place an AGENT into subject position, the next preference being for a RECIPIENT or BENEFACTIVE, then THEME/PATIENT, then other roles. From our English examples, it seems that INSTRUMENT is then preferred to LOCA-TION. This is sometimes described as an *implicational hierarchy*. There are various versions of such a hierarchy proposed in the literature, e.g. in Fillmore (1968) and Givón (1984b), but we can construct a simple example of a universal subject hierarchy like 6.48 below:

6.48   AGENT > RECIPIENT/BENEFACTIVE > THEME/PATIENT > INSTRUMENT >
          LOCATION

(extrema izquierda)

This diagram can be read in two equivalent ways: one is that the leftmost elements are the preferred, most basic and expected subjects, while moving rightward along the string gives us less expected subjects. A second way to read this diagram is as a kind of rule of expectation, going from right to left: if a language allows the LOCATION role to be subject, we expect that it will allow all the rest. If, however, it allows the role INSTRUMENT to be subject, we expect that it allows those roles to the left, but we don't know if it allows the LOCATION role as subject. The idea is that languages can differ in what roles they allow to occur as subject but they will obey this sequence of preference, without any gaps. So, for example, we should not find a language that allows AGENT and INSTRUMENT to be subject but not THEME/PATIENT.

It is a little difficult to think of English examples with LOCATION as sub-ject, unless we include sentences like 6.49a–b below:

6.49   a.   **This cottage** sleeps five adults.
          b.   **The table** seats eight.[1]

but the other positions on the hierarchy occur regularly, as we can see from the following examples:

6.50   AGENT subjects:
          The thief stole the wallet.
          Fred jumped out of the plane.

6.51   EXPERIENCER subjects:
          I forgot the address.
          Your cat is hungry.

6.52   RECIPIENT subjects:
          She received a demand for unpaid tax.
          The building suffered a direct hit.

6.53   PATIENT subjects:
          The bowl cracked.
          Una died.

6.54   THEME subjects:
Joan fell off the yacht.
The arrow flew through the air.

6.55   INSTRUMENT subjects:
The key opened the lock.
The scalpel made a very clean cut.

See Comrie (1981) and Croft (1990) for discussion of this and other implicational hierarchies.

6.4   Verbs and Thematic Role Grids

As we saw earlier with the verbs *raise, rise* and *drive*, verbs have particular requirements for their thematic roles. Since this is part of a speaker's semantic knowledge about a verb, we might expect it to be part of the lexical information stored for verbs. Thus we need to know not only how many arguments a verb requires (i.e. whether it is intransitive, transitive, etc.) but also what thematic roles its arguments may hold.

In the generative grammar literature, this listing of thematic roles is often called a **thematic role grid**, or **theta-grid** for short.[2] A simple example might be:

6.56   **put** V: <<u>AGENT</u>, THEME, LOCATION>

This entry tells us that *put* is a three-argument, or ditransitive, verb and spells out the thematic roles the three arguments may carry. Here we show Williams's (1981) suggestion of underlining the AGENT role to reflect the fact that it is this role that typically occurs as the subject of the verb (or 'external argument' in Williams's terminology). Clearly this is just the start of the job that a grammatical description must do of mapping between thematic roles and grammatical categories and structures. Our thematic grid for *put* in 6.56 predicts that this verb, when saturated with the correct arguments, might form a sentence like 6.57:

6.57   John$_{\text{AGENT}}$ put the book$_{\text{THEME}}$ on the shelf$_{\text{LOCATION}}$[3]

Of course, not all nominals in a sentence are arguments of a verb and thus specified in verbal theta-grids in the lexicon. We will make the assumption that one can employ grammatical tests to identify arguments: for example, to distinguish between the role of argument played by the prepositional phrase *in the bathroom* in 6.58 below and its status as a non-argument in 6.59:

6.58   [$_S$ Roland [$_{VP}$ put [$_{NP}$ the book] [$_{PP}$ in the bathroom]]]

6.59   [$_S$ Roland [$_{VP}$ read [$_{NP}$ the book]] [$_{PP}$ in the bathroom]]

The square brackets in 6.58–9 reflect the fact that while *in the bathroom* is an argument of the verb *put*, explaining why it cannot be omitted:

6.60   *Roland put the book.

it is not an argument of the verb *read*, on the other hand, which can form a sentence without it:

6.61   Roland read the book.

In grammatical terms, while *in the bathroom* is an argument in 6.58, it is an **adjunct** in 6.59. As well as not being required by the verb, adjuncts are seen as less structurally attached to the verb, explaining why 6.62 below is a much more unusual word order than 6.63, and usually requires a marked intonation pattern:

6.62   In the bathroom Roland put a book.

6.63   In the bathroom Roland read a book.

See Radford (1988) and Haegeman (1994) for discussion of the grammatical status of arguments and adjuncts. We will assume that all verbs may co-occur with adjuncts (usually adverbials of time, place, manner, etc.) and that requirements need only be listed in the lexicon for arguments.

Another way of making this distinction is to distinguish between **participant roles** and **non-participant roles**. The former correspond to our arguments: they are needed by the predication, in the sense we have been discussing; the latter are optional adjuncts which give extra information about the context, typically information about the time, location, purpose or result of the event. Of course only participant roles will be relevant to verbal thematic grids, and our discussion in this chapter focuses on these participant roles.

Listing thematic grids soon reveals that verbs form classes which share the same grids. For example, English has a class of TRANSFER, or GIVING, verbs which in one subclass includes the verbs *give, lend, supply, pay, donate, contribute*. These verbs encode a view of the transfer from the perspective of the AGENT. They have the thematic grid in 6.64; 6.65 is an example:

6.64   V: <AGENT, THEME, RECIPIENT>

6.65   Barbara$_{AG}$ loaned the money$_{TH}$ to Michael$_{RE}$.[4]

Another subclass of these TRANSFER verbs encodes the transfer from the perspective of the RECIPIENT. These verbs include *receive, accept, borrow, buy, purchase, rent, hire.* Their thematic grid is in 6.66, with an example in 6.67, paralleling 6.65 above:

6.66   V: <RECIPIENT, THEME, SOURCE>

6.67   Michael~RE~ borrowed the money~TH~ from Barbara~SO~.

Thematic grids such as these are put to use in the literature for a variety of descriptive jobs. We can look at some of these in section 6.6, when we ask more generally: what purpose do thematic roles serve in linguistic analysis? First, though, we discuss some of the problems associated with the simple picture of thematic roles we have outlined so far.

6.5 Problems with Thematic Roles

In our introductory discussion, we mentioned that the lists of roles given in the literature have varied from author to author. Authors disagree about what, if any, distinctions are to be made between PATIENT and THEME, for example, or between AGENT and related roles like ACTOR, EXPERIENCER, etc.

We can see these debates as reflections of two general problems with thematic roles (usually abbreviated to 'theta-roles', sometimes also called θ-roles). The first problem is really about delimiting particular roles. The extreme case would be to identify individual thematic roles for each verb: thus we would say that a verb like *beat* gives us two theta-roles, a BEATER-role and a BEATEN-role. This would of course reduce the utility of the notion: if we lose the more general role-types like AGENT, PATIENT etc., then we cannot make the general statements about the relations between semantic roles and grammatical relations discussed earlier, nor put theta-roles to any of the uses we describe in the next section.

But if we are to classify individual theta-roles roles like BEATER and BEATEN into theta-role types like AGENT and PATIENT, we will have to find some way of accommodating variation within the role type. Let us take the example of PATIENT in a typical grid:

6.68   V: <AGENT, PATIENT, INSTRUMENT>

A typical example would be 6.69:

6.69   The child~AG~ cracked the mirror~PA~ with his toy~IN~.

Earlier we defined the PATIENT as the entity affected by the action of the verb. However, attempts to examine particular verbs, such as Dixon (1991), reveal that both the type of 'affectedness' and the role of the INSTRUMENT vary between verb types. For example, Dixon (1991: 102–13) identifies eight types of affectedness: a range including the minimal contact of the verb *touch* in 6.70, where possibly no change occurs in the PATIENT, through *rub* in 6.71, where the surface of the PATIENT might be affected, and *squeeze* in 6.72 where a temporary change of shape in the PATIENT occurs, to *smash* in 6.73, where the PATIENT loses its physical integrity:

6.70   John touched the lamp with his toe.

frotar

6.71   The captain rubbed the cricket ball with dirt.

presionó

6.72   Henry squeezed the rubber duck in his hands.

6.73   Alison smashed the ice cube with her heel.

The questions which face semanticists here are: do the differences between the affectedness of the PATIENT reduce the usefulness of this label, or can the differences be explained in some way?

The second problem is more general: how do we define theta-roles in general? That is, what semantic basis do we have for characterizing roles? Facing both of these problems, Dowty (1991) proposes a solution where theta-roles are not semantic primitives but are defined in terms of **entailments** of the predicate. In this view a theta-role is a cluster of entailments about an argument position which are shared by some verbs. He gives examples like *x murders y*, *x nominates y*, *x interrogates y*, where:

6.74   entailments they all share include that *x* does a volitional act, that *x* moreover intends this to be the kind of act named by the verb, that *x* causes some event to take place involving *y* (*y* dies, *y* acquires a nomination, *y* answers questions – or at least hears them), and that *x* moves or changes externally (i.e. not just mentally). (1991: 552)

Such a set of shared entailments about *x* will serve to define the nominal which denotes *x* as AGENT. Thus theta-roles are defined in terms of shared verbal entailments about nominal referents.[5] We will see something of how these entailments are used in this approach in the rest of this section.

falta de claridad

In this view of theta-roles as clusters of entailments, we can see a solution to the problem of the fuzziness of roles. Dowty proposes that we view the roles not as discrete and bounded categories but instead as **prototypes**, where there may be different degrees of membership. He suggests that there are two basic prototypes: Proto-Agent and Proto-Patient,[6] each of which would contain characteristic lists of entailments such as those in 6.75 and 6.76 below:

(Definiciones prototípicas)

6.75   Properties of the Agent Proto-Role (Dowty 1991: 572):

entailment

    a. volitional involvement in the event or state
    b. sentience (and/or perception)
    c. causing an event or change of state in another participant
    d. movement (relative to the position of another participant)

6.76   Properties of the Patient Proto-Role (Dowty 1991: 572):

    a. undergoes change of state *(some case)*
    b. incremental theme[7] *(que es progresivo)*
    c. causally affected by another participant
    d. stationary relative to movement of another participant

grupo

The idea is that these clusters of entailments would allow various kinds of shading. For example, some arguments might have more of the entailments than others. So, for example, *John* in *John cleaned the house* would include all four of the entailments in 6.75 above: volition, sentience, causation and movement. By contrast *John* as an argument of *drop* in *John fainted and dropped the vase* would involve no volition, and *the storm* in *The storm destroyed the house* would involve neither sentience nor volition. We can see that this approach allows variation amongst AGENTS: some will be more typical and involve a greater number of characteristic entailments; others will be more marginal. Similar variation would hold for PATIENTS.

    This approach would also allow other forms of fuzziness: some entailments might be viewed as more important than others; or each entailment itself might be fuzzy-edged. As several commentators have pointed out, speakers sometimes blur the distinction between sentient and non-sentient when they talk about computers, saying things like *The computer thinks these are the same file* or *This program doesn't realize that the memory is full.*

    These proposals by Dowty to view thematic roles in terms of prototypical clusters of entailments allow flexibility in defining thematic roles. One result of his classification is that traditional role-types fall out as more-or-less prototypical versions of the two main categories. Thus, as we have seen, a centrally prototypical AGENT like *Maggie* in 6.77a below involves all four entailments in 6.75, while an EXPERIENCER, like *Joan* in 6.77b can be seen as a more marginal AGENT, including sentience but not volition or causation; and an INSTRUMENT like *the scalpel* in 6.77c includes causation and movement but not volition or sentience:

6.77   a. **Maggie** pruned the roses.
      b. **Joan** felt the heat as the aircraft door opened.
      c. **The scalpel** cut through the muscle.

Similarly a centrally prototypical PATIENT, like *the roses*, in 6.77a and repeated in 6.78a below, will involve all four entailments in 6.76 above, but a PERCEPT like *the game* in 6.78b does not undergo a change of state nor is it causally affected:

6.78   a.   Maggie pruned **the roses**.
         b.   Roberto watched **the game**.

Having seen something of an attempt to cope with the problem of defining
theta-roles on a more systematic basis, in the next section we examine some
of the uses of such roles.

6.6   The Motivation for Identifying Thematic Roles

From our discussion so far it is clear that linguists employ thematic roles to
describe aspects of the interface between semantics and syntax, in particular
to characterize the links between the semantic classification of its participants that is inherent in a verb's meaning and the grammatical relations it
supports. Thus, to recap our discussion in its simplest terms, when we use
an English verb like *feel* in *Joan felt the heat as soon as the aircraft door was
opened*, we identify a relationship between an EXPERIENCER and a PERCEPT.
This can be viewed as one of many conventional ways of viewing relations
that are coded in the language. Grammatically, of course, the verb *feel* is
transitive, taking a subject and direct object. As we have seen, one fact we
have to account for is that there is a conventional linkage between the
participant roles and the grammatical relations, such that in this case the
EXPERIENCER will be subject and the PERCEPT, direct object.[8]

Predicting such linkages, and more general patterns amongst individual
cases, is one of the primary functions of thematic roles. To take one example, in Dowty's prototype and entailments approach described in the
last section, this linkage is described as below by an argument selection
principle (1991: 576) (together with a couple of ancillary principles and the
characteristics in 6.79d):

6.79   a.   *Argument Selection Principle*: In predicates with grammatical
              subject and object, the argument for which the predicate
              entails the greatest number of Proto-Agent properties will be
              lexicalized as the subject of the predicate; the argument having
              the greatest number of Proto-Patient entailments will be
              lexicalized as the direct object.
         b.   *Corollary 1*: If two arguments of a relation have (approximately)
              equal numbers of entailed Proto-Agent and Proto-Patient prop-
              erties, then either or both may be lexicalized as the subject
              (and similarly for objects).
         c.   *Corollary 2*: With a three-place predicate, the non subject
              argument having the greater number of entailed Proto-Patient
              properties will be lexicalized as the direct object and the non sub-
              ject argument having fewer entailed Proto-Patient properties
              will be lexicalized as an oblique or prepositional object (and if

two non subject arguments have approximately equal numbers of entailed P-Patient properties, either or both may be lexicalized as direct object).

d. *Non discreteness*: Proto-roles, obviously, do not classify arguments exhaustively (some arguments have neither role) or uniquely (some arguments may share the same role) or discretely (some arguments could qualify partially but equally for both proto-roles).

Though the phrasing of these principles makes it sound as if theta-roles are in competition for grammatical slots in the formation of each sentence, Dowty intends these observations as a set of constraints on verbal linking rules. As the term *lexicalized* in the above suggests, these principles are viewed as constraints on possible verbs.

We can give an idea of how such principles might work by looking again at the type of example we have already discussed: the relations between subject position and theta-roles in the sentences in 6.80 below:

6.80   a.   Captain Nemo sank the ship with a torpedo.
        b.   The torpedo sank the ship.
        c.   The ship sank.

In 6.80a *Captain Nemo* has the Proto-Agent properties of volition, sentience, causation and movement and is thus linked to subject position, as predicted by the selection principles. In 6.80b *the torpedo* has the Proto-Agent properties of causation and movement, and thus, in the absence of an entity with a stronger cluster of such properties, becomes subject. Finally in 6.80c *the ship* has just the property of movement, but in this sentence that is enough for it to become the subject.

This idea of stronger and weaker candidates for subject, and other grammatical roles, leads naturally to the idea of a hierarchy, as we discussed in section 6.3. Dowty's version of a subject hierarchy is as in 6.81 (1991: 578):[9]

$$6.81 \quad \text{Agent} > \begin{Bmatrix} \text{Instrument} \\ \text{Experiencer} \end{Bmatrix} > \text{Patient} > \begin{Bmatrix} \text{Source} \\ \text{Goal} \end{Bmatrix}$$

As before, the candidates move from left to right in decreasing strength of linkage to the subject position. In this version, though, the roles themselves are not primitives but convenient labels for clusterings of the proto-role entailments.

So far we have been talking about theta-roles as explanatory devices in accounting for linkage between semantic and syntactic argument structure. A second justification for using thematic roles is to help characterize semantic verbal classes. For example, we can identify in English two classes of psychological verbs both of which take two arguments (i.e. are transitive), one of which is an EXPERIENCER and the other a STIMULUS.[10] The classes differ, however, in their linking between these roles and subject and object position. The first class has the theta-grid in 6.82a below, and can be exemplified by the verbs in 6.82b, while the second class has the theta-grid in 6.83a and includes verbs like those in 6.83b:

6.82   Psychological verbs type 1
    a. V: <EXPERIENCER, STIMULUS>
    b. *admire, enjoy, fear, like, love, relish, savour*

6.83   Psychological verbs type 2
    a. <STIMULUS, EXPERIENCER>
    b. *amuse, entertain, frighten, interest, please, surprise, thrill*[11]

Thus we say *Claude liked the result* but *The result pleased Claude*.

Such classifications of verbs can help predict the grammatical processes individual verbs will undergo. Thus, though the motivation for grammatical rules is often multifactorial, theta-role grids have been used to describe argument changing processes like **passive**, as we shall see shortly, or argument structure alternations like those in 6.84–5 below, where in each case the example sentences are in a, the link between theta-grids and syntactic arguments is given in b, and some example verbs in c:

6.84   a. He banged the broom-handle on the ceiling.
        He banged the ceiling with the broom-handle.
        She tapped the can against the window.
        She tapped the window with the can.
    b. V: <AGENT, INSTRUMENT & THEME,[12] LOCATION>
          NP   NP   PP
        V: <AGENT, LOCATION, INSTRUMENT & THEME>
          NP   NP   PP
    c. *bang, bash, beat, hit, knock, pound, rap, tap, whack*[13]

6.85   a. The whole community will benefit from the peace process.
        The peace process will benefit the whole community.
    b. V: <BENEFICIARY, SOURCE>
        NP   PP
        V: <SOURCE, BENEFICIARY>
        NP   NP
    c. *benefit, profit*[14]

These alternations are just two of a large range identified for English in Levin (1993). The conditional factors for such alternations are often a mix of semantic information, such as the verb's meaning and its theta-grid (as shown above), and its syntactic environment.

We can look at one further type of justification for thematic roles which comes from another area of grammar: the claim that in some languages they play a role in the morphology of verbal agreement. Mithun (1991: 514) gives examples of the pronominal verbal prefixes in Lakhota (Siouan; USA, Canada). In the transitive verbs in 6.86a below we see a prefix *wa* which marks an AGENT argument and in 6.86b a prefix *ma*, which marks a PATIENT:

6.86   a.   **awá**ʔu   'I brought it.'
              waktékte   'I'll kill him.'
        b.   **amá**ʔu   'He brought **me**.'
              maktékte   'He'll kill **me**.'

We can see that these prefixes do not mark subject or object agreement because a subject, for example, can take either prefix depending on whether it is an AGENT (as in 6.87a below) or PATIENT (as in 6.87b) (Mithun 1991: 514):

6.87   a.   AGENT subjects
              wapsíča   'I jumped'
              wahí   'I came'
        b.   PATIENT subjects
              makʰúže   'I'm sick'
              maxwá   'I'm sleepy'

In other words, what would be a subject pronoun in English corresponds to either an AGENT or PATIENT pronoun affix in Lakhota. Thus Lakhota morphological marking is sensitive to theta-roles rather than grammatical relations. Mithun gives similar examples from Guaraní (Tupi; Paraguay, Bolivia), and the Pomoan languages of California. The implication for our discussion is clear: if we need theta-roles to explain morphological patterns, this is strong evidence that they are significant semantic categories.

We have seen then in this section a number of different motivations for identifying thematic roles: to explain linking rules in verbal argument structure, to reflect semantic classes of verbs, to predict a verb's participation in argument structure alternations, and finally to describe morphological rules adequately. For many linguists this utility motivates their continuing use, despite the definitional problems discussed in the last section. In the next section we look at the category of **voice**, which, as we shall see, adds new dimensions to the relationship between theta-roles and grammatical relations.

6.7 Voice

6.7.1 Passive voice

The grammatical category of *voice* affords speakers some flexibility in viewing thematic roles. Many languages allow an opposition between *active voice* and *passive voice*. We can compare, for example, the English sentences in 6.88 below:

6.88   a.   Billy groomed the horses.
        b.   The horses were groomed by Billy.

In the active sentence 6.88a *Billy*, the AGENT, is subject and *the horses*, the PATIENT, is object. The passive version 6.88b, however, has the PATIENT as subject and the AGENT occurring in a prepositional phrase, the structure often associated with INSTRUMENT, as we saw in the last section. This is a typical active–passive voice alternation: the passive sentence has a verb in a different form – the past participle with the auxiliary verb *be* – and it allows the speaker a different perspective on the situation described. This passive sentence (6.88b) allows the speaker to describe the situation from the point of view of the PATIENT rather than that of the AGENT. In some cases indeed passive constructions are used to obscure the identity of an AGENT, as in 6.89 below:

6.89   The horses were groomed.

Here the AGENT is so far backgrounded that it becomes merely an implied participant. Many writers describe this foregrounding of the PATIENT and backgrounding of the AGENT in terms of promoting the PATIENT and demoting the AGENT (for example Givón 1990) or as reflecting the speaker's greater empathy with the PATIENT rather than the AGENT (Kuno 1987). There are other lexical and syntactic strategies which alter perspective in this way. For example, in 6.90 below the alternation relies in part on the lexical relation between *in front of* and *behind*; while in 6.91 it is accomplished by the syntactic patterns known as **pseudo-cleft** in a and **cleft** in b:

6.90   a.   The house stood in front of the cliff.
        b.   The cliff stood behind the house.

6.91   a.   What Joan bought was a Ferrari.
        b.   It was Joan who bought the Ferrari.

In 6.91 above the same situation is described but in a the speaker is interested in Joan's purchase, while in b she is interested in the Ferrari's purchaser. This kind of choice of perspective presumably depends on a speaker's judgements of conversational salience. We can use the terms **figure** and **ground**[15] to describe this kind of linguistic perspective: if we call the situation described a **scene**, then the entity that the speaker chooses to foreground is the figure, and the background is the ground. So in 6.90a above *the house* is the figure and *the cliff* the ground, and vice versa in 6.90b.

Passive constructions allow the foregrounding of roles other than PATIENT. In 6.92–4 we see English examples of THEME, PERCEPT and RECIPIENT roles occurring as the subject of passives:

6.92   **This money** was donated to the school. (THEME)

6.93   **The UFO** was seen by just two people. (PERCEPT)

6.94   **He** was given a camera by his grandmother. (RECIPIENT)

The qualifications for foregrounding in a passive in English are complex: partly grammatical, partly semantic and partly due to the flow of discourse and the speaker's choice of viewpoint. The importance of grammatical information can be shown by observing that each of the roles occurring as passive subjects in 6.92–4 above occur in object position in a corresponding active sentence:

6.95   Someone donated **this money** to the school.

6.96   Just two people saw **the UFO**.

6.97   His grandmother gave **him** a camera.

The typical pattern is that a nominal occupying object position is fronted to subject in passives. When a theta-role normally occurs as a prepositional phrase in an active sentence, this is less likely to be foregrounded in a passive. Neither moving the full prepositional phrase nor extracting just the nominal seems to work, as shown below:

6.98   a.   This house stood **on the corner**. (LOCATION)
        b.   *__On the corner__ was stood by this house.
        c.   ?**The corner** was stood **on** by this house.

6.99   a.   John built a garage for **her**. (BENEFICIARY)
        b.   *__For her__ was built a garage by John.
        c.   ?**She** was built a garage by John.

6.100   a.   He opened the door **with this key**. (INSTRUMENT)
        b.   *__With this key__ was opened the door by him.
        c.   *__This key__ was opened the door **with**.

Some apparent exceptions to this rule are possible, however, e.g.

6.101   a.   Three monarchs lived in **this house**. (LOCATION)
        b.   **This house** was lived in by three monarchs.[16]

To further underline this grammatical aspect of passives, i.e. that it is the object position that is relevant to passivization, we can look at a class of English verbs called the *spray/load* verbs. These verbs allow the speaker to select either their THEME role (as in 6.102a and 6.103a) below, or the GOAL (as in 6.102b and 6.103b), to be the verb's direct object and thus be the focus of the effect of the action:

6.102   a.   He sprayed paint on the car.
         b.   He sprayed the car with paint.

6.103   a.   He loaded hay on to the tractor.
         b.   He loaded the tractor with hay.

We can easily show that whichever argument occupies object position can be passivized, while the argument in the prepositional phrase cannot: corresponding to 6.102 above we find the patterns:

6.104   a.   Paint was sprayed on the car.
         b.   *The car was sprayed paint on.
         c.   The car was sprayed with paint.
         d.   *Paint was sprayed the car with.

See Rappaport and Levin (1985, 1988), Jeffries and Willis (1984) and Levin (1993) for further discussion of these *spray/load* verbs.[17]

The discourse factors affecting passives have been described in a number of frameworks: for example, as mentioned above, Kuno (1987: 209–16) employs the notion of speaker empathy. He gives an example of a person relating a story about their friend Mary and her experiences at a party. In the narrative the speaker's empathy is with Mary and thus events are viewed from her perspective. This explains why a passive is fine in 6.105b below but not in 6.106b (treating these as two independent reports of events):

6.105   Mary had quite an experience at the party she went to last night.
         a.   An eight-foot-tall rowdy harassed her.
         b.   She was harassed by an eight-foot-tall rowdy.

6.106   Mary had quite an experience at the party she went to last night.
         a.   She slapped an eight-foot-tall rowdy in the face.
         b.   *An eight-foot-tall rowdy was slapped in the face by her.

The passive construction works in 6.105b because the fronted nominal refers to the entity the speaker empathizes with, but not in 6.106b where the other participant is fronted.

Passive constructions have received a great deal of attention in the linguistics literature. This is not surprising: even from our brief discussion, we can see that while the general effect of passive is to allow a shift in linkage between theta-roles and grammatical relations, the process is subject to a complex of grammatical and discourse factors. It is this interdependence of different levels of analysis that makes passives an interesting arena for theoretical debate.

6.7.2 Comparing passive constructions across languages

While many languages have passive-type constructions, the comparison of passives across languages reveals that there is considerable variation around the pattern of the English passive outlined in the last section, i.e. where the AGENT is demoted from subject position, a non-AGENT role is promoted to subject, and the verb shows a distinct form which agrees with the promoted subject: the total package being what we have called **passive voice**. Often languages have more than one passive construction: in English, for example, it is possible to distinguish between *be*-passives and *get*-passives, as in 6.107 (R. Lakoff 1971; Givón and Yang 1994):

6.107   a.   Mary was shot on purpose.
          b.   Mary got shot on purpose.

As noted by Lakoff, these sentences differ in the amount of control over the event associated with Mary.[18]

   Other languages have a special type of passive, often called the **impersonal passive**, which does not allow the AGENT to be mentioned in the sentence. In Irish, for example, we can distinguish between one type of passive associated with verbal noun constructions, as shown in the active/ passive pair in 6.108 below, and another, the impersonal passive, with verbs, as is shown in 6.109 (Noonan 1994: 282–6):

6.108   a.   Bhí sí   ag bualadh   Sheáin.
               was she at hit-NOMIN John-GEN
               'She was hitting John.'
          b.   Bhí Seán á   bhualadh   aici.
               was John to+his hit-NOMIN at-her
               'John was being hit by her.'

6.109   a.   Thug   siad Siobhán abhaile inniu.
               brought they Joan   home   today
               'They brought Joan home today.'
          b.   Tugadh   Siobhán abhaile inniu.
               brought-IMPERS Joan   home   today.
               'Joan was brought home today.'

This impersonal passive in 6.109 does not straightforwardly correspond to the translation given: i.e. to an English passive where no AGENT is expressed. In 6.109b we can see how both in Irish and in the English translation the passive verb form is differentiated from the active, and how in both the AGENT is often omitted. However the Irish passive in 6.109b differs from its English translation because the THEME, *Siobhán*, remains in its original position as an object while in the English passive *Joan* becomes subject. In other words, the PATIENT is not promoted to subject in the Irish impersonal passive in 6.109b, but the AGENT is omitted. See Noonan (1994) for discussion.

This example from Irish is of a transitive impersonal passive. In many languages the term *impersonal passive* is used to describe passives of intransitive verbs: Kirsner (1976: 387) gives the following pair of examples from Dutch:

6.110   a.   De jongens fluiten.
                the boys   whistle.
                'The boys whistle/are whistling.'
         b.   Er   wordt   door de jongens gefloten.
                there becomes by   the boys   whistling
                'By the boys (there) is whistling.'

In 6.110b the AGENT is backgrounded, but there is no other argument to be foregrounded and subject position is taken by the word *er* 'there', which does not refer directly to any entity and which has no theta-role. It is also possible to delete the AGENT altogether in this passive, giving:

6.111   Er   wordt   gefloten.
         there becomes whistling
         'There is whistling/People whistle/Someone whistles.'

Similar impersonal passives have been reported for other languages, including German, Welsh and Latin; see Perlmutter (1978) and Perlmutter and Postal (1984) for discussion.

These impersonal passives imply that in comparing languages we need to separate out the two functions of the passive: firstly, the demotion of AGENTS, and secondly, the promotion of non-AGENTS. Thus an English passive like *Spike was arrested by the police* combines both functions: the AGENT argument is demoted to a prepositional phrase, and the PATIENT is promoted to subject. We can see the related sentence *Spike was arrested* as a special case of this, where demotion reaches its extreme in the suppression of the AGENT. In the Dutch impersonal passives in 6.110b, on the other hand, we see a passive strategy which just embodies the first function: demotion of AGENT, with no concomitant promotion function. Since this example has an intransitive verb, the further step of suppressing the AGENT leaves a sentence with no theta-role bearing nominal as in 6.111.

The third characteristic of English passives described in the last section was a special verb form and associated verbal agreement with the promoted subject. This too is subject to cross-linguistic variation. Passive verbs are often semantically distinguished from their active counterparts, for example by being more **stative**, though this is not always so, and they may show agreement with the promoted non-AGENT nominal (as in English), or the demoted AGENT, or neither, since agreement inflections may be neutralized; see Givón (1990: 563–644) for discussion of variations along this parameter as well as along the parameters of AGENT demotion and non-AGENT promotion.

One conclusion from comparing passives across languages seems to be that the phenomenon is typically a cluster of functions: in each case following the general pattern of allowing the speaker planning her discourse some variation in the linkage between thematic and grammatical roles, but with considerable variation in the associated semantic and grammatical elements of the cluster.

In most active–passive systems the active form is usually grammatically simpler and we may ask why this should be so. It has been argued that we as humans naturally view situations from the point of view of any human beings involved, and if there are none, of other living creatures. This preference, sometimes called an **animacy hierarchy** (see for example Dixon 1979, Hopper and Thompson 1980), is coded into the lexical semantics of a language so that a verb like *drive*, for example, in 6.112 sets up a thematic role frame which requires an AGENT as the subject:

6.112   Ann drove the truck across the field.

and since agency, as we have seen, requires wilful action, AGENTS are typically people, or higher animals. It is difficult to think of a verb which describes the action in 6.112 from the point of view of the truck. We might say:

6.113   The truck carried Ann across the field.

but this sentence has a different meaning: we have not specified that Ann was driving. So it seems that the meaning of the verb *drive* is set up to prioritize the role of any human or volitional agent. Passive voice allows the speaker to get around this in-built bias, so that to switch the viewpoint from Ann to the truck, or to the field, she can use passive constructions, as in 6.114–15:

6.114   The truck was driven across the field by Ann.

6.115   The field was driven across by a truck (*by Ann).

We can see that in 6.115 there is no longer a slot for the AGENT, Ann. So passive constructions do allow a change of perspective but the conventional bias towards animate subjects means that the active *drive* is grammatically simpler than the passive *was driven*.

6.7.3 Middle voice

While very many languages display this active/passive voice contrast, some languages have a three-way distinction between active, passive and **middle**

voice. As we might expect, the use of middle voice varies from language to language but a central feature is that middle forms emphasize that the subject of the verb is affected by the action described by the verb. This **affectedness**, as it is often termed (e.g. Klaiman 1991), can be of several types, and we can select four typical uses as examples: neuters, bodily activity and emotions, reflexives, and autobenefactives. Though we will use examples from several languages, to keep the discussion brief we will concentrate on two unrelated languages, well separated in space and time: classical Greek and the modern Cushitic language Somali.[19] In both these languages middle voice is marked by verbal inflection.

Neuter intransitives   This type of middle is where the subject undergoes a non-volitional process or change of state. The external cause is not represented but can often be shown in a related active form, as shown in 6.116 below, an example from Sanskrit (Klaiman 1991: 93):

6.116   a.   So   namati   daṇḍam.
             he-NOM bends-3sg ACTIVE stick-ACC
             'He bends the stick.'
        b.   Namate   daṇḍaḥ.
             bends-3sg MIDDLE stick-NOM
             'The stick bends.'

Middle-voice verb forms of this neuter type, where the subject undergoes a process over which it has no control, occur in classical Greek, as shown in 6.117 (Bakker 1994: 30) and Somali,[20] as in 6.118:

6.117   phú-e-**sthai**   'grow'
        tréph-e-**sthai**   'grow up'
        sêp-e-**sthai**   'rot'
        têk-e-**sthai**   'melt'
        rhêgnu-**sthai**   'break'

6.118   kab-**o**   'recover, set (of a bone)'
        qub-**o**   'fall (of leaves and fruit)'
        dhim-**o**   'die'
        haf-**o**   'drown'
        garaads-**o**   'reach maturity'

Bodily activity and emotion   In some languages the verb occurs in a middle voice when the activity involves the body or emotions of the subject. These would seem to be clear cases of affectedness since the subject is so overtly involved. Examples of such middle-voice verbs are in 6.119–20:

6.119   Classical Greek (Bakker 1994)
        klín-e-**sthai**   'lean'
        hêd-e-**sthai**   'rejoice'

6.120   Somali (Saeed 1999)
         fadhiis-**o**   'sit down'
         baroor-**o**   'mourn, wail'

Reflexives   In some languages the middle is used where the subject's action
affects the subject himself, or a possession or body part of the subject. To
take another example from classical Greek (Barber 1975: 18–19):

6.121   Lou – omai.
         wash-1sg MIDDLE
         'I wash myself.'

This use means that in many languages verbs of grooming occur in the
middle voice, with no need for a reflexive pronoun as object; see 6.122 for
some further examples from Somali, and examples from other languages in
6.123 from Kemmer (1994: 195):

6.122   feer-**o**   'comb one's hair'
         maydh-**o**   'wash oneself, bathe'
         labbis-**o**   'dress up, put on one's best clothes'

6.123   Latin   orno-**r**   'adorn oneself'
         Quechua   arma-**ku**-y   'bathe'
         Turkish   giy-**in**   'dress'
         Hungarian   mosa-**kod**-   'wash oneself'

Autobenefactives   This type of middle is used to signify that the action of the
subject is done for his or her own benefit. Once again this use occurred in
classical Greek, as in 6.124 (Barber 1975: 18), and is a regular process in
Somali, as 6.125 shows (Saeed 1993: 58):

6.124   a.   hair-ō   moiran.
               take-1sg-ACTIVE share
               'I take a share.'
         b.   hari-oumai   moiran.
               take-1sg-MIDDLE share
               'I take a share for myself.'

6.125   Active verbs: Middle verbs:
         wad   'to drive'   wad-**o**   'to drive for oneself'
         beer   'to cultivate'   beer-**o**   'to cultivate for oneself'
         qaad   'to take'   qaad-**o**   'to take for oneself'
         sid   'to carry'   sid-**o**   'to carry for oneself'

In the examples so far, middle voice has been marked by verbal inflection.
In some languages a pronoun marks middle forms, often the same form as a

reflexive pronoun, e.g. German *sich*, French *se*, Spanish *se*, or a closely related form, e.g. Russian reflexive *sebja*, middle *-sja*, Dutch reflexive *zichzelf*, middle *-zelf* (Kemmer 1994). In such languages the overlap between middle voice and reflexivity, seen in examples 6.119–25 above, becomes overt. In French and Spanish, for example, we might identify our first three types of middle:

6.126   French middle reflexives
    a. neuter: s'écrouler   'collapse'
                                  s'évanouir   'vanish'
    b. bodily activity: s'asseoir   'sit down'
           emotion: se plaindre   'complain'
    c. reflexive: s'habiller   'dress oneself'
                                  se peigner   'comb one's hair'

6.127   Spanish middle reflexives
    a. neuter: helarse   'freeze (intr.)'
                                  recuperarse   'get well'
    b. bodily activity: tirarse   'jump'
           emotion: enamorarse (de)   'fall in love (with)'
    c. reflexive: afeitarse   'shave'
                                  quitarse   'take off (clothes)'

However, even in languages where the middle and reflexives are marked by the same pronoun, there are usually clear cases where the meaning distinguishes between true reflexives and the middle, e.g. in German (Kemmer 1994: 188):

6.128   Er sieht **sich**   'He sees himself'   (Reflexive)
        Er fürchtet **sich**   'He is afraid'   (Middle – emotion)

In English there is no inflectional or pronominal marker of the middle: the distinction is only shown by alternations between transitive active verbs and intransitive middle verbs, where the agent is omitted, e.g.

6.129   a. They open the gates very smoothly.   (Active)
        b. The gates open very smoothly.   (Middle – neuter)

These intransitive middles in English are often used to describe the success of a non-AGENT in some activity, e.g.

6.130   a. These clothes wash well.
        b. This model sells very quickly.
        c. These saws don't cut very efficiently.

See Dixon (1991: 322–35) for more examples of this type of construction in English. Because of the similar suppression of the AGENT in this type of middle and in the passive, some writers use the term **medio-passive** to cover both.

6.8 Summary

In this chapter our topic has been the ways in which a speaker may portray the roles of participants in a situation. We outlined a classification of such semantic roles, termed **thematic roles** or **theta-roles**, including AGENT, PATIENT, THEME etc. and described the relationship between these roles and grammatical relations like **subject** and **object**. It has been claimed that as part of its inherent lexical specification a verb requires its arguments to be in specific thematic roles, and that this can be reflected by formulating thematic role **grids**, or **theta-grids**. We discussed the difficulties there are in fixing tight definitions for individual thematic roles, and presented one approach, from Dowty (1991), which seeks to provide a solution in terms of fuzzy categories. This difficulty with precision notwithstanding, it seems that the notion of thematic roles has proved a useful descriptive tool in a number of areas of the semantics–grammar interface.

The grammatical category of **voice** allows speakers different strategies for relating thematic roles and grammatical relations. We concentrated on relations with **subject** position, in particular the way in which **passive voice** allows the foregrounding of non-AGENT roles to subject and the backgrounding of AGENT roles away from subject. We also looked at **middle voice**, which reflects the **affectedness** of the subject in the action of the verb: thus offering a different view of the relationship between subject and verb from the **active voice**.

FURTHER READING

An important study of thematic roles is Dowty's (1991) article. Palmer (1994) is a survey of thematic roles, the different ways they are grammaticalized and the role of passive and middle voice. Dixon (1991) discusses the ways in which the grammar of English verbs reflects semantic distinctions, and includes sections on thematic roles and voice. Givón (1994) is a collection of studies on argument structure changing processes, including passive. Keenan (1985) reviews passive constructions in a range of languages, while Klaiman (1991) does a similar job for middle voice. Wilkins (1988), Grimshaw (1990) and Williams (1994) shed light on the interaction of thematic roles and grammatical processes. These works are quite technical, however, and require some background in syntactic theory.

EXERCISES

6.1 On the basis of the informal definitions in section 6.2, try to assign a single **thematic role** label to each of the expressions in bold in the following sentences:

  a. **Helen** drove **to the party**.
  b. **He** swatted **the fly** with **a newspaper**.
  c. **The baboon** was asleep **on the roof of my car**.
  d. **Joan** drank **the yard of ale**.
  e. **Campbell** saw **the gun** first.
  f. **George** gave **the doorman a tip**.

6.2 For each of the **theta-roles** below, construct an English sentence where an argument bearing that role occurs as **subject**. For example, as an example of an EXPERIENCER subject we could provide the sentence: ***The agents*** *saw the robbers leaving the bank*.

  a. AGENT
  b. PATIENT
  c. THEME
  d. INSTRUMENT
  e. RECIPIENT

[handwritten annotations:]
Sally broke the ice
The roses were crushed
The ball was passed
I stepped on the fly with his foot
She recieved a bouquet of flowers.

6.3 As we saw, Jackendoff (1990) proposes a distinction between a **thematic tier** of thematic roles (relating to movement and location) and an **action tier** (relating to ACTOR–PATIENT type relations). An argument may have role at each level and thus fulfil two roles. For example, the underlined argument in *The car smashed into* <u>*the shop window*</u> can be analysed as both PATIENT and GOAL. For each of the combinations of roles below, try to invent a sentence where a single argument fulfils the combination:

  a. AGENT and GOAL
  b. PATIENT and THEME
  c. AGENT and SOURCE
  d. AGENT and THEME

6.4 In sections 6.5 and 6.6 we discussed proposals from Dowty (1991) to characterize thematic roles in terms of **clusters of entailments**, and to describe the rules linking thematic roles and grammatical relations like subject and object in terms of **argument selection principles**. Using the selection principles in 6.79 in the chapter and the properties of Proto-roles in 6.75 and 6.76, discuss the selection of subject and object positions in the following sentences:

     a.   The butler is polishing the silverware.
     b.   The dogs will smell the food.
     c.   The train hit the cow.

What problems are posed for these principles by the selection of subject and objects in the pairs of sentences below?

1   a.   He fears AIDS.
     b.   AIDS frightens him.

2   a.   Patricia resembles Maura.
     b.   Maura resembles Patricia.

3   a.   Joan bought a sportscar from Jerry.
     b.   Jerry sold a sportscar to Joan.

6.5   We saw how **passive** allows the foregrounding of non-AGENT theta-roles into subject position. Compare for example the active sentence 1 below with the passive equivalent in 2:

1   Craig$_{AG}$ devoured the ice-cream$_{PA}$.
2   The ice-cream$_{PA}$ was devoured by Craig$_{AG}$.

Assume 2 is formed from 1 by a simple rule: (a) Place the non-AGENT argument at the beginning of the sentence; (b) change the active verb to a passive verb (e.g. *devoured* → *was devoured*); (c) place the word *by* in front of the AGENT and place the AGENT at the end of the sentence. Below are some active sentences with a non-subject argument underlined. For each one, use our simple rule to try to create a corresponding passive where the underlined non-AGENT argument becomes subject.

     a.   The court fined <u>Emma</u> five hundred francs.
     b.   Aliens abducted <u>me</u> in the middle of my examination.
     c.   The professor mailed <u>the answer</u> to the student.
     d.   The professor mailed the answer to <u>the student</u>.
     e.   The professor mailed <u>the student</u> the answer.
     f.   The professor mailed the student <u>the answer</u>.

Were any of the resulting passives ungrammatical? If so, what explanation can you give?

6.6   The rule of passive formation is not entirely regular. Using the rule in the last exercise as your model, try to create passives by foregrounding the underlined arguments below. What problems do you meet? Can you think of any semantic reasons to explain the results of the passive rule in these cases?

    a. A pleasant smell filled <u>the room</u>.
    b. Roy likes <u>linguine in a clam sauce</u>.
    c. Your paper included <u>a nice conclusion</u>.
    d. The fans crowded <u>the hall</u>.
    e. We were just watching <u>television</u>.
    f. Fritz hated <u>war</u>.
    g. He watched <u>himself</u>.

6.7   As we saw, in some languages (e.g. Somali) when a speaker describes a reflexive act of grooming, say for example the equivalent of *I wash myself*, the verb occurs in a **middle voice** form with no object. In others (e.g. French) a **reflexive pronoun** is used as the object. In English we find another strategy: some verbs which are normally transitive allow the speaker to omit the object in order to convey a reflexive meaning. For example, we know that *hide* is normally a transitive verb because of sentences like *She hid the money*; however *She hid* means of course *She hid herself*. So English has verbs like *hide*, which by omitting an argument can convey an **understood reflexive object**. Unlike Somali, though, the English verbs in these constructions do not have a special middle-voice ending. Below are some verbs which describe what we could call acts of grooming. Decide which of these allow an understood reflexive object.

    undress   towel
    wash   bathe
    brush   shampoo
    soap   shave
    strip   lather

    Is there any semantic differences between those verbs which allow this understood reflexive object and those which do not? If you think there is, test your hypothesis with other verbs from this semantic field of grooming.

6.8   Design **lexical theta-grids** for the verbs in bold in the sentences below. For example, a theta-grid for *buy* in *Dee-dee **bought** the car for his mistress* would be: **buy** <<u>AGENT</u>, THEME, BENEFICIARY>.

    a. Brenda **reported** the incident to her boss.
    b. Frogs **fell** from the sky.
    c. Our headquarters will **remain** in London.
    d. Batman **received** a commendation from the mayor.
    e. Harvey **noticed** a strange smell.

NOTES

1   One might also think of examples like: *In the village stands a pump*. But here
    the subject still seems to be *a pump* rather than *in the village*, as can be shown
    by the pattern of agreement in: *In the village stand several pumps*. But see Levin
    and Rappaport Hovav (1995: 261–4) for arguments, couched in the theory of
    Lexical-Functional Grammar (e.g. Bresnan 1994), that the preverbal PP is, at
    some level of analysis, a subject.
2   See the introductory discussion of theta-grids in Haegeman (1994: 33–73).
3   Hereafter we will use just the two first letters of a thematic role with this
    subscript notation, e.g. Joan$_{AG}$ for Joan$_{AGENT}$.
4   In Jackendoff's (1990) two-tier representation described earlier, these 'transfer'
    verbs would have a more complicated thematic grid: we could, for example,
    assign both AGENT and SOURCE roles to *Barbara* in 6.65.
5   Note that in this view, theta-roles convey a speaker's classifications of things in
    the world: in other words, the roles are borne by real-world entities rather than
    grammatical elements like NPs. See for example the following example and
    comment from Laduslaw and Dowty (1988: 63):

    1   a.   Fido chased Felix.
        b.   Felix was chased by Fido.

    . . . The only sense in which it is reasonable to think of the subject NP of
    (1a) as the Agent is the sense in which it is shorthand for saying that the
    object (in the world) referred to by the subject is the Agent in the action
    described by the sentence. What makes Fido an agent in the event described
    by (1a) and (1b) is information about Fido and his role in the event, not
    about the grammatical category or function of anything in the sentence.

6   For a related idea, see Foley and van Valin's (1984) theory of **macro-roles**,
    where all thematic roles fall into two main categories: **actor** and **undergoer**.
7   This term arises from Dowty's (1991) examination of different types of what
    he calls THEME roles, some of which would be PATIENT roles in our classifica-
    tion. He proposes a class of **incremental themes** for the THEME/PATIENT roles
    of achievement and accomplishment verbs, e.g. *mow* <u>*the lawn*</u>, *eat* <u>*an egg*</u>, *build*
    <u>*a house*</u>, *demolish* <u>*a building*</u>. The observation is that the action (for example, the
    mowing action) and the state of the associated THEME/PATIENT (e.g. the lawn)
    are in a proportional relationship: some mowing cuts some of the grass, more
    mowing, more of the grass, etc. until completing the action cuts all of the grass.
    Dowty extends this idea of incremental themes to other types of role, e.g. *swim*
    <u>*from England to France*</u>, where the path is incrementally affected, and *memorize*
    <u>*a poem*</u>, where there is a similar incremental relationship between the action
    and a representation of the THEME entity. See Dowty (1991) for further details.
8   In our discussion we focus on languages like English which have the grammat-
    ical relations, **subject** and **object**. We therefore leave aside the different pattern
    of mapping between theta-roles and grammatical relation shown by **ergative**
    languages. Briefly, in a typical ergative system one grammatical relation, called
    absolutive, is used for the single argument of an intransitive verb, whatever its
    theta-role (and in this resembles English subject), but is also used in ditransitive
    verbs for the PATIENT argument (and here resembles English object). A second

grammatical relation, called **ergative**, is used for the AGENT/EXPERIENCER in ditransitive verbs (as is English subject). There is therefore no correspondence between the absolutive/ergative distinction and the subject/object distinction. They represent two different strategies for mapping between theta-roles and grammatical relations. See the following simple example of an ergative system from Tongan (Austronesian: Tonga), given by Anderson (1976):

a. na'e lea   '**a** etalavou.
    PAST speak ABS young.man
    'The young man spoke.'

b. na'e alu '**a**   Tevita ki Fisi.
    PAST go ABS David to Fiji
    'David went to Fiji.'

c. na'e tamate'i '**a** Kolaiate '**e**   Tevita.
    past kill   ABS Goliath ERG David
    'David killed Goliath.'

d. na'e ma'u   '**e**   siale   '**a** e   me'a'ofa.
    past receive ERG Charlie ABS DEF gift
    'Charlie received the gift.'

Note that in these Tongan sentences the verb comes first in the sentence, and the case-marking particles (in bold) precede their nominals. Sentences a and b have intransitive verbs and the verb's only argument is in the absolutive case. Sentences c and d have transitive verbs. Here the AGENT in c and the RECIPIENT in d are in the ergative case. The PATIENT in c and the THEME in d are in the absolutive case. The reader may compare this with the mapping for subject–object languages like English. Ergative languages are found all over the world and include Basque in southern Europe, the Australian language Dyirbal, Tongan from the Pacific, and the Inuit languages of Canada, Greenland, etc. See Dixon (1979) for discussion and Croft (1990) and Palmer (1994) for cross-linguistic overviews.

9   Note that Dowty's hierarchy here has INSTRUMENT and PATIENT in reverse order to our earlier hierarchy. We won't try to arbitrate between these claims here: compare the discussion in Dowty (1991) and Croft (1990).

10 These are labels commonly used in the literature for the thematic roles associated with these verbs. We leave aside discussion of how these roles would correlate with the Agent-properties and Patient-properties in a Dowty-style approach.

11 See Grimshaw (1990) and Levin (1993) for discussion of these classes of psychological verbs.

12 Here we follow Jackendoff (1990) in allowing one argument to have two theta-roles, as described earlier.

13 See Dowty (1991: 594–5), Levin (1993: 67–8).

14 See Levin (1993: 83).

15 This is similar to the use of 'figure' and 'ground' in the analysis of motion verbs by Talmy (1975), and others, as discussed in chapter 9. There the *figure* is the entity in motion and the background is called the *ground*.

16 But only under some special conditions, which have been much debated in the literature. Levin and Rappaport Hovav (1995: 143–4), for example, discuss examples of this type like *This platform has been stood on by an ex-president* under

the label **prepositional passives**. They provide a restriction on the construction in English that mixes grammatical and semantic factors: that it is only possible with **unergative verbs** which take an animate subject. **Unergative** is a term introduced by Perlmutter (1978) for intransitive verbs like *sit* and *stand* whose single argument is an AGENT and whose grammatical behaviour contrasts with **unaccusative verbs** which are intransitive verbs like *grow* or *drown* and whose single argument is essentially a PATIENT. Dixon (1991: 298–321), on the other hand, proposes syntactic restrictions, which include the absence of a direct object in the active sentence, and a lack of an alternative active construction in which the passivized NP could occur as direct object. For an in-depth study of these prepositional passive constructions see Couper-Kuhlen (1979).

17   Other English verbs allow alternations into object position, e.g.:

1   a.   He wrapped cling-film around the food.
      b.   He wrapped the food in cling-film.

2   a.   David gave the keys to Helen.
      b.   David gave Helen the keys.

3   a.   She bought some flowers for her husband.
      b.   She bought her husband some flowers.

Alternations like 2 and 3 are often called *Dative Shift*. Givón (1984a) describes these, and similar alternations in other languages, as *promotion to object*, a process paralleling passive. By comparison with passive, though, the process is more restricted to particular verbs and is less likely to be marked on the verb by a distinct inflection of voice.

18   Though this is less true of pairs like:

1   Mary was killed.
2   Mary got killed.

See Givón and Yang (1994) for a discussion of the English *get*-passive; and Weiner and Labov (1983) for a sociolinguistic approach.

19   For a survey of the meanings of middle voice in Somali, see Saeed (1995).

20   Note that not all neuter middles in Somali have an active form: the verbs *jabo*, *qubo*, *hafo* do, but *garaadso* does not, and the middle verb *dhimo* 'to die' has as its active equivalent a different lexical verb *dil* 'to kill'. It seems that all languages which have a middle voice have some verbs that are inherently middle and have no morphologically related active forms. See Klaiman (1991) for discussion.

chapter 7

Context and Inference

7.1 Introduction

In this chapter we examine how speakers and hearers rely on context in constructing and interpreting the meaning of utterances. We have already seen instances of this: in chapter 2 we mentioned the role of assumed knowledge in the use of proper names and definite noun phrases. The use of the names in bold in 7.1–2 below is only licensed by an assumption that the hearer can identify the individuals:

7.1   It'll take more than a pair of Levis to make you into **James Dean**.

7.2   I'm starting to talk like **Michael Jackson**.

We discuss this kind of assumed or background knowledge in section 7.6. Sometimes this kind of knowledge is called **non-linguistic knowledge** because it is argued that knowing who James Dean or Michael Jackson is does not form part of one's knowledge of English, in the same way as knowing the meaning of *pair* or *talk*. For, of course, knowledge about film stars or music personalities is not restricted to speakers of any single language in the way that knowledge of a particular noun or verb's meaning is. We will see, though, that this non-linguistic knowledge about the world does perform an important role in understanding utterances.

Of course, to understand these sentences the hearer also has to be able to identify the *you* of 7.1 and the *I* of 7.2. This information is normally instantly understood from the context, but if we provide an odd enough situation, e.g. finding these sentences written on pieces of paper, we can clearly see the essential role of knowing contextual information like who wrote the sentence, to whom it is addressed, etc. The reason of course is that, as we have seen in earlier chapters, pronouns like *I*, *you*, *he*, etc. are shorthand devices which need various forms of contextual support. Elements of language that are so contextually bound are called **deictic**, from the noun **deixis** (from classical Greek *deiknymi* 'to show, point out'). In chapter 5 we called tense a deictic category because, for example, past tense and future tense identify time phases relative to the 'now' of utterances. We noted how commonly references to time are oriented towards the time of speaking, as in 7.3 below:

7.3   We'll put the letters in the post later.

In this sentence both the future tense of the verb and the temporal adverb *later* set up a division of time which is 'in the future of now', where 'now' is whenever the sentence is uttered.

In chapter 1 we discussed the relationship between semantics and pragmatics. One proposal we reviewed suggested that while both areas of study are concerned with meaning, semantics is the study of conventional, linguistic meaning and pragmatics is the study of how we use this linguistic knowledge in context. In this view, pragmatics is the study of how hearers, for example, have to combine semantic knowledge with other types of knowledge and make inferences in order to interpret a speaker's meaning. In this chapter we focus on areas of meaning where there is very clear evidence of this combination of different types of knowledge. By doing this we move our attention to the study of language use and to what are therefore, for many linguists, pragmatic aspects of meaning. We begin with deixis.

7.2   Deixis

7.2.1   Spatial deixis

The deictic devices in a language commit a speaker to set up a frame of reference around herself. As we will see, every language carries an implicit division of the space around the current speaker, a division of time relative to the act of speaking, and, via pronouns, a shorthand naming system for the participants involved in the talk. To take a simple example, adverbs of location can be used deictically as in 7.4:

7.4   It's too hot **here** in the sun, let's take our drinks into the shade over
        there.

The adverbs *here* and *there* pick out places according to their proximity to the location of the speaker. We can see this because, of course, if the speaker moves, the interpretation of the adverbs will change. When the speaker and her addressee in 7.4 have moved, they can call the shade *here* and their original place in the sun *there*, as in 7.5:

7.5   I'm glad we moved **here**, I was melting **over there.**

Demonstratives work in a similar way: English has a two-term opposition between *this/these* and *that/those*. Once again the current speaker occupies the reference point: items closer to her will be described as *this/these*, items further away as *that/those*. While languages contain such deictic divisions of space, their use has to be calculated by the participants in actual contexts. For example, how big an area is meant by *here* depends on context: a speaker might use *here* to refer to a country, a city, a room, a part of a room, etc. This plasticity is inherent: the use of *here* does not even always have to include the location of the speaker. We can use *here* pointing to locations on a map, but there will be an actual or implicit contrast with *there*, a place further away from the speaker.

Other languages vary in the number of deictic divisions of space available to the speaker. We can compare English's two-term adverbial distinction between *here* and *there* with Spanish's three-term *aquí* 'here', *ahí* '(just) there', and *allí*, '(over) there'. Spanish parallels this with a three-term demonstrative system: *esto* 'this', *eso* 'that (just there)', and *aquello* 'that (over there)'. These demonstratives can be used to give three zones of proximity to the speaker, as shown in 7.6. They can also be used to relate to the position of an addressee, as in 7.7:

7.6   near speaker   further away   furthest from speaker
       *speaker   ───→

                   esto   *eso*   *aquello*

7.7   *esto*   'close to speaker'
       eso   'close to addressee'
       aquello   'distant from both'

Languages differ in both how many divisions of space are coded in their demonstratives and what other information is obligatorily included. We can look at some examples. In the West African language Hausa (Afroasiatic; Nigeria, Niger), as 7.8 below shows, the demonstrative and adverbial systems include terms which obligatorily make reference to the location of the addressee (Jaggar 2001: 323–30, 645–7):

7.8   (SP = speaker; ADR = addressee, â = falling tone; a = high tone)
       nân   'here' (near the SP)
       nan   'there' (near the ADR)
       cân   'there' (away from both)
       can   'there' (further away from both)

The English translation 'there' for *nan* in 7.8 is, of course, inaccurate: as Jaggar and Buba (1994) observe, *nan* has to relate to the vicinity of the addressee and thus a sentence like 7.9 below is impossible:[1]

7.9 ʔjèe-ka nan!
'OFF you go there!'

Similar reference to the addressee is reported for Japanese demonstratives and adverbs by Kuno (1973).

Other languages incorporate more complex divisions of space in their demonstratives, for example Malagasy (Austronesian; Madagascar), as shown in 7.10 (Anderson and Keenan 1985: 294):

7.10   Near SP   Increasingly far from SP
——————————————————————→
ity   io   itsy   iny   iroa   iry

More unusual is the addition of a vertical dimension, as is described by Anderson and Keenan (1985: 291) for Daga (Trans-New Guinea; Papua New Guinea), shown in 7.11:

7.11 *oea* 'overhead'   *ea* 'underneath'   *ata* 'same level'
      ao 'up, high'   *ae* 'down, low'   *ase* 'same level, far'

      uta 'higher   *ita* 'lower   *ma* 'near SP, this'
           (near)'   (near)'
      utu 'higher   *isi* 'lower (far)'   *ame* 'near ADR, that'
           (far)'
      use 'higher   *ise* 'lower
           (remote)'   (remote)'

As 7.11 shows, these Daga demonstratives distinguish locations in space above, below and on the same level as the speaker's position.

The examples so far have been of deictic elements relating to location and proximity relative to the speaker. Deictic elements may also include information about motion towards and away from the speaker. We can see this in English: the comparison between *come* and *go* in 7.12 and 7.13 below tells us something about the location of the speaker:

7.12   Don't come into my bedroom.

7.13   Don't go into my bedroom.

This explains why the sentences in 7.14 and 7.15 below sound odd at first:

7.14   ?Fred went to me.

7.15   ?Fred came from me.

We have to interpret the situations described in a rather complicated way
to accept these sentences. Some languages have specific deictic motion
morphemes: Somali for example has two: *soo* 'towards the speaker' and *sii*
'away from the speaker', which combine freely with verbs, as in 7.16:

7.16   a.   Soo soco!
              DEIC walk
              'Come this way!, Approach!'
        b.   Sii   soco!
              DEIC walk
              'Go on over there!, Go away!'

Finally we can end this look at spatial deixis with an example of a very
complex system, and one which includes information other than distance
and position: Yup'ik (Eskimo-Aleut; Alaska) in 7.17 (Anderson and Keenan
1985: 295):

7.17

Extended	**Restricted**	**Obscured**	
man'a	*una*		'this (near SP)'
tamana	*tauna*		'that (near ADR)'
		imna	'the aforementioned one'
ukna			'the one approaching the speaker'
aug̑na	*ingna*	*amna*	'the one going away from the speaker'
agna	*ikna*	*akemna*	'the one across there'
qaug̑na	*kiug̑na*	*qamna*	'the one inland, inside, upriver'
qagna	*keggna*	*qakemna*	'the one outside'
un'a	*kan'a*	*camna*	'the one below, towards river'
unegna	*ugna*	*cakemna*	'the one downriver, by the exit'
paug̑na	*pingna*	*pamna*	'the one up there, away from river'
pagna	*pikna*	*pakemna*	'the one up above'

The headings in 7.17 describe a semantic classification of the objects to which
the demonstratives refer: 'extended' forms are for either large expanses of
land or water, or objects that are lengthy or moving; 'restricted' applies to
objects that are stationary, or moving within a confined area, and fairly
small in extent, relatively near, and visible; and 'obscured' describes objects
that are farther away and not clearly in sight. See Anderson and Keenan
(1985) for details.

7.2.2   Grammaticalization of context

We can see from the Yup'ik example above that languages vary in the type of semantic information that is obligatorily included in deictic terms. When semantic distinctions are obligatory in this way we will say that they are **grammaticalized**. We can make an informal distinction between, on the one hand, the obligatory 'wired-in' ways a language divides up space and time in its function words (like demonstratives and pronouns) or its morphology, and on the other hand, the ability which seems to exist in all languages to talk about any division of space and time by paraphrase. Thus we can use the latter ability to provide English translations for the Yup'ik demonstratives above. To use a different example: a language like Arabic obligatorily includes information about the gender of the addressee. If, for example, one wants to refer to a single addressee, the choice is as in 7.18 below:

7.18   *'anta*   'you (masculine, singular)'
        'anti   'you (feminine, singular)'

These pronouns have corresponding verbal forms. There is no 'you (singular)' pronoun which does not include a gender specification. English, on the other hand, does not distinguish the gender of the addressee in its pronouns and verbal morphology. To come back to our distinction, this does not mean, of course, that English speakers cannot make reference to the gender of an addressee, merely that this information is not obligatory, i.e. grammaticalized. In our discussion of deixis we are concerned with cases where contextual features are grammaticalized in language.

7.2.3   Extensions of spatial deixis

Systems of spatial deixis are also used in other domains. For example they are often used as a form of orientation within a discourse, in what we could therefore call **discourse** or **textual deixis**,[2] as when we say *Here our argument runs into some difficulties* or *At this point we have to look back to our initial premises*. In many languages too, spatial deixis terms, such as demonstratives, are extended to refer to time.[3] An example of this use of the demonstratives is below:

7.19   **That** year was much hotter than **this** one is.

This transference is often described as a metaphorical shift from the more concrete domain of physical space to the more abstract domain of time. The belief that there is a general human tendency to extend spatial terms in this way to a range of other linguistic domains is sometimes called **localism** (as in, for example, Lyons 1977). A commonly used example is languages where semantic notions like possession and states are expressed spatially, as in the Irish examples below:

7.20   Tá Porsche agam.
        is Porsche at.me
        'I have a Porsche.'

7.21   Tá slaghdán orm.
        is cold   on.me
        'I have a cold.'

7.22   Tá gliondar orm.
        is delight on.me
        'I am delighted.'

In 7.20 possession is expressed spatially, while in 7.21 and 7.22 physical
and emotional states are so expressed.[4] A more complicated example which
is sometimes quoted is the use of the verb *go* in English and other languages
for immediate future tenses, as in the future-tense reading of *He is going to
leave the country*, where the idea of spatial movement away from the speaker
is mapped into time as a future event. See Fleischman (1982, 1989) for
discussion of these ideas.

7.2.4   Person deixis

Thus far we have concentrated on deictic divisions of space. A further
deictic system grammaticalizes the roles of participants: the current speaker,
addressee(s) and others. This information is grammaticalized by pronouns:
typically a first person singular pronoun is used for the speaker, second
person pronouns for addressee(s) and minimally, a third person category for
a category 'neither-speaker-nor-addressee(s)'. This basic three-way system is
the basis of most pronoun systems but once again languages differ in the
amount of other contextual information that is included in pronouns. We
can show this by continuing our comparison of Arabic and English, using
just subject pronouns for brevity:

7.23 | **Singular** | **Plural** | **Singular or Plural** |
        |--------------|------------|------------------------|
        | I | we | you |
        | he | they | |
        | she | | |
        | it | | |

7.24 | **Singular** | | **Dual** | | **Plural** | |
        |----------|-----------|--------|-----------------|---------|---------------|
        | *'anaa* | 'I' | | | *nah.nu* | 'we' |
        | *'anta* | 'thou (m)' | *'antumaa* | 'you (two)' | *'antum* | 'you (m)' |
        | *'anti* | 'thou (f)' | | | *'antunna* | 'you (f)' |
        | *huwa* | 'he, it' | *humaa* | 'they (two) | *hum* | 'they (m)' |
        | *hiya* | 'she, it' | | | *hunna* | 'they (f)' |

We can see that the Arabic pronouns in 7.24 encode more information about number than the English pronouns in 7.23: there is an extra category *dual*, which is used for 'exactly two'. The coding of gender is also different: English has a neuter pronoun 'it' which does not occur in Arabic, where all third persons have to have either masculine or feminine gender. On the other hand, Arabic pronouns encode gender more widely: English only distinguishes between *he* and *she*. So both languages have an economic and 'portable' reference system for participants that can be used in any context, but we can see that the packaging of information about participants differs.

One point worth mentioning here is that for obvious reasons there is a difference between the notion of plurality applied to the role of speaker and to non-speaker roles. Since (in normal situations) the speaker is singular, what are called first person plural pronouns actually encode information about some form of identification between the speaker and others. In English it is as simple as that; other languages are more specific. The Ethiopian Omotic language Zayse, for example, has two distinct first person plural pronouns, as shown below (again in subject forms) (Hayward 1990):

7.25   *núy*   'we' (including the addressee(s))
        níi   'we' (not including the addressee(s))

Thus in Zayse, saying the equivalent of 'We're going to the party' overtly communicates whether the addressee is included, whereas English speakers have to rely on the context.

7.2.5 Social deixis

The pronoun systems of some languages also grammaticalize information about the social identities or relationships of the participants in the conversation. Some writers, for example Levinson (1983), call this phenomenon **social deixis**. The most obvious example is the distinction in many European languages between 'familar' and 'polite' pronouns, e.g. *tu/vous* in French, *tu/usted* in Spanish, *du/Sie* in German. Speakers of these languages are committed to revealing their calculations of relative intimacy and formality to their addressees. If we identify this category of social deixis, then Asian languages like Japanese, Korean and Balinese have much richer systems for grammaticalizing social relations. In Japanese, for example, distinctions are marked by the speaker not only in relation to an addressee but also to third persons referred to, as in 7.26 and 7.27 below (Kuno 1973):

7.26   a.   *Tanaka-san ga kudasaimashita.*
              'Mr Tanaka gave it to me.'
              [where hearer is on a somewhat formal basis with speaker]
        b.   *Tanaka-san ga kudasatta.*
              'Mr Tanaka gave it to me.'
              [where hearer is a friend of speaker]

According to Kuno (1973), in both the sentences above Mr Tanaka is in a higher social position than the speaker; we can see the effect of changing the relationship between the speaker and the third person in 7.27 below:

7.27   a.   *Jiroo-kun ga kuremashita.*
              'Jiro gave it to me.'
              [where hearer is in a semi-formal relationship with speaker]
        b.   *Jiroo-kun ga kureta.*
              'Jiro gave it to me.'
              [where hearer is a friend of speaker]

In these sentences Jiro is in a lower social position than the speaker. Comparing 7.26 and 7.27 we can see that distinctions of social relationship have a marked effect on the form of sentences: the speaker's judgements of these are encoded by the choice of verb 'to give' and by the verbal endings.

7.3   Reference and Context

Deictic expressions have been extensively studied, but it would be wrong to see their context-dependence as exceptional, as a special part of language. Much of reference involves reliance on context, together with some calculation on the part of the speaker and hearers. A clear example of this is what Clark (1978) calls **short-hands**. Turning on the radio recently, I heard this sentence:

7.28   It's a struggle keeping the barnacles from off the crops.

After a while it became clear that *barnacles* was a shorthand for *barnacle geese*. The reference would have been clear, of course, if I had listened from the beginning of the programme. This simple example is characteristic of normal language use: speakers calculate how much information their hearers need to make successful references, and where they can, they economize. To give another personal example, I once overheard 7.29 below in a bookshop:

7.29   I'm looking for the new wolf (i.e. Wolfe).

where the speaker obviously felt that *the new Wolfe* was sufficient for the bookseller to identify *the new book by Tom Wolfe*. Another example might be 7.30 below, said during a snooker game:

7.30   He's got two reds left.

Shorthands are sometimes grouped with the rhetorical devices **metonymy** and **synecdoche**. The former is where we identify the referent by something associated with it, as in 7.31 below:

7.31   a. The cover-up extends to **the Oval Office**.
        b. Who were all **those suits** drinking in the pub last night?
        c. Have you cleared this deal with **the top floor**?

Synecdoche is a form of reference where the part stands for the whole, as in 7.32:

7.32   a. All of his cattle are affected; he'll lose more than fifty **head**.
        b. It's good to see some new **faces** in here.

The use of technical terms like **shorthands, metonymy** and **synecdoche** has the disadvantage that it suggests that these are rhetorical devices, special uses of language, whereas they are just specific examples of the routine calculation involved in making reference. We can see this use of context and calculation if we parallel examples from Clark (1978) with a hypothetical situation where someone wants to buy two bottles of Heineken lager. In a pub, they might say *Two bottles of Heineken, please*! In a theatre bar, where only bottled beer is available, their order might be: *Two Heinekens, please*! At a sponsor's stall at an open-air concert, which only serves Heineken beer, in bottle and on draught, they could say: *Two bottles, please*! If the stall only sold bottles, they might say just *Two please*! The point here is that the ordinary use of referring expressions involves calculations of retrievability, which take account of contextual information.

7.4 Knowledge as Context

These calculations of retrievability are really guesses about knowledge: a speaker choosing how to make reference to an entity must make estimations of what her hearers know. So if someone were to rush up to you and shout:

7.33   The baby's swallowed the canary!

their choice of words reveals that they think you can identify both the baby and the canary involved. To discuss the role of knowledge it is useful to divide it into different types. This is not a scientific classification but just a way of organizing our discussion. We might, for example, distinguish between three different sources for the knowledge a speaker has to estimate:

   1 that computable from the physical context;
   2 that available from what has already been said;
   3 that available from background or common knowledge.

Under the first heading we can put the knowledge gained from filling in the deictic expressions, as described in section 7.2, i.e. who is speaking to whom, the time and location of the conversation. Let us examine what might come under the second and third headings.

7.4.1 Discourse as context

Under the second heading, we might view the talk itself, often called the **discourse,** as a kind of context. One clear example of this is the interpretation of sentence fragments. In isolation, fragments like *Ronan did* or *Me too* cannot be interpreted, but in the right conversational context they are meaningful:

7.34   a.   Who moved these chairs?
        b.   Ronan did.

7.35   a.   I'm starving.
        b.   Me too.

Participants would have no difficulty interpreting *Ronan did* as *Ronan moved these chairs*; or *Me too* as *I'm starving too*. Clearly the preceding discourse licenses these interpretations.

We can see another example of the role of the discourse itself as context when we look at the notion of **discourse topic**. It seems clear that in conversing, participants construct a notion of what the discourse is about – a kind of current topic. This topic is a form of knowledge which then influences the way they interpret the meaning of what they subsequently hear. There have been a number of experiments which support this picture. One simple one is described by Brown and Yule (1983: 139–40), from a study by Anderson et al. (1977). Subjects were asked to read the story in 7.36 below, with the 'Prisoner' title, then were asked questions about it.

7.36   **A Prisoner Plans His Escape**
        Rocky slowly got up from the mat, planning his escape. He hesit-
        ated a moment and thought. Things were not going well. What
        bothered him was being held, especially since the charge against
        him had been weak. He considered his present situation. The lock
        that held him was strong, but he thought he could break it.

It was generally agreed 'that Rocky was alone, that he had been arrrested by the police, and that he disliked being in prison' (p. 139). When the same text was presented under another title, the 'Wrestler' title in 7.37 below, other subjects agreed that 'Rocky was a wrestler who was being held in some kind of wrestling hold and was planning to get out of this hold' (p. 140). In this interpretation there is no prison cell and no police.

7.37   **A Wrestler in a Tight Corner**
        Rocky slowly got up from the mat, planning his escape. He hesitated
        a moment and thought. Things were not going well. What bothered
        him was being held, especially since the charge against him had
        been weak. He considered his present situation. The lock that held
        him was strong, but he thought he could break it.

The main point here is that listeners add their own inferences when they
interpret utterances, fleshing out the material in ways that depend on knowledge provided by the discourse topic. We look at these inferences in more
detail a little later in sections 7.6 and 7.7.

7.4.2 Background knowledge as context

Our third type of knowledge has been called many things, including background, common-sense, encylopaedic, sociocultural and real-world knowledge. What is usually meant is the knowledge a speaker might calculate
others would have before, or independently of, a particular conversation, by
virtue of membership in a community. We are all, of course, members of
many overlapping communities: speakers of our native language, citizens of
the same state, city or neighbourhood, members of the same sports teams,
churches or political groups, fellow university students, co-workers, etc.
Each community implies certain types of knowledge which might be shared
with other members and which conversationalists must seek to calculate as
they interact. We can use an example that is so obvious that we may not
notice its reliance on cultural knowledge:

7.38   A: I'm hungry.
        B: I'll lend you some money.

This exchange gains coherence from the knowledge that money can be
exchanged for food, which is cultural knowledge not present in any reasonable dictionary entry for the words *food* or *money*. Much of the fleshing out
of an utterance via inference that we mentioned above relies on this kind of
background knowledge. To take another invented exchange, in 7.39:

7.39   A: Shall we go and get some ice cream?
        B: I'm on a diet.

Here speaker A might reasonably infer that B's reply is a refusal; that B's
reply implies 'No'. We will look at the use of such implications in section
7.7, but what's important here is that the implication and inference both
rely on cultural knowledge about diets and ice cream. The fact that it is
cultural knowledge which is providing the basis for the inference can be
shown by using an example that is less familiar to some readers, like the
exchange in 7.40 below:

7.40   A: Come over next week for lunch.
          B: It's Ramadan.

If A and B are Muslims then A will probably infer that B's reply means 'No'.[5]

In chapter 4 we discussed Stalnaker's (1974) use of the term **common ground** for the presuppositions in a discourse. Clark (1994) adopts this term and distinguishes between **communal** common ground for the knowledge shared by co-members of communities and **personal** common ground for the knowledge two people share from their past experience of each other.

Some slightly different evidence for the importance of background knowledge comes from a study by Kess and Hoppe (1985) on how listeners detect and resolve ambiguity. It is a well-known fact about English sentence structure that adding a prepositional phrase to a verb phrase can cause ambiguity, as in 7.41 below:

7.41   a.   John chased the dog.
          b.   John chased the dog with a stick.

The ambiguity in 7.41b is in whether John or the dog has the stick. Kess and Hoppe provide a list of similar sentences, as in 7.42:

7.42   John chased the dog with the stick.
          John chased the dog with the bone.
          John chased the dog with the broom.
          John chased the dog with the trombone.
          John chased the dog with the white tail.
          John chased the dog with the pointed ears.
          John chased the dog with the black spot.
          John chased the dog with the wound.

They suggest that while, structurally, ambiguity should be present in all of these sentences, in fact background knowledge about dogs and people will mean that for most people there is no ambiguity in any but the first sentence in the list. Of course these sentences are given without a context: since 'background knowledge' here is a prediction of how typically dogs and people behave, based on experience, the 'normal' interpretation can be overruled in a particular context.

7.4.3   Mutual knowledge

One important point about this backgound knowledge is that, while the speaker makes guesses about the knowledge her listeners have, there is no certainty. It is probably a mistake to identify this background knowledge with **mutual knowledge**.[6] This is a topic that has been heavily debated in the philosophical and semantic literature; see for example the collection of papers in N. V. Smith (1982). As linguists have pointed out (e.g. Gibbs 1987), the problem is that if we take from philosophers a tight definition like 7.43 below, the notion is too strong (Gibbs 1987: 565):

7.43   (where S = speaker, A = addressee)
        S and A mutually know a proposition P, if and only if:
        S knows that P
        A knows that P
        S knows that A knows that P
        A knows that S knows that A knows that P,
        . . . and so on, *ad infinitum.*

For an example of a proposition that might be mutual knowledge in this sense, we can go back to our example 7.39, and extend it slightly below:

7.44   A: Shall we go and get some ice cream?
        B: I'm on a diet.
        A: Oh, okay.

We could take the mutually known proposition P to be something like 'Diets usually prohibit ice cream (because it's too fattening)'. So B knows this, and relies for her implication on A knowing it. Since A seems to understand the refusal correctly, then A did know P, and also knows that for B to imply it, A must have known it, and so on.

While there doesn't seem to be a principled way of stopping this chain of reciprocal knowledge as in 7.43, this is obviously not a promising definition for linguists, leading as it does to at least the two following problems:

7.45   a.   How can speakers and hearers compute an infinite series of
             propositions in a finite (actually very small) piece of time?
        b.   How do S and A ever coordinate what they mutually believe if
             there's always one more belief statement to be established?

It seems that a plausible pragmatic theory of how participants use back-ground knowledge will have to employ a weaker form of knowledge than this philosophical notion of mutual knowledge. We will not pursue this issue any further here, but see Sperber and Wilson (1995) and Blakemore (1992) for discussions of solutions to this problem. What seems intuitively clear is that the participants' access to background knowledge must be based on guesswork rather than certain knowledge and must involve relatively quick and economic calculations.

7.4.4 Giving background knowledge to computers

The importance of background knowledge to language understanding was quickly recognized in the field of Artificial Intelligence (AI). One typical application is the design of computer programs to process and store information from texts, e.g. newspaper articles, so that users can later interrogate the databases. These programs quickly revealed the extent to which human readers make inferences to gain an understanding of a text; inferences that are often based on background knowledge. Various forms of knowledge representation have been proposed to model this background information. Roger Schank and his colleagues (Schank and Abelson 1977; Cullingford 1978) devised **scripts** to do this. Scripts are descriptions of what typically goes on in various social settings. One well-known example is a restaurant script, of which 7.46 below is a simplified version (written in English rather than a computer language) (Schank and Kass 1988: 190):

7.46   1   <u>Actor</u> goes to a <u>restaurant</u>.
        2   <u>Actor</u> is seated.
        3   <u>Actor</u> orders a <u>meal</u> from <u>waiter</u>.
        4   <u>Waiter</u> brings <u>meal</u> to the <u>actor</u>.
        5   <u>Actor</u> eats the <u>meal</u>.
        6   <u>Actor</u> gives money to the <u>restaurant</u>.
        7   <u>Actor</u> leaves the <u>restaurant</u>.

In this very basic script the underlined elements are variables that have to be filled in from any specific restaurant text the script is applied to. A fuller script than 7.46, with more details of what goes on in a typical restaurant, allowed the computer program Script Applier Mechanism (SAM) to interpret a text about a restaurant visit by using inferences to fill in the gaps in the text. Such a text is in 7.47 below with an interpretation in 7.48 (both based on Schank and Abelson 1977), which includes inferences based on the script in 7.46:

7.47   John went to a restaurant. The waiter gave John a menu. The waiter came to the table. John ordered a lobster. John was served quickly. John left a large tip.

7.48   John went to a restaurant. John looked for a table. John went to the table. John sat down in the chair. John got the menu from the waiter. John read the menu. The waiter went to the table. John ordered lobster. The cook pepared the lobster. The waiter got the lobster from the cook. The waiter served John the lobster. John ate the lobster. John indicated to the waiter he would like to get the bill from him. John got the bill from the waiter. John left the waiter a large tip. John paid the bill. John left the restaurant.

As can be seen, inferences based on a script allow a much fuller version of what went on in the visit than is explicit in the text, and SAM is then able to respond to questions about the visit, as shown in an example interrogation 7.49 (based on Schank and Abelson 1977):

7.49   Q: What did John eat?
        A: LOBSTER.
        Q: Who gave John the menu?
        A: THE WAITER.
        Q: Who gave John the lobster?
        A: PROBABLY THE WAITER.
        Q: Who paid the bill?
        A: PROBABLY JOHN.
        Q: What happened when John went to the table?
        A: JOHN SAT DOWN AND THE WAITER GAVE HIM A MENU.
        Q: Why did John get a menu?
        A: SO HE COULD ORDER.
        Q: Why did John give the waiter a large tip?
        A: BECAUSE HE WAS SERVED QUICKLY.

In subsequent work Schank and his colleagues have developed this approach further, replacing scripts with knowledge representations which are more flexible and which share components more easily; see Schank and Kass (1988) for a brief overview.

7.5 Information Structure

We have been looking at how different types of knowledge provide a contextual background for understanding utterances, and at how speakers routinely make guesses about the knowledge accessible to their listeners. In this section we briefly examine how linguistic structure reflects these guesses, or to put it another way: how these estimates of knowledge are grammaticalized. We will see that speakers 'package' their utterances to take account of these estimates of knowledge. This packaging is often called **information structure** or, alternatively, **thematic structure**.

Perhaps the most universally grammaticalized distinction is the basic one between the information which the speaker assumes her hearers already know and the information that the speaker is presenting as additional or new. This distinction is so ubiquitous and grammaticalized in so many different ways that there are a number of different terminologies describing it, as we shall see in the following sections. As a starting-point it is simplest to call the already present knowledge **given**, and the additional information, **new**.[7] In the next sections we look at some linguistic markers of this distinction.

7.5.1 The information status of nominals

One basic way for a speaker to convey her assumption that something is given is to use a definite nominal. One way to do this in English is to use the definite article *the*; compare for example:

7.50   a.   I'm going to the party.
         b.   I'm going to a party.

The definite article in 7.50a signals that the speaker assumes the hearer can
identify the referent, the party. The normal conversation pattern is for items
to be introduced by an indefinite nominal, remain conversationally salient
for a time, then fade from salience, perhaps later to be reintroduced.
This is a very complicated and little understood process but a simple sketch
might go as follows: a nominal will be introduced with a marker that it is
new, perhaps an indefinite noun phrase, as in 7.51 below:

7.51   I'm going to **a party** tonight.

Thereafter a definite article can be used to show that it is now given:

7.52   **The party** begins at eleven.

If the party is not mentioned again, it fades from salience and will need to
be referred to by various support structures: *that party*, *that party you mentioned*, etc. While an entity is accessible, it can be referred to by pronouns,
e.g.

7.53   The party begins at eleven and **it**'ll go on for hours.

The sensitivity of nominal types to information structure has been described
in various approaches. Gundel et al. (1993), for example, identify a Givenness
Hierarchy for English nominals as below:

7.54   Givenness Hierarchy (Gundel et al. 1993)[8]
         in focus > activated > familiar > uniquely identifiable
         {*it*}   ⎧*that* ⎫   {*that* N}   {*the* N}
                         ⎨*this* ⎬
                         ⎩*this* N⎭

         > referential > type identifiable
         ⎧indefinite⎫ {*a* N}
         ⎩*this* N   ⎭

This hierarchy identifies different information states of a referent, moving
left to right from most given to most new. Beneath each states are examples
of English nominals typically used for it. These writers use examples like
7.55–6 below (from Gundel et al. 2000), where 7.55 is the first sentence
providing the context and 7.56 provides different continuations appropriate
in different information states, with the relevant nominal in bold:

7.55   I couldn't sleep last night.

7.56   a.   **A dog next door** kept me awake.
        b.   **This dog next door** kept me awake.
        c.   **The dog next door** kept me awake.
        d.   **That dog next door** kept me awake.
        e.   **This dog/that/this** kept me awake.
        f.   **It** kept me awake.

In this approach the indefinite article *a* used with the nominal in 7.56a signals the rightmost end of the Givenness Hierarchy: its use just assumes that the hearer can identify the type of thing referred to. The referentially indefinite use of *this* in the b version signals an extra message: that the speaker intends to refer to a particular dog subsequently. The definite article *the* in c signals the assumption that the hearer can identify the referent. The demonstrative *that* in d assumes previous familiarity with the referent on the hearer's part. The demonstrative article *this* and the pronominal versions *this* and *that* in e signal that the referent has been mentioned, or 'activated' in the discourse.[9] Finally the pronoun *it* in f shows that the referent is both activated and currently under discussion. Other hierarchies of informational status have been discussed by Ariel (1988) and Prince (1981, 1992).

In a sentence like 7.53 above, *The party begins at eleven and **it**'ll go on for hours*, the reference of *it* is supported by the preceding nominal *the party*. This relationship of indirect reference is called **anaphora**. The nominal *the party* is termed the antecedent and the pronoun *it* is termed an **anaphoric pronoun**. Of course there are constraints on how far apart the antecedent and the anaphoric pronouns may be;[10] moreover, if they are in the same sentence, there are complicated structural conditions on their co-occurrence: see Chomsky (1988) for proposals for describing the latter within generative grammar. We will not pursue these issues here, simply recognizing that the use of anaphoric pronouns is part of this process of grammaticalizing the information status of nominals. As seen in the hierarchy in 7.54 above, for hearers to be able to make reference on the basis of such abbreviatory forms as pronouns, they have to be maximally accessible. We can see the parallel between the anaphoric use of pronouns, where the referents have been introduced into the discourse, and the **deictic** use of pronouns, where the referents are also maximally accessible because they are physically present in the context of the utterance, e.g. if I point to someone and say:

7.57   That's **him**.

Another way of viewing this process of using indefinite nominals, definite nominals and pronouns to refer to entities is to see it as a kind of filing system, a way of tracking entities through the discourse. We might think of it as a spoken version of the coloured lines some novelists are said to use for keeping track of characters and plotlines in their stories. See Givón (1983) for a detailed discussion of the grammaticalization of referential accessibility and the knowledge base of discourse participants.

7.5.2 Focus and topic

Another marker of information structure in English is intonation, where the assignment of primary stress can be used to bring parts of the sentence into prominence. One of the main functions of this prominence is to mark new information. In the following examples, capitals show this primary stress, and we divide the given and new elements of the sentence:

7.58   a. HENRY cleaned the kitchen.
          b. Given: Someone cleaned the kitchen.
          c. New: It was Henry.

7.59   a. Henry cleaned THE KITCHEN.
          b. Given: Henry cleaned something.
          c. New: It was the kitchen.

7.60   a. Henry CLEANED the kitchen.
          b. Henry did something to the kitchen.
          c. He cleaned it.

For a detailed discussion of this use of intonation see Allan (1986, 2: 59–163). What the English intonation system is doing here is to allow the speaker to partition the sentence into two elements: a prominent part and the rest.[11] This prominent part is usually called the **focus**. As we see here, one function of focus is to mark new information. Another function allows the speaker to pick out one of a number of alternatives, as in:

7.61   a. Did HARRY take the car?
          b. No, GEORGE did.

Here both nominals may be activated in the conversation and the focus now has a **contrastive** function.

In other languages this function of intonation is taken over by specific, otherwise meaningless, words which mark elements of the sentence as in focus or not. Somali, for example, has focus words which include the nominal focus particle *baa*, as shown in 7.62a and b:

7.62   a. *Amina baa   wargeyskii keentay.*
             Amina FOCUS newspaper brought
             'AMINA brought the newspaper, It was AMINA who brought the newspaper.'

          b. *Amina wargeyskii bay   keentay.*
                              baa + ay
             Amina newspaper FOCUS + she brought
             'Amina brought THE NEWSPAPER, It was THE NEWSPAPER Amina brought.'

This word *baa* follows a nominal and places it in focus. Once again one of the primary uses of this focus system is to mark new information: sentence 7.62a fits a conversational context where it was known that someone brought the newspaper and the sentence asserts it was Amina, while in 7.62b, it was known that Amina brought something, and the sentence asserts that it was the newspaper she brought.

These Somali focus words also have the contrastive function described above, as we can see from the proverb below:

7.63   *Libàaxyeedháyiyo libàax aammusáy, libàax aammusáy bàa   xún.*
        lion roared and lion   kept:silent lion   roared   FOCUS bad
        '(Of) a roaring lion and a silent lion, A SILENT LION is worse.'[12]

As indicated by the English glosses to the examples 7.62a and b above, another way of marking information structure in English is by syntactic constructions. Certain constructions serve to place parts of the sentence in focus, for example the constructions known as **clefts** in 7.64, and the **pseudo-cleft** in 7.65, where the focus elements are underlined:

7.64   a. It was <u>yesterday</u> that Bob came.
        b. It was <u>Bob</u> who came yesterday.

7.65   What we want is <u>a living wage</u>.

Once again we can see that focus is part of information structure: in 7.64a and b the basic situation described is the same: *Bob came yesterday*, but the information is packaged differently to fit different states of participants' knowledge at the specific point in the conversation.

There is another important information structure role that is marked in languages, that of **topic**. We discussed in section 7.4.1 the notion of discourse topic; that is, a general idea among participants of what the current topic of discussion is. As Halliday and Hasan (1976) pointed out, such discourse topics are maintained by a battery of conversational devices, including anaphora, using related lexemes, repetition of lexemes, all of which create a cohesion to discourses that make them more than a collection of unrelated sentences. In addition, some languages have **sentence topics**: see for example the Japanese sentences below, from Kuno (1973: 44):

7.66   *Kuzira wa   honyuu-doobutu desu*
        whale TOPIC mammal   is
        'Speaking of whales, they are mammals, A whale is a mammal.'

7.67   *John wa   watakusi no tomodati desu*
        John TOPIC I   's friend   is
        'Speaking of John, he is my friend.'

In these examples the topic occurs at the beginning of the sentence and is identified by a following particle *wa*. In the following Mandarin Chinese example from Li and Thompson (1976: 468) the topic is again initial but there is no special morphmeme:

7.68   *Nèike shù yèzi   dà*
        that   tree leaves big
        'That tree (topic), the leaves are big.'

The major characteristic of topics is that they must be 'entered into the registry of the present discourse', as Kuno (1973: 45) put it. The function of this kind of topic is characterized by Chafe (1976: 50) as limiting the applicability of the rest of the sentence:

7.69   Typically, it would seem, the topic sets a spatial, temporal, or individual framework within the main predication holds.

As the translations in 7.66–7 show, there is no exact correspondence in English to these sentence topics. Many of the features of topics are typical of subjects in English, for example: that they are typically given information, often activated elements; that they tend to occur at the beginning of sentences; and that they are in some sense what the sentence is 'about'. There are also, especially in spoken English, sentences like those below:

7.70   As for the referendum, it's a foregone conclusion.

7.71   Me, I've been a Liverpool fan all my life.

In such sentences the first part, before the comma, seems rather like a topic. These though are rather marginal constructions in the language and speakers tend to avoid using them in writing. Li and Thompson (1976) argue that languages differ systematically in their use of sentence topics and subjects. They identify four types: subject-prominent languages (like English); topic-prominent languages (like Chinese); languages where both topics and subjects are important (like Japanese); and finally, languages where neither is important. For this last type they suggest as an example Tagalog (Austronesian: Philippines). Traditionally observers speak of the first type having a subject-predicate structure to their sentences; while the second type have a topic-comment structure. In each case the claim is that the basic organization of the sentence is related to the speaker's decisions about its information structure.

7.5.3 Information structure and comprehension

Brown and Yule (1983: 128) cite an example from a talk by M. A. K. Halliday which demonstrates the importance of information structure to

comprehension. Halliday, who has written detailed studies of discourse structure (e.g. Halliday and Hasan 1976), quoted a US radio report describing
an official welcome for astronauts, as in 7.72 below:

7.72   The sun's shining, it's a perfect day. Here come the astronauts.
         They're just passing the Great Hall; perhaps the President will
         come out to greet them. No, it's the admiral who's taking the
         ceremony . . .

Halliday then altered the markers of information structure to produce the
text in 7.73:

7.73   It's the sun that's shining, the day that's perfect. The astronauts
         come here. The Great Hall they're just passing; he'll come out to
         greet them the President. No, it's the ceremony that the admiral's
         taking . . .

As can be seen, the use of inappropriate markers of information structure,
in effect disregarding the reader's evolving state of knowledge, makes the
text incoherent and difficult to read. The point is, of course, that in reality
speakers continually assess their audience's knowledge, and package their
utterances accordingly.

7.6   Inference

Throughout our discussion of the role of context, we have seen examples of
the way that listeners actively participate in the construction of meaning, in
particular by using inferences to fill out the text towards an interpretation
of speaker meaning. We now turn to look at examples of conversational inference, first with a general discussion in this section, then with a look at one
important approach to inference, conversation implicature, in section 7.7.
   We can begin our examples of inference with anaphora. As described
above, this is a special sub-type of **coreference**, a referential relation between
expressions where they both refer to the same entity. There are many types
of coreference: a nominal may be repeated, as in 7.74; there may be an
independent nominal, used as an epithet, as in 7.75, or very commonly, an
anaphoric pronoun may be used, as in 7.76. As mentioned earlier, anaphoric
pronouns differ from full nominals in that they have no independent reference
and must rely on an antecedent.

7.74   I fell down a hole yesterday. **The hole** was very deep.

7.75   I saw your brother this morning. **The old fool** still doesn't recognize
         me.

7.76   I trod on a slug this morning. **It** died.

Very commonly interpreting anaphora across sentences involves inference. Take for example the interpretation of the pronoun **it** (shown in bold) in 7.77 below:

7.77   The plane was late, the hotel wasn't fully built, there were crowds everywhere she went. I think **it** really disappointed her.

If we are to look for a nominal antecedent for the pronoun *it* in 7.77, possible candidates are *the plane, the hotel, crowds*. It seems more likely, though, that it is the whole situation that *it* refers back to: a kind of composite antecedent we could call something like *the holiday*. This cumulative antecedent has to be constructed by the listener. This kind of 'sloppy' use of pronouns is very common, but seems to cause listeners no difficulty.[13]

There are other inferential links routinely made between sentences. Some have been called **bridging inferences** by Clark (1977). Below are a few of his examples:

7.78   a.   I looked into the room. **The ceiling** was very high.
        b.   I walked into the room. **The windows** looked out to the bay.
        c.   I walked into the room. **The chandeliers** sparkled brightly.
        d.   John went walking out at noon. **The park** was beautiful.

In each of these examples, the nominal in bold occurs with a definite article, showing that the speaker assumes that referent is accessible to the listener, i.e. that it is given. In each case the question is: how, if it has not been mentioned earlier, nor is physically present at the utterance, did this nominal become part of given information? The answer seems to be that the listener makes a bridging inference which links the nominal to the preceding sentence and creates coherence. In these examples the basis for the inferences seems to be background knowledge. People know that rooms usually have ceilings, commonly have windows, may have chandeliers, and that one of the conventional places to go for a walk is in a park. With this knowledge, the listener can infer, for example, that the park referred to in 7.78d is the one that John went walking in.

What the listeners seem to be doing here is making inferences to preserve a notion of coherence in what they are told. Speakers seem confident that their listeners will do this and they take advantage of it to speak less explicitly than they might. The following are examples of where the speaker seems to rely on listener inferences:

7.79   I left early. I had a train to catch.
        INFERENCE: Speaker left **because** of having to catch the train.

7.80   A: Did you give Mary the money?
        B: I'm waiting for her now.
        INFERENCE: B did not give Mary the money.

Knowing that their listeners will flesh out their utterances with inferences gives speakers the freedom to imply something rather than state it. In the next section we look at one particular type of implication identified in the pragmatics literature, **conversational implicature**.

7.7 Conversational Implicature

The term 'conversational implicature' was introduced by the philosopher H. Paul Grice. In lectures and a couple of very influential articles (Grice 1975, 1978), he proposed an approach to the speaker's and hearer's cooperative use of inference. As we suggested above, there seems to be enough regularity in the inference-forming behaviour of listeners for speakers to exploit this by implying something, rather than stating it. Grice argued that this predictability of inference formation could be explained by postulating a **cooperative principle**: a kind of tacit agreement by speakers and listeners to cooperate in communication. It would be a mistake to interpret this too widely: we may assume that Grice is not identifying in human interaction a utopian ideal of rational and egalitarian cooperation. As sociolinguists have shown us, people use language as an integral part of their social behaviour, whether competing, supporting, expressing solidarity, dominating or exploiting. Grice's observations are focused at a different, more micro level: if I am in conflict with you, I still may want to communicate my intentions to you, and assume you will work out the implications of my utterances. It is at the underlying level of linguistic communication that Grice identifies this cooperation between speakers and listeners.

7.7.1 Grice's maxims of conversational cooperation

The assumptions that hearers make about a speaker's conduct seemed to Grice to be of several different types, giving rise to different types of inference, or, from the speaker's point of view, implicatures. In identifying these, Grice called them **maxims**, and phrased them as if they were injunctions: Do *thus*! This can be misleading: it is important to realize that the conversational principles that Grice proposed are not rules, like phonological or morphological rules, which people have to follow to speak a language; nor are they moral principles. Perhaps the best way to intepret a maxim *Do X!* is to translate it into a descriptive statement: the hearer seems to assume that the speaker is doing *X* in communicating. We can see this by looking at the maxims and some examples.

Grice's four main maxims are as follows (Grice 1975, 1978):

7.81 *The Maxim of Quality*
        Try to make your contribution one that is true, i.e.
        1 Do not say what you believe is false.
        2 Do not say that for which you lack adequate evidence.

The Maxim of Quantity
1   Make your contribution as informative as is required
    (for the current purposes of the exchange).
2   Do not make your contribution more informative than is
    required.

The Maxim of Relevance (Relation)
Make your contributions relevant.

The Maxim of Manner
Be perspicuous, and specifically:
1   Avoid ambiguity
2   Avoid obscurity
3   Be brief
4   Be orderly.

As suggested above, these maxims can be viewed as follows: the listener will assume, unless there is evidence to the contrary, that a speaker will have calculated her utterance along a number of parameters: she will tell the truth, try to estimate what her audience knows and package her material accordingly, have some idea of the current topic, and give some thought to her audience being able to understand her. To repeat: these are assumptions the listener starts out with; any or all may be wrong, and he may realize this or not, but this is a kind of baseline for talking.

We can look at a couple of examples of how these maxims help the hearer arrive at implicatures; we focus on the maxims of relevance and quantity:

7.82   Relevance
        A: Can I borrow £5?
        B: My purse is in the hall.
        (Implicature: Yes.)

Here it is A's assumption that B's reply is intended to be relevant that allows the inference: yes. The implicature in 7.82 has three characteristics: firstly, that it is implied rather than said; secondly, that its existence is a result of the context, the specific interaction – there is, of course, no guarantee that in other contexts *My purse is in the hall* will mean 'yes'; the third characteristic is that such implicatures are cancellable, or **defeasible** in the terminology we used in chapter 4, without causing a contradiction. Thus the implicature 'yes' in 7.82 can be cancelled in 7.83 below by the addition of extra clauses:

7.83   Defeasibility of implicature
        A: Can I borrow £5?
        B: My purse is in the hall. But don't you dare touch it. I'm not
            lending you any more money.

Our next example involves the maxim of quantity:

7.84   Quantity
        A: Did you do the reading for this week's seminar?
        B: I intended to.
        (Implicature: No.)

Here B's answer would, of course, be true if B intended to do the reading
and then did, but then the answer would violate the maxim of quantity. A,
assuming the maxim to be observed, is likely to infer the answer no. Once
again the implicature is implied, contextual and cancellable. Another typical
example is 7.85 below:

7.85   Quantity
        A: Did you drink all the bottles of beer in the fridge?
        B: I drank some.
        (Implicature: B didn't drink them all.)

Once again, logically if B drank all of the beer, then B drank some of the
beer. So B's reply would be true in this case. However, the maximum of
quantity would lead A to the implicature above, assuming that B would
otherwise make the more informative reply.
    As mentioned above, these maxims are basic assumptions, not rules, and
they can be broken. Grice distinguished between the speaker secretly breaking them, e.g. by lying, which he termed **violating** the maxims; and overtly
breaking them for some linguistic effect, which he called **flouting**. We take
an example of the creative flouting of the maxim of manner from Flann
O'Brien's novel *At-Swim-Two-Birds* (1967: 38):

7.86   The three of us were occupied in putting glasses of stout into the
        interior of our bodies and expressing by fine disputation the resulting
        sense of physical and mental well being.

From a linguist's point of view cases of flouting are more interesting than
violations of maxims. Irony, for example, can be seen as a flouting of the
maxim of quality, as for example, if you say to a friend who has done
something terrible to you: *You're a fine friend*. Indeed the cooperative principle often forms an important part of the **literal language theory** described in chapter 1. In this theory the principle is often viewed as the
engine which drives the interpretation of non-literal utterances. The explanation goes like this: if a listener interprets an utterance as literally untrue
or nonsensical, the principle may lead him to search for a further level of
meaning, **figurative** language, which preserves the maxim of quality. Thus
the listener will be led to interpret rather than reject as impossible the
metaphors as in 7.87 below, or **hyberbole** in 7.88:

7.87   a. He lit the stage with his talent.
        b. She just lapped up all the compliments.

7.88   a. I've read this millions of times.
        b. You're the only woman in my life.

One possible criticism of these maxims, for example the maxim of manner, is that they contain a built-in assumption of one type of language use: one that is clear and informative. By contrast, most cultures have types of language use where obscurity and ambiguity are expected and valued: perhaps poetry and riddles, or more mundanely, advertising. One solution might be to relativize the maxims to some classification of talk interaction, such as is discussed in studies in the ethnography of communication; see, for example, Gumperz and Hymes (1972).

A number of writers have proposed cooperative principles like the ones we have been discussing. Brown and Levinson (1978), for example, have identified a politeness principle, as discussed in Leech (1983) and Allan (1986), which we will return to in the next chapter. Meanwhile, Grice's cooperative principle and maxims have been much developed in subsequent work; we discuss two strands of this work in the next two sections.

7.7.2 Generalizing the Gricean maxims

Subsequent writers have attempted to reduce Grice's original four maxims (and eight sub-maxims). In one tradition the Quality maxim is elevated to a higher level than the others and seen as a prerequisite for all others. Thereafter Horn (1984, 1989, 1996), for example, collapses several maxims into two general principles: a Q-principle and an R-principle, which are held to be in tension with each other. The Q-principle draws together Grice's first Quantity maxim and the first two sub-maxims of Manner. It is a kind of guarantee of informational adequacy to the hearer. It may be informally characterized as:

7.89   Q-Principle: Say as much as you can, balancing against the R-principle.

The R-principle is a principle of speaker economy; it subsumes the Relevance maxim and the last two maxims of Manner, and can be represented as:

7.90   R-principle: Say no more than you must, balancing against the Q-principle.

One area where the Q-principle is held to operate is in scalar implicatures (Horn 1989; Gazdar 1979). This is the claim that certain linguistic expressions form a scale of strength, $<x, y>$, where x is stronger than y, for example:

7.91   Q-principle scales
         a.   <all, some>
         b.   <be certain that, think that>
         c.   <succeed in, try to>

Strength here is a notion of informational content and also involves an asymmetrical relation of entailment, the semantic relation discussed in chapter 4. The stronger expression *x* entails *y* but *y* does not entail *x*. Thus *all* entails *some* but *some* does not entail *all*. The idea is that when a speaker utters a weaker expression from a scale, the Q-principle ensures that the hearer infers that the speaker believes the stronger expression does not hold. This explains the following implicatures:

7.92   a.   Jane ate some of the biscuits IMPLICATES Jane didn't eat all of
               them.
         b.   I think she's at home IMPLICATES I'm not certain she's at home.
         c.   I tried to buy you some flowers IMPLICATES I didn't buy you
               some flowers.

In simple terms, if Jane in 7.92a did eat all the biscuits she surely ate some of them; to use *some* when *all* would apply is held to be a violation of the Q-principle and therefore uncooperative, in Gricean terms.

   The R-principle is used to explain why longer forms have different interpretations than shorter ones, when they seem to be paraphrases of each other. See for example the pairs:

7.93   a.   Leonora caused her husband to die.
         b.   Leonora killed her husband.

7.94   a.   I don't not like you.
         b.   I like you.

In 7.93a the periphrastic use of two clauses weakens the chain of cause and effect relative to 7.93b. It would be odd to use 7.93a if for example Leonora stabbed her husband to death in a violent rage. The sentences in 7.94 show that a double negative often has a different interpretation than a corresponding positive: in ordinary use 7.94a doesn't quite mean the same as 7.94b. In both these examples the shorter form is assumed to be the expected form because of the R-principle; the longer forms, as violations, will therefore carry extra levels of meaning.[14]

7.7.3   Relevance theory

A more radical development of Grice's maxims is Relevance Theory (Sperber and Wilson 1995). This approach seeks to unify the Gricean cooperative principle and conversational maxims into a single principle of relevance that will motivate a hearer's inferential strategy:

7.95   Principle of relevance
         Every act of ostensive communication communicates the presump-
         tion of its own optimal relevance.   (Sperber and Wilson 1995: 158)

For these writers the term **ostensive communication** describes a situation where there is interaction: the communicator wants to signal something and create a mutual environment of communication and this intention is recog-nized by her hearers. This is the situation of ordinary conversation.

This principle follows Grice in recognizing that hearers can assume a speaker has a communicative intent. In this theory it is this intent that leads her to calculate the relevance of her utterance with the hearer's role in mind. In Relevance Theory this is often described as a speaker calculating a bal-ance between communicative profit and loss from the hearer's point of view. The profit is the extent to which the communication produces cognitive effects (e.g. changing existing knowledge); the loss is the processing cost where the closer the new information is to already existing knowledge, the less 'expensive' it is to assimilate it. The hearer takes this speaker calculation for granted when making his inferences.

One characteristic of Relevance Theory is the argument that the inferential processes that we identify as leading from the basic meaning of an utterance to its conversational implicatures are also involved in getting to the 'basic' meaning in the first place. Blakemore (1992: 58) discusses a traditional example of implicature in 7.96 below, where B's answer produces the implicature shown.

7.96   A: Did you enjoy your holiday?
         B: The beaches were crowded and the hotel was full of bugs.
             (B's implicature: No, I didn't enjoy my holiday.)

Blakemore argues that pragmatic processes of another more basic sort are involved in the interpretation of B's utterance. The hearer A has a number of problems to solve because of the sketchiness of the linguistic input. For example, what were the beaches crowded with? Which hotel is referred to? Which meaning of the word bug is involved, e.g. electronic listening device, or insect? She argues that we get the answers to these by pragmatic processes, and that these processes necessarily produce an intervening phase which underlies the production of implicatures. This two-phase interpretation gives us 7.97a and b from B's reply in 7.96:

7.97   a. The beaches at the holiday resort that the speaker went to were
             crowded with people and the hotel he stayed at was full of
             insects.
         b. The speaker did not enjoy his holiday.

To get to 7.97a the hearer must perform certain tasks, including, for example, determining which hotel is referred to. In this theory the correct target for reference will be the one that makes the resulting proposition maximally relevant to the accessible context. Clearly the most relevant hotel to B's holiday story is the one he stayed in. This information being accessible in the context relies on the real-world knowledge that beach holidays often involve staying in hotels. Other tasks involve expanding elliptical expressions: that the beaches were crowded with people; and resolving lexical ambiguity: that the bugs are insects. Clearly, in a context where A and B are spies, the most accessible interpretation might have bugs as listening devices. These interpretations, which are expansions of the original underspecified linguistic input, are called **explicatures** in this theory. They too are licensed by the principle of relevance and they form the basis for further inferential steps to arrive at the conversational implicature in 7.97b.

In their account of implicature, writers in this theory make a distinction between **implicated premises** and **implicated conclusions**. We can illustrate these terms by modifying an example from Sperber and Wilson (1995: 194):

7.98   a.   Peter: Would you drive a Saab?
        b.   Mary: I wouldn't drive ANY Swedish car.
              (Mary's implicature: I would not drive a Saab.)

Mary's implicature is called an implicated conclusion and fits what is traditionally called a conversational implicature. However, for it to be derived, Mary has introduced into the context the linking assumption:

7.99   A Saab is a Swedish car.

In this theory 7.99 is called an implicated premise. It is not directly stated and therefore is implicated but it is provided as an inferential support for the final implicature, or implicated conclusion. Note that the implicated premise 7.99 need not be known by the hearer; in 7.98 if Peter doesn't know a Saab is Swedish he will infer it in order to preserve the relevance of Mary's reply in 7.98b.

In summary, in this theory one overarching principle of relevance is used to describe a whole range of inferential behaviour. The theory stresses the underdetermination of meaning and its reliance on context and inference. Through the notion of explicatures these writers take the process of inference in understanding deep into traditional areas of semantics and reduce the importance of literal or context-free meaning.

7.8   Summary

One basic conclusion from this chapter is that to understand an utterance hearers have to access and use contextual information of different types. We

have seen, for example, that a hearer has to be able to perform the interpretative tasks in 7.100:

7.100   a. Fill in deictic expressions.
         b. Fix the reference of nominals.
         c. Access background knowledge.
         d. Make inferences.

Each of these tasks involves calculation. Hearers have to create meaning by
combining linguistic and contextual information; in doing so, they make
inferences as a matter of course. We have seen several examples of this,
including shorthand expressions and conversational implicature. These tasks
draw upon different types of knowledge, which we can classify as in 7.101:

7.101   a. the language used (e.g. English, French, Arabic),
         b. the local contextual information (e.g. when and where uttered,
             and by whom),
         c. background knowledge (e.g. cultural practices).

In this chapter we have concentrated on fleshing out the second and third
types of knowledge. For the first, of course, the hearer needs to know
linguistic facts, for example that the activity of writing is described by the
verb *kataba* in Arabic and *escribir* in Spanish, or that the current speaker
calls herself *je* in French or *ég* in Icelandic.

   This distinction between types of knowledge brings us back to the
issue of the division between semantics and pragmatics, discussed in chapter 1. Is only the use of the first type of knowledge in 7.101 above properly part of semantics, leaving the use of the second and third types to
pragmatics? If so, and many linguists would accept this, many of the
processes of interpreting meaning that we have discussed in this chapter, for
example interpreting deictic expressions and forming conversational
implicatures, are part of pragmatics. One related problem is what to call
this first type of knowledge: if we call it 'meaning', then what do we call
the result of combining it with contextual information to get the final
message?

   One response is to distinguish between three types of meaning: the conventional meaning of words and sentences in the language, the speaker's
intended meaning, and the hearer's constructed meaning. Another possibility is to call the sentence meaning, simply **meaning**; the speaker meaning,
content; and the hearer meaning, **interpretation**.[15] If we use these latter
terms, then our basic observation in this chapter has been that meaning
underrepresents content and that the hearer must enrich meaning to get an
interpretation. The extent to which this interpretation corresponds to content will determine the success of the communication. As pointed out by the
American linguist W. D. Whitney over a hundred years ago, communication
is a process of interpretation (1971 [1867]: 14–15):

7.102   Sentences are not images of thoughts, reflected in a faultless mirror; or even photographs, needing only to have the colour added: they are but imperfect and fragmentary sketches, giving just outlines enough to enable the sense before which they are set up to seize the view intended, and to fill it out to a complete picture; while yet, as regards the completeness of the filling out, the details of the work, and the finer shades of coloring, no two minds will produce pictures perfectly accordant with one another, nor will any precisely reproduce the original.

FURTHER READING

Levinson (1983) has comprehensive sections on deixis and conversational implicature. Fillmore (1982a) is an interesting article on spatial deixis, while Fillmore (1997) is an accessible discussion of deixis in general. Brown and Yule (1983) include discussions of information structure, discourse topic and coherence. Culicover and McNally (1998) has a number of papers on the influence of information structure on grammar. Levinson (2000) presents a development of Grice's approach to conversational implicature similar to that described in 7.7.2. Blakemore (1992) is an accessible introduction to Relevance Theory, while an authoritative account is in Sperber and Wilson (1995). Kempson (1988a, 1988b) discusses reference and anaphora from this perspective. Finally, Mey (2001) covers many of the points raised here in his discussion of pragmatics.

EXERCISES

7.1   Give two examples of each of the following:

      a.   shorthand expressions
      b.   metonymy
      c.   synecdoche

For the shorthands you should give the contextual information that would allow their use.

7.2   Underline the deictic expressions in the following sentences and describe which type of deixis (**person, time, space**) is involved.

      a.   She was sitting over there.
      b.   This is the biggest room in the house.
      c.   Bring him in whenever you're ready.

d. I'll see you tomorrow.

e. They were here, looking at this Cadillac.

7.3 We discussed how the use of a **definite nominal** reflects a speaker's confidence that the referent is **accessible** to her audience. We saw that this confidence can derive from several sources, including the referent being unique in the wider discourse (e.g. *the sun, the Pope, the President*); being physically present in the context (i.e. via **deixis**); being already talked about (e.g. **anaphora**); being available from lexical relations like **meronymy** (e.g. *the kitchen* when talking about a house), or being **inferrable**.

In the following pairs of sentences, the definite nominal (marked in bold) in the second sentence is accessible because of the first sentence. We could say that its definiteness is **licensed** by the first sentence. Decide whether this licensing relationship is due to:

1 **anaphora**
2 **hyponymy**
3 **meronymy**
4 none of these and the link must be based on an **inference** by the listener.

a. I chose a dog for her. **The animal** turned out to be vicious.

b. He made a sandwich for me. **It** was delicious.

c. I went sailing last week and I hated it. **The motion** made me really sick.

d. She walked into the cinema. **The seats** had all been removed.

e. Don't buy this car. **The engine** is useless.

f. He drove the car very erratically. I kept **the vehicle** in sight.

g. They drove me to the airport. I couldn't believe **the traffic jams**.

7.4 We also saw that speakers keep track of nominal referents, using different types of nominals (indefinite NPs, definite NPs, pronouns) to form **chains of reference**, e.g. *a house . . . the house . . . this house . . . it . . . it*, etc.

Below is an extract from the screenplay of Woody Allen's film *Interiors* (1983: 115–17).

a. Select from it two examples of chains of reference and identify the types of nominal used.

b.   Then identify five or six **referring** uses of the pronoun *it*, and try to establish how the hearers might identify the referents: i.e. is the referent available from **deixis, anaphora, inference**, or some combination?

MIKE   Can I get you anything?

EVE   Oh, just some coffee . . . if you don't mind.

MIKE   No, it's no trouble at all.
Eve places her shopping bag on the table while Mike walks to the kitchen area to prepare the coffee.

EVE   I think I found a very nice vase for the foyer.

MIKE   (*Absently, getting the coffee materials together*) Uh huh.

EVE   (*Taking out a box from the shopping bag and opening it*) You'll probably think it's an extravagance, but it's not, all things considered. These pieces are becoming increasingly rare. (*Holding up a delicate blue vase*) Isn't that exquisite? (*Mike, filling a kettle of water at the sink, looks up at Eve; she walks toward the foyer*) I hope you like it, because it's perfect for what I have in mind for the foyer.

MIKE   (*Placing the kettle on the range*) We already have a vase in the foyer, Eve.

EVE   (*Speaking from the foyer*) Yes, but this will never look right when we redo the floors.

MIKE   (*Preparing a tray with a jar of instant coffee and sugar bowl*) I never understood why the floors have to be redone.
Eve is busy rearranging a basket of dried flowers on the cabinet in the foyer next to the vase she's just bought; she holds the vase that had been there in her hand.

EVE   Why, we've discussed all that, Michael. Don't you remember? You agreed.

MIKE   (*Bringing the tray to the dining table*) You know, it costs money to have these things done and redone two or three times over.

EVE   (*Walking back into the dining area*) But the – It's such a large floor space. That's why we agreed that the paler tones would make a more subtle statement. The pale woods would be lovely.

MIKE   I never agreed about anything! I'm always being told.

EVE   Well, I wouldn't put it that way.

MIKE   Well, how would you put it, Eve? I mean, first the living room was finished, then it wasn't. Then the, uh, bedroom needed more work. Now the floors have to be stripped again. You picked a sofa, then you hated it.

EVE   It was a lovely piece. It just was the wrong scale, that's all. It's not an exact science. (*Fidgeting with the collar of her suit*) Sometimes you just have to see it . . . then you get the feel of it. (*Glancing at a lamp sitting on a cabinet in the dining area*) You didn't like that in the bedroom?

MIKE   (*Looking at the lamp*) I knew you were gonna say something. I get better use of it out here.

EVE   (*Walking over to the lamp*) Well, if you utilized it in here, that's fine. It's meant to be used. It's just that it was part of what we were trying to do in the bedroom. (*Pointing at the lamp-shade*) It's the shade and the bedspread. They set each other off so nicely, I thought.

MIKE   How much is the vase?

EVE   (*Looking down*) Uh . . . they're asking four hundred dollars.

MIKE   Uh! Give me a break, Eve!

EVE   (*Fingering her forehead and hairline, still holding the small vase from the foyer*) All right, Michael, I'll return it. Would you mind closing the window? The street noises are just unnerving. *Joey, in a white bathrobe, enters the dining area.*

JOEY   I hope you two aren't having another argument.

EVE   (*Sitting down at the table*) Not at all.

JOEY   Oh, I love that suit. It's a unique color.

EVE   Renata calls it ice-gray.

JOEY   Well, it makes you look very beautiful. Isn't she beautiful, Michael?

MIKE   (*Bringing the kettle with boiling water and a carton of milk to the table*) Very lovely.

EVE   Well, I don't feel lovely. I'm exhausted. I've been running up and down Second Avenue all day.

JOEY   (*Walking into the foyer, seeing the new vase*) Oh, wow! Is this for us? It's exquisite!

EVE   No, I was just showing it to Michael.

MIKE   It's too expensive, Joey.

7.5   We saw that the **information structure** of a sentence reflects its context in the conversation. The examples below consist of a sentence followed by several candidates for a continuing sentence. In each case the candidates describe the same basic situation but have the information packaged differently in their information structure. Choose the continuation sentences (there may be more than one) which best fit the previous sentence. Discuss how differences in earlier sentences, not given below, might influence your choice.

    1   Was it Henry who brought in the groceries?
       a.   No, Fred brought the groceries in.
       b.   No, it was the groceries that Fred brought in.
       c.   No, what Fred brought in was the groceries.
       d.   No, it was Fred who brought the groceries in.

2   Watching the house, Maguire saw a car arrive.
    a. The car turned into the driveway.
    b. It was the driveway the car turned into.
    c. What turned into the driveway was the car.
    d. It was the car that turned into the driveway.

3   I just want to know who made this coffee.
    a. I made the coffee.
    b. The coffee was made by me.
    c. What was made by me was the coffee.
    d. What I made was the coffee.

4   Kelly picked up her jacket and walked out of the kitchen.
    a. The hall was dark.
    b. What was dark was the hall.
    c. It was the hall that was dark.
    d. It was dark, the hall.

7.6   Below are a series of invented exchanges. Using Grice's notion of
      conversational implicature, give for each a likely implicature of
      B's reply. Discuss, firstly, the contextual information you have
      to supply in order to support your proposal, and, secondly, the
      reasons B might have for using an implicature rather than a
      simple statement.

      a. A: Are you coming out for a pint tonight?
          B: My in-laws are coming over for dinner.
      b. A: How did United play this afternoon?
          B: Well, eleven guys wearing United shirts ran out onto
              the pitch.
      c. A: I'm going to tell those young thugs to stop smoking
              in this compartment.
          B: Do you have life insurance?
      d. A: Are you going to wear those trousers?
          B: They're brand new. I just bought them.
      e. A: Does my smoking bother you?
          B: I can't say that it doesn't.

7.7   In discussing Horn's notion of Q-principle scales in section 7.7.2 we
      noted that in a scale $<x, y>$, where x is a stronger term, uttering
      y implicates 'not x'. Thus *some* implicates *not all*. Use this behavi-
      our to discuss whether the following are valid scales in this sense:

      a. <certainly, possibly>
      b. <hot, warm>

c. \<more than, as many as\>
d. \<five, four\>
e. \<none, not all\>

7.8 Below is a joke from the British comedian Les Dawson (1979). Discuss the boy's behaviour in terms of Grice's **conversational maxims**:

> Not too bright, that particular lad. A salesman found him sitting on the doorstep one day. 'Is your mother at home sonny?' he asked. 'Yes,' replied the boy. So the salesman knocked on the door for a few minutes, then tried ringing the bell; finally he resorted to bashing on the window – all to no avail. 'I thought you said your mother was at home,' he snapped at the boy. 'She is,' came the reply, 'only this isn't our house.'

NOTES

1 In this transcription, ` = low tone, e.g. è.
2 Lyons (1977: vol. 2, 668ff.) distinguishes between **textual deixis**, where reference is made to the surface form of words and sentences and **impure textual deixis**, where reference is made to some underlying unit of discourse like a point made, or an argument. He gives an example of the former involving an anaphoric use of **it**:

A: That's rhinocerous.
B: A what? Spell **it** for me.

where B is using **it** to refer not to a real rhinocerous but to the word *rhinocerous* just used by A. In this distinction, our examples here are of the impure variety.
3 In chapter 5 we saw that **tense** is a deictic system too: dividing zones of time around the current act of speaking, i.e. the speaker's position in time.
4 Other examples of such spatial metaphors include the one below which is the normal Irish equivalent to English *I enjoyed it*:

Bhain mé taitneamh as.
took I   enjoyment out of.it
'I enjoyed it.'

5 The study of the role of cultural or common-sense knowledge is an important focus of investigation in the field of study known as the **ethnography of communication**. See Schiffrin (1994: 137–89) for an introductory survey.
6 The term **mutual knowledge** is often used as a more inclusive term than our use of background knowledge, i.e. to cover knowledge gained from all the sources mentioned above, including deixis, the discourse and background

knowledge. However, the problems discussed below apply to any application of the term.

7   Other labels for given information have included **old information**, the **theme** or the **presupposition**; and new information has been called the **rheme**, or **focus** (in a sense related to but distinct from how we shall use the term in 7.5.2 below).

8   Note the use of the term **focus** here is consistent with the psychology and psycholinguistics literature, where it signifies a notion of current topic and therefore given information. This is diametrically opposed to the use in general linguistics, as discussed in 7.5.2 below, where focus is used for elements given prominence in some way because they represent new information, or for contrast. We follow the general linguistic use in this chapter. The hierarchy in 7.54 is treated as a kind of scale: a nominal may be used for the status conventionally associated with it, or for any status to the left, i.e. higher in familiarity. The explanation for why there is a tendency to use an expression for its minimal status and not for higher points on the scale is usually given in terms of Gricean scalar implicatures, discussed in 7.7 below.

9   See Chafe (1976) and Dryer (1996) for discussion of activation in discourse.

10   See Givón (1983) for quantitative studies of the distances between coreferential elements in discourse.

11   As is well known, English intonation does not always uniquely identify the focused constituent. When the sentential nuclear stress falls on the final constituent, for example, the scope of the focus (marked [$_{FOC}$] below), is ambiguous:

> 1a   What is he drinking?
> b   He's drinking [$_{FOC}$ BEER].
> 2a   What's he doing?
> b   He's [$_{FOC}$ drinking BEER).

See Vallduví and Engdahl (1996) for discussion.

12   Saeed (1984) and (2000) are studies of these markers of informational structure in Somali.

13   See Kuno (1987) and Levinson (1991) for discussions of anaphora in discourse.

14   This discussion is based on Horn's development of Gricean implicature. A related approach is outlined by Levinson (2000), which presents a slightly different systematization of the maxims.

15   See Barwise (1988) for a discussion of the role of context in meaning, which includes proposals for terms similar to these.

chapter 8

Functions of Language: Speech as Action

8.1 Introduction

In this chapter we maintain our focus on language use and we look at the idea that part of the meaning of an utterance is its intended social function. It seems clear that learning to communicate in a language involves more than acquiring the pronunciation and grammar. We need to learn how to ask questions, make suggestions, greet and thank other speakers. In other words, we need to learn the uses to which utterances are conventionally put in the new language community and how these uses are signalled, if we are to use the language in a realistic way. Similarly, as hearers, part of understanding the meaning of an utterance is knowing whether we have been asked a question, invited to do something, etc. In a terminology introduced by J. L. Austin (1975), which we discuss in section 8.2, such functions of language are called *speech acts*.

In the last chapter we discussed areas of meaning which highlight the role of context and speaker–hearer interpretation. We recognized that if we admit a distinction between semantics and pragmatics, some of these topics, e.g. conversational implicature, seem to fall under pragmatics, while others, like reference and deixis, seem to straddle the semantics–pragmatics divide. The study of speech acts occupies a similar border area. In many cases the intended function is linguistically coded: languages often have, for example, specific morphemes, intonation and sentence patterns to mark questions, wishes, orders, etc. However, as we shall see, communicating functions also relies on both general knowledge of social conventions and specific knowledge of the local context of utterance. This area, then, reveals the pattern we saw in the last chapter: hearers have to coordinate linguistic and non-linguistic knowledge to interpret a speaker's intended meaning.

We can begin our discussion by identifying two important characteristics of speech acts: **interactivity** and **context-dependence**. The first is a crucial feature: communicating functions involves the speaker in a coordinated activity with other language users. For some uses of language this interactivity is more explicit than others. We can take as an example Akindele's description of a typical afternoon greeting between persons of equal age and status in the Nigerian language Yoruba (1990: 4)[1]:

8.1   **Greetings**:   **Gloss**:
       F: Ẹ káàsán.   F: Good afternoon.
       MT: Ẹ káàsán.   MT: Good afternoon.
       F: Ṣ'álàáfíà ni?   F: How are you?
       MT: A dúpẹ́.   MT: We thank (God).
       F: Ilé ńkọ́?   F: How is your house(hold)?
       MT: Wó.n wà.   MT: They are (in good health).
       F: Ọmọ nkọ́?   F: How are your children?
       MT: Wọ́n wà.   MT: They are (in good health).
       F: Bá mi kí wọn.   F: Help me to greet them.
       MT: Wọ́n á gbọ́.   MT: They will hear.

A similar, if less extended, interactivity is characteristic of one of Austin's well-known examples: bets in English. As Austin described, a bet only comes into existence when two or more parties interact. If I say to someone *I bet you five pounds he doesn't get elected*, a bet is not performed unless my addressee makes some response like *Okay* or *You're on*. While other speech acts, like asking a question or greeting someone, do not need explicit responses to make them questions or greetings, they nonetheless set up the expectation for an interactive response. Studies in the discourse analysis approach known as **conversational analysis** (for example, Schegloff 1972, 1979; Schegloff and Sacks 1973; Goodwin 1979; Atkinson and Heritage 1984), have revealed that failure to respond to a question, say by silence, triggers certain types of compensatory behaviour: the speaker may repeat the question, seek to evade the perceived rejection, or others may try to repair the lapse.[2] Similarly, Akindele (1990: 3) says of Yoruba greetings like 8.1 above:

8.2   Another factor is the Yoruba ethical code in which it is a duty to greet people engaged in different activities. Hence there is a salutation for every conceivable occasion and situation. . . . Greeting persons at work is regarded as a matter of respect in one's occupation.

Failure to offer such greetings in the appropriate context usually gives rise to bad feelings especially among close friends and relatives to the extent that it can lead to suspicion of sorcery or witchcraft.

The second feature, context dependence, has two aspects. The first is that many speech acts rely on social conventions to support them. Sometimes this is very explicit, where the speech act is supported by what Searle (1969) called **institutional facts**. Thus every society has procedures and ceremonies where some participants' words carry a special function. Examples commonly used in the literature include a judge saying *I sentence you to hang by the neck until dead*, a priest in the marriage ceremony saying *I now pronounce you man and wife*, a country's president announcing *I declare a state of national emergency*, and so on. These speech acts of sentencing prisoners, pronouncing a couple married, etc. can only be performed by the relevant people in the right situations, where both are sanctioned by social laws and conventions. Again though these are just the most explicit cases: it is clear that social conventions also govern ordinary uses of language in society. Sociolinguistic and ethnographical studies have shown us how the forms of asking questions, making greetings, etc. are influenced by a particular society's conventions for the participants' age, gender, relative social status, degree of intimacy, etc.[3]

The second aspect of context dependence is the local context of a speech act. An utterance may signal one speech act in one situation and another elsewhere. Questions in English are notoriously flexible in this way. If the asker already knows the answer then an utterance with the form of a question can be, for example, a request, as if I see you are wearing a watch and I say *Can you tell me the time?* Or the question might have the force of a statement *No* as in B's possible replies in the invented exchange in 8.3 below:

8.3   A: Are you going to buy his car?
       B: a.   Are you crazy?
            b.   Do you think I'm crazy?

We can find a parallel use of questions with known answers in the popular use of sentences like *Is the Pope a catholic?*, *Do dogs have fleas?* or *Do Bears shit in the woods?* as livelier and more informal ways of saying *Yes of course*.[4]

Because of this flexibility, we have to be careful about terminology. Some sentences have a particular grammatical form which is conventionally associated with a certain speech act. Thus questions in English, which of course include several types, usually have a special rising intonation pattern and an inverted subject-verb word order which differentiates them from statements, as 8.4b and c below are distinguished from 8.4a:

8.4   a.   He is leaving.
       b.   Is he leaving?
       c.   When is he leaving?

When there is a conventional match between grammatical form and speech act function we can identify a **sentence type**. We need to use separate terms for sentence types and speech acts, though, so that we can identify cases where the matching does not hold. Thus we might identify the sentence types in 8.5 below:

8.5   a.   declarative, e.g. *Siobhán will paint the anaglypta.*
         b.   interrogative, e.g. *Will Siobhán paint the anaglypta?*
         c.   imperative, e.g. *Siobhán, paint the anaglypta!*
         d.   optative, e.g. *If only Siobhán would paint the anaglypta!*

The conventional, or literal, use of these sentence types will be to perform the speech acts with the corresponding letter in 8.6 below:

8.6   a.   assertions
         b.   questions
         c.   orders
         d.   wishes

However, as we have already seen, interrogatives can be used for other speech acts than asking questions, and the same is true to a greater or lesser degree of the other sentence types. We discuss this variability in section 8.4.

Both of the features we have outlined, interactivity and context dependence, emphasize that in discussing speech acts we are examining the union of linguistic and social behaviour. We will begin our discussion of this behaviour by reviewing J. L. Austin's theory of speech acts in section 8.2., then go on to examine revisions of the theory by J. R. Searle and others in 8.3. Thereafter in section 8.4 we look at an interesting and difficult area for the theory: variability and indirect speech acts. Finally, in section 8.5 we come back to the identification of sentence types.

8.2   Austin's Speech Act Theory

8.2.1   Introduction

Speech act theory was developed by the Oxford philosopher J. L. Austin, whose 1955 lectures at Harvard University were published posthumously as *How to Do Things with Words* (1975). The approach has been greatly developed since so that there is a large literature. One of the most important writers on speech acts has been the philosopher John R. Searle (for example: 1969, 1975, 1976), and within linguistics studies and surveys have included Sadock (1974), Cole and Morgan (1975), Bach and Harnish (1979), Gazdar (1981) and Sadock and Zwicky (1985). We look at Austin's proposals in this section and discuss subsequent developments in section 8.3.

Austin's work is in many respects a reaction to some traditional and influential attitudes to language. We can risk simplifying these as a starting-point. The attitudes can be said to involve three related assumptions, as follows:

8.7   a.   that the basic sentence type in language is declarative (i.e. a statement or assertion);

        b.   that the principal use of language is to describe states of affairs (by using statements);

        c.   that the meaning of utterances can be described in terms of their truth or falsity.

Some of these assumptions are discernible in recent formal approaches to semantics, as we shall see in chapter 10. Among Austin's contemporaries these assumptions are associated with the philosophers known as **logical positivists**, a term originally applied to the mathematicians and philosophers of the Vienna Circle; see Ayer (1959) for discussion. An important issue for logical positivist approaches is how far the meaning of a sentence is reducible to its verifiability, i.e. the extent to which, and by which, it can be shown to be true or false.

Austin's opposition to these views is the 'common-sense' one that language is used for far more than making statements and that for the most part utterances cannot be said to be either true or false. He makes two important observations. The first is that not all sentences are statements and that much of conversation is made up of questions, exclamations, commands and expressions of wishes, like the examples in 8.8 below:

8.8   a.   Excuse me!

        b.   Are you serving?

        c.   Hello.

        d.   Six pints of stout and a packet of peanuts, please!

        e.   Give me the dry roasted ones.

        f.   How much? Are you serious?

        g.   *O tempora! O mores!*

Such sentences are not descriptions and cannot be said to be true or false.

Austin's second observation was that even in sentences with the grammatical form of declaratives, not all are used to make statements. Austin identified a subset of declaratives that are not used to make true or false statements, such as the examples in 8.9 below:

8.9   a.   I promise to take a taxi home.

        b.   I bet you five pounds that he gets breathalysed.

        c.   I declare this meeting open.

        d.   I warn you that legal action will ensue.

        e.   I name this ship *The Flying Dutchman*.

Austin claimed of these sentences that they were in themselves a kind of action: thus by uttering 8.9a a speaker makes a promise rather than just describing one. This kind of utterance he called **performative** utterances: in these examples they perform the action named by the first verb in the sentence, and we can insert the adverb *hereby* to stress this function, e.g. *I hereby request that you leave my property.* We can contrast performative and non-performative verbs by these two features. A speaker would not, for example, expect the uttering of 8.10a below to constitute the action of cooking a cake, or 8.11a the action of starting a car. These sentences describe actions independent of the linguistic act. Accordingly the use of *hereby* with these sentences as in 8.10b and 8.11b sounds odd.

8.10   a.   I cook this cake.
         b.   ?I hereby cook this cake.

8.11   a.   I start this car.
         b.   ?I hereby start this car.

8.2.2   Evaluating performative utterances

Austin argued that it is not useful to ask whether performative utterances like those in 8.9 are true or not, rather we should ask whether they work or not: do they constitute a successful warning, bet, ship-naming etc.? In Austin's terminology a performative that works is called **felicitous** and one that does not is **infelicitous**. For them to work, such performatives have to satisfy the social conventions that we mentioned in section 8.1: for a very obvious example, I cannot rename a ship by walking up to it in dock and saying *I name this ship the Flying Dutchman.* Less explicitly, there are social conventions governing the giving of orders to co-workers, greeting strangers, etc. Austin's name for the enabling conditions for a performative is **felicity conditions**.

Examining these social conventions that support performatives, it is clear that there is a gradient between performatives that are highly institutionalized, or even ceremonial, requiring sophisticated and very overt support, like the example of a judge pronouncing sentence, through to less formal acts like warning, thanking, etc. To describe the role of felicity conditions, Austin (1975: 25–38) wrote a very general schema:

8.12   A1   There must exist an accepted conventional procedure having a certain conventional effect, the procedure to include the uttering of certain words by certain persons in certain circumstances . . .
         A2   The particular persons and circumstances must be appropriate for the invocation of the particular procedure invoked . . .

B1 The procedure must be executed by all the participants correctly . . .

B2 . . . and completely. . . .

Austin went on to add **sincerity** clauses: firstly that participants must have the requisite thoughts, feelings and intentions, as specified by the procedure, and secondly, that if subsequent conduct is called for, the participants must so conduct themselves. If the speech act is unsuccessful by failing the A or B conditions in 8.12, then he described it as a **misfire**. Thus my casually renaming any ship visiting Dublin docks is a misfire because A2 above is not adhered to. If the act is insincerely performed, then he described it as an **abuse** of a speech act, as for example saying *I bet* . . . with no intention to pay, or *I promise* . . . when I already intend to break the promise. Linguists, as opposed to philosophers, have tended not to be so interested in this second type of infelicity, since the primary speech act has, in these cases, been successfully communicated.

8.2.3 Explicit and implicit performatives

Looking at examples of performative utterances like those in 8.9 earlier, we can say that they are characterized by special features, as in 8.13:

8.13   a. They tend to begin with a first person verb in a form we could describe as simple present: *I bet, I warn,* etc.

         b. This verb belongs to a special class describing verbal activities, for example: *promise, warn, sentence, name, bet, pronounce.*

         c. Generally their performative nature can be emphasized by inserting the adverb *hereby,* as described earlier, thus *I hereby sentence you to.* . . .

Utterances with these characteristics we can call **explicit** performatives. The importance of speech act theory lies in the way that Austin and others managed to extend their analysis from these explicit performatives to other utterances. The first step was to point out that in some cases the same speech act seems to be performed but with a relaxation of some of the special characteristics mentioned in 8.13 above. We regularly meet utterances like those in 8.14 below, where this is so:

8.14   a. You are (hereby) charged with treason.

         b. Passengers are requested to avoid jumping out of the aircraft.

         c. Five pounds says he doesn't make the semi-final.

         d. Come up and see me sometime.

We can easily provide the sentences in 8.14 above with corresponding explicit performatives, as below:

8.15   a. I (hereby) charge you with treason.
         b. We request that passengers avoid jumping out of the aircraft.
         c. I bet you five pounds that he doesn't make the semi-final.
         d. I invite you to come up and see me sometime.

It seems reasonable to say that the sentences in 8.14 could be uttered to perform the same speech acts as those in 8.15. In fact it seems that none of the special characteristics of performative utterances is indispensable to their performance. How then do we recognize these other performatives, whch we can call **implicit** performatives? Answers to this have varied somewhat in the development of the theory but Austin's original contention was that it was an utterance's ability to be expanded to an explicit performative that identified it as a performative utterance. Austin discussed at length the various linguistic means by which more implicit performatives could be marked, including the mood of the verb, auxiliary verbs, intonation, etc. We shall not follow the detail of his discussion here; see Austin (1975: 53–93). Of course we soon end up with a situation where the majority of performatives are implicit, needing expansion to make explicit their force. One positive advantage of this translation strategy is that it focuses attention on the task of classifying the performative verbs of a language, a task we shall take up in section 8.3. For now, the basic claim is clear: explicit performatives are seen as merely a specialized subset of performatives whose nature as speech acts is more unambiguous than most.

8.2.4   Statements as performatives

Austin's original position was that performatives, which are speech acts subject to felicity conditions, are to be contrasted with declarative sentences, which are potentially true or false descriptions of situations. The latter were termed **constatives**. However, as his analysis developed, he collapsed the distinction and viewed the making of statements as just another type of speech act, which he called simply **stating**. Again, we needn't follow his line of argument closely here: see Austin (1975: 133–47) and the discussion in Schiffrin (1994: 50–4). In simple terms, Austin argued that there is no theoretically sound way to distinguish between performatives and constatives. For example, the notion of felicity applies to statements too: statements which are odd because of presupposition failure, like the sentence *The king of France is bald* discussed in chapter 4, are infelicitous because the speaker has violated the conventions for referring to individuals (i.e. that the listener can identify them). This infelicity suspends our judgement of the truth or falsity of the sentence: as we saw in chapter 4, it is difficult to say that *The king of France is bald* is false in the same way as *The president of France is a woman*, even though they are both not true at the time of writing this.

So we arrive at a view that all utterances constitute speech acts of one kind or another. For some the type of act is explicitly marked by their containing a verb labelling the act, *warn, bet, name, suggest, protest* etc.; others are more implicitly signalled. Some speech acts are so universal and fundamental that their grammaticalization is the profound one of the distinction into sentence types we mentioned in section 8.1. In their cross-linguistic survey of speech acts Sadock and Zwicky (1985: 160) observe:

8.16   It is in some respects a surprising fact that most languages are similar in presenting three basic sentence types with similar functions and often strikingly similar forms. These are the declarative, interrogative, and imperative. As a first approximation, these three types can be described as follows: The declarative is used for making announcements, stating conclusions, making claims, relating stories, and so on. The interrogative elicits a verbal response from the addressee. It is used principally to gain information. The imperative indicates the speaker's desire to influence future events. It is of service in making requests, giving orders, making suggestions, and the like.

Though the authors go on to discuss the many detailed differences between the uses of these main forms in individual languages, it seems that sentence type is a basic marker of primary performative types.

   This conclusion that all utterances have a speech act force has led to a widespread view that there are two basic parts to meaning: the conventional meaning of the sentence (often described as a proposition) and the speaker's intended speech act. Thus we can view our earlier examples in 8.5, repeated in 8.17 below, as divisible into propositional meaning (represented in small capitals in 8.18 below) and a sentence type marker, uniting to form a speech act as shown in 8.18 below:

8.17   a.   *Siobhán is painting the anaglypta.*
        b.   *Is Siobhán painting the anaglypta?*
        c.   *Siobhán, paint the anaglypta!*
        d.   *If only Siobhán would paint the anaglypta!*

8.18   a.   SIOBHÁN PAINT THE ANAGLYPTA + declarative = statement
        b.   SIOBHÁN PAINT THE ANAGLYPTA + interrogative = question
        c.   SIOBHÁN PAINT THE ANAGLYPTA + imperative = order
        d.   SIOBHÁN PAINT THE ANAGLYPTA + optative = wish

We have to remember, though, that the matching in 8.18 is only a typical one; we return to this question in section 8.4.

8.2.5   Three facets of a speech act

Austin proposed that communicating a speech act consists of three elements: the speaker says something, the speaker signals an associated speech act, and the speech act causes an effect on her listeners or the participants. The first element he called the **locutionary act,** by which he meant the act of saying something that makes sense in a language, i.e. follows the rules of pronunciation and grammar. The second, the action intended by the speaker, he termed the **illocutionary act.** This is what Austin and his successors have mainly been concerned with: the uses to which language can be put in society. In fact the term **speech acts** is often used with just this meaning of illocutionary acts. The third element, called the **perlocutionary act,** is concerned with what follows an utterance: the effect or 'take-up' of an illocutionary act. Austin gave the example of sentences like *Shoot her!* In appropriate circumstances this can have the illocutionary force of ordering, urging or advising the addressee to shoot her, but the perlocutionary force of persuading, forcing, frightening etc. the addressee into shooting her. Perlocutionary effects are less conventionally tied to linguistic forms and so have been of less interest to linguists. We know, for example, that people can recognize orders without obeying them.

8.3 Categorizing Speech Acts

After Austin's original explorations of speech act theory there have been a number of works which attempt to systematize the approach. One important focus has been to categorize the types of speech act possible in languages.[5] J. R. Searle, for example, while allowing that there is a myriad of language-particular speech acts, proposed that all acts fall into five main types, as in 8.19 below (1976: 10–16):

8.19   1   REPRESENTATIVES, which commit the speaker to the truth of the expressed proposition (paradigm cases: asserting, concluding);
       2   DIRECTIVES, which are attempts by the speaker to get the addressee to do something (paradigm cases: requesting, questioning);
       3   COMMISSIVES, which commit the speaker to some future course of action (paradigm cases: promising, threatening, offering);
       4   EXPRESSIVES, which express a psychological state (paradigm cases: thanking, apologizing, welcoming, congratulating);
       5   DECLARATIONS, which effect immediate changes in the institutional state of affairs and which tend to rely on elaborate extralinguistic institutions (paradigm cases: excommunicating, declaring war, christening, marrying, firing from employment).

Searle uses a mix of criteria to establish these different types, including the act's **illocutionary point;** its '**fit**' with the world; the **psychological state** of the speaker; and the **content** of the act. The illocutionary point is the purpose or aim of the act: thus the point of directives is get the hearer to do something. The 'fit' concerns direction of the relationship between language and the world: thus speakers using representatives, for example assertions, are seeking to get their words to match the world, while users of directives, for example requests or orders, are seeking to change the world so that it matches their words. The criterion of *psychological state* relates to the speaker's state of mind: thus statements like *It's raining* reflect belief, while expressives like apologies and congratulations reveal the speaker's attitude to events. Finally, *content* relates to restrictions placed on speech acts by what they are about, their propositional content.[6] Thus one cannot properly promise or predict things that have already happened. Or for another example: one way of viewing the difference between a promise and a threat is in terms of whether the future event is beneficial or harmful to the addressee.

In distinguishing these acts, Searle further developed Austin's notion of felicity conditions into a classification of conditions that must hold for a successful speech act. Searle (1969) distinguishes between **preparatory**, **propositional**, **sincerity** and **essential** conditions for an act. See for example 8.20 below where we give examples of his conditions for the act of *promising*:

8.20   Conditions for promising (Searle 1969: 62ff.)
        [where S = speaker, H = hearer, A = the future action, P = the proposition expressed in the speech act, e = the linguistic expression]
        a.   Preparatory 1: H would prefer S's doing A to his not doing A and S believes H would prefer S's doing A to not doing A.
        b.   Preparatory 2: It is not obvious to both S and H that S will do A in the normal course of events.
        c.   Propositional: In expressing that P, S predicates a future act A of S.
        d.   Sincerity: S intends to do A.
        e.   Essential: the utterance e counts as an undertaking to do A.

Among these conditions we might note that the second preparatory condition suggests that one does not normally promise what would happen as a matter of course. Thus saying *I'll be home at five* to one's spouse when leaving for work might not be considered a typical promise. The propositional condition, as we mentioned earlier, reflects that in a promise a future act must be predicated of the speaker, so that something that has already happened cannot be promised.

The conditions for questions include those in 8.21 below:

8.21   Conditions for questioning (Searle 1969: 66)
        [where S = speaker, H = hearer, P = the proposition expressed in the speech act]

a. Preparatory 1: S does not know the answer, i.e. for a yes/no question, does not know whether P is true or false; for an elicitative or WH-question, does not know the missing information.[7]
b. Preparatory 2: It is not obvious to both S and H that H will provide the information at that time without being asked.
c. Propositional: Any proposition or propositional function.
d. Sincerity: S wants this information.
e. Essential: The act counts as an attempt to elicit this information from H.

It is clear that this characterization relates to a prototypical question: it does not apply, of course, to rhetorical questions, nor the questions of a teacher in the classroom, a lawyer in court etc. Note that the propositional condition simply says that there are no semantic restrictions on the content of a question as a speech act.

Searle provides felicity conditions like those in 8.20 and 8.21 for each type of speech act: we shall be satisfied for now with looking at just these two. Elsewhere in the literature, there have been a number of taxonomies of speech act types suggested, for example Schiffer (1972), Fraser (1975), Hancher (1979) and Bach and Harnish (1979).[8] One assumption that seems to underlie all such classification systems, and one we have assumed so far in talking about speech acts, is that there is some linguistic marking (no doubt supported by contextual information) of a correlation between form and function. In other words, we recognize a sentence type and are able to match it to a speech act. There are two problems with this: the first is how to cope with cases where what seems to be the conventional association between a sentence form and an illocutionary force is overridden. We discuss this in the next section under the heading of **indirect speech acts**. The second problem, which we discuss in section 8.5, arises from difficulties in identifying sentence types.

8.4 Indirect Speech Acts

8.4.1 Introduction

In 8.2.4 we discussed the typical matching between certain sentence types and speech acts. Thus we discussed the matching between the interrogative sentence type in English and the act of questioning. However, as we noted there, quite often this conventional matching is superseded by an extra, more immediate interpretation. The conventionally expected function is known as the **direct speech act** and the extra actual function is termed the **indirect speech act**. Thus we can find examples like those in 8.22 below:

8.22	**Utterance**	**Direct act**	**Indirect act**
	Would you mind passing me the ashtray?	question	request
	Why don't you finish your drink and leave?	question	request
	I must ask you to leave my house.	statement	order/request
	Leave me and I'll jump in the river.	order and statement	threat

The problem is: how do people recognize the indirect act? There are a number of possible answers to this. We look first at Searle's (1975) approach.

The first question is whether hearers are only conscious of the indirect act, or whether they have both available and choose the indirect act as most contextually apt. Searle (1975) argues that speakers do indeed have access to both: he terms the direct use the **literal** use of the speech act and the indirect, the **non-literal** use. He gives as examples the sentences in 8.23a– 8.25a below, all of which can be requests, but none of which have the form of imperatives in the (b) versions, but instead are interrogatives and declaratives:

8.23   a. Can you pass the salt?
        b. Please pass the salt.

8.24   a. I wish you wouldn't do that.
        b. Please don't do that.

8.25   a. Aren't you going to eat your cereal?
        b. Please eat your cereal.

Searle argues that in the a cases above two speech acts are available to the hearer: the literal act is backgrounded or secondary while the non-literal act is primary – 'when one of these sentences is uttered with the primary illocutionary point of a directive, the literal illocutionary act is also performed' (1975: 70). The question he raises is: how is it that these but not all non-literal acts will work, i.e. why is it that stating *Salt is made of sodium chloride* will not work as a request like *Can you pass the salt?* (p. 75). Searle's solution relies on the system of felicity conditions mentioned in the last section. The conditions for making requests include the following:

8.26   Conditions for requesting (Searle 1975: 71)
        [where S = speaker, H = hearer, A = the future action]
        a. Preparatory condition: H is able to perform A.
        b. Sincerity condition: S wants H to do A.
        c. Propositional condition: S predicates a future act A of H.
        d. Essential condition: Counts as an attempt by S to get H to do A.

Searle argues that other sentence types can only work as indirect requests when they address one of the conditions for requests. Thus sentence 8.23a *Can you pass the salt?* addresses the preparatory condition in 8.26. This example shows that an indirect request can be made by asking whether (or stating that) a preparatory condition holds.

The sentence *I wish you wouldn't do that* in 8.24a above, forms an indirect request by addressing another felicity condition: it states that the sincerity condition in 8.26 holds.[9]

Searle's third example, *Aren't you going to eat your cereal?* in 8.25a, works by asking whether the propositional content condition holds. Perhaps we can add another example: if a teacher uses an imperative as a directive to a student: *Return that book to the library!*, the propositional content involves predicating the future act: *You will return that book to the library*. Searle's point is that a corresponding indirect directive can be made by questioning this, i.e. *Aren't you going to return that book to the library?* or *Are you going to return that book to the library?*

So in this view, indirect speech acts work because they are systematically related to the structure of the associated direct act: they are tied to one or another of the act's felicity conditions. This still leaves the question of how the hearer works out which of the two acts, the backgrounded direct act or the primary indirect act, is meant. We look briefly at Searle's proposal for this in 8.4.2.

8.4.2   Understanding indirect speech acts

Searle's view of how we understand indirect speech acts is that we combine our knowledge of three elements to support a chain of inference. The elements are: the felicity conditions of direct speech acts, the context of the utterance, and principles of conversational cooperation, such as the Gricean maxims of relevance, quality etc. that we discussed in chapter 7. We can briefly sketch how these three types of knowledge are used in this chain of reasoning by looking at the example of *Can you pass the salt?* (following Searle 1975: 73–5). In an everyday situation, the context will tell the hearer that the speaker should already know that he can pass the salt, and thus he recognizes that the question violates the felicity conditions for a question. The assumption of cooperative principles, however, leads the hearer to search for some other point for the utterance. This is essentially the search for an indirect speech act, i.e. the hearer asks himself, as it were, if it can't be a genuine question, what is the purpose of this utterance? The hearer knows that a condition for requests is that the hearer can actually carry out the desired act *A* (see 8.26a above), and also recognizes that to say *yes* here is to confirm that a preparatory condition for doing *A* has been met. The hearer also knows as part of general background knowledge that passing salt around a table is a usual part of meals, so this is a reasonable goal for the speaker to entertain. From these pieces of knowledge the hearer infers that the speaker's utterance is likely to be a request.

One problem with this account is that it does not take into account the **idiomatic** quality of many indirect acts. As Searle, and others, have noted, it is not at all clear that a parallel question *Are you able to pass me the salt?* would be interpreted in the same way, even though *can* and *be able* are largely synonymous. This difference is confirmed by the different possibilities of occurrence with *please*, usually an optional marker of requests. Thus *Can you please pass me the salt?* sounds fine while *Are you able to please pass me the salt?* sounds decidedly odd.

Searle's response to this seems to be that while the account of inference we have just outlined stands, there is a certain degree of conventionality about forms like *Can you . . . ?* being used as requests. Other writers strike the balance differently: Gordon and Lakoff (1975), for example, see hearers as employing short cuts known as **conversational postulates**. These are rules that are engaged whenever the hearer is encouraged by conversational principles to search for an indirect speech act, as described above. The postulates reduce the amount of inference involved in tracing the indirect act. The relevant postulate for our present example would be as in 8.27:

8.27   Conversational postulate (Gordon and Lakoff 1975: 86)
         ASK (*a*, *b*, CAN (*b*, *Q*)) → REQUEST (*a*, *b*, *Q*)

In their formalism, 8.27 is to be interpreted as 'when a speaker *a* asks whether *b* can do *Q*, this implies a request for *b* to do *Q*'. Thus these postulates can be seen as a reflection of the conventionality of some indirect acts. More generally Gordon and Lakoff agree with Searle's suggestion that stating or questioning a felicity condition of a direct act will produce an indirect version. Thus, to add to our earlier examples, if we look at the conditions for requests in 8.26 earlier, we can predict that instead of using the sentence *Please come home!*, the following indirect strategies are possible:

8.28   a.   Question the preparatory condition: *Can you please come home?*
         b.   State the sincerity condition: *I want you to please come home.*
         c.   Question the propositional content condition: *Will you please come home?*

Clearly both of these accounts, by Searle and by Gordon and Lakoff, view the understanding of indirect act as involving inference. The question remains of balance: how much of the task is inferential and how much is conventionalized into strategies or rules for forming indirect acts. A position at the opposite extreme from Searle's would be that indirect speech acts are in fact idioms and involve no inferences from a direct to an indirect act.[10] In this view an utterance like *Can you pass me the salt?* is simply recognized and interpreted as a request, with no question perceived. This position is undercut by the common-sense fact that hearers deciding to be uncooperative, or trying to be funny, can choose to address utterances like *Can you tell me the time?* as direct questions, and simply say *Yes*. There is also some psychological evidence that hearers have access to the direct act in indirect requests:

Clark and Lucy (1975), for example, is a psycholinguistic study which concludes from testing subjects' responses to sentences like *Please colour the circle blue*, *Why colour the circle blue?*, *I'll be very happy if you colour the circle blue*, etc. that direct speech acts are understood more quickly and that hearers seem to have access to the literal meaning of indirect acts. Experiments by Clark and Schunk (1980) seem to confirm this: they suggest that the literal meaning of an indirect request is an important element in the perceived politeness of the act. Thus among indirect requests, *May I ask you what time it is?* is more polite than *Won't you tell me what time it is?* because the first sentence's literal meaning places the onus on speaker action, while the second places it on hearer action. Also, in answering *May I ask you what time it is?* the response *Yes, it's six* is more polite than just *It's six* because the former addresses both the direct and indirect speech acts, answering the question and complying with the request.

This last point raises an interesting issue: why do speakers employ these indirect acts? One motivation might be politeness, a hypothesis we examine in 8.4.3.

8.4.3   Indirect acts and politeness

Most commentators on indirect speech acts have remarked on the role of politeness. Searle (1975: 64), for example, writes:

8.29   In the field of indirect illocutionary acts, the area of directives is the most useful to study because ordinary conversational requirements of politeness normally make it awkward to issue flat imperative statements (e.g. *Leave the room*) or explicit performatives (e.g. *I order you to leave the room*), and we therefore seek to find indirect means to our illocutionary ends (e.g. *I wonder if you would mind leaving the room*). In directives, politeness is the chief motivation for indirectness.

Similarly, Ervin-Tripp's (1976) study of the social implications of indirect requests and orders in American English concludes that speakers do calculate issues of social power and politeness in framing speech acts. She suggests that indirect interrogative requests are useful because they give 'listeners an out by explicitly stating some condition which would make compliance impossible' (p. 38), as in the following example of an indirect request and response (Ervin-Tripp 1976: 38):

8.30   [Daughter to father]
         You ready?
         Not yet.

This is even more pronounced with negative questions used indirectly as requests, e.g. (Ervin-Tripp 1976: 38):

8.31   [Motorist to gas station attendant]
          You don't happen to have any change for the phone do you?

Her study shows that the use of imperatives and *need* statements as directives is commoner from superiors to subordinates, e.g. (1976: 29):

8.32   [Doctor to nurse in hospital]
          I'll need a 19 gauge needle, IV tubing, and a preptic swab.

while questions with modals like *can, could, may* etc. as requests are commoner with superiors and non-familiars, e.g. (1976: 38):

8.33   [Salesman to clerk]
          May I have change for a dollar?

8.34   [Employee to older employer]
          May I have the salt?

Ervin-Tripp points out that, as we all know, getting the calculation right is
important in maintaining social relationships: she gives the example 8.35
below (1976: 63), where the more polite form a is felt to be less appropriate
than b:

8.35   [Young file clerks who have worked together for four months]
          I got the applications done finally.
          a.   Could you take these back to Emma, please?
               or
          b.   Take these with you.

As Ervin-Tripp remarks, 'To address a familiar peer as a non-peer is to be
cold and distancing' (p. 63).

     The role of politeness in social interaction and conversation has been an
important topic in sociology and conversational studies: we cannot hope to
review this large literature here but a few remarks might shed useful light
on the issue of indirect speech acts. We can begin by noting that the work
of the sociologist Ervin Goffman (1967, 1971, 1981)[11] on the social construction of the self, and his notion of **face** (roughly, the public image an
individual seeks to project), has influenced a number of linguistic studies
which have dealt with politeness, including Brown and Levinson (1978,
1987), Leech (1983) and Tannen (1984, 1986).

     In Brown and Levinson's version, face is 'the public self image that every
member of society wants to claim for himself' (1978: 66). For them, face
has two components: **positive face**, which represents an individual's desire
to seem worthy and deserving of approval, and **negative face**, which represents an individual's desire to be autonomous, unimpeded by others. A
kind of mutual self-interest requires that conversational participants maintain

both their own face and their interactors' face. In this view, many verbal interactions are potential threats to face. Threats to negative face, which potentially damage an individual's autonomy, include orders, requests, suggestions and advice. Threats to positive face, which potentially lower an individual's self and social esteem, include expressions of disapproval, disagreements, accusations and interruptions. Speakers can threaten their own face by their words: such self-threats to positive face include apologies and confessions.

In the continual interactive balancing of one's own and others' face, politeness serves to diminish potential threats. In other words, speakers seek to weaken face-threatening acts by using a series of strategies, which together can be called politeness or tact. One of these strategies is the use of indirect speech acts.[12] These indirect acts can be seen to follow the distinction between positive and negative face. Negative indirectness helps to diminish the threat of orders and requests: examples would include giving an explanation for a request rather than the request itself, e.g. saying *It's very hot in here* instead of *Please open the window*; or as we saw earlier, querying a preparatory condition for the request, as in *Could you open the window?* Positive indirectness weakens the threat provided by disagreements, interruptions etc.: for example, by prefacing them with apologies or explanation as in *I'm sorry but you're wrong* instead of simply *You're wrong*, or *I have to say that I don't agree* instead of *I don't agree*.

While the notion of politeness does seem to have explanatory value for the study of indirect speech acts, one important issue which it raises is cross-cultural variation. Researchers have applied the notion of politeness to a number of different languages and some have argued that the account of politeness strategies we have outlined, including the use of indirect speech acts, is too firmly based on European and North American cultural norms. The notion of face, according to Brown and Levinson, is universal: every language community will have a system of politeness but the details of the system will vary because face is related to 'the most fundamental cultural ideas about the nature of the social persona, honour and virtue, shame and redemption, and thus to religious concepts' (Brown and Levinson 1987: 13). Thus politeness strategies, and individual speech acts, will vary from culture to culture. This has been investigated by a number of studies containing implicit or explicit comparison with English, including Blum-Kulka (1983, 1987) on Hebrew, Wierzbicka (1985) on Polish, Matsumoto (1988, 1989) on Japanese, Hwang (1990) on Korean, Gu (1990) on Chinese, and Sifianou (1992) on Greek. These studies give us insights into the politeness systems of their languages but the overall conclusion about a universal system is unclear: some have successfully applied a general system to the specific languages, while others, like Matsumoto (1988) and Gu (1990), have claimed that Brown and Levinson's system does not adequately reflect conversational practices in the highly deferential societies they describe.

It seems safe, though, to conclude that both speech acts in general (thanks, apologies, compliments, invitations, etc.) and indirectness will vary from culture to culture. In terms of our current interest in indirect speech acts, comparisons have been made between requests in English and German (House and Kasper 1981) and English and Russian (Thomas 1983) which seem to suggest consistent differences, with a greater use of indirectness in English than the other two languages. However Sifianou's (1992) study of requests in Greek and English reveals the complexity and difficulty of such comparisons. Her conclusion is that the Greek politeness system is more oriented towards positive face strategies and the (British) English to negative face, leading to different expectations of what conversational politeness is.

8.5   Sentence Types

Our final section takes us back to an issue we raised in chapter 5: how to decide whether a given grammatical category, say subjunctive, is a marker of a sentence type, or some semantic category like mood.[13] We have defined a sentence type as a conventional matching between a grammatical form and a speech act. Thus some languages have a question word which contrasts with a declarative word, as in the Somali examples 8.36a and b below, where there is also a contrast with a lack of such a word (or zero marking) for the imperative as in 8.36c:

8.36   a.   Warkii   miyaad dhegeysatay?
              war+kii   ma+aad dhegeysatay
              news+the Q+you   listen.to-2sg-PAST
              'Did you listen to the news?'
         b.   Warkii   waad   dhegeysatay.
              war+kii   waa+aad   dhegeysatay
              news+the DECL+you   listen.to-2sg-PAST
              'You listened to the news.'
         c.   Warkii   dhegeyso!
              news+the listen to-2sg-IMP
              'Listen to the news!'

As these sentences show, the question word in 8.36a is *ma*, while *waa* in 8.36b marks a declarative; these words are called **classifiers** in Saeed (1993). Greenlandic marks a similar distinction with different verbal inflections for person, etc. (Sadock and Zwicky 1985: 167):

8.37   a.   Igavoq
              cook(INDIC 3-sg)
              'He cooks.'
         b.   Igava
              cook(Q 3-sg)
              'Does he cook?'

Table 8.1　Possible Somali markers of sentence type

a. Positive forms

Sentence type	Forms		Meaning
	Classifier	*Verb*	
Declarative	*waa*	*keenaa*	'He brings it'
Interrogative	*ma*	*keenaa*	'Does he bring it?'
Imperative	–	*kèen*	'Bring (sg) it!'
Optative	*há*	*keeno*	'May he bring it!'
Potential	*shòw*	*keenee*	'Possibly he'll bring it, He may bring it'

b. Negative forms

Sentence type	Forms			Meaning
	Classifier	*Negative word*	*Verb*	
Declarative	–	*má*	*keenó*	'He doesn't bring it'
Interrogative	*sòw*	*má*	*keenó*	'Doesn't he bring it?'
Imperative	*ha*	–	*kéenin*	'Do not bring (sg) it!'
Optative	*yaan-u**	–	*kéenin*	'May he not bring it!'

*$*u$ = 'he'

Source: Saeed (1993: 80–1)[14]

The problem, however, is that such marking by special words or inflections can be used for a variety of semantic distinctions. We can use some examples from Somali to show the difficulties, beginning with the lists in table 8.1, where the verb *keen* 'bring' is used to show the forms.

As these tables show, the marking here is quite complicated: the system uses gaps as a marker in several places and tone is important: distinguishing the positive question word *ma* from the negative word *má*, and the optative word *há* from the negative imperative marker *ha*. Note too that the distinctions combine specific classifiers and verbal inflection.

For our current purposes, the question that tables like those in table 8.1 raise is: does every classifier and negative morpheme in table 8.1 mark a distinct sentence type? The answer we would like to give is: only when it regularly and conventionally matches a corresponding speech act. Unfortunately, however, we do not have a pre-existing list of speech acts to help us decide this. The situation, though not clear-cut, is not totally gloomy, however. Sadock and Zwicky (1985), for example, suggest some rules of thumb for identifying sentence types, which we can modify slightly as follows:

8.38   a. The sentence types should form a system, so that there should be corresponding versions of a sentence in each type;

b. similarly, the types should be mutually exclusive, i.e. there should be no combinations of two sentence-type markers in the same sentence;

c. as we have noted, there should be a conventional association with a speech act.

On the basis of rules like these, we can probably discount the **negative** morpheme *má* in table 8.1 as a marker of sentence type in Somali. Negation co-occurs with declarative and interrogative sentences, thus breaking rule 8.38b. This fact also indicates that this marker does not conventionally convey a speech act of denial in Somali, since it is used in, for example, negative questions, thus breaking rule 8.38c. The decisions are more diffi-cult with the **optative** and **potential** markers in table 8.1. These occur in a regular correspondence with interrogative and other sentences but do not co-occur with them: no sentences are optative and interrogative, potential and declarative, etc. Thus they seem to pass rules 8.38a and b. When it comes to 8.38c, the optative does seem a likely candidate for a sentence type because it is conventionally associated with **wishes** (like *Soomaaliya há noolaato!* 'May Somalia live! Long live Somalia!'), which we know from other languages is a likely speech act. So we can add optative to interrogat-ive, declarative and imperative as sentence types for Somali. However, the potential is a little more problematic: the type seems to pass our rules 8.38a and b since it doesn't co-occur with other markers; but note that there is no negative potential form. It is also difficult to view expressions of possibility as a distinct speech act rather than as a type of statement, differing from *waa* statements in showing a different part of the semantic range of modality.

Luckily, solving this descriptive problem is not necessary for our point here and we can leave the issue to one side. What this brief excursion into Somali sentence-type marking shows us is that it is not necessarily an easy process to set up the sentence-type half of the match-up between sentence type and speech act we identified in section 8.1. It also seems to indicate that markers of sentence type may also have functions in other semantic systems.

8.6   Summary

In this chapter we have seen that the social function of an utterance is an important part of its meaning. We reviewed J. L. Austin's very influential theory of **speech acts**, which emphasizes the role of language in commun-icating social acts like requesting, questioning, promising, thanking, stating, as well as more institutional verbal acts like pronouncing sentence in court, or performing ceremonies of baptizing, marrying etc.

We saw that understanding the speech act force, or **illocutionary force** in Austin's terms, of an utterance involves the hearer in combining linguistic knowledge about grammatical marking with both background cultural knowledge and knowledge of the immediate local context. The determination of the linguistic marking of speech act force is in itself not a simple task: we saw that the markers may have other roles to perform in the grammar. Moreover, even when we can identify sentence types, the correlation between these and speech acts is not a steady one: the investigation of indirect speech acts reveals that inference and conversational principles play a role in hearers' recognition of a speech act.

Overall the study of speech acts is a fascinating area: partly because their role is so crucial to the social interaction in a speech community (so that we have no choice but to study them) but also because they give us another glimpse of the interpretive powers that interactants routinely employ in order to communicate: unconsciously and seamlessly combining linguistic and other forms of knowledge in order to reach meaning.

FURTHER READING

In addition to the primary sources already mentioned, speech act semantics is reviewed in Schiffrin (1994), Mey (1993) and Levinson (1983). Leech (1983) gives an account which explores the role of politeness in this and related areas of conversational interaction. As mentioned earlier, Sadock and Zwicky (1985) is an interesting cross-linguistic survey of speech act grammaticalization. Vanderveken (1990) is an extended study of speech acts which proposes an integration with formal semantic approaches, and is thus best approached after reading chapter 10.

EXERCISES

8.1   Decide which of the following sentences, when uttered, would count as a performative utterance, in Austin's terms:

    a.   I suggest you take a holiday soon.
    b.   I'm warning you it won't end here.
    c.   I think you're taking this press attention too seriously.
    d.   I deny all knowledge of this scandal.
    e.   I promised them there'd be no fuss.

8.2   Replace the following explicit performatives with corresponding implicit versions, e.g. *I predict that it will rain before teatime* → *It'll rain before teatime, mark my words.*

    a.   I insist that you come with us.
    b.   We order you to return to your unit.

    c.   I confess that I stole the money.

    d.   We invite you to join us for the weekend.

8.3   Below are some examples of **indirect speech acts**. For each one, try to identify both the direct and indirect act, e.g.

    [Customer at a railway ticket-office window]
    I'd like a day return to Galway.
    Direct act: *statement* Indirect act: *request*

    a.   [Travel agent to customer]
        Why not think about Spain for this summer?

    b.   [Customer to barman]
        I'll have the usual.

    c.   [Mother to child coming in from school]
        I bet you're hungry.

    d.   [Bank manager to applicant for an overdraft]
        We regret that we are unable to accede to your request.

    e.   [Someone responding to a friend's money-making schemes]
        Get real!

    f.   [Doorman at a nightclub to aspiring entrant]
        Don't make me laugh.

8.4   In example 8.26 in the chapter we gave a set of felicity conditions for **requests**. Based on these, and using your own examples, try to form one indirect request for each of the following strategies:

    a.   by stating the preparatory condition of the direct request;
    b.   by querying the preparatory condition of the direct request;
    c.   by stating the sincerity condition of the direct request;
    d.   by querying the propositional content of the direct request.

8.5   Repeat exercise 8.4 but for the speech acts of **promising** and **questioning**, whose felicity conditions are given in examples 8.20 and 8.21 in the chapter. Discuss which of the strategies in exercise 8.4 work for these speech acts.

8.6   It is often claimed that cross-cultural differences in the use of direct versus indirect speech acts can lead speakers of one language to stereotype speakers of another language as impolite. Discuss any experience you may have had of such misunderstandings. If you speak a second language, reflect on how requests and other speech acts might differ in their directness in your two languages. Try to come up with specific examples of differences.

NOTES

1   These examples are in the standard Yoruba orthography, which includes the following: Tones: ´ = high tone, no mark = mid tone, ` = low tone. The subscript dot indicates distinct sounds: ọ = [ɔ], ẹ = [ɛ], ṣ = [ʃ]; and p and gb are labiovelar plosives [kp] and [gb].

2   In this approach questions and answers are an example of a more general interactional unit: the **adjacency pair**. This is a pair of utterances, which might consist of question–answer, summons–answer, compliment–acceptance/rejection, etc., which form an important structural unit in this theory's view of conversational interaction. The expectation of a response that is set up by the first part is called **conditioned relevance** by Schegloff (1972). See Levinson (1983: 226–79) and Schiffrin (1994: 232–81) for discussion.

3   See Saville-Troike (1989) for an introduction to the study of the conventions governing types of communication in different societies.

4   Such answers have been called **indirect answers** (Nofsinger 1976), **indirect responses** (Pearce and Conklin 1979) and **transparent questions** (Bowers 1982). These studies discuss how speakers infer that such answers are equivalent to 'yes' and 'no', and investigate the different attitudes hearers have to such answers compared to literal answers.

5   We omit discussion of Austin's original five-fold classification of speech acts into *verdictives, exercitives, commissives, behabitives* and *expositives* (Austin 1975: 148–64) since his proposals, which influence subsequent systems, are proposed in a very tentative way, e.g. 'I distinguish five very general classes: but I am far from equally happy about all of them' (1975: 151) and 'The last two classes are those which I find most troublesome, and it could well be that they are not clear or are cross-classified, or even that some fresh classification altogether is needed. I am not putting any of this forward as in the very least definitive' (1975: 152).

6   This somewhat inaccurately suggests that all speech acts have propositional content. As is well known, some speech acts do not, for example *Sorry!* or *Excuse me!* for apologies, *Huh?* for a question, *Hello!* or *Hi!* as greetings, etc.

7   A **yes–no** (or elicitative) question seeks confirmation or denial of a proposition, and thus expects an answer yes or no, as in *Is Bill going to London?* An **elicitative** or WH-question seeks new information to augment what is already known, as in the following example, where the speaker knows that Bill is going but seeks extra information:

    a.   Where is Bill going?
    b.   When is Bill going?
    c.   Why is Bill going?

8   We can take a brief look at the last of these as an example: Bach and Harnish (1979: 39–59) establish a general taxonomy very like Searle's in example 8.19, though they use six categories rather than five, and employ slightly different labels: **constatives** (e.g. assertions), **directives** (e.g. questions), **commissives** (e.g. promises), **acknowledgements** (e.g. greetings), **effectives** (e.g. naming a ship) and **verdictives** (e.g. finding a defendant guilty). For their constative class, for example, which correponds to Searle's representatives, they identify fifteen sub-types, each characterized by a description of the act performed and

exemplified by English verbs. We can provide a few of their examples of constative and directive class:

1 Bach and Harnish's (1979) **constative speech acts**
   [where S = speaker, H = hearer, e = linguistic expression, P = the proposition expressed in the speech act]
   a. *Assertives* (simple): (affirm, allege, assert, aver, avow, claim, declare, deny (assert . . . not), indicate, maintain, propound, say, state, submit)
       In uttering e, S asserts that P if S expresses:
       i.   the belief that P, and
       ii. the intention that H believe that P.
   b. *Predictives*: (forecast, predict, prophesy)
       In uttering e, S predicts that P if S expresses:
       i.   the belief that it will be the case that P, and
       ii. the intention that H believe that it will be the case that P.
   c. *Concessives*: (acknowledge, admit, agree, allow, assent, concede, concur, confess, grant, own)
       In uttering e, S concedes that P if S expresses:
       i.   the belief that P, contrary to what he would like to believe or contrary to what he previously believed or avowed, and
       ii. the intention that H believe that P.

2 Bach and Harnish's (1979) **directive speech acts**
   [where S = speaker, H = hearer, e = linguistic expression, P = the proposition expressed in the speech act, A = the future action]
   a. *Requestives*: (ask, beg, beseech, implore, insist, invite, petition, plead, pray, request, solicit, summon, supplicate, tell, urge)
       In uttering e, S requests H to A if S expresses:
       i.   the desire that H do A, and
       ii. the intention that H do A because (at least partly) of S's desire.
   b. *Questions*: (ask, enquire, interrogate, query, question, quiz)
       In uttering e, S questions H as to whether or not P if S expresses:
       i.   the desire that H tell S whether or not P, and
       ii. the intention that H tell S whether or not P because of H's desire.
   c. *Requirements*: (bid, charge, command, demand, dictate, direct, enjoin, instruct, order, prescribe, require)
       In uttering e, S requires H to A if S expresses:
       i.   the belief that his utterance, in virtue of his authority over H, constitutes sufficient reason for H to A, and
       ii. the intention that H do A because of S's utterance.

9   Searle (1975: 72) notes that asking whether the sincerity condition holds won't work. So asking *Do I wish you wouldn't do that?* will not work as an indirect form of a request, *Please don't do that.*
10 A position close to this is adopted by Sadock (1974).
11 See Schiffrin (1994: 97–136) for a discussion of Goffman's work and its influence on conversational analysis.

12 See Brown and Levinson (1978, 1987) for a discussion of other possible strat-
    egies for performing face-threatening acts.
13 Or both: see note 14 below.
14 In Saeed (1993: 79–85) words like *waa, ma, shòw*, etc. are taken to be part of
    the mood system. This is because, as our discussion here hints, the two systems
    of modality and sentence-type marking overlap in these forms. For example we
    can analyse the distinction between positive statements with *waa*, negative
    statements with *má*, and potential sentences with *shòw* as being part of the
    system of mood marking, i.e. marking a distinction between (for proposition
    P): certainty that-*P*, possibility that-*P* and certainty that not-*P*. As we note here,
    waa also seems to mark the speech act of stating.

Theoretical Approaches

part III

chapter 9

Meaning Components

9.1 Introduction

In chapter 3 we reviewed a range of lexical relations, including the MALE–FEMALE and ADULT–YOUNG relations in sets of words like those below:

9.1   man–woman–child   ram–ewe–lamb
         dog–bitch–pup   bull–cow–calf
         stallion–mare–foal   hog–sow–piglet

As we saw, these and other relations are characteristic of the lexicon. To explain this networking, some semanticists have hypothesized that words are not the smallest semantic units but are built up of smaller components of meaning which are combined differently (or **lexicalized**) to form different words.

Thus, to take perhaps the commonest examples in the literature, words like *woman, bachelor, spinster* and *wife* have been viewed as being composed of elements such as [ADULT], [HUMAN] etc.:

9.2   *woman*   [FEMALE]   [ADULT]   [HUMAN]
       bachelor   [MALE]   [ADULT]   [HUMAN]   [UNMARRIED]
       spinster   [FEMALE]   [ADULT]   [HUMAN]   [UNMARRIED]
       wife   [FEMALE]   [ADULT]   [HUMAN]   [MARRIED]

The elements in square brackets in 9.2 above are called **semantic components**, or **semantic primitives**, and this kind of analysis is often called
componential analysis (CA for short). As we shall see in this chapter,
there are three related reasons for identifying such components. The first is
that they may allow an economic characterization of the lexical relations
that we looked at in chapter 2, and the sentence relations we discussed in
chapter 4, like the contradiction between 9.3a and b below, or the entailment between 9.4a and b:

9.3   a.   Ferdinand is dead.
        b.   Ferdinand is alive.

9.4   a.   Henrietta cooked some lamb chops.
        b.   Henrietta cooked some meat.

In the next section, 9.2, we discuss how semantic components might be
used to capture lexical relations, and in 9.3 we look briefly at Jerrold Katz's
semantic theory, a componential theory designed to capture such semantic
phenomena.

   A second, related, justification for semantic components is that they have
linguistic import outside semantics: that only by recognizing them can we
accurately describe a range of syntactic and morphological processes. We
look at this claim in section 9.4. The third and most ambitious claim is that
in addition to these two important uses, such semantic primitives form part
of our psychological architecture: that they provide us with a unique view
of conceptual structure. We look at two versions of this approach when we
examine the work of Ray Jackendoff in section 9.6 and James Pustejovsky
in 9.7.

9.2   Lexical Relations in CA

One use for semantic components is that they might allow us to define the
lexical relations we looked at earlier. Take, for example, **hyponymy** (inclusion). Below we can see that *spinster* is a hyponym of *woman*, and their
components might be given as shown:

9.5   *woman*   [FEMALE]   [ADULT]   [HUMAN]
        spinster   [FEMALE]   [ADULT]   [HUMAN]   [UNMARRIED]

We can see that by comparing the sets of components we could define
hyponymy as:

9.6   A lexical item P can be defined as a hyponym of Q if all the features
        of Q are contained in the feature specification of P.

Similarly we might be able to deal with some kinds of antonymy, or more generally **incompatibility**, as in 9.7 below. The words *spinster, bachelor, wife* are incompatible and from a comparison of their components we might suggest a definition like 9.8:

9.7   *bachelor*   [MALE]   [ADULT]   [HUMAN]   [UNMARRIED]
         spinster   [FEMALE]   [ADULT]   [HUMAN]   [UNMARRIED]
         wife   [FEMALE]   [ADULT]   [HUMAN]   [MARRIED]

9.8   Lexical items P, Q, R . . . are incompatible if they share a set of features but differ from each other by one or more contrasting features.

Thus *spinster* is incompatible with *bachelor* by contrast of gender specification; and with *wife* by the marital specification. Note that these definitions are not exact but are meant to give a general idea of how this approach might proceed. Componential analysts also often make use of **binary features** and **redundancy rules**, which we can briefly describe.

9.2.1   Binary features

Many linguists use a binary feature format for these components, similar to that used in phonology and syntax. Our original examples will, in this format, be as below:

9.9   *woman*   [+FEMALE]   [+ADULT]   [+HUMAN]
         bachelor   [−FEMALE]   [+ADULT]   [+HUMAN]   [−MARRIED]
         spinster   [+FEMALE]   [+ADULT]   [+HUMAN]   [−MARRIED]
         wife   [+FEMALE]   [+ADULT]   [+HUMAN]   [+MARRIED]

Note that this allows a characterization of antonyms by a difference of the value plus or minus a feature, and so is considered a more economical format by many writers.

9.2.2   Redundancy rules

The statement of semantic components is also more economical if we include some redundancy rules which predict the automatic relationships between components. An example of such a rule is:

9.10   HUMAN   →   ANIMATE
           ADULT   →   ANIMATE
           ANIMATE   →   CONCRETE
           MARRIED   →   ADULT
           etc.

If we state these rules once for the whole dictionary, we can avoid repeating the component on the right of a rule in each of the entries containing the component on the left: so every time we enter [HUMAN], for example, we don't have to enter [ANIMATE]. With redundancy rules like 9.10, an entry like 9.11a below for *wife* might be stated more economically as in 9.11b:

9.11   a.   *wife*   [+FEMALE]   [+HUMAN]   [+ADULT]   [+MARRIED]
                         [+ANIMATE]   [+CONCRETE], etc.
         b.   *wife*   [+FEMALE]   [+ADULT]   [+MARRIED]

To sum up: in this approach each lexical item will be entered in the dictionary with a complex of semantic components. There will be in addition a set of redundancy rules for these components which apply automatically to reduce the number of components stated for each item. Lexical relations can then be stated in terms of the components.

9.3   Katz's Semantic Theory

9.3.1   Introduction

One of the earliest approaches to semantics within generative grammar was componential: it appeared in Katz and Fodor (1963), and has been refined since, notably in Katz and Postal (1964) and Katz (1972):[1] for simplicity we will refer to it as **Katz's theory**. Two central ideas of this theory are:

1   Semantic rules have to be **recursive** for the same reasons as syntactic rules: that the number of possible sentences in a language is very large, possibly infinite.
2   The relationship between a sentence and its meaning is not arbitrary and unitary, i.e. syntactic structure and lexical content interact so that *John killed Fred* and *Fred killed John* do not have the same meaning despite containing the same lexical elements; nor do *The snake frightened Mary* and *The movie delighted Horace* despite having the same syntactic structure. In other words, meaning is **compositional**. The way words are combined into phrases and phrases into sentences determines the meaning of the sentences.

Katz's theory reflects this by having rules which take input from both the syntactic component of the grammar, and from the dictionary. For these linguists the aims of the semantic component, paralleling the aims of syntax, are:

1   to give specifications of the meanings of lexical items;
2   to give rules showing how the meanings of lexical items build up into the meanings of phrases and so on up to sentences;
3   to do this in a universally applicable metalanguage.

The first two aims are met by having two components: firstly, a dictionary which pairs lexical items with a semantic representation; and secondly, a set of **projection rules**, which show how the meanings of sentences are built up from the meanings of lexical items. The third aim is partially met by the use of semantic components. We can look at the dictionary and the projection rules in turn.

9.3.2 The Katzian dictionary

The details of the form of dictionary entries changed considerably during the development of this theory; we can risk abstracting a kind of typical entry for the most famous example: the word *bachelor* (adapted from Katz and Fodor 1963, Katz and Postal 1964):[2]

9.12   *bachelor* {N}
  a.   (human) (male) [one who has never been married]
  b.   (human) (male) [young knight serving under the standard of another knight]
  c.   (human) [one who has the first or lowest academic degree]
  d.   (animal) (male) [young fur seal without a mate in the breeding season]

The conventions for this entry are as follows. Information within curly brackets {*i*} is grammatical information; here simply that the four readings are all nouns. Our entry in 9.12 contains two types of semantic component: the first, the elements within parentheses (*i*), are **semantic markers**. These are the links which bind the vocabulary together, and are responsible for the lexical relations we looked at earlier. The second type, shown within square brackets [*i*], are **distinguishers**. This is idiosyncratic semantic information that identifies the lexical item. So Katz and his colleagues built into their theory the common-sense idea that part of a word's meaning is shared with other words, but part is unique to that word.

9.3.3 Projection rules

These rules are responsible for showing how the meaning of words combines into larger structures. Since this theory was designed to be part of a Chomskyan generative grammar, the rules interfaced with a generative syntactic component. So typically the projection rules operated on syntactic phrase markers, or 'trees', as in figure 9.1. The projection rules used these trees to structure the amalgamation of word meanings into phrase meanings, and then phrase meanings into the sentence's meaning. Again we can select a standard example from Katz and Fodor (1963) in figure 9.1. In this figure the subscripts (1–4) on the syntactic labels show the order of amalgamation of semantic readings, once the individual words had been attached to the

Figure 9.1 Projection rules

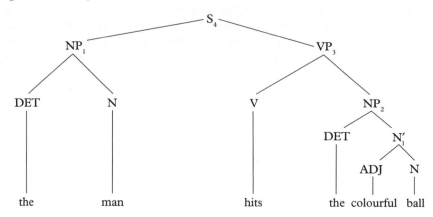

Source: Katz and Fodor (1963)

bottom of the tree. To keep the figure readable, we just include the words, not their associated dictionary entries, which are of course what is actually being amalgamated; we'll look at this fuller version a little later. Thus the projection rules begin at the bottom of the syntactic tree by amalgamating the semantic readings of *the* and *man* to give the semantics of the NP *the man*. Similarly, the rules combine the semantics of *colourful* and *ball*, then adds the semantics of *the*, to form the NP *the colourful ball*. Thereafter the rules move up the tree combining elements until a semantic representation for the whole sentence *The man hits the colourful ball* is reached. We can see that these projection rules are clearly designed to reflect the compositionality of meaning.

The main constraint on the amalgamation processes involved in these rules is provided by **selection restrictions**. These are designed to reflect some of the contextual effects on word meaning. We can stay with the same example and look at the dictionary entries for *colourful* and *ball* in 9.13 and 9.14 below, with the selectional restrictions shown on the adjective in angle brackets < >:

9.13   **colourful** {ADJ}
   a.   (colour) [abounding in contrast or variety of bright colors] <(physical object) or (social activity)>
   b.   (evaluative) [having distinctive character, vividness or pictur-esqueness] <(aesthetic object) or (social activity)>

9.14   **ball** {N}
   a.   (social activity) (large) (assembly) [for the purpose of social dancing]
   b.   (physical object) [having globular shape]
   c.   (physical object) [solid missile for projection by engine of war]

Thus the dictionary provides two readings for *colourful* and three for *ball*; and, as we noted, the selection restrictions which restrict co-occurrence are attached to the adjective. To see how this works we can observe that by simple arithmetic the two readings for *colourful* and the three for *ball* should produce six combinations for *colourful ball*. However, some combinations are blocked by the selection restrictions: the second reading of *colourful*, being restricted to (aesthetic object) or (social activity) will not match the second or third readings for *ball*.

As the projection rules successively amalgamate readings, the selection restrictions will limit the final output. We will not spell out the process in any great detail here except to show one legal output of the amalgamation rules for figure 9.1:

9.15   *The man hits the colourful ball.*
        [Some contextually definite] – (physical object) – (human) – (adult)
        – (male) – (action) – (instancy) – (intensity) [strikes with a blow
        or missile] – [some contextually definite] – (physical object) –
        (colour) – [[abounding in contrast or variety of bright colours]
        [having globular shape]]

From this brief outline of the Katzian approach to meaning, we can see that an essential part of the theory is the attempt to establish a semantic metalanguage through the identification of semantic components: in simple terms, the theory is **decompositional**. It is these components that Katz (1972) uses to try to characterize the semantic relations of hyponymy, antonymy, synonymy, contradiction, entailment, etc. We can take just one example of this: Katz (1972: 40) provides the simplified dictionary entry for *chair* in 9.16:

9.16   *chair*
        (Object), (Physical), (Non-living), (Artefact), (Furniture), (Portable),
        (Something with legs), (Something with a back), (Something with
        a seat), (Seat for one)

Katz argues that the internal structure of components in 9.16 can explain the entailment relation between 9.17 below and each of 9.18a–h:

9.17   There is a chair in the room.

9.18   a.   There is a physical object in the room.
        b.   There is something non-living in the room.
        c.   There is an artefact in the room.
        d.   There is a piece of furniture in the room.
        e.   There is something portable in the room.
        f.   There is something having legs in the room.
        g.   There is something with a back in the room.
        h.   There is a seat for one in the room.

This then is a semantic justification for meaning components: in the next section we review arguments that semantic components are necessary for the correct description of syntactic processes too.

9.4   Grammatical Rules and Semantic Components

As mentioned earlier, some linguists claim that we need semantic components to describe grammatical processes correctly, i.e. that it is grammatically necessary to recognize that certain units of meaning are shared by different lexical items. Thus two verbs might share a semantic concept, e.g. MOTION, or CAUSE. We could reflect this in two complementary ways: one is by setting up verb classes, e.g. of **motion verbs** or **causative verbs**; the other is to factor out the shared element of meaning and view it as a semantic component. In this section we review some components that have been proposed in the analysis of grammatical processes and we begin by looking at the basic methodology of this approach.

9.4.1   The methodology

To see the effect of these assumptions on methodology, we can look at an example from Beth Levin's study of the semantics of English verbs (Levin 1993). As part of this study, she investigates the semantic features of four English verbs by examining their grammatical behaviour. The verbs are *cut, break, touch, hit* (Levin 1993: 5ff.). All four are transitive verbs, as shown in:

9.19   a.   Margaret cut the bread.
         b.   Janet broke the vase.
         c.   Terry touched the cat.
         d.   Carla hit the door.

Levin looks at how these four verbs interact with three different constructions which are usually seen as involving alternations of argument structure: **middle** constructions as in 9.20;[3] **conative** constructions involving *at*, as in the b sentences in 9.21 and 9.22; and what she terms **body-part ascension** constructions, as in the b sentences in 9.23 and 9.24:

Middle construction:

9.20   a.   These shirts wash well.
         b.   This car drives very smoothly.

Conative construction:

9.21   a. He chopped the meat.
        b. He chopped at the meat.

9.22   a. They shot the bandits.
        b. They shot at the bandits.

Body-part ascension construction:

9.23   a. Mary slapped Fred's face.
        b. Mary slapped Fred in the face.

9.24   a. Igor tapped Lavinia's shoulder.
        b. Igor tapped Lavinia on the shoulder.

As Levin's examples in 9.25–7 below show, not all of these four verbs occur
in each of these constructions:

9.25   Middle
        a. The bread cuts easily.
        b. Crystal vases break easily.
        c. *Cats touch easily.
        d. *Door frames hit easily.

9.26   Conative
        a. Margaret cut at the bread.
        b. *Janet broke at the vase.
        c. *Terry touched at the cat.
        d. Carla hit at the door.

9.27   Body-part ascension
        a. Margaret cut Bill's arm.
        b. Margaret cut Bill on the arm.
        c. Janet broke Bill's finger.
        d. *Janet broke Bill on the finger.
        e. Terry touched Bill's shoulder.
        f. Terry touched Bill on the shoulder.
        g. Carla hit Bill's back.
        h. Carla hit Bill on the back.

In fact the four verbs have distinct patterns of occurrence with the three
grammatical processes, as shown in 9.28 (Levin 1993: 6–7).

9.28

	touch	*hit*	*cut*	*break*
Conative	No	Yes	Yes	No
Body-part ascension	Yes	Yes	Yes	No
Middle	No	No	Yes	Yes

On the basis of this grammatical behaviour, the semanticist can hypothesize that each of these verbs belongs to a different set, and indeed further investigations of this sort would confirm this. Other verbs which belong to these sets are shown in 9.29:

9.29   a.   *Break* verbs: break, crack, rip, shatter, snap . . .
        b.   *Cut* verbs: cut, hack, saw, scratch, slash . . .
        c.   *Touch* verbs: pat, stroke, tickle, touch . . .
        d.   *Hit* verbs: bash, hit, kick, pound, tap, whack . . .

We have dealt with this example at length because it provides an example of how verb classes can be set up within this type of approach. The next move in a decompositional approach, as we described earlier, would be to try to establish what meaning components might be responsible for this bunching of verbs into classes. Levin's conclusion, based on further analysis, is as in 9.30 (1993: 9–10):

9.30   touch is a pure verb of contact, hit is a verb of contact by motion, cut is a verb of causing a change of state by moving something into contact with the entity that changes state, and break is a pure verb of change of state.

This might provide us with the semantic components in 9.31 below; and suggests that whatever other elements of meaning they might contain, we might analyse these four verbs as in 9.32:

9.31   CHANGE, MOTION, CONTACT, CAUSE

9.32   *cut*   CAUSE, CHANGE, CONTACT, MOTION
        break   CAUSE, CHANGE
        touch   CONTACT
        hit   CONTACT, MOTION

So from a componential point of view, the presence of these different semantic components in these verbs causes them to participate in different grammatical rules. It follows then that correctly identifying the semantic components of a verb will help predict the grammatical processes it undergoes.

Of course the semantic components identified in 9.32 are only part of the meaning of these verbs. For a discussion of the relationship between these components and other elements of a verb's meaning, see Pinker (1989: 165ff.) and his 'Grammatically Relevant Subsystem' hypothesis. This hypothesis is that only some components of a word's meaning, such as those in 9.32, which are shared by a number of words, are relevant to grammatical processes; other item-specific elements are not. Pinker gives the example of the English verb *to butter* (Pinker 1989: 166):

9.33   Thus a verb like *to butter* would specify information about butter
          and information about causation, but only the causation part could
          trigger or block the application of lexical rules or other linguistic
          processes.

We can perhaps liken this distinction among semantic information to Katz's
distinction, discussed earlier, between semantic **markers** and **distinguishers**.
Components like those in 9.32 which form part of Pinker's grammatically
relevant subset would correspond to Katz's markers, though Pinker's focus
is on lexical rules rather than lexical relations. It is clear that Pinker, along
with other writers, considers the grammatically relevant subset to be the
main focus of research into language universals and language acquisition.
The aim is to establish:

9.34   a set of elements that is at once conceptually interpretable, much
          smaller than the set of possible verbs, used across all languages,
          used by children to formulate and generalize verb meanings, used in
          specifically grammatical ways (for example, being lexicalized into
          closed-class morphemes), and used to differentiate the narrow classes
          that are subject to different sets of lexical rules.   (Pinker 1989: 169)

A number of different terms have been used to make this binary distinction
in the meaning of lexical items, including the following:

9.35   Grammatically relevant subsytem *versus* unrestricted conceptual
          representation (Pinker 1989)
          Semantic structure *versus* semantic content (Grimshaw 1994)
          Semantic form *versus* conceptual structure (Wunderlich 1997)
          Semantic structure *versus* conceptual structure (Mohanan and
          Mohanan 1999)

9.4.2   Thematic roles and linking rules

Semantic components have been used to investigate several areas of the
syntax–semantics interface. It has been claimed, for example, that they
might allow a more satisfactory account of the interaction of verbal argument
structure with the **thematic roles** discussed in chapter 6. There we discussed the mapping between a verb's syntactic arguments, like subject and
object, and its thematic roles like AGENT and PATIENT. One problematic area
much discussed in the literature is the mapping of thematic roles in various
types of what have been called **locative alternation verbs** (Rappaport and
Levin 1988; Pinker 1989; Levin and Rappaport Hovav 1991; Gropen et al.
1991). In chapter 6 we discussed a subset of these, the *spray/load* verbs
which allow the alternation shown below:

9.36   a.   He loaded newspapers onto the van.
        b.   He loaded the van with newspapers.

9.37   a.   She sprayed pesticide onto the roses.
        b.   She sprayed the roses with pesticide.

The description we proposed there is that the speaker can choose between alternate mappings, or **linkings**, between grammatical and theta-roles: in 9.36a and 9.37a the direct object represents the THEME, while in 9.36b and 9.37b it is the GOAL. As has been pointed out in the literature (e.g. Anderson 1971), however, this analysis overlooks a semantic difference between a and b sentences, namely that in the b versions there is an interpretation of completeness: the van is completely loaded with newspapers and the roses are all sprayed with pesticide. This is not true of the a sentences. The difference is not explicable in our description of alternate mappings to theta-roles.

Other problems arise when we try to characterize similar variations in other movement-to-location verbs. Rappaport and Levin (1985), Pinker (1989) and Gropen et al. (1991) discuss locative verbs like *pour*, which describe an agent moving something into or onto a place, for example:

9.38   Adele poured oil into the pan.

In a theta-role analysis we would describe a linking pattern of AGENT, THEME and GOAL mapping into subject, direct object and prepositional phrase, respectively. Some verbs, like *pour*, show this linking and do not allow the GOAL to be direct object, as we can see in 9.39:

9.39   *Adele poured the pan with oil.

Other verbs, however, like *fill*, reverse this pattern:

9.40   a.   Adele filled the pan with oil.
        b.   *Adele filled the oil into the pan.

Here the GOAL is direct object and the THEME must be in a prepositional phrase. Still other verbs, like *brush*, allow both mappings as alternatives:

9.41   a.   Adele brushed oil onto the pan.
        b.   Adele brushed the pan with oil.

It is not clear that a simple listing of mappings to theta-roles sheds any light on these differences. We may simply have to list for each verb an idiosyncratic theta-grid. Levin, Rappaport Hovav, Pinker and other writers have argued that this approach would ignore the fact that verbs form natural classes and that we can make general statements about how these classes link to certain argument structure patterns. It is proposed that a more satisfactory account of the semantic–syntax interface requires a finer-grained analysis of verbal semantics and that a decomposition of the verb's meaning is the answer.[4]

Rappaport and Levin (1985), for example, and Pinker (1989), propose that the variation in argument structures in 9.38–41 reflects different semantic classes of verb, as in 9.42 and 9.43:

9.42   Verbs of movement with the semantic structure 'X causes Y to move into/onto Z':
    a.   Simple motion verbs, e.g. *put, push*.
    b.   Motion verbs which specify the motion (especially manner), e.g. *pour, drip, slosh*.

9.43   Verbs of change of state with the semantic structure 'X causes Z to change state by means of moving Y into/onto it', e.g. *fill, coat, cover*.

The verb class in 9.42 typically has an argument structure where the THEME argument occurs as object and the GOAL argument occurs in an *into/onto*-prepositional phrase as in 9.44:

9.44   a.   Ailbhe pushed the bicycle into the shed.
    b.   Harvey pulled me onto the stage.
    c.   Joan poured the whiskey into the glass.

The verb class in 9.43 typically has an argument structure where the PATIENT occurs as the object and what we might call the INSTRUMENT[5] occurs in a *with*-prepositional phrase as in 9.45:

9.45   a.   Joan filled the glass with whiskey.
    b.   Libby coated the chicken with oil.
    c.   Mike covered the ceiling with paint.

A third semantic class has the characteristics in 9.46:

9.46   Verbs of movement which share the semantic structure 'X causes Y to move into/onto Z' with the verbs in 9.42 and thus can have the same argument structure, but which also describe a kind of motion which causes an effect on the entity Z, e.g. *spray, paint, brush*.

This third class allows the speaker a choice: either to emphasize the movement, thus giving the argument structure in 9.47a below, shared with verbs in 9.42, or to focus on the change of Z's state, giving the argument structure in 9.47b below, shared with 9.43. This choice is what has been termed **locative alternation**.

9.47   a.   Vera sprayed paint onto the wall.
         b.   Vera sprayed the wall with paint.

The authors whose work we have cited here would argue that the mapping between individual verbs and particular argument structures, and phenomena like locative alternation, can only be described by investigating the internal semantic structure of the verbs.

A similar pattern occurs with locative verbs describing removal (Levin and Rappaport Hovav 1991), where we find related verbs like *clear*, *wipe* and *remove*:

9.48   Robert cleared ashtrays from the bar.

9.49   Christy wiped the lipstick from the glasses.

9.50   Olivia removed the empties from the crate.

Once again an assumption of a canonical mapping between AGENT–subject, THEME–direct object and SOURCE–prepositional phrase will not adequately characterize the behaviour of these verbs. See 9.51–3 below, for example:

9.51   Robert cleared the bar.

9.52   Christy wiped the glasses.

9.53   ?Olivia removed the crate.

In 9.51 and 9.52 *clear* and *wipe* allow the SOURCE as direct object, and the THEME to be missing; but *remove* does not allow this pattern: 9.53 is semantically different and cannot mean that Olivia took something from the crate. Another pattern allowed by *clear* also has the SOURCE as direct object but retains the THEME in an *of*-phrase:

9.54   Robert cleared the bar of dishes.

9.55   ?Christy wiped the glasses of lipstick.

9.56   ?Olivia removed the crate of empties.

As we can see from 9.55, *wipe* is less acceptable with this pattern and again *remove* does not permit it: sentence 9.56 cannot mean that Olivia took empties out of the crate. Again, the proposal is that these differences in syntactic argument structure reflect three semantic classes of removal verb (Levin and Rappaport Hovav 1991: 129):

9.57   *Clear* verbs: clear, clean, empty.
        Wipe verbs: buff, brush, erase, file, mop, pluck, prune, rake, rinse,
        rub, scour, scrape, scratch, scrub, shear, shovel, sponge, sweep,
        trim, vacuum, wipe, etc.
        Remove verbs: dislodge, draw, evict, extract, pry, remove, steal,
        uproot, withdraw, wrench, etc.

Here again it seems that we might be missing something if we describe
the differences between these verbs simply by listing alternate mappings
between syntactic functions and theta-roles. Levin and Rappaport Hovav
suggest setting up semantic verb classes, which we can represent as in 9.58–
60 below.

9.58   Verbs of removal with the semantic structure 'X causes Y to go
        away from Z', e.g. *remove, take*.

9.59   Verbs which share the same semantic structure 'X causes Y to go
        away from Z' but include specification of the means of removal,
        either:
        a.   the manner of removal, e.g. *wipe, rub, scrub*; or
        b.   the instrument of removal, e.g. *brush, hose, mop*.

9.60   Verbs which have the semantic structure 'X causes Z to change by
        removing Y', i.e. change-of-state verbs which focus on the resultant
        state, e.g. *clear, empty, drain*.

As we saw in our examples 9.48–56 above, each semantic class has a
different pattern of syntactic argument structure. The *remove* verbs in 9.58
have the THEME as direct object and the SOURCE in a *from*-prepositional
phrase, and no other pattern. The *wipe* verbs in 9.59 occur with the same
pattern but can also occur with the SOURCE as direct object and no overt
THEME. Finally the *clear* verbs in 9.60 allow an alternation between two
patterns: the first is the argument structure shared with the other two classes,
where the THEME is direct object and the SOURCE is in a *from*-prepositional
phrase, and the second is where the SOURCE occurs as direct object and the
THEME in an *of*-prepositional phrase. The reader can check these patterns
against the sentences in 9.48–56.
    Clearly there are generalizations to be made about the way that change-
of-state verbs in both the *spray*-type class earlier and the *clear*-type class here
allow a locative alternation; see Pinker (1989) and Levin and Rappaport
Hovav (1991) for discussion. For now we can see the force of the claim that
only an examination of the verb-internal semantic structure allows the analyst to characterize these variations correctly in verbal argument structure.
Semantic components, it is argued, allow us to give a motivated explanation
of the links between individual verbs, their argument structures, and the
alternations they undergo.

9.5 Components and Conflation Patterns

A similar research programme of using semantic components to characterize the syntax–semantics interface has been followed by Leonard Talmy
(1975, 1983, 1985), who has studied how elements of meaning are combined not only in single words but across phrases. Talmy has, for example,
identified semantic components associated with verbs of motion. These
include the following (Talmy 1985: 60–1):

9.61   the **Figure**:   an object moving or located with respect to an-
                             other object (the **Ground**);
          the **Motion**:   the presence *per se* of motion or location in the
                             event;
          the **Path**:   the course followed or the site occupied by the
                             Figure object with respect to the Ground object;
          the **Manner**:   the type of motion.

Thus in 9.62:

9.62   Charlotte swam away from the crocodile.

Charlotte is the Figure; the Ground is *the crocodile*; the Path is *away from*; and
the verb encodes the Manner of motion: *swam*. In 9.63 below:

9.63   The banana hung from the tree.

the banana is the Figure; *the tree* is the Ground; *from* is the Path; and
Manner is again expressed in the verb *hung*.
   Talmy has pointed out differences between languages in how these semantic
components are typically combined or **conflated** in verbs and verb phrases,
comparing for example how Path and Manner information is conflated in
English, as in 9.64 below, and Spanish, as in 9.65:

9.64   a.   He ran out of the house.
          b.   He ran up the stairs.

9.65   a.   Salió de   la   casa   corriendo.
               left from the house running
               'He ran out of the house.'
          b.   Subió   las ecaleras corriendo.
               went-up the stairs   running
               'He ran up the stairs.'

In the English sentences 9.64 the Manner, 'running', is incorporated in the
verbs while the direction, or Path, is encoded in an external prepositional

phrase. This strategy for the verb is schematically represented as in 9.66 below:

9.66   Conflation of Motion with Manner (Talmy 1985: 62)
          Figure   Motion   Path   Ground   Manner/Cause

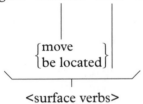

          <surface verbs>

Other examples of this pattern from English are in 9.67:

9.67   a.   The flag *drooped* on the mast.
          b.   The ball *spun* across the line.
          c.   She *pirouetted* out of the lecture hall.
          d.   They *rolled* the beer keg into the seminar.

In the Spanish sentences 9.65 the information is differently packaged: the Path is encoded in the verb and the Manner is encoded in external phrases. The conflation in the verb can be represented as in 9.68:

9.68   Conflation of Motion with Path (Talmy 1985: 69)
          Figure   Motion   Path   Ground   Manner/Cause

          ⎰move   ⎱
          ⎱be located⎰

          <surface verbs>

Some further examples of this from Spanish are in 9.69 (Talmy 1975, 1985):

9.69   a.   La botella *entró*   a la cueva (flotando).
               the bottle moved-in to the cave (floating)
               'The bottle floated into the cave.'
          b.   La botella *salió*   de   la cueva (flotando).
               the bottle moved-out from the cave (floating)
               'The bottle floated out of the cave.'
          c.   El globo   *subió*   por   la chimenea (flotando).
               the balloon moved-up through the chimney (floating)
               'The balloon floated up the chimney.'

d. *Metí*   el barril a la bodega   rodandolo.
I moved in the keg to the storeroom rolling it
'I rolled the keg into the storeroom.'

e. *Quité*   el papel del paquete   cortandolo.
I moved off the paper from the package cutting it
'I cut the wrapper off the package.'

A third possible pattern of conflation combines the Figure with the Motion: that is, instead of information about Manner – about *how* something is moving – being incorporated into the motion verb, as in English *running/swimming/hopping/cartwheeling etc. into the cave*, such a pattern would include information about *what* is moving. Talmy (1985) identifies the Californian Hokan language, Atsugewi, as a clear instance of this pattern, and he includes the following examples (p. 73):

9.70   Atsugewi verb roots of Motion with conflated figure
-lup-   'for a small shiny spherical object (e.g. a round candy, an eyeball, a hailstone) to move/be-located'
-t'-   'for a smallish planar object that can be functionally affixed (e.g. a stamp, a clothing patch, a button, a shingle, a cradle's sunshade) to move/be-located'
-caq-   'for a slimy lumpish object (e.g. a toad, a cow dropping) to move/be-located'
-swal-   'for a limp linear object suspended by one end (e.g. a shirt on a clothesline, a hanging dead rabbit, a flaccid penis) to move/be-located'
-qput-   'for loose dry dirt to move/be-located'
-st'aq'- 'for runny icky material (e.g. mud, manure, rotten tomatoes, guts, chewed gum) to move/be-located'

In Atsugewi, then, semantic features of the Figure are encoded in the verbs of motion. Spherical Figures, for example, occur with a different verb than small flat Figures, and so on. We can select just one of Talmy's examples of how these verb roots and other elements build into an Atsugewi verb (1985: 74):

9.71   a. Morphological elements:
            locative suffix: -ik·   'on the ground'
            instrumental prefix: uh–   'from "gravity" (an object's own weight) acting on it'
            inflectional affix-set: '-w- -ª   '3rd person subject (factual mood)'
        b. Combined underlying form
            /'-w-uh-st'aq'-ik·-ª'/
        c. Pronounced as
            [w'ost'aq'ík·a]

> Literal meaning: 'Runny icky material is located on the
>   ground from its own weight acting on it'
> Instantiated: 'Guts are lying on the ground'

This pattern is represented schematically as in 9.72 (Talmy 1985: 73):

9.72   Conflation of Motion with Figure

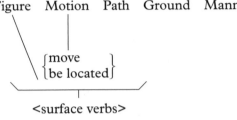

Figure   Motion   Path   Ground   Manner/Cause

{move / be located}

<surface verbs>

Talmy (1985) suggests that languages can be classified into different types, depending upon how their semantic components characteristically map into grammatical categories such as verbs. The word *characteristically* is used here to identify a normal or **unmarked**[6] pattern in the language:

9.73   Any language uses only one of these types for the verb in its most characteristic expression of Motion. Here, 'characteristic' means that: (i) It is colloquial in style, rather than literary, stilted, etc. (ii) It is frequent in occurrence in speech, rather than only occasional. (iii) It is pervasive, rather than limited, that is, a wide range of semantic notions are expressed in this type. (Talmy 1985: 62)

The idea is that languages fall into different types on the basis of their patterns of conflation, and thus a classification or **typology** can be set up, as in 9.74 (based on Talmy 1985: 75):

9.74
Language/language family	**Verb conflation pattern**
a. Romance, Semitic, Polynesian, Nez Perce, Caddo	Path + fact-of-Motion
b. Indo-European except Romance*, Chinese	Manner/Cause + fact-of-Motion
c. Atsugewi and all of North Hokan*, Navajo	Figure + fact-of-Motion

* as far as has been investigated

Talmy's work has led to a number of cross-linguistic studies of how semantic components are conflated into lexical and grammatical structures, for example Choi and Bowerman's (1992) comparison of how Korean and English-speaking children learn verbs.

In the last two sections we have looked at investigations into how semantic components influence grammatical processes and grammatical structures. Next we look at work which builds on this to propose that such semantic components are part of our conceptual structure.

9.6 Jackendoff's Conceptual Structure

9.6.1 Introduction

The semanticist Ray Jackendoff has, in a series of works (e.g. 1972, 1983, 1987, 1990, 1992), developed a decompositional theory of meaning which he calls **conceptual semantics**. The central principle of this approach is that describing meaning involves describing mental representations; in Jackendoff (1987: 122) this is called the **Mentalist Postulate**:

9.75   Meaning in natural language is an information structure that is mentally encoded by human beings.

So the meaning of a sentence is a conceptual structure. Since Jackendoff also believes that sentence meaning is constructed from word meaning,[7] a good deal of attention is paid to lexical semantics in this approach.

Jackendoff endorses the justifications for semantic components discussed in the previous sections. These components are seen as having an important role in describing rules of semantic inference. He argues, for example (1990: 39ff.), that a major argument for identifying a semantic component CAUSE is economy. One of the aims of a semanticist is to explain the relationship between the sentences below:

9.76   George killed the dragon.

9.77   The dragon died.

As we saw in earlier chapters, the label **entailment** is used for this relation: to recognize a speaker's intuitions that if 9.76 is true then so 9.77 must be; or to put it another way, just from hearing 9.76, we know 9.77.[8] Jackendoff's argument is that if our analysis remains above the level of the word, all we can do for 9.76 and 9.77 above is recognize the relationship between the two words *kill* and *die*, as in 9.78:

9.78   x killed y *entails* y died

However, we then have to have similar but distinct rules for lots of other pairs, including:

9.79   a.   x lifted y   *entails*   y rose
        b.   x gave z to y   *entails*   y received z
        c.   x persuaded y that P   *entails*   y came to believe that P

Jackendoff claims that to do this is to miss a generalization: namely that all such cases share the schema:

9.80   x cause E to occur   *entails*   E occur

In other words, there is a semantic element CAUSE which occurs in many lexical items and which, as a result, produces many entailment relations.

Jackendoff's work also shares the aims of Levin and others, as described in section 9.4, that semantic decomposition can be used to investigate the mapping between semantics and grammatical processes. We shall see later in this section examples of conceptual structure being used to describe grammatical rules and structures.

9.6.2   The semantic components

Jackendoff's work identifies an inventory of universal semantic categories, or concepts, which include: **Event, State, Material Thing** (or **Object**), **Path, Place** and **Property**.[9] At the level of conceptual structure a sentence is built up of these semantic categories. The two basic conceptual situations are **Event** and **State**, and if we look at examples of these, we can see something of the role of the other semantic components. We can show an example of an **Event** by looking at a sentence describing motion: 9.81 below gives first the syntactic structure, 9.81a, then the conceptual structure, 9.81b, of the same sentence *Bill went into the house* (Jackendoff 1992: 13):

9.81   a. $[_S [_{NP}$ Bill] $[_{VP} [_V$ went] $[_{PP} [_P$ into] $[_{NP}$ the house]]]]
        b. $[_{Event}$ GO $([_{Thing}$ BILL], $[_{Path}$ TO $([_{Place}$ IN $([_{Thing}$ HOUSE])])])]$

The structure in 9.81b concentrates on the semantics of motion and thus the entity (or 'Thing') *the house* is given as an unanalysed atom of meaning. Jackendoff is claiming here that the motion event in 9.81 has three main semantic categories: the motion itself, **Go**, which is then composed of two further categories: the entity or **Thing**, moving, and the trajectory, or **Path**, followed by the entity. This Path may have a destination or **Place**, where the motion ends. In 9.81 the motion is *went*, the Thing is *Bill*, the Path is *into the house*, and the Place is *the house*.

We can bring out the articulated nature of this semantic representation if we follow Pinker (1989) and represent 9.81 as a tree structure, where a mother node tells us the type of constituent, the leftmost daughter stands for the function and the other daughters are its arguments. This is shown

Figure 9.2   Conceptual structure of example 9.81 as a tree structure

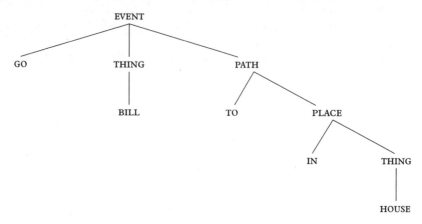

in figure 9.2. Thus Jackendoff's conceptual structure has a syntax of its own: semantic categories are built up from simpler elements by rules of combination. The conceptual structure in 9.81b is formed by such rules of combination. The elements GO, TO and IN, which describe movement, direction and location, act like functions in a semantic algebra, combining elements to form the major semantic categories. Thus the overall **Event** in 9.81b is formed by GO combining a **Thing** with a **Path** to form an event of a particular type: something moving in a direction. The category **Path** is formed by the element TO, combining with a **Place** to describe the direction (or trajectory) taken by the object. Lastly, the **Place** is formed by IN, called a **place-function**, combining with an entity (or 'thing') to describe an area inside the object which serves as the destination of the movement. Jackendoff paraphrases the conceptual structure in 9.81b as 'Bill traverses a path that terminates at the interior of the house.' (1992: 13).[10]

We can take 9.82a below as an example of a sentence describing a **State**, with its conceptual structure shown in 9.82b, and in tree form in figure 9.3.

Figure 9.3   Conceptual structure of example 9.82 as a tree structure

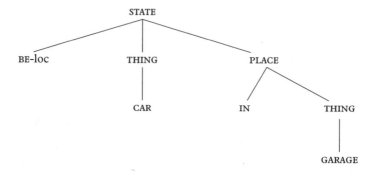

Figure 9.4   Conceptual structure of example 9.84 as a tree structure

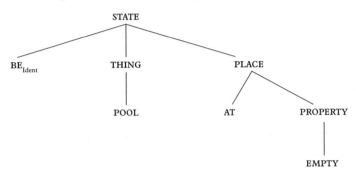

9.82   a.   [$_s$ [$_{NP}$ The car] [$_{VP}$ [$_V$ is] [$_{PP}$ [$_P$ in] [$_{NP}$ the garage]]]]

         b.   [$_{State}$ BE ([$_{Thing}$ CAR], [$_{Place}$ IN ([$_{Thing}$ GARAGE])])]

9.6.3   Localist semantic fields

Sentence 9.82 describes a state of being in a spatial **location,** and this is
reflected in Jackendoff (1990) by giving the semantic component BE a subscript to identify this subcategory of state: BE$_{Loc}$ is used for a **locational** BE
('be in a place'), giving us the conceptual structure in 9.83:

9.83   [$_{State}$ BE$_{Loc}$ ([$_{Thing}$ CAR], [$_{Place}$ IN ([$_{Thing}$ GARAGE])])]

We can compare this with an example of a state consisting of having a
property, which is represented by the **identifying** or **copulative** BE$_{Ident}$ in
9.84. Again, figure 9.4 shows the conceptual structure in tree format.

9.84   a.   [$_s$ [$_{NP}$ The pool] [$_{VP}$ [$_V$ is [$_{AP}$ [$_{ADJ}$ empty]]]]]

         b.   [$_{State}$ BE$_{Ident}$ ([$_{Thing}$ POOL], [$_{Place}$ AT ([$_{Property}$ EMPTY])])]

We can see that having a property is given a spatial interpretation in 9.84.
This is a version of the approach which we called **localism** in chapter 7.
In Jackendoff (1990) the function BE is used to represent four subcategories
of STATE, which Jackendoff calls **semantic fields.** These extend spatial
conceptualizations into non-spatial domains, as shown in the example sentences below:

9.85   a.   Carl is in the pub.

         b.   [$_{State}$ BE$_{Loc}$ ([$_{Thing}$ CARL], [$_{Place}$ IN ([$_{Thing}$ PUB])])]

9.86   a.   The party is on Saturday.

         b.   [$_{State}$ BE$_{Temp}$ ([$_{Thing}$ PARTY], [$_{Place}$ AT ([$_{Time}$ SATURDAY])])]

9.87   a.   The theatre is full.
        b.   [$_{\text{State}}$ BE$_{\text{Ident}}$ ([$_{\text{Thing}}$ THEATRE], [$_{\text{Place}}$ AT ([$_{\text{Property}}$ FULL])])]

9.88   a.   This book belongs to John.
        b.   [$_{\text{State}}$ BE$_{\text{Poss}}$ ([$_{\text{Thing}}$ BOOK], [$_{\text{Place}}$ AT ([$_{\text{Thing}}$ JOHN])])]

Example 9.85 shows the function BE$_{\text{Loc}}$ which represents location in space; 9.86 shows BE$_{\text{Temp}}$, which describes location in time; 9.87 shows BE$_{\text{Ident}}$ which represents the ascription of a property in locational terms; and in 9.88 we see BE$_{\text{Poss}}$ which represents possession as location. Thus the four kinds of state are given a localist interpretation.

The same four subcategories or semantic fields apply to Event functions like GO. Spatial GO$_{\text{Loc}}$ would be used to describe movement in space as in sentence 9.81, *Bill went into the house*; GO$_{\text{Temp}}$ would be used for movement in time, for example *The party has been moved from Saturday to Sunday*; GO$_{\text{Ident}}$ might be used for movement between properties, as in *Joan went from being depressed to being elated*; and GO$_{\text{Poss}}$ would represent a movement in possession like *The prize went to Kate*. So in this approach these four localist semantic fields **spatial location**, **temporal location**, **property ascription** and **possession** cross-classify the basic ontological categories of EVENT and STATE.

9.6.4   Complex events and states

A more complicated example of an **Event** would be sentence 9.89 below, where we see the semantic component CHANGE OF STATE, or INCHOATIVE (abbreviated to INCH), which operates as a function mapping a state into an event.

9.89   a.   [$_s$ [$_{\text{NP}}$ The pool] [$_{\text{VP}}$ [$_v$ emptied]]]
        b.   [$_{\text{Event}}$ INCH ([$_{\text{State}}$ BE$_{\text{Ident}}$ ([$_{\text{Thing}}$ POOL], [$_{\text{Place}}$ AT ([$_{\text{Property}}$ EMPTY])])])]

Here the event is the pool changing to the state of being empty.

A further complex event is created by the semantic function CAUSE, which maps an event into a further event, as in 9.90:

9.90   a.   John emptied the pool.
        b.   [$_{\text{Event}}$ CAUSE ([$_{\text{Thing}}$ JOHN], [$_{\text{Event}}$ INCH ([$_{\text{State}}$ BE$_{\text{Ident}}$ ([$_{\text{Thing}}$ POOL], [$_{\text{Place}}$ AT ([$_{\text{Property}}$ EMPTY])])])])]

We might paraphrase 9.90 by saying that the complex event is that John caused the event of the pool changing to the state of being empty.

The structure of the events and states we have seen so far can be represented in formation rules like 9.91 below, where we collapse the various subclasses of GO and BE:

9.91   a.   [EVENT]   →   [$_\text{Event}$ GO ([THING], [PATH])]
        b.   [STATE]   →   [$_\text{State}$ BE ([THING], [PLACE])]
        c.   [PATH]   →   [TO ([PLACE])]
        d.   [PLACE]   →   [IN ([THING])]
        e.   [PLACE]   →   [AT ([TIME])]
        f.   [PLACE]   →   [AT ([PROPERTY])]
        g.   [PLACE]   →   [AT ([THING])]
        h.   [EVENT]   →   [$_\text{Event}$ INCH ([STATE])]
        i.   [EVENT]   →   [$_\text{Event}$ CAUSE ([THING], [EVENT])]

These rules exemplify the conceptual elements identified in Jackendoff (1990). Each type of rule in 9.91 would of course need to be extended for further English examples. For example 9.91d expands PLACE into a complex expression: a place-function IN which defines a region of its THING argument, its interior. Other place-functions would include UNDER, OVER, AROUND, etc. which define other regions with respect to their arguments.

Having seen something of the composition of conceptual structures, we look next at one category in more detail: the category **Thing**.

9.6.5   THINGS: Semantic classes of nominals

So, to repeat, in this approach semantic components break down into smaller, simpler semantic components. We can see this clearly if we look at some properties of the category **Thing**, that is, at the semantics of nouns. We can begin with Jackendoff's semantic feature [±BOUNDED]. This distinguishes, for example, between count nouns like *banana* or *car*, and mass nouns like *water* or *oxygen*. The idea is that count nouns are basically units: if we divide up a banana or a car, by slicing or dismantling, we don't get further instances of the basic unit. We can't call each of the pieces a *banana* or a *car*. Mass nouns, on the other hand, are not units and can be divided into further instances of themselves: if you divide a gallon of water into eight pints, each of the eight pints can still be called *water*. This is reflected by describing count nouns as [+BOUNDED], or [+b], and mass nouns as [−BOUNDED], or [−b].

Plurals of count nouns, on the other hand, act like mass nouns in many ways. They occur with similar determiners, for example:

9.92   Singular count nouns
        a.   She offered me a banana.   [with *a*]
        b.   I didn't get a banana.   [with *a*]

9.93   Plural count and mass nouns
        a.   She offered me water/bananas.   [with no article]
        b.   I didn't get any water/any bananas. [with *any*]

Figure 9.5 Semantic classes of nominals

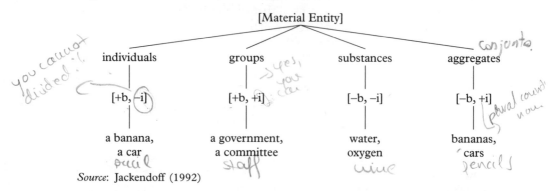

Source: Jackendoff (1992)

Count plurals can also be divided into their composite units. These plural count nouns are of course different from mass nouns in being composed of individual units and Jackendoff proposes a feature ±INTERNAL STRUCTURE to distinguish between the two types: plural count nouns are +INTERNAL STRUC-TURE, or [+i], while mass nouns are −INTERNAL STRUCTURE, or [−i].

What is happening here is that nouns are being cross-classified by these two semantic features. One further type is possible: a collective noun like *the Government* contains individual units – its members – and therefore is like a plural and [+i]; however, if we do divide it, we cannot call each of the results a *government*, and thus it is bounded, [+b]. The resulting typology of semantic classes of nouns is in figure 9.5 with the matching of these to noun classes being as follows:

9.94   *individuals*:   count nouns
        groups: collective nouns
        substances: mass nouns
        aggregates: plural nouns

9.6.6 Cross-category generalizations

One aspect of this use of these semantic features is typical of Jackendoff's work: a feature like [±BOUNDED] doesn't just cross-classify nouns: it is also used to describe verbs. Thus verbs which describe on-going processes that are not overtly limited in time, are analysed as [−b]. An example is *sleep*, as in 9.95:

9.95   John is sleeping.

Verbs which describe events with clearly defined beginnings and ends are classified as [+b], like the verb *cough* in 9.96, which is a very short, limited, event:

9.96   John coughed.

We discussed the way that different verbs describe different types of event in chapter 5, where we used the term **situation type** to describe it. Thus Jackendoff is making the interesting claim that there are common conceptual elements to both number in nouns and situation type in verbs.

9.6.7 Processes of semantic combination

We have already seen Jackendoff's claim for the advantages of semantic components in accounting for semantic inference. Jackendoff also employs his conceptual primitives to investigate the relationship between semantics and grammar, in a similar way to the work of the linguists described in section 9.4. We can briefly look at some examples.

When we discussed situation type in chapter 5 we noted the fact that in English some combinations of a semelfactive verb and a durative adverbial do not result in an anomalous sentence but are given instead an iterative interpretation, e.g.

9.97   a.   The beacon flashed.
          b.   The beacon flashed for two minutes.

Thus sentence 9.97a describes a single flash; however, adding the durative adverbial *for two minutes* as in 9.97b does not extend this single flash over the period but describes a series of flashes. The way Jackendoff (1992) approaches this process is to view it in terms of levels of embedding in conceptual structure. Introducing a durative adverbial is taken to have the effect of taking an unbounded event, like 9.98a below, and producing a bounded event, like 9.98b:

9.98   a.   Ronan read.
          b.   Ronan read until 5 a.m.

However in an iterative sentence like:

9.99   The beacon flashed until 5 a.m.

the adverbial *until 5 a.m.* is taking an inherently bounded event and producing a further bounded, multiple event. Jackendoff describes this as involving a rule of construal that inserts a PLURAL (PL) component as an intermediate level between the two events, as in 9.100.

9.100
$$
\begin{bmatrix}
+b \\[2pt]
\text{until}\quad
\begin{bmatrix}
-b \\[2pt]
\text{pl}\quad
\begin{bmatrix}
\begin{bmatrix}
+b \\
\text{beacon flashed} \\
\text{Event}
\end{bmatrix}
\end{bmatrix}, \ [5\ \text{am}] \\[2pt]
\text{Event}
\end{bmatrix} \\[2pt]
\text{Event}
\end{bmatrix}
$$

This is a simplified version of the sentence's conceptual structure; Jackendoff (1992) gives a more formal and detailed account of this and similar analyses of situation type and aspect.

This account is part of a larger enterprise to provide a semantic account of a range of morphological and syntactic processes of combination. If we look at nouns, for example, these combinatory processes include plural formation, the construction of compounds like *chicken curry*, and the various semantic uses of *of*-constructions, as in *a grain of rice, a wall of the house, a house of bricks*, etc. Staying with the features [±BOUNDED] and [±INTERNAL STRUCTURE], Jackendoff (1992) proposes six combinatory functions which map features of [*b*] and [*i*] together. These are divided into two types as in 9.101 below:

9.101   Including functions   Extracting functions
           plural (PL)   **element of** (ELT)
           composed of (COMP)   **partitive** (PART)
           containing (CONT)   **universal grinder** (GR)

The headings **including** and **extracting** in 9.101 identify two different types of part–whole relation that results from the process of combination: the including functions map their arguments into a larger entity containing the argument as a part, while the extracting functions pull out a sub-entity of their arguments. We can see these characteristics if we look briefly at these functions in turn.

The **plural function**, for example, reflects the process of pluralizing nouns and changes their feature specifications for boundedness and internal structure, for example:

9.102   brick [+b, −i]   →   bricks [−b, +i]

The semantic representation for the plural noun *bricks* is represented as in 9.103 below:

9.103
$$
\begin{bmatrix}
-b, +i \\
pl \quad \begin{bmatrix} \begin{bmatrix} +b, -i \\ brick \\ Mat \end{bmatrix} \end{bmatrix} \\
Mat
\end{bmatrix}
$$

This diagram represents the fact that the plural function (PL) has overridden the original [+b, −i] specification of *brick*.

If we move to the second including function **composed of** (COMP), we can take as an example the nominal *a house of wood*, which is given the representation below:

9.104
$$\begin{bmatrix} \text{+b, } -\text{i} \\ \text{house} \\ \text{comp} \begin{bmatrix} \begin{bmatrix} -\text{b, } -\text{i} \\ \text{wood} \\ \text{Mat} \end{bmatrix} \end{bmatrix} \\ \text{Mat} \end{bmatrix}$$

Here COMP links an individual entity *house*, [+b, −i], with a substance *wood*, [−b, −i], and the whole unit has the semantic features of the grammatical head of the construction, *house*. An example of where the COMP function links an individual with a plural aggregate is in 9.105 below, where the semantic structure of a *house of bricks* is shown:

9.105
$$\begin{bmatrix} \text{+b, } -\text{i} \\ \text{house} \\ \text{comp} \begin{bmatrix} -\text{b, } +\text{i} \\ \text{pl} \begin{bmatrix} \begin{bmatrix} +\text{b, } -\text{i} \\ \text{brick} \\ \text{Mat} \end{bmatrix} \end{bmatrix} \\ \text{Mat} \end{bmatrix} \\ \text{Mat} \end{bmatrix}$$

Here we can see the effect of the two semantic processes PL and COMP on the features [±b] and [±i]. Once again the construction as a whole has the features of the head, *house*. This function is also used to reflect uses where a mass noun like *coffee, tea* or *beer* is used as a count noun, as for example in 9.106 below:

9.106   a. I'll have a coffee.
          b. Table four want three coffees and two teas.
          c. Me, drunk? I've only had three beers.

Here the interpretation of *a coffee* is of course 'a unit of coffee', where the unit is some contextually appropriate one, perhaps a cup. Calling this rule which allows the counting of mass nouns **the universal packager**, Jackendoff argues for a parallel with the combination of the durative adverbial and semelfactive verb described earlier. In the case of *a cup of coffee*, the incompatibility of the indefinite article with a mass noun triggers a rule of construal, inserting the operator COMP, which causes the reading 'a portion composed of coffee'. The quantifiers *two* and *three* and the plural endings in 9.106b and c trigger the same process.

The third including function is **containing** (CONT), which is used to describe compound nominals like *chicken curry* or *cheese sandwich*, where the first element describes an important, identifying element of the second. In examples like *chicken curry*, the CONT function does not change the values of the features, mapping the mass nouns, i.e. [−b, −i], *chicken* and *curry* into the [−b, −i] compound *chicken curry*.

If we move on to the three extracting functions: **element of** (ELT) describes the semantics of phrases like *a grain of rice* and *a stick of spaghetti*,
where the first noun picks out an individual from the aggregate described
by the second noun, creating overall a count noun. The second function
partitive (PART) describes the semantics of partitive constructions, N of
NP, like *leg of the table* or *top of the mountain*, where the phrase identifies a
bounded part (the first noun) of a larger bounded entity (the second NP).
These constructions often have semantically equivalent compound nominals
like *table leg* or *mountain top*. The final extracting function, with the rather
strange name of **universal grinder**, is used for instances where what are
usually count nouns are used to describe substances, as in Jackendoff's
unpleasant example 9.107 below:

9.107   There was dog all over the road.

Here using a count noun *dog* without an article triggers a rule of construal
where *dog* loses its boundedness and is construed as a substance. We can see
this perhaps as the opposite process to COMP in *I'll have a coffee* where a
mass noun (i.e. a substance) is interpreted as a count noun. This GR function also allows us to use animal names for their meat as in 9.108 below:

9.108   a.   Have you ever eaten *crocodile*?
           b.   *Impala* tastes just like mutton.

From these examples we can see that Jackendoff's approach, like the work
of Levin, Rappaport Hovav, Pinker, and the other writers cited in section
9.4, uses lexical decomposition to investigate the semantics–grammar interface. Jackendoff's approach in particular presents a view of semantic primitives occurring in highly articulated semantic representations. In this theory
these representations are proposed as conceptual structures underlying linguistic behaviour.

9.7   Pustejovsky's Generative Lexicon

James Pustejovsky (in particular 1992, 1995) has proposed a compositional
account of lexical semantics which is broadly in sympathy with the Jackendoff
approach described in the last section, but which both extends the
compositional representation in some areas and incorporates more general
or encyclopedic knowledge into the account. The central thrust of this
approach is computational. Pustejovsky argues that lexical meaning is best
accounted for by a dynamic approach including rules of combination and
inference, rather than the essentially lexicographic tradition of listing senses
of a lexeme, as we described in chapter 3. Pustejovsky (1995: 61) proposes
four levels of semantic representations for lexical items, as shown below:

9.109   a.   Argument structure: the semantic arguments of an item and
               the linking rules to syntax
          b.   Event structure: the situation type of an item
          c.   Qualia structure: a classification of the properties of an item
          d.   Lexical inheritance structure: how the item fits into the network
               of the lexicon

In our discussion we will concentrate on two of these representations and
two grammatical categories: event structure and verbs, and qualia structure
and nouns.

9.7.1 Event structure

Pustejovsky provides a compositional account of the situation type distinctions we discussed in chapter 5. There we reviewed several classifications
systems, including Vendler's (1967) influential division into states, activities,
accomplishments and achievements. As we saw, these distinctions are viewed
as part of the lexical semantics of verbs. We saw in the last section that
Jackendoff includes semantic components of event structure in his representations, namely EVENT and STATE, with constituent components of CHANGE
(INCHOATION) and CAUSE. These categories combine in semantic representations with other categories like THING and PLACE. As we shall see, Pustejovsky
argues for finer distinctions among situation types and for a level of event
structure distinct from other semantic information.

   In this literature the term **event structure** is used for what we have called
situation type, that is, for the lexically encoded aspectual distinctions in
verbs. Since events in this use also include states, a more neutral term like
Bach's **eventualities** (Bach 1986) might be preferable, but we will continue to
use the term event structure in the present discussion. As we saw in chapter
5, a verb's event structure is modified as it combines with other elements,
including noun phrases and adverbials, to build verb phrases and sentences.

   A major feature of Pustejovsky's approach is the claim that events are
composed of smaller events (sub-events) and that this relationship needs to
be represented in an articulated way, by a form of syntax. We can briefly
review from Pustejovsky (1991: 56f.) how the three main event types that
he identifies are represented:

9.110   States (S) are single events that are evaluated relative to no other
          event, represented as:

$$
\begin{array}{c}
S \\
| \\
e
\end{array}
$$

Examples are stative verbs like *understand, love, be tall*.

9.111   Processes (P) are sequences of events identifying the same semantic expression, represented as:

Examples are verbs like *sing, walk, swim*.

9.112   Transitions (T) are events identifying a semantic expression that is evaluated relative to its opposition, represented as follows (where *E* is a variable for any event type):

Examples are verbs like *open, close, build*.

These representations just give information about event structure. This event structure (ES) representation is united with other semantic information at two other levels: a level of logic-like predicate decomposition called LCS and an interface level which incorporates lexical semantic elements but maintains the event structure more transparently, called LCS'. The relations between them can be shown in the causative/inchoative alternations *John closed the door/The door closed*:

9.113   a.   The door closed.
         b.   ES:

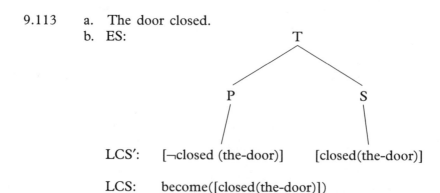

9.114   a. John closed the door.
         b. ES:

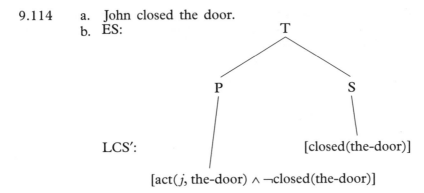

LCS':   [closed(the-door)]

[act(j, the-door) ∧ ¬closed(the-door)]

LCS: cause([act(j, the-door)], become([closed(the-door)]))

The corresponding state is shown in 9.115:

9.115   a. The door is closed.
         b. ES: S

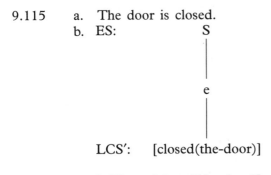

LCS':   [closed(the-door)]

LCS: [closed(the-door)]

These diagrams show the claim that inchoative and causative versions of the verb *close* represent a transition from the state of being not-closed to its opposite, being closed. In Vendler terms, the inchoative *close* is an achieve-ment and the causative *close* is an accomplishment. The difference is here recognized by the presence or absence of an agent acting on the changing entity (*John* is the agent in the example above). There is no other structural distinction between these two event types.

One main justification for this type of sub-event structural description is that it allows the recognition of regular differences in adverbial interpreta-tion, such as the ambiguity in 9.116a, shown by the paraphrases in b and c:

9.116   a. Joan rudely departed.
         b. Joan departed in a rude way.
         c. It was rude of Joan to depart.

The representations in 9.113–15 above allow such differences to be analysed as adverbial scope over a sub-event rather than the whole event: narrow scope versus wide scope readings. Pustejovsky (1991) proposes that the interpretation in 9.116b is a result of the adverb having scope over the process sub-event, shown below:

9.117   ES:

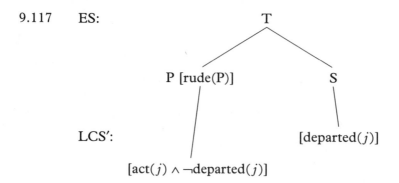

The interpretation in 9.116c, on the other hand, has the adverb taking wide scope over the whole event, shown as:

9.118   ES:

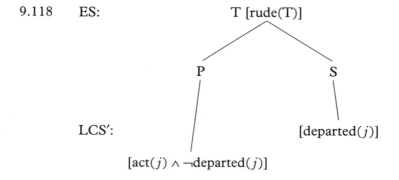

Thus the ambiguity of adverbial interpretation is given a structural account.

Another related example discussed by Pustejovsky (1991) and Alsina (1999) in this approach concerns an ambiguity of interpretation with *almost* that occurs in accomplishments but not in other event types.[11] To use Alsina's cruel example, *John almost killed the cat* has the two readings: John's action resulted in the near-death of the cat and John nearly undertook an action that would have killed the cat. In the former *almost* has scope over the resulting State, while in the latter *almost* has scope over the Process.[12] This account correctly predicts that an achievement verb like *walk* will have only one reading, the 'nearly undertook the action' reading, as in *I almost walked*, because there is only one undifferentiated event constituent in the event structure (as in diagram 9.111 earlier).

The essential claim made by this approach is that a representation which does not have access to sub-events, such as the activity and state sub-events above, will lack explanatory power.

9.7.2   Qualia structure

In his treatment of nouns Pustejovsky claims that listing senses in a dictionary, making what he terms Sense Enumeration Lexicons (Pustejovsky 1995),
cannot adequately account for polysemy. He discusses examples like the
variation in the meaning of *good* in *a good meal, good soccer player, good book,
good husband* or *fast* in *a fast car, fast driver, fast decision, fast food* etc. As we
discussed in chapter 3, there are two traditional approaches to such variation:
we can decide that there are a number of related senses here or alternatively
that these adjectives are simply vague, so that *good*, for example, is simply
a general term of approbation whose meaning must be derived by contextual
rules of inference. Pustejovsky argues for a variation of the multiple senses
approach and against an explanation via general reasoning. His arguments
are firstly that any inferences must rely on linguistic information in the
accompanying nouns and secondly that the variation is systematic, with
different classes of items patterning together. However, rather than treating
this by listing senses Pustejovsky views the variants as products of specific
rules of semantic composition tied to systematic properties of the lexical
item. These properties are called **qualia** (plural of the Latin noun *qale* 'quality,
nature') in this theory.

  Although all types of words have a qualia structure, we concentrate our
discussion on nouns. Qualia structure has four dimensions, viewed as roles,
shown below with characteristic values for nominals:

9.119   Qualia Structure (Pustejovsky 1995: 85)
         a.   CONSTITUTIVE: the relation between an object and its constitu-
              ents, or proper parts.
              For example: i. Material ii. Weight iii. Parts and component
              elements.
         b.   FORMAL: that which distinguishes the object within a larger
              domain.
              For example: i. Orientation ii. Magnitude iii. Shape iv.
              Dimensionality v. Colour vi. Position.
         c.   TELIC: the purpose and function of the object.
              For example: i. Purpose that an agent has in performing
              an act. ii. Built-in function or aim which specifies certain
              activities.
         d.   AGENTIVE: factors involved in the origin or 'bringing about' of
              an object.
              For example: i. Creator ii. Artefact iii. Natural kind iv. Causal
              chain.

Without going into the formal detail we can sketch how the knowledge
about nouns represented by qualia can be used to account for polysemy.
One example is the different interpretations of *bake* in the following:

9.120   a.   Joan baked the potato.
         b.   Joan baked the cake.

In 9.120a the verb has a change-of-state interpretation while in b it has an additional creation sense, i.e. the act of baking creates a cake that didn't exist previously. For Pustejovsky this polysemy is explained by rules of combination between the verb and noun. The verb itself has only one meaning: it entails a change of state. The difference between a and b above results from the qualia structures of the nominals. The noun *cake* will have as part of its agentive role that it is created by an act of baking by an agent, i.e. that it is an artefact. The verb *bake* will have as part of its agentive qualia that it describes an act of baking by an agent. When the verb and noun combine to form a verb phrase, their qualia structures merge and unite the two representations of the baking event to form the creation interpretation. In other words it is the unification of qualia structures between verb and this particular type of object that produces the creation reading. In this view an extended meaning is created by rules of composition. Hence we gain a dynamic view of polysemy which specifies the context for the extended reading. For technical details see Pustejovsky (1995: 122–5).

A further example is the variations in meanings of adjectives like *fast* and *good* mentioned earlier. Pustejovky's approach is to treat these as modifiers of events (event predicates) and therefore applicable to events represented in the qualia structure of nominals that they combine with. The noun *typist* is given the qualia structure below:

9.121
$$
\begin{bmatrix}
\textbf{typist} \\
\text{ARGSTR} = [\text{ARG}\,1 = \textbf{x:human}] \\
\text{QUALIA} = \begin{bmatrix} \text{FORMAL} = \text{x} \\ \text{TELIC} = \textbf{type(e, x)} \end{bmatrix}
\end{bmatrix}
$$

The combination of argument and qualia structure tells us that the activity associated with this noun is an event of a human being typing. Combining this noun with the event modifier *fast* will automatically give the reading that a fast typist types fast.

Similarly the qualia structure for *knife* is given as:

9.122
$$
\begin{bmatrix}
\textbf{knife} \\
\text{ARGSTR} = [\text{ARG}\,1 = \textbf{x:tool}] \\
\text{QUALIA} = \begin{bmatrix} \text{FORMAL} = \text{x} \\ \text{TELIC} = \textbf{cut(e, x, y)} \end{bmatrix}
\end{bmatrix}
$$

The telic quale tells us that a knife is used for cutting. Treating *good* as an event predicate means it can apply to this event of cutting incorporated in representation of this noun, ensuring that a good knife is one that cuts well. This of course generalizes across other adjectives and nouns, ensuring that a good driver drives well, a slow runner runs slowly, etc. Once again variation in interpretations, this time in adjectives, is triggered by specific types of knowledge represented in the nouns with which they combine.

This sketch is necessarily only suggestive but we hope that the general approach to polysemy in this theory is clear. It is accounted for by dynamic rules of combination, unifying different forms of knowledge represented in lexical entries. It is possible to discern a distant, and dynamic, family resemblance here to the use of selectional restrictions in the Katzian semantics that we described at the beginning of this chapter.

9.8 Problems with Components of Meaning

The compositional approaches we have been looking at have been criticized in two important ways. The first concerns the identification of semantic primitives. These primitives have been attacked from both philosophical and psychological perspectives. The former (e.g. J. A. Fodor 1970, Fodor et al. 1980) claims that these semantic components are simply a variation of, and equivalent to, the necessary and sufficient conditions approach to word meaning that we discussed in chapter 2. As we saw there, it proves impossible to agree on precise definitions of word meaning. The resulting practical problems for the decompositional semanticist include knowing how to validate any proposed set of primitives, and when to stop identifying them, i.e. knowing what are the right features and how many is enough.

There have also been psychological criticisms, for example J. D. Fodor et al. (1975), which claim that there is no experimental evidence for semantic primitives. Though there is not a large literature on the topic, some experiments have shown little or no support for varying degrees of internal complexity in words. These studies seem to show that in processing language we seem to treat words as atoms of meaning, and therefore do not divide them into subcomponents in order to understand them.[13]

The second focus for attack has been on the use of metalanguages. As we have seen, there have been various proposals, using a range of symbols and diagrams. The criticism has been that these devices are *ad hoc* and unsystematic: at best another arbitrary language; at worst, a kind of garbled version of the English, French, etc. of the writer. This criticism is related to the more serious philosophical criticism that attaching a set of primitives to a word or phrase is not a semantic analysis in the deepest sense. We can recall the point discussed in chapter 2, deriving from observations by the philosopher W. V. O. Quine, that this is in effect a form of translation into another language, a language of primitive elements which is sometimes pejoratively called **Markerese**, after Lewis (1972), by linguists making this point. The claim is that to translate from the object language into an arbitrary invented language doesn't advance semantic analysis very far, if you then have to translate the metalanguage. If the process doesn't have an anchor in reality, the criticism goes, it is merely circular.[14] As we said earlier, the basic idea is that since the expressions of language are symbols, they must be **grounded** somehow. This grounding may be of different types: in the next chapter we shall see how **formal semanticists** attempt to ground semantic analysis in the external world; and in chapter 11 we will see an attempt by **cognitive semanticists** to ground their analyses in primitive-level concepts derived from bodily experience. But, the criticism goes, the type of componential analysis we have reviewed in this chapter begs the question of such grounding.

To decompositional semanticists, none of these attacks seems fatal. Responses to the psychological attack, e.g. Jackendoff (1990: 37ff.), point out that we would expect words to be the relevant unit for processing, not components. After all, goes this reply, that's why semantic features are bunched into word units: because these particular bunchings have cognitive utility, i.e. they are useful sizes and mixtures for thinking and talking about the world. In reply to the complaint about the never-ending identification of primitives, these linguists tend to claim that this is an empirical question, not solvable in advance by stipulation, e.g.

> 9.123   there should eventually come a point when increasing the complexity of a semantic theory by adding new markers no longer yields enough advantage in precision and scope to warrant the increase. At that point the system of markers should reflect the systematic features of the semantic structure of the language. (Katz and Fodor 1963: 190)

Or we might note the response in Jackendoff (1990: 4) where he makes a comparison with physics, where physicists haven't worried about identifying smaller and smaller particles, if there is sufficient justification for them.

Responses to the criticism of metalanguages have varied: some semanticists agree with it and conduct their inquiry through the medium of a natural language like English, see for example Wierzbicka (1980), and Allan (1986: 265–70) for discussion. This is in effect to give up the search for a neutral metalanguage. Another response is to rely more firmly on tried and tested metalanguages from other disciplines like logic, as in Dowty (1979).[15] Still others, like Jackendoff, rely on empirical justification for the formalisms they use: in this view the machinery is justified to the extent it allows the analyst to capture significant generalizations.

9.9   Summary

In this chapter we have reviewed the proposal that semantic representation should involve semantic components. These components are primitive elements which combine to form units at the level of grammar. The nature of their combination differs from author to author: from, for example, the original Katz and Fodor listings of components at the word level to the more articulated representations used by Jackendoff, where the components are arranged as functions and arguments which can be successively embedded within one another, and Pustejovsky, who proposes a syntax of event structure.

Linguists have argued that these components help characterize semantic relations: both lexical relations and sentential relations like entailment. As we have seen, they have also been used to investigate the semantic basis for morphological and syntactic processes. From the viewpoint of linguistic analysis these are claims that such components are important units at the level of semantics. From a wider perspective the question arises: are these components psychologically real? Do they form part of our cognitive structures? For some linguists, like Jackendoff, the answer is yes. These elements play a role in our thinking and by identifying them correctly we are establishing meaning.

FURTHER READING

A detailed discussion of Katz's semantic theory is in Allan (1986). A special edition of the journal *Cognition*, containing an interesting range of work in decompositional semantics, was published as Levin and Pinker (1992). Pustejovsky (1993) contains contributions from a wide range of approaches, including work in computational linguistics. For discussions of the role of semantic properties of verbs in their grammatical behaviour see Pinker (1989) and Levin (1993). An example of the use of semantic components to investigate the semantics–syntax interface is Levin and Rappaport Hovav (1995). For an introduction to Jackendoff's work, see his *Semantic Structures* (1990). For Pustejovky's notion of a generative lexicon see his (1995) book. A collection of papers on event structure, some using approaches described in this chapter, is in Tenny and Pustejovsky (2000). Mohanan and Wee (1999) is a collection of papers that investigate the semantics–grammar interface via decompositional approaches. For an influential attack on componential approaches see J. A. Fodor (1981b).

EXERCISES

9.1 Use **semantic components** to characterize the semantic relations between the following words:

mother father daughter son sister brother grandmother grandfather granddaughter grandson uncle aunt cousin nephew niece

Discuss whether a **binary format** would be an advantage for the semantic components you decide on.

9.2   In chapter 6 we met the argument structure alternation in English called **Dative Alternation**, where some verbs, such as *give*, allow both of the patterns below:

    a.   Aideen gave the shoes to her neighbour.
          [NP_X - V - NP_Z - *to* NP_Y]
    b.   Aideen gave her neighbour the shoes.
          [NP_X - V - NP_Y - NP_Z]

This alternation seems to be restricted to certain semantic subclasses of verbs. We can adapt from Pinker (1989: 110ff.) an initial hypothesis to distinguish two semantic verb classes, as follows:

(1)   Class 1a: the *give*-class: verbs whose semantic structure is 'X causes Y to have Z', e.g. *Paul gave some money to the beggar*.

        Class 1b: the *send*-class: verbs which share the basic semantic structure of (1a) but where the change of possession involves separation in time and/or space, which X tries to bridge by a means of transfer, e.g. *Harry sent the check to his wife*.

(2)   Class 2:   the *carry*-class: verbs whose semantic structure is 'X moves Z to Y in a certain manner', e.g. *He carried the books to the clerk*.

The difference between classes 1 and 2 can be viewed in terms of CHANGE OF POSSESSION. In class 1a verbs this change is a necessary part of the meaning. In Class 1b verbs the change is intended though not necessary (we can say *I sent her the letter but she never got it* unlike **I gave her the money but she never got it*); while in class 2 verbs Y's taking possession of Z is simply not part of the verb's meaning, although it may occur incidentally. We could then postulate a condition on Dative Alternation: class 1 verbs allow Dative Alternation but class 2 verbs do not. Thus we find *Paul gave the beggar some money, Harry sent his wife the check* but not **Mary carried the clerk the books*.

   For the following verbs, decide which of these semantic classes they belong to and whether our prediction about Dative Alternation works. If not, discuss any further semantic qualification that might be necessary, for example, are there further classes to be set up; and if so, how would you characterize them?

mail, push, kick, pass, sell, lower, hand, push, flip, throw, bring, haul, ferry, take.

9.3 **Dative Alternation** also occurs with some verbs of communication. Once again we can set up semantic classes to try to explain which verbs show the alternation and which do not:

  a. Class 3: the *tell*-class: verbs whose semantic structure is 'X causes Y to cognitively possess Z', where 'cognitively possess' includes Y knowing, perceiving, learning, etc. Z. For example: *Joan told the answer to Kate*.

  b. Class 4: the *shout*-class: verbs whose semantic structure is 'X communicates Z to Y in a certain manner', e.g. *Joan shouted the answer to Kate*.

Pinker (1989) calls class 3 'illocutionary verbs of communication' because the verb gives information about what kind of illocutionary act the speaker intends. Thus *tell* in our example signals a **representative** act in the terminology of Searle (1976), discussed in chapter 8. Pinker (1989) and Levin (1993) follow Zwicky (1971) in calling class 4 verbs 'manner of speaking' verbs. We could claim that class 3 verbs show the Dative Alternation, *Joan told Kate the answer*; while class 4 verbs do not, **Joan shouted Kate the answer*.

As in the last exercise, examine the verbs below and decide to which of these two semantic classes they belong and whether our prediction about Dative Alternation works. Again, for any problematic cases, discuss whether you would add qualifications to our characterization of the classes above, or set up further semantic classes.

  teach, read, whisper, mention, quote, murmur, say, show, scream, yell, cite.

9.4 The alternation **Dative Alternation** also occurs with examples like the one below:

  a. She bought a car for her daughter.
   [NP$_X$ - V - NP$_Z$ - *for* NP$_Y$]
  b. She bought her daughter a car.
   [NP$_X$ - V - NP$_Y$ - NP$_Z$]

These structures are called **benefactive** structures because X performs the action of the verb for the benefit of Y. Using your own examples, discuss whether this benefactive Dative Alternation exhibits the same restrictions that we saw in exercises 9.1 and 9.2, i.e. is the alternation determined by a verb's membership of a semantic class?

9.5   Levin (1993), reporting on several earlier studies, notes that there seems to be a further type of lexical constraint on Dative Alternation: verbs derived from Latin roots do not undergo the alternation, even when they belong to the right semantic class. See for example 1 and 2 below which parallel verbs in exercises 9.2 and 9.3:

1   a.   He gave the books to the college.
     b.   He gave the college the books.
     c.   He donated the books to the college.
     d.   *He donated the college the books.

2   a.   He told the news to his father.
     b.   He told his father the news.
     c.   He communicated the news to his father.
     d.   *He communicated his father the news.

Using your own examples, investigate the range of this constraint on the semantic verb classes allowing Dative Alternation. If you find exceptions, do they form a coherent class or classes?

9.6   In this chapter we reviewed Talmy's (1985) investigations of how semantic components of motion events (Figure, Ground, Motion, Path, Manner) are conflated in verbs. Croft (1991a) discusses the example 1 below:

1   The boat sailed into the cave.

where the verb *sailed* conflates both the Manner and the Motion. Croft compares this with 2:

2   The boat burned into the cave.

where this cannot mean that the boat entered the cave whilst burning. Croft's explanation is that the Manner and Motion can only be conflated in the same verb when the Manner causes the Motion. So in 1 sailing causes the motion into the cave; but in 2 burning does not.
        Now look at the following English examples, where the verb is in bold. How many of these fit in with Croft's generalization? If

any do not, try to establish what other semantic factors might be at work.

   3 a. They **waltzed** onto the balcony.
       b. The wind **howled** through the trees.
       c. The grenade **bounced** into the bunker.
       d. The ball **thudded** into his chest.
       e. We **cycled** along the canal.
       f. The cart **creaked** along the path.
       g. The jet **flashed** across the sky.
       h. The bees **swarmed** into the kitchen.

9.7   We mentioned tests to distinguish between singular count nouns (typically representing individuals) and mass nouns (typically representing substances). One such test is **divisibility**: if you divide an example of the noun into, say quarters, can the same name be applied to each part? The answer is yes for mass nouns, and no for singular count nouns. Another test is occurrence with **determiners** like *a* and *some*, for example in a frame like *I brought X*. Compare the singular count noun in a with the mass noun in b:

    a. I brought **a saucepan**.
    b. I brought **rice/some rice**.

Use these tests to classify the following nouns as singular count nouns or mass nouns:

    racoon, barley, computer, manure, waiter, chair, soil.

What problems do the following nouns cause for these tests?

    Type 1: beer, coffee, tea, icecream, lemonade.
    Type 2: chicken, turkey, ham, potato, carrot.

[handwritten note: used determiners in order not to be a substance.]

Try to provide some further examples of these two types.

9.8   Using the format for Jackendoff's conceptual structure described in section 9.6, provide a conceptual structure for each of the following sentences:

    a. Maura has a cold.
    b. Her birthday is on Thursday.
    c. John went out of the room.

> d. The house is Helen's.
> e. The cat is on the roof.
> f. The legacy went to a dog's home.

9.9 Using the same format, provide a Jackendoff-style conceptual structure for the following sentences:

> 1 a. The window is closed.
>   b. The window closed.

> 2 a. Peg became angry.
>   b. Bob angered Peg.

> 3 a. George had the money.
>   b. George gave the money to Cindy.

> 4 a. The prisoners walked into the yard.
>   b. The guards walked the prisoners into the yard.

NOTES

1   J. D. Fodor (1983) provides a good overview of Katz and Fodor's theory. See also Katz (1987) for a more recent discussion of this approach.

2   See Allan (1986, vol. 1: 274–391) for a very detailed description of the evolution of the theory and the resulting changes in dictionary entries.

3   We discussed middle constructions in chapter 6. As described there, 'argument structure alternation' is a term used to describe processes which change the usual matching of semantic roles and grammatical positions. So in 9.20a we find *shirts*, which would normally be the object of a verb like *wash*, occurring as the subject.

4   A view shared by other writers, like Jackendoff (1990, 1992) whose work we discuss below, and Pustejovsky (1995).

5   Pinker (1989) calls this thematic role the 'state changer' argument, while Rappaport and Levin (1985) call it the 'displaced theme'. These terms are used because these elements are not simple instruments but carry a role we might paraphrase as: 'entities which by being moved cause a change of state in something to/from which they are moved'.

6   This term **unmarked** comes from **markedness theory**. This is a theory of naturalness where the more marked an element is, the less natural it is. This notion can be applied both within a language, as in this case, or cross-linguistically, as when we say, for example, that back rounded vowels like French [u] in *tout* [tu] 'all', are less marked than front rounded vowels like French [y] in *tu* [ty] 'you'. This implies that back rounded vowels are commoner in the languages of the world, will be learned earlier by children, are less

likely to be lost in language change or in language disorders, etc. See Jakobson (1968) for discussion.

7   'It is widely assumed, and I will take for granted, that the basic units out of which a sentential concept is constructed are the concepts expressed by the words in the sentence, that is *lexical* concepts' (Jackendoff 1990: 9).

8   We discussed this notion of entailment in chapter 4.

9   See Jackendoff (1990: 43; 1992: 13ff.) for further details.

10 Verbs of motion have received a lot of attention in the semantics literature: see for example Miller and Johnson-Laird (1976) and Talmy (1975, 1983, 1985).

11 These and similar scope ambiguities are discussed in a formal approach by Dowty (1979).

12 Alsina (1999) in fact claims a third reading for this sentence: a wide scope interpretation. He distinguishes this with the explanation: for example John shoots at the cat intending to kill it, but misses.

13 But see Gentner (1975, 1981) for some counter-arguments and suggestions that the evidence of these earlier studies is not convincing.

14 This is reminiscent of Daniel Dennett's criticism of psychological approaches which only concern themselves with the internal state of the mind, ignoring the individual's interaction with the environment:

> The alternative of ignoring the external world and its relations to the internal machinery . . . is not really psychology at all, but just at best abstract neurophysiology – pure internal syntax with no hope of a semantic interpretation. Psychology 'reduced' to neurophysiology in this fashion would not be psychology, for it would not be able to provide an explanation of the regularities it is psychology's particular job to explain: the reliability with which 'intelligent' organisms can cope with their environments and thus prolong their lives.   (Dennett 1987: 64)

15 But see Jackendoff (1983: 14–15) for an attack on the use of logic-based formalisms.

chapter 10

Formal Semantics

10.1 Introduction

In this chapter we look at the approach known as **formal semantics**. Although any approach might be formalized, this label is usually used for a family of denotational theories which use logic in semantic analysis. Other names which focus on particular aspects or versions of this general approach include **truth-conditional semantics, model-theoretic semantics** and **Montague Grammar**.[1] As we shall see, another possible label might be **logical semantics**.

This approach elaborates further the use of truth, truth-conditions and logic discussed in chapter 4. There we reviewed the strategy of borrowing from logic the notion of **truth** and the formalism of **propositional logic** to characterize semantic relations like entailment. In this chapter we shall see how further tools from logic can be used to help characterize aspects of sentence-internal semantics. In discussing formal semantics we touch on an important philosophical divide in semantics: between **representational** and **denotational** approaches to meaning. In chapter 9 we saw examples of the representational approach: for semanticists like Jackendoff semantic analysis involves discovering the conceptual structure which underlies language. For such linguists the search for meaning is the search for mental representations. Formal semanticists, on the other hand, come at meaning from another angle: for them a primary function of language is that it allows us to talk about the world around us. When communicating with others and in our own internal reasoning we use language to describe, or model, facts and situations. From this perspective, understanding the meaning of an utterance is being able to match it with the situation it describes. Hence the search for meaning, from the denotational perspective, is the search for how the symbols of language relate to reality.

How is this relation characterized? Formal semanticists employ the **correspondence theory** of truth discussed in chapter 4. Speakers are held to be aware of what situation an utterance describes and to be able to tell whether the utterance and the situation match up or **correspond**. Thus knowing the meaning of an English sentence like *It's raining in Belfast* involves understanding what situation in the world this sentence would correspond to, or fit. A successful match is called **true**; an unsuccessful match is **false**. Another way of describing this is to say that the listener who understands the sentence is able to determine the **truth conditions** of the uttered sentence, that is, know what conditions in the world would make the sentence true. In the basic version of this approach used in logic there are no *almost*s or *nearly*s: an utterance either describes a situation, and is therefore true of that situation, or not, in which case it is false. See for example, the characterization from a logic text, Bradley and Swartz (1979: 11):

10.1   The account of truth which we are espousing here has been described variously as 'the Correspondence Theory', 'the Realist theory', or even 'the Simple Theory' of truth. In effect, it says that a proposition, P, is true if and only if the (possible) states of affairs . . . is as P asserts it to be. It defines 'truth' as a property which propositions have just when they 'correspond' to the (possible) states of affairs whose existence they assert. It is a 'realist' theory insofar as it makes truth a real or objective property of propositions, i.e. not something subjective but a function of what states of affairs exist in this or that possible world. And it is a 'simple' theory of truth insofar as it accords with the simple intuitions which most of us – before we try to get too sophisticated about such matters – have about the conditions for saying that something is true or false.[2]

Some objections to this might quickly occur to a linguist seeking to borrow these notions to describe natural languages. On a practical descriptive level, this characterization seems to apply just to statements, since intuitively it is hard to see how other utterance types like questions and orders can be viewed as descriptions of situations. Yet, as we saw in our discussion of speech acts in chapter 8, many utterances are not statements. On a more general level the idea of correct or incorrect matches seems to remove the subjectivity of the speaker. We saw in chapter 5 that the certainty shown by a statement might be just one of a range of speaker attitudes to, or confidence in, a proposition. We described such ranges with terms like **modality** and **evidentiality**. In section 10.8 we discuss how formal approaches might take account of such notions.

Formal semanticists have to meet these and related objections to the extension of logical mechanisms to ordinary language. Nonetheless, this approach has become one of the most important and liveliest in the semantics literature. Why is this? We can perhaps outline at this preliminary stage a number of advantages. One great advantage comes from using logical expressions as a semantic metalanguage. It enables semanticists to import into linguistics the economy and formality of the traditional discipline of logic and the benefits of the long struggle to establish mathematics and logic on common principles.[3] Logicians try to make as explicit as possible both the relations between logical symbols and what they represent and the effects of combining symbols. Consequently logic, as a potential semantic metalanguage, has the important advantage of precision.

Denotational approaches, if successful, have another advantage: they escape the problem of circularity discussed in chapter 1. We raised the problem that if we interpret English in terms of a metalanguage, another set of symbols, then we have just translated from one language to another. This second language then needs a semantics, and so on. As we shall see, formal semanticists do translate a natural language like English into a second, logical language, but this translation is only part of the semantic analysis. This logical language is then semantically grounded by tying it to real-world situations. The aim of a denotational approach is not just to convert between representations: it seeks to connect language to the world.

There are other less obvious advantages claimed for such theories: it has been suggested, for example by Chierchia and McConnell-Ginet (1990), that denotational approaches allow us to see more clearly the connection between human languages and the simpler signs systems of other primates like vervet monkeys, baboons and chimpanzees. These systems are clearly referential: primates often have distinct conventional signs for different types of predators like eagles, snakes or big cats.[4] Perhaps this basic matching between a symbol and entities in the environment was the starting-point for human languages.

Whatever the advantages to this approach, we should mention one temporary, practical disadvantage for students new to the theory: this is a very technical and highly formalized approach. Employing the tools of logic means having to become familiar with them and this involves a substantial expenditure of time and effort. Beginners will not see a return on this investment, in terms of improved semantic analyses of real language, very quickly. For an introductory survey like this one, this poses problems of coverage. How much of this large and complicated technical apparatus can we cover in a chapter like this? Our proposal is to sketch in the basic features of the approach without too steep an immersion into mathematical formulae. In particular we will not investigate the formal proofs that a logical language must support. We mention some book-length introductions to this approach in our suggestions for further readings at the end of the chapter, which will allow the interested reader to pursue these topics more fully.

10.2   Model-Theoretical Semantics

Much of the investigation of logic and natural language semantics has been conducted by philosophers, logicians and mathematicians: for example, the predicate logic we describe in this chapter derives largely from the work of the logician and mathematician Gottlob Frege,[5] the notion of truth owes much to Alfred Tarski (1944, 1956), and much of the recent and contemporary debate has been undertaken by philosophers like Donald Davidson (e.g. 1980, 1984). For many linguists, interest in this approach was sparked by the work in the 1960s of the logician Richard Montague, mentioned earlier. As we shall see, an important element in this theory is a **model**, a formal structure representing linguistically relevant aspects of a situation. Consequently one term for Montague's work and similar approaches is **model-theoretical semantics**. The application of this approach to linguistic description by linguists and computer scientists has led both to further development of the model-theoretical approach and the emergence of a number of related but distinct approaches, like **situation semantics** (Barwise and Perry 1983) and **discourse representation theory** (Kamp and Reyle 1993). Since our discussion will remain at an introductory level, we begin by outlining a kind of embryonic model-theoretic approach. Our description will be influenced by Montague Grammar but we will not attempt an introduction to this theory here[6] (see Montague 1974, Dowty, et al. 1981). In such an approach semantic analysis consists of three stages: firstly, a translation from a natural language like English into a logical language whose syntax and semantics are explicitly defined. Secondly, the establishment of a mathematical model of the situations that the language describes. Thirdly, a set of procedures for checking the mapping between the expressions in the logical language and the modelled situations. Essentially these algorithms check whether the expressions are true or false of the modelled situations. Each of these three stages can throw light on the semantic capabilities of natural languages.

We look at these stages in order: we discuss the translation in section 10.3, where we use English as our example and we concentrate on the syntax of the logical metalanguage. We discuss models and mapping algorithms in 10.4–5, where the emphasis is on adding a semantics to the metalanguage. In 10.6 we discuss word meaning in formal semantics.

Subsequently we review some key areas where this basic model has been extended to reflect more accurately the semantics of natural languages. In 10.7 we look at quantifiers in more detail; in 10.8 we discuss intensionality;

and in 10.9 we look at an approach which takes account of the dynamic nature of communication, discourse representation theory (DRT).

10.3   Translating English into a Logical Metalanguage

10.3.1   Introduction

As we have said, the first stage of this semantic analysis consists of translation. The basic idea is that we can translate from a sentence in an individual language like English into an expression in a universal metalanguage. One such metalanguage is **predicate logic**. As mentioned in chapter 4, predicate logic builds on the investigation of sentence connectives in propositional logic and goes on to investigate the internal structure of sentences, for example the truth-conditional effect of certain words like the English quantifiers *all, some, one,* etc. In chapter 4 we briefly introduced a set of logical connectives which parallel in interesting ways some uses of English expressions like *and, or, if . . . then,* and *not.* These connectives are summarized in 10.2 below; for each connective the table gives its symbol, an example of its syntax, i.e. how it combines with sentence constants **p**, **q** etc., and an approximate English equivalent:

10.2   Connectives in propositional logic

Connective	**Syntax**	**English**
$\neg$	$\neg\mathbf{p}$	it is not the case that **p**
$\wedge$	$\mathbf{p} \wedge \mathbf{q}$	**p** and **q**
$\vee$	$\mathbf{p} \vee \mathbf{q}$	**p** and/or **q**
$\vee_e$	$\mathbf{p} \vee_e \mathbf{q}$	**p** or **q** but not both
$\rightarrow$	$\mathbf{p} \rightarrow \mathbf{q}$	if **p**, then **q**
$\equiv$	$\mathbf{p} \equiv \mathbf{q}$	**p** if and only if **q**

We will be using these connectives in our translations into predicate logic, which we begin in section 10.3.2.

10.3.2   Simple statements in predicate logic

If we begin with simple statements like 10.3 and 10.4 below:

10.3   Mulligan is sleeping.

10.4   Bill smokes.

we can identify a subject-predicate structure where the subject is a referring expression (*Mulligan, Bill*) and the predicate tells us something about the subject (*is asleep, smokes*). The predicate logic assigns different roles to these two elements: the predicate is treated as a skeletal function which requires the subject argument to be complete. Our first step is to represent the predicate by a capital **predicate letter**, e.g.

10.5   is asleep: A
        smokes: S

The subject argument can be represented by a lower-case letter (usually chosen from a to t and called an **individual constant**), e.g.

10.6   Mulligan: m
        Bill: b

The convention is that predicate logic forms begin with the predicate, followed by the subject constant. Thus our original sentences can be assigned the representations in 10.7:

10.7   Mulligan is asleep: $A(m)$
        Bill smokes: $S(b)$

If we want to leave the identity of the subject unspecified we can use **variables** (lower-case letters from the end of the alphabet: w, x, y, z), e.g.

10.8 x is asleep: $A(x)$
        y smokes: $S(y)$

As we shall see later, these variables have a special use in the analysis of quantifiers.

We have been looking at the representation of intransitive sentences. The verbs in transitive sentences like 10.9 below require more than one nominal:

10.9   Bill resembles Eddie.
        Tommaso adores Libby.

These predicates are identified as relations between the arguments and represented as follows:

10.10   Bill resembles Eddie: $R(b, e)$
        Tommaso adores Libby: $A(t, l)$

Other relational sentences will be represented in the same way, e.g.

10.11   Pete is crazier than Ryan: $C(p, r)$

Note that the order of constant terms after the predicate letter is significant: it mirrors English sentence structure in that the subject comes before the object. Three-place relations are of course possible; we show an example with its logical translation below:

10.12   Fatima prefers Bill to Henry: $P(f, b, h)$

In our examples so far we have included the English sentence and the logical translation. Alternatively, we can keep track of what the letters in the logical form correspond to by providing a key, e.g.

10.13 $P(f, b, h)$
          Key: P: prefer
                 f: Fatima
                 b: Bill
                 h: Henry

Our notation so far can reflect negative and compound sentences by making use of the connectives shown earlier in 10.2, for example:

10.14   Máire doesn't jog: $\neg J(m)$

10.15   Fred smokes and Kate drinks: $S(f) \wedge D(k)$

10.16   If Bill drinks, Jenny gets angry: $D(b) \rightarrow A(j)$

We might also wish to translate sentences containing **relative clauses** like (*the student*) *who passed the exam*, (*the dress*) *that she wore*, etc. We can represent complex sentences containing relative clauses by viewing them as a form of conjunction, i.e. by using $\wedge$ 'and', as in 10.17–19 below:

10.17   Carrick, who is a millionaire, is a socialist: $M(c) \wedge S(c)$

10.18   Emile is a cat that doesn't purr: $C(e) \wedge \neg P(e)$

10.19   Jean admires Robert, who is a gangster: $A(j, r) \wedge G(r)$

In the next section we extend the logic further to cope with quantified noun phrases.

10.3.3   Quantifiers in predicate logic

One important feature of natural languages that formal semanticists have to deal with in their translation into logical form is **quantification**. All languages have strategies for allowing a proposition to be generalized over ranges or sets of individuals. In English, for example, quantifiers include words like *one, some, a few, many, a lot, most* and *all*. We can look at a simple example. Let's say that we want to predicate the verb phrase *wrote a paper* of various members of a class of students. We could assert this predicate will be true of (at least) one member, by saying 10.20 below:

10.20   A student/some student wrote a paper.

or vary the range of its applicability, as below:

10.21   a.   A few students wrote a paper.
         b.   Many students wrote a paper.
         c.   Most students wrote a paper.
         d.   All students wrote a paper.
         e.   Every student wrote a paper.

We could also deny it applies to any of them by using:

10.22   No student wrote a paper.

The simple logical representation we have developed so far isn't able to reflect this ability to generalize statements over a set of individuals. One way to do this is to follow a proposal of Frege's that statements containing quantifiers be divided into two sections: the quantifying expression which gives the range of the generalization; and the rest of the sentence (the generalization), which will have a place-holder element, called a **variable**, for the quantified nominal. We can show how this approach works for the quantifiers *all*, *every*, *some* and *no*, though as we shall see in section 10.6 later the other quantifiers in example 10.21 will require a different account. To show this we look first at the quantifiers *all* and *every*. Both of these English quantifiers are represented in predicate logic by the **universal quantifier**, symbolized as $\forall$. We can take as an example 10.21e above. This will be given the representation 10.23a below, which can be read as 10.23b:

10.23   a. $\forall x\ (S(x) \rightarrow W(x, p))$
         b.   For every thing x, if x is a student then x wrote a paper.

The universal quantifier establishes the range by fixing the value of x as everything; the expression in parentheses is the generalization. By itself the generalization is an incomplete proposition, called an **open proposition**: until the value of x is set for some individual(s) the expression cannot be true or false. As we shall see, the quantifier serves to set the value of x and close the proposition. Expressions with the universal quantifier can be paraphrased in English by *all* or *every* as in *All students wrote a paper* or *Every student wrote a paper* in 10.23.[7]

We can see that the quantifier phrase can be associated with different positions in the predicate if we compare 10.24a and b below:

10.24   a.   Every student knows the professor: $\forall x \ (S(x) \rightarrow K(x, p))$
         b.   The professor knows every student: $\forall x \ (S(x) \rightarrow K(p, x))$

Here the logical representations emphasize more than English does that both 10.24a and b are predicating something about all of the students. The relationship between the quantifier phrase and the rest of the formula is described in two ways: the quantifying expression is said to **bind** the variable in the predicate expression; and the predicate expression is said to be the **scope** of the quantifier.

Next we turn to the quantifier *some* in example 10.20. *Some* is represented in predicate logic by the **existential quantifier**, symbolized as ∃. We can thus translate our example as 10.25 below:

10.25 $\exists x \ (S(x) \wedge P(s, e))$
         There is (at least) one thing x such that x is a student and x wrote a paper.

We can paraphrase such expressions in English by using noun phrases like *a student, some student,* and *at least one student.* The existential quantifier can also be associated with different positions in the predicate:

10.26   (At least) One student kissed Kylie: $\exists x \ (S(x) \wedge K(x, k))$

10.27   Kylie kissed (at least) one student: $\exists x \ (S(x) \wedge K(k, x))$

Once again the existential quantifier is said to bind the variable and the predicative expression is described as the scope of the quantifier.

The English determiner *no* can be represented by a combination of the existential quantifier and negation, as shown below:

10.28 $\neg\exists x \ (S(x) \wedge W(x, p))$
         It is not the case that there is a thing x such that x is a student and x wrote a paper, There is no x such that x is a student and x wrote a paper.

This corresponds to the sentence *No student wrote a paper.* Another way of representing this is by using the material implication:

10.29 $\forall x \ (S(x) \rightarrow \neg P(x, e))$
         For everything x, if x is a student then it is not the case that x wrote a paper.

With the introduction of these quantifiers we can now summarize the syntax of the predicate logic so far. The syntax includes the vocabulary of symbols in 10.30 below and the rules for the formation of logical formulae in 10.31:

10.30   The symbols of predicate logic
         Predicate letters: A, B, C, etc.
         Individual constants: a, b, c, etc.
         Individual variables: x, y, z, etc.
         Truth functional connectives: $\neg$, $\wedge$, $\vee$, $\vee_e$, $\rightarrow$, $\equiv$
         Quantifiers: $\forall$, $\exists$

10.31   The rules for creating logical formulae
         a. Individual constants and variables are terms.
         b. If A is an n-place predicate and $t_1 \ldots t_n$ are n terms, then
             $A(t_1 \ldots t_n)$ is a formula.[8]
         c. If ϕ is a formula, then $\neg\phi$ is a formula.
         d. If ϕ and ψ are formulae, then $(\phi \wedge \psi)$, $(\phi \vee \psi)$, $(\phi \vee_e \psi)$,
             $(\phi \rightarrow \psi)$, $(\phi \equiv \psi)$ are all formulae.
         e. If ϕ is a formula and x is a variable, then $\forall x\phi$, and $\exists x\phi$ are
             formulae.

We can add to these rules the convention that the outer parentheses of a
complete formula can be omitted, i.e. instead of writing $(\phi \wedge \psi)$, we can
write $\phi \wedge \psi$.

10.3.4   Some advantages of predicate logic translation

The predicate logic we have been looking at is used by logicians to demon-
strate the validity of arguments and reasoning. Thus in addition to a syntax
and semantics, the logical language requires rules of inference. This, however, is a topic we will not pursue here. From a linguist's perspective there
are a number of advantages to the representations we have introduced. We
can take as an example the way that the representation of quantifiers, as
introduced above, clarifies some ambiguities found in natural languages.
One of these is **scope ambiguity**, which can occur when there is more than
one quantifier in a sentence. For example the English sentence 10.32a
below has the two interpretations paraphrased in 10.32b and c:

10.32   a. Everyone loves someone.
         b. Everyone has someone that they love.
         c. There is some person who is loved by everyone.

Version 10.32b involves a many-to-many relationship of loving, while version
10.32c involves a many-to-one relationship. While the English sentence is
structurally ambiguous between these two interpretations, the difference is
explicitly shown in predicate logic by the ordering of the quantifiers. The
interpretation in 10.32b is represented by the formula in 10.33a and that
in 10.32c by 10.33b below:

10.33   a. $\forall x \exists y \; (L(x, y))$
        b. $\exists y \forall x \; (L(x, y))$

The formula in 10.33a says that for every person x, there is some person y that they love. The universal quantifier comes leftmost and therefore contains the existential quantifier in its scope. This situation is described as the universal quantifier having **wide scope**. In 10.33b we have the reverse: the existential quantifier contains the universal in its scope and therefore takes wide scope. Thus the scope of one quantifier may be contained within the scope of another.

Negative words, like English *not*, also display scope over a predication and a second advantage of this type of representation is that it allows us to disambiguate some sentences which contain combinations of quantifiers and negation. The sentence *Everybody didn't visit Limerick*, for example, can have the two interpretations given in 10.34 and 10.35 below, where we give a paraphrase in b and the predicate logic translation in c:

10.34   a. Everybody didn't visit Limerick.
        b. For every person x, it's not the case that x visited Limerick.
        c. $\forall x \; \neg(V(x, l))$

10.35   a. Everybody didn't visit Limerick.
        b. It's not the case that every person x visited Limerick.
        c. $\neg\forall x \; (V(x, l))$

As we can see, the ambiguity is clearly distinguished in the predicate logic translations. In 10.34c the universal quantifier has wide scope over the negative connector $\neg$, while in 10.35c the negative has wide scope over the universal quantifier.

These examples have shown some of the advantages of semantic clarity gained by the translation into predicate logic. In fact, though, as we mentioned earlier, the real purpose of this translation is to allow a denotational semantic analysis to be carried out. In the next section we look at how this logical representation is given a semantics.

10.4   The Semantics of the Logical Metalanguage

10.4.1   Introduction

As we have said, the aim of this approach is to devise a denotational semantics. Clearly our first stage alone is not such a semantic analysis. Translating from an English sentence into a logical formula is not enough: we then have to relate this second set of symbols to something outside – the situation described. To do this we need to add three further elements:

10.36   1.   a **semantic interpretation** for the symbols of the predicate logic;
          2.   a **domain**: this is a model of a situation which identifies the linguistically relevant entities, properties and relations; and
          3.   a **denotation assignment function**: this is a procedure, or set of procedures, which match the logical symbols for nouns, verbs etc. with the items in the model that they denote. This function is also sometimes called a **naming function**.

The domain and naming function are together called a **model**. We look at each of these constituents in turn.

10.4.2   The semantic interpretation of predicate logic symbols

We can adopt a simple denotational theory of reference, as discussed in chapter 2, for the units of the predicate logic. We will identify three such units for discussion: whole sentences, constant terms and predicates, and we will use some simple **set theory** notions to help us define denotation.[9]

Sentences
Following the correspondence theory of truth we will take the denotatum of a whole sentence to be the match or lack of match with the situation it describes. A match will be called **true** (**T**), also symbolized by the numeral **1**. A mismatch will be called **false** (**F**), symbolized by the numeral **0**. So using a variable v for situations, we might say 'a sentence **p** is true in situation v', and symbolize it as $[\mathbf{p}]^v = 1$. Here we use square brackets to symbolize the denotatum of an expression, so $[x]^v$ means the denotatum of x in the situation v. Thus the notation $[\mathbf{p}]^v = 1$ means 'the denotatum of **p** in v is **true**'. By contrast the expression $[\mathbf{p}]^v = 0$ will be read as 'the denotatum of **p** in v is **false**' or, equivalently, 'the sentence **p** is false in situation v'. Since, as we have acknowledged, meaning is compositional, we want the truth value of a sentence to be determined by the semantic value of its parts: the nouns, verbs, connectives etc. of which it is constructed.

Individual constant terms
We will assume the denotation of individual constant terms to be individuals or sets of individuals in the situation. So if we adopt as our situation the 1974 world heavyweight title fight between Muhammad Ali and George Foreman in Zaire, we could use an individual constant term a to denote Ali, another individual constant f to denote Foreman and a third, r, to denote the referee in this situation v.

Predicate constants
We will assume that predicate constants, abbreviated with capital letters, P, Q, R etc., identify sets of individuals for which the predicate holds. Thus a

one-place predicate like *be standing* will pick out the set of individuals who are standing in the situation described. This can be described in a set theory notation as either $\{x \mid \ldots\}$ or $\{x: \ldots\}$, both of which can be read as 'the set of all x such that...'. So a notation like $\{x: x$ is standing in $v\}$ can be read as 'the set of individuals who are standing in situation v'.

Two-place predicates identify a set of ordered pairs: two individuals in a given order. Thus the predicate *punch* will pick out an ordered pair where the first punches the second in v, represented in set theory terms as: $\{<x, y>: x$ punches y in $v\}$. Similarly a three-place predicate like *hand to* will identify a 3-tuple $\{<x, y, z>: x$ hands y to z in $v\}$.

10.4.3   The domain

The domain is a representation of the individuals and relationships in a situation, which we will continue to call v. Let's invent an example by imagining a situation in the Cavern Club, Liverpool in 1962 where the Beatles are rehearsing for that evening's performance. If we use this as our domain, let's say we can identify several individuals in the situation: the Beatles themselves – John, Paul, George and Ringo – their manager Brian Epstein and one stray fan we'll call Bob. In the format we are using here we will say that the situation v contains a set of individuals, U, such that in this case U = {John, Paul, George, Ringo, Brian Epstein, Bob}.

10.4.4   The denotation assignment function

This function matches symbols from the logical representation with elements of the domain, according to the semantic nature of the symbols. For our simple example, we can divide its work into two parts: (a) the matching of individual constant terms with individuals in the situation v; and (b) the matching of predicate constants with sets of individuals in v.

Matching individual constant terms
The assignment is a function, which we can symbolize as $F(x)$. This function will for any symbol x of the logical formula always return its **extension** in the situation. Thus we can establish a matching for individual constant terms as follows:

10.37   Assignment of individual constant terms
             $F(j) = $ John
             $F(p) = $ Paul
             $F(g) = $ George
             $F(r) = $ Ringo
             $F(e) = $ Brian Epstein
             $F(b) = $ Bob

In other words, the individual constant j denotes the entity John in the situation v, p denotes Paul, and so on.

Matching predicate constants
Our function $F(x)$ will return the extensions of predicates, as described a little earlier on for the semantics of predicates. Thus the function will return individuals, ordered pairs or 3-tuples, depending on the type of predicate. For our current example the matching will be as follows:

10.38   Assignment of predicate letters
         $F(B)$ = was a Beatle   = {John, Paul, George, Ringo}
         $F(M)$ = was a manager   = {Brian Epstein}
         $F(F)$ = was a fan   = {Bob}
         $F(S)$ = sang   = {John, Paul}
         $F(G)$ = played guitar   = {John, Paul, George}
         $F(D)$ = played the drums   = {Ringo}
         $F(J)$ = joked with   = {<John, George>}
         $F(I)$ = idolized   = {<Bob, John>, <Bob, Paul>, <Bob, George>, <Bob, Ringo>}

Thus the extension of J '*joked with*' in the situation is the set of the ordered pair, John and George.

At this point then we have defined the semantic (denotational) behaviour of some of the logical constituents and established a model, which we take to be a combination of a domain and the assignment function. Such a model is often schematically described as $M_n = <U_n, F_n>$, where M = the model, U = the set of individuals in the situation, and F is our denotation assignment function. The subscript **n** (for 1, 2, 3 . . . **n**) on each element relativizes the model to one particular situation. So we can identify our situation as $M_1 = <U_1, F_1>$. For a different situation we would need a second model, $M_2 = <U_2, F_2>$, and so on.

Next we need to have some evaluation procedure to reflect a listener's ability to evaluate a sentence's truth value relative to a situation. Basically this means a set of algorithms to check whether a given sentence is true or not of the situation. We outline a simple informal version of this in the next section.

10.5   Checking the Truth Value of Sentences

As we mentioned earlier, our procedures for checking the truth value of a sentence must reflect the compositionality of meaning. If this is done correctly, then we will have shown something of how the constituents of a sentence contribute to the truth value of the whole sentence. To keep our discussion within bounds, we will look at this procedure for just three basic types of sentence: a simple statement, a compound sentence with $\land$ 'and', and sentences with the universal and existential quantifiers, $\forall$ and $\exists$.

10.5.1 Evaluating a simple statement

If we take our model M_1, we might construct some relevant sentences in predicate logic as in 10.39 below, some of which are true of M_1 and some of which are false:

10.39   a. $D(r)$
          b. $G(b)$
          c. $\mathcal{J}(e, b)$
          d. $G(p)$
          e. $S(j)$

The reader may routinely translate these back into English, for example, 10.39a as *Ringo played the drums*, etc. Let's take 10.39e as an example and test its truth value in M_1. The procedure for checking if $S(j)$ is true is based on the denotational definitions we gave earlier and can be schematized as in 10.40 below:

10.40 $[S(j)]^{M_1} = \mathbf{1}$ iff $[j]^{M_1} \in [S]^{M_1}$

This rather forbidding schema employs various elements of our notation so far and can be paraphrased in English as in 10.41:

10.41   The sentence *John sang* is true if and only if the extension of *John* is part of the set defined by *sang* in the model M_1.

Now to check this we have to check the extensions returned by the denotation assignment function for the individual constant j and the predicate constant S to see if $F_1(j) \in F_1(S)$. We know from our model and assignment that:

10.42 $F_1(j) = \text{John}$

and we also know:

10.43 $F_1(S) = \{\text{John, Paul}\}$

So since it is clearly true that John $\in$ {John, Paul}, then our sentence is true, i.e. schematically $[S(j)]^{M_1} = \mathbf{1}$.

10.5.2 Evaluating a compound sentence with $\wedge$ 'and'

Evaluating a compound sentence follows basically the same procedure we have just outlined. Let's take as an example sentences containing $\wedge$ 'and'. We can create such sentences as 10.44 below for our model M_1:

10.44   a. $S(j) \wedge S(p)$
        b. $\mathcal{J}(j, g) \wedge \mathcal{J}(r, b)$
        c. $M(e) \wedge F(b)$
        d. $S(j) \wedge I(b, e)$

Once again 10.44 contains some true and some false sentences for M_1. We can take as our example 10.44d, $S(j) \wedge I(b, e)$. To evaluate any compound sentence **p** ∧ **q** we first establish the independent truth value of **p** and then of **q**. Then we evaluate the effect of joining them with ∧. The truth-functional effect of ∧ was given in the form of a truth table in chapter 4: essentially a compound with ∧ is only true when **p** is true and **q** is true. In the format we are using here this behaviour can be expressed as in 10.45 below:

10.45   Truth behaviour of ∧
        $[\mathbf{p} \wedge \mathbf{q}] = 1$ iff $[\mathbf{p}] = 1$ and $[\mathbf{q}] = 1$

In effect 10.45 says that both conjuncts must be true for the compound to be true. If we turn again to our example 10.44d above, we can run through the procedure for evaluating its truth value relative to M_1. For this particular sentence and model, the behaviour of ∧ can be expressed as below:

10.46 $[S(j) \wedge I(b, e)]^{M_1} = 1$ iff $[S(j)]^{M_1} = 1$ and $[I(b, e)]^{M_1} = 1$

That is, both of these conjuncts have to be true in M_1 for the sentence to be true in M_1. Well, we already know from our discussion of simple statements that $S(j)$ is true, so we can go on to evaluate $I(b, e)$ in the same way. The relevant rule is 10.47:

10.47 $[I(b, e)]^{M_1} = 1$ iff $[<b, e>]^{M_1} \in [I]^{M_1}$

We can paraphrase this in English as 10.48 below:

10.48   The sentence *Bob idolized Brian Epstein* is true if and only if the extension of *Bob* and the extension of *Brian Epstein* are an ordered pair which is part of the set defined by *idolized* in the model M_1.

Thus $I(b, e) = 1$ iff <Bob, Brian Epstein> $\in F_1(I)$. We can easily check this. The denotation assignment function will give the relevant values for this sentence as in 10.49 below:

10.49   a. $F_1(b) = \{Bob\}$
        b. $F_1(e) = \{Brian\ Epstein\}$
        c. $F_1(I) = \{<Bob, John>, <Bob, Paul>, <Bob, George>, <Bob, Ringo>\}$

We can see that the ordered pair <Bob, Brian Epstein> is not part of the set defined by the predicate I, i.e. <Bob, Brian Epstein> ∉ {<Bob, John>, <Bob, Paul>, <Bob, George>, <Bob, Ringo>}, so our sentence $I(b, e)$ is **false**.

Since our first conjunct $S(j)$ is true and our second, $I(b, e)$, false, then by the rule in 10.45 the whole sentence $S(j) \wedge I(b, e)$ is false. This evaluation procedure may seem rather laborious as we step through it in this simple way, but the importance for semantic analysis is that the procedure is explicit, is based on our semantic definitions of logical elements and the well-proven behaviour of logical connectives, and is productive: it can be applied in the same way to more and more complicated structures. The other truth-functional connectives can be treated in the same way as $\wedge$ by reflecting their respective truth-functional behaviours, described in truth tables in chapter 4, in rules paralleling 10.45 above, thus allowing the evaluation of sentences containing ¬ 'not', ∨ 'or', → 'if . . . then', etc.

10.5.3 Evaluating sentences with the quantifiers ∀ and ∃

The same procedure can, with some modification, be used to evaluate sentences with the universal and existential quantifiers, ∀ and ∃. We won't give the step-by-step detail here but we can outline the spirit of the approach, using a different example. Let's imagine a sad situation of a house that has three cats (*Tom, Felix* and *Korky*) and just one mouse (*Jerry*). Tom and Felix hunt Jerry but Korky does not. Without setting up a model for this we can see that one might say of the situation the (false) statement below:

10.50   Everyone hunts Jerry. ∀x $(H(x, j))$

As we saw earlier the quantifier phrase ∀x expresses the range of the generalization $H(x, j)$ and the quantifier binds the variable x. The evaluation procedure can exploit this structure as follows. We reflect the meaning of ∀, *every*, by establishing the rule that a sentence with this quantifier is true if the generalization is true for **each** denotation of x, otherwise false. Thus we need to test the truth of the expression x *hunts Jerry* for each individual in the situation that x can denote.

We already have a function F_n that matches individual constant terms with their denotation in the situation; we need another function, let's call it g_n, to do the same for variables. Such a function would successively match each individual in the situation with the variable x. In this situation the following are possible matchings:[10]

10.51   a. x = Tom
          b. x = Felix
          c. x = Korky

All we need to do then is test the generalization with each value for x, i.e. use the procedure we used for simple statements earlier to evaluate each of the following versions:

10.52   a. x = Tom: is $H(x, j)$ true/false?
          b. x = Felix: is $H(x, j)$ true/false?
          c. x = Korky: is $H(x, j)$ true/false?

Once again, we won't step through the evaluation for each. Since of course 10.52a and b are true and 10.52c is false of this situation, then we know that the universal quantifier sentence $\forall x \ (H(x, j))$ is false.

Sentences containing the existential quantifier $\exists$ can be evaluated in the same way, except that the rule for this quantifier is that if the generalization is true of **at least one** individual in the range, the quantified sentence is true. Let's take for example the sentence 10.53 below:

10.53   Some cat hunts Jerry. $\exists x \ (C(x) \wedge H(x, j))$

Once again the possible denotations for x are the three cats and we would evaluate the truth of $C(x) \wedge H(x, j)$ with x set for the three values in 10.51:

10.54   a. x = Tom: is $C(x) \wedge H(x, j)$ true/false?
          b. x = Felix: is $C(x) \wedge H(x, j)$ true/false?
          c. x = Korky: is $C(x) \wedge H(x, j)$ true/false?

The truth table for $\wedge$ will tell us that 10.54a and 10.54b are true in our situation, while 10.54c is false. Consequently the existential quantifier rule that at least one must be true is satisfied and the sentence $\exists x \ (C(x) \wedge H(x, j))$ is true.

We have, of course, only sketched this evaluation procedure for quantifiers; for example, we haven't given the formal detail of the function g_n which assigns denotations to variables. For a fuller account of this approach see Chierchia and McConnell-Ginet (2000: 126f.).

We have outlined in this section a denotational semantics for the predicate logic translations we introduced in 10.3. As we have observed, such a semantics has a number of advantages. From a methodological point of view, it has the advantages of being formal and explicit.[11] More generally it adopts the denotational programme of relating utterances to specific situations. The semantics also embodies certain key features of natural languages in that it is compositional and productive; and more specifically, it allows the identification of individuals, sets of individuals and relations and, in a so far limited way, allows quantification. In the next section we look at how this approach accounts for word meaning.

10.6   Word Meaning: Meaning Postulates

As we have seen, when it comes to dealing with word meaning, the model-theoretic approach we have been looking at places great emphasis on the denotational properties of words. This is consistent with this approach's general assumption that the focus of semantic enquiry is sentence meaning: the idea is that the meaning of words is something best not pursued in isolation but in terms of their contribution to sentence meaning. Thus most formal approaches define a word's meaning as the contribution it makes to the truth value of a sentence containing it.

However, the original structuralist position that words gain their significance from a combination of their denotation (reference) and their sense still seems to have force. We can return to our example from chapter 3: that if an English speaker hears 10.55 below, he knows 10.56:

10.55   I saw my mother just now.

10.56   The speaker saw a woman.

As we saw in chapter 3, speakers and hearers have knowledge about many kinds of sense relations between words, or what we termed **lexical relations**. The question for formal approaches is how to capture this lexical knowledge in a format compatible with the model-theoretical approach we have been looking at. One solution is to use **meaning postulates**, a term from logic (see Carnap 1952), and an approach advocated by J. D. Fodor et al. (1975) and Kintsch (1974).

The meaning postulates approach would recognize that 10.56 follows automatically from knowledge of 10.55 but rather than state this in terms of components of meaning of either word, this approach simply identifies this relationship as a form of knowledge,[12] using some basic connectives from propositional logic. These connectives are those used in our earlier discussion and are repeated below:

10.57   Logical connectives in meaning postulates
          $\rightarrow$ 'if . . . then'
          $\wedge$ 'and'
          $\neg$ 'not'
          $\vee$ 'or'
          $\equiv$ 'if and only if'

Let's look at some lexical relations in this approach, beginning with **hyponymy**. The hyponymy relationship between, for example, *dog* and *animal* can be represented using $\rightarrow$, the '*if . . . then*' connective, by writing a rule like 10.58:

10.58 $\forall x(DOG(x) \rightarrow ANIMAL(x))$

In the representation in 10.58 we use italic capitals to represent the translation of lexical items into predicate logic: 10.58 is to be read 'for all x, if x is a dog, then x is an animal', or more simply 'if something is a dog, then it is an animal'. In principle, all of the lexical relations described in chapter 3 can be represented using meaning postulates. We can look at a few further examples.

Binary antonyms   Here we can use the 'not' symbol ($\neg$) as in 10.59 below:

10.59 $\forall x(DEAD(x) \rightarrow \neg ALIVE(x))$

This is to be read 'if something is dead then it is not alive'.

Converses   The lexical relation between the words *parent* and *child* can be captured as in 10.60:

10.60   a. $\forall x \, \forall y(PARENT(x, y) \rightarrow CHILD(y, x))$
           b. $\forall x \, \forall y(PARENT(x, y) \rightarrow \neg CHILD(x, y))$

The formula in 10.60a tells us that if x is the parent of y then, y is the child of x. The second formula in 10.60b reflects the asymmetry of this relationship: if x is y's parent, x cannot be y's child.

Synonymy   To capture the relation of synonymy we have to use two mirror-image *if. . . then* rules, i.e. both of the rules in 10.61 below for a speaker for whom *couch* and *sofa* are synonyms:

10.61   a. $\forall(COUCH(x) \rightarrow SOFA(x))$
           b. $\forall x(SOFA(x) \rightarrow COUCH(x))$

If both of these are true then *couch* and *sofa* are synonymous. We can abbreviate this double implication with the symbol $\equiv$ as in 10.62:

10.62 $\forall x \, (COUCH(x) \equiv SOFA(x))$

From these few examples we can see that this approach thus allows the formal semanticist to reflect the network of sense relations that we detect in the vocabulary of a language, in a format consistent with translation into predicate logic and interpretation via model theory.

   These meaning postulates can be seen as a way of restricting or constraining denotation, e.g. 'if something is a dog, then it is an animal' tells us something about the denotational behaviour of the word *dog*. If we take the view that the source for such information is the knowledge that speakers have, then we can see meaning postulates as an example of the effect of the subject's knowledge on the denotational properties of expressions.

The version of sentence and word meaning that we have outlined so far is only the starting-point for a formal semantics of natural languages. The account has to be broadened to reflect the range of semantic features we find in all languages. In the next sections we discuss some of these developments.

10.7   Natural Language Quantifiers and Higher Order Logic

The theory of quantifiers that we have outlined so far suffers from several disadvantages as an account of quantifiers that are found in natural languages. One major problem, as we mentioned earlier, is that there are some common types of quantifiers which cannot be modelled in this standard form of the predicate calculus. We can briefly show why this is so by looking at the English quantifier *most*. It is impossible to establish *most* on a par with the universal quantifier $\forall$ and existential quantifier $\exists$, using the logical connectives $\wedge$ and $\rightarrow$.

Neither 10.63b or c below seem to have the same truth conditions as 10.63a:

10.63   a.   Most students read a book.
          b.   Most $x(S(x) \wedge R(x, b))$
          c.   Most $x(S(x) \rightarrow R(x, b))$

The expression in b has the interpretation 'For most x, x is a student and x reads a book' which suggests the likeliest paraphrase in English 'Most things are students and read books', which is of course quite different from the meaning of 10.63a. The formula in c has the interpretation 'For most x, if x is a student then x reads a book' which suggests 'Most things are such that if they are students they read a book'. The problem here is that *most* is quantifying over all the individuals in the domain rather than over all students. We can show how this will cause a divergence from the meaning of 10.63a. First we may recall the truth table for the material implication $\rightarrow$, given in chapter 4. We can apply this to our expression as follows:

10.64

	$S(x)$	$R(x, b)$	$(S(x) \rightarrow R(x, b))$
1	T	T	T
2	T	F	F
3	F	T	T
4	F	F	T

Next let us decide for argument's sake that *most* means more than 50 per cent of the individuals concerned. So whenever the expression $(S(x) \rightarrow R(x, b))$ is true of more than 50 per cent of the entities in the situation, the sentence in 10.63a will be true. However the truth table in 10.64 tells us that $(S(x) \rightarrow R(x, b))$ is true in a number of situations, for example when the individual is not a student (i.e. $S(x)$ is false) but does read (i.e. $R(x, b)$ is true), as in line 4 of the table. Consequently we would predict that 10.63c is true in a number of situations that do not reflect the meaning of *Most students read a book*, for example if a majority of students do not read a book but they are outnumbered by the non-students who do read a book.

What seems to be going wrong here is that our form of interpretation has quantifiers ranging over all individuals in the relevant situation whereas in noun phrases like *most students* the quantifier in determiner position seems to have its range restricted by the type of thing named by the following noun.

A second problem with our predicate logic account of quantifiers also concerns the interpretation of noun phrases. In chapter 1 we discussed the compositionality of meaning and claimed that semantic rules need to parallel the compositionality and recursion that we find in grammar. However, we can compare the following sentences and their translations into predicate logic:

10.65   a. $[_{\text{NP}} \text{ Ray}]\ [_{\text{VP}} \text{ is hardworking}]$
        b. $H(r)$

10.66   a. $[_{\text{NP}} \text{ One student}]\ [_{\text{VP}} \text{ is hardworking}]$
        b. $(\exists x)(S(x) \wedge H(x))$

10.67   a. $[_{\text{NP}} \text{ All students}]\ [_{\text{VP}} \text{ are hardworking}]$
        b. $(\forall x)(S(x) \rightarrow H(x))$

In these examples the syntactic structure is the same: a noun phrase followed by a verb phrase. While in 10.65 the noun phrase corresponds to a unit in the logical form, i.e. *Ray* = r, in the following two examples the noun phrase does not correspond to a unitary expression in the logical formulae. In 10.67, for example, the English noun phrase corresponds to no single logical expression. The meaning of *all students* is split: part of the meaning is to the left of the head noun *students* in the choice of the quantifier $\forall$, while part occurs to the right in the choice of the connective $\rightarrow$. The NP *one student* is similarly divided between $\exists$, *student* and the connective $\wedge$. We can call this the problem of **isomorphism**.

Both of these problems can be solved by taking a different approach to the semantics of noun phrases, as described in the next sections.

10.7.1   Restricted quantifiers

One step is to express the restriction placed on quantifying determiners by their head nominals. This can be done by adopting a different notation: that of **restricted quantification**. A sentence like *All students are hardworking* would be represented in the restricted format by 10.68a below, compared to the standard format in 10.68b:

10.68   a. $(\forall x: S(x))\ H(x)$
          b. $(\forall x)(S(x) \rightarrow H(x))$

Here the information from the rest of the noun phrase is placed into the quantifying expression as a restriction on the quantifier. Similarly *One student is hardworking* is represented in the restricted format by 10.69a below, again contrasting with the standard format in 10.69b:

10.69   a. $(\exists x: S(x))\ H(x)$
          b. $(\exists x)(S(x) \wedge H(x))$

Restricted quantification helps solve the problem of isomorphism: it has the advantage that the logical expressions correspond more closely to natural language expressions. If we compare 10.68a and b above, for example, in a the English noun phrase *all students* has a translation into a unitary logical expression: $(\forall x: S(x))$. *Most students* would be represented as $(\text{Most } x: (S(x))$; *few students* as $(\text{Few } x: S(x))$, etc.

We should note that in English some quantifiers can stand alone, e.g. *everything, everybody, everywhere*. These will have to be translated into complex expressions in predicate logic, as in 10.70 and 10.71 below:

10.70   *everything*   every thing $(\forall x: T(x))$
          everybody   every person $(\forall x: P(x))$
          everywhere   every location $(\forall x: L(x))$

10.71   Everything is either matter or energy: $(\forall x: T(x))\ (M(x) \vee E(x))$
          Barbara hates everyone: $(\forall x: P(x))\ H(b, x)$
          Everywhere is dangerous: $(\forall x: L(x))\ D(x)$

As with the universal quantifier, some English words seem to incorporate an existential quantifier, e.g. *something, someone, somewhere*. These will be expanded in the translation into predicate logic, as shown below:

10.72   *something*   some thing $(\exists x: T(x))$
          someone   some person $(\exists x: P(x))$
          somewhere   some location $(\exists x: L(x))$

10.7.2   Generalized quantifiers

Though restricted quantification seems to have advantages for representing the syntax–semantics interface, we still need to develop a way to provide a semantic interpretation for noun phrase formulae like (Most x: ($S(x)$)) *most students*, ($\forall x$: $S(x)$) *all students*, etc. Some influential recent research on the formal semantics of noun phrase semantics has focused on an application of set theory from mathematical logic, called **generalized quantifier theory**. We can outline this approach, beginning with an example of a simple sentence like *John sang* from sections 10.5.1–2 earlier, where we used set membership to interpret it. We used 10.73 below to claim that this sentence is true if the subject is a member of the set identified by the predicate.

10.73   a. $[S(j)]^{M_1} = \mathbf{1}$ iff $[j]^{M_1} \in [S]^{M_1}$
         b.   The sentence *John sang* is true if and only if the extension of *John* is part of the set defined by *sang* in the model M_1.

A different approach is to reverse this and evaluate the truth of *John sang* by checking whether singing is one of the properties that are true of John in the situation. In other words, we look for singing to be among the set of things John did for the sentence to be true. To do this, however, we need to give a new predicate-argument structure to the sentence (10.74b below) and a new semantic rule (10.74c) to replace those in 10.40 earlier:

10.74   a.   John sang
         b.   John (sang)
         c. $[\text{John (sang)}]^{M_1} = \mathbf{1}$ iff $[\text{sang}]^{M_1} \in [\text{John}]^{M_1}$

We can paraphrase 10.74c as *John sang* is true if and only the denotation of the verb phrase *sang* is part of the denotation of the name *John* in the model M_1. To capture this procedure by a rule like 10.74c involves viewing John as a set of properties: a set of sets. For our model in sections 10.4–5 above this might include properties like 'is a Beatle', 'sang', 'played guitar', etc. The noun phrase *John* denotes this set of sets. This is a shift from the standard predicate logic analysis of the denotation of a noun phrase like *John* as an individual.

   This translation of a noun phrase as a set of sets was proposed by Montague (1969) and developed by Barwise and Cooper (1981) as an application of the mathematical notion of generalized quantifiers. Since sets of sets and the formula in 10.66b are not part of the predicate logic we have been using so far, this constitutes an extension into a higher order, or second-order logic.

   In this approach the semantic interpretation of the sentence *Most students are hardworking* will interpret *most students* as a set of properties and the sentence will be judged true if the set *are hardworking* is an element of the set *most students*. The semantic rule for *most* can be given as follows:[13]

10.75   Most (A, B) = $\mathbf{1}$ iff $|A \cap B| > |A - B|$

We can paraphrase this as '*Most A are B* is true if the cardinality of the set of things that are both A and B is greater than the cardinality of the set of things which are A but not B', or more succinctly 'if the members of both A and B outnumber the members of A that are not members of B'. This assumes our earlier definition of *most* as more than 50 per cent and therefore claims that *Most students are hardworking* is true if the number of students who are hardworking is greater than the number who aren't.

Other quantifiers can be given similar definitions in terms of relations between sets, for example:

10.76   All (A, B) = **1** iff A ⊆ B
         All A are B is true if and only if set A is a subset of set B

10.77   Some (A, B) = **1** iff A ∩ B ≠ Ø
         Some A are B is true if and only if the set of things which are members of both A and B is not empty

10.78   No (A, B) = **1** iff A ∩ B = Ø
         No A are B is true if and only if the set of things which are members of both A and B is empty

10.79   Fewer than seven (A, B) = **1** iff | A ∩ B | < 7
         Fewer than seven As are B is true if and only if the cardinality of the set of things which are members of both A and B is less than 7

This analysis of noun phrases as generalized quantifiers has stimulated a large literature investigating the formal properties of quantifiers in natural languages and has led researchers to propose solutions to a number of descriptive problems. We cannot do justice to this literature here but in the next two sections we will select examples to illustrate this field of inquiry. The reader is referred to Keenan (1996) for an overview.

10.7.3   The strong/weak distinction and existential *there* sentences

One descriptive problem, discussed by Milsark (1977) and subsequently by Barwise and Cooper (1981), de Jong (1987) and Keenan (1987), concerns the distribution of NPs in existential *there* sentences. Some examples are below:

10.80   a.   There is/isn't a fox in the henhouse.
         b.   There are/aren't some foxes in the henhouse.
         c.   There are/aren't two foxes in the henhouse.
         d.   ?There is/isn't every fox in the henhouse.
         e.   ?There are/aren't most foxes in the henhouse.
         f.   ?There are/aren't both foxes in the henhouse.

These sentences are used to assert (or deny in negative versions) the existence of the noun phrase following *be*.[14] As can be seen, some quantifying determiners, including *every*, *most* and *both*, are anomalous in this construction. The explanation proposed by Milsark (1977) is that there are two classes of noun phrases, weak and strong, and that only weak NPs can occur in these sentences. Subsequent work has sought to characterize this distinction correctly. One proposal, from Keenan (1987) uses the format of generalized quantifiers to explain the difference in terms of **symmetry**. One group of quantifiers expresses asymmetrical relations, that is to say that the order of their set arguments is significant. We can take the example of *all* and *most*. The form *All A are B* is not equivalent to *All B are A*, so that *All my friends are cyclists* does not have the same meaning as *All cyclists are my friends*. Similarly *Most A are B* is not equivalent to *Most B are A*, so that *Most football players are male* does not mean the same as *Most males are football players*. We can schematize this pattern as below, where **det** is the quantifying determiner:

10.81   Asymmetrical quantifiers
          det (A, B) ≠ **det** (B, A)

Another group expresses symmetrical relations. Here we can use *some* and *two* as examples. *Some A are B* is equivalent to *Some B are A*, so that *Some skiers are Sudanese* can describe the same situation as *Some Sudanese are skiers*. Similarly *Two Nobel prize winners are Welshmen* is equivalent to *Two Welshman are Noble prize winners*. These can be schematized as:

10.82   Symmetrical quantifiers
          det (A, B) = **det** (B, A)

The asymmetrical class is also called **proportional** because they express a proportion of the restricting set identified by the nominal. So for example to interpret NPs like *most foxes, all foxes, few foxes* etc. we need access to the number of the relevant set of *foxes*. The symmetrical class is not proportional in this sense. If we say *two foxes* we don't need to know how many other foxes are in the set in order to interpret the noun phrase. This class is called, by distinction, **cardinal** quantifiers since they denote the cardinality of the intersection of the sets A and B, i.e. the intersection of *two* and *foxes* in our example. Some quantifiers have both a cardinal and proportional reading, for example *many* and *few*. Compare the sentences in 10.83:

10.83   a.   There are many valuable stamps in this collection.
          b.   Many of the stamps in this collection are valuable.

The interpretation of *many* in a is cardinal in that the sentence means that the number of valuable stamps is high. The interpretation in b is proportional since *many* is here calculated relative to the collection. It is reasonable to use b but not a if the collection is in fact a small one.

The proposal is that the asymmetrical, proportional class are strong quantifiers and create strong NPs. These strong NPs form the class of items that cannot be used in existential *there* sentences. Symmetrical, cardinal quantifiers on the other hand form weak NPs and can be used in these sentences. The theory of generalized quantifiers allows us to characterize the difference in quantifiers reflected in the English data. One possible line of explanation for the difference is that the necessity in strong NPs for access to the restriction on the domain of quantification somehow clashes with the semantic function of existential *there* sentences. In other words, when interpreting *most foxes* we have to access the whole set of foxes, including those outside the set of *most*. The idea is that accessing a presupposed set of foxes clashes with the normal assertion or denial of the existence of foxes in sentences like 10.80a–c, creating a tautology or a contradiction respectively. See Barwise and Cooper (1981) for discussion.

10.7.4   Monotonicity and negative polarity items

A further descriptive problem that has been investigated in the generalized quantifier literature is how to account for the distribution of negative polarity items like English *any, ever, yet*, which seem dependent on the presence of negation in the sentence:

10.84   a.   She doesn't ever eat dessert.
          b.   ?She ever eats dessert.

10.85   a.   I haven't seen the movie yet.
          b.   ?I have seen the movie yet.

However, as discussed in Laduslaw (1979, 1996) and van der Wouden (1997), the restriction seems to be wider than strictly sentence negation. As shown below, negative polarity items are also licensed by certain quantifiers like *nobody, few* and adverbials like *seldom, rarely*, as well as other items; see Laduslaw (1996) for more examples.

10.86   a.   Nobody sees any difficulty.
          b.   ?Everybody sees any difficulty.

10.87   a.   Few people have seen the movie yet.
          b.   ?Many people have seen the movie yet.

10.88   a.   Rarely has she ever been late.
          b.   ?Often has she ever been late.

An influential proposal, deriving from Laduslaw (1979), is that the licensing expressions are not simply negative but have a particular property of

monotonicity. The term monotonicity applied to quantifiers describes patterns of entailment between sets and subsets. **Upward entailment** is characterized by entailment from a subset to a set. **Downward entailment** involves entailment from a set to a subset. Let's take as an example (*NP*) *is driving home* which is a subset of (*NP*) *is driving*. By placing different quantified nominals into the subject position we can test the monotonicity of the quantifiers:

10.89   *Everyone is driving* does not entail *Everyone is driving home*.
          Everyone is driving home does entail *Everyone is driving*.
          Therefore: *every* involves upward entailment.

10.90   *No one is driving* does entail *No one is driving home*.
          No one is driving home does not entail *No one is driving*.
          Therefore: *no* involves downward entailment.

10.91   *Someone is driving* does not entail *Someone is driving home*.
          Someone is driving home does entail *Someone is driving*.
          Therefore: *some* involves upward entailment.

10.92   *Few people are driving* does entail *Few people are driving home*.
          Few people are driving home does not entail *Few people are driving*.
          Therefore: *few* involves downward entailment.

Quantifiers which trigger upward entailment are described as monotone increasing while those involving downward entailment are described as monotone decreasing.

The specific explanatory proposal in this literature is that negative polarity items are licensed by downward entailing expressions. We can see even from our simple examples that this correctly predicts the following pattern:

10.93   a.   Few people are ever driving home.
          b.   No one is ever driving home.
          c.   ?Everyone is ever driving home.
          d.   ?Someone is ever driving home.

Our examples so far have been of sets and subsets identified by the right argument of the quantifier, corresponding to the VP arguments, for example *Few* (*people, driving*) and its subset *Few* (*people, driving home*). The same quantifiers may show the same or different entailment patterns in the sets and subsets in the left argument, corresponding to the NP, for example *Few* (*people, driving*) and its subset *Few* (*drunk people, driving*). The examples below show that *few* is downward entailing in the left argument as it is in the right (10.92 above) but that *every* is downward entailing in the left argument though it is upward entailing in the right (as in 10.89 above):

10.94   *Few people are driving* does entail *Few drunk people are driving.*
         Few drunk people are driving does not entail *Few people are driving.*
         Therefore: *few* involves downward entailment (left argument).

10.95   *Every person is driving* does entail *Every drunk person is driving.*
         Everyone drunk person is driving does not entail *Every person is driving.*
         Therefore: *every* involves downward entailment (left argument).

This difference correctly predicts that *every* licenses negative polarity items in the NP but not in the VP:

10.96   a.   [Everyone who has ever driven drunk] will be ashamed by these figures.
         b.   ?[Everyone who has driven drunk] will ever be ashamed by these figures.

10.7.5   Section summary

In this section we have seen something of the formal investigation of quantifiers in natural language. We can identify two claims which emerge from this literature. The first is that formal models can be successfully developed to describe natural language quantifiers. The second, more ambitious, claim is that these formal models help identify and characterize features of quantifier behaviour that would otherwise remain mysterious.

10.8   Intensionality

10.8.1   Introduction

As we mentioned in the introduction, section 10.1, one disadvantage of the simple version of the denotational approach is that it downplays the speaker-hearer's **subjectivity**. The procedures we have been outlining allow a mechanical-seeming matching between statements and situations. However, as we have seen in our previous chapters, it is clear that natural languages largely communicate **interpretations** between speakers and hearers. For example, languages contain a whole range of verbs which describe different mental states. Instead of a flat statement **S**, we can say in English for example:

10.97   a.   Frank knows that **S**.
         b.   Frank believes that **S**.
         c.   Frank doubts that **S**.

    d.   Frank regrets that **S**.
    e.   Frank suspects that **S**.
    f.   Frank hopes that **S**.
    g.   Frank imagines that **S**, etc.

As we saw in chapter 5, one way of describing this, which comes to us from the philosophy of language, is to say that in sentences like 10.97 we have a range of speaker attitudes to the proposition expressed by **S**, or, more briefly, that we have a set of **propositional attitudes**.

As we discussed in chapter 5, propositional attitudes are not only conveyed by embedding **S** under a higher verb. We might say that if a speaker chooses between the sentences in 10.98 below, the choice reflects a difference in propositional attitude between certainty and degrees of lack of certainty:

10.98   a.   Phil misrepresented his income.
           b.   Phil probably misrepresented his income.
           c.   Phil may have misrepresented his income.

In another terminology, sentences which reveal this interpretative or cognitive behaviour are said to be **intensional** and the property is called **intensionality**. More generally these terms are applied whenever linguistic behaviour reveals a relation between an agent and a thought. The notion was discussed by Frege in his 1893 article 'Sense and Reference' (*Über Sinn und Bedeutung*; see Frege 1980) in relation to cases where we need access to the sense of an expression as well as its denotation, as discussed in chapter 2. The classical cases are the verbs of propositional attitudes mentioned above, which in one terminology are said to form **opaque** contexts. The term opaque figuratively describes the fact that the truth or falsity of the subordinate clause seems to be independent of the truth or falsity of the whole sentences. As Quine (1980: 22–3) points out for the statements in 10.99:

10.99   a.   Jones believes that Paris is in France.
           b.   Jones believes that Punakha is in Bhutan.

sentence 10.99a may be true and b false even though the components 'Paris is in France' and 'Punakha is in Bhutan' are true. Similarly for 10.100:

10.100   a.   Jones believes that Punakha is in Nepal.
           b.   Jones believes that Paris is in Japan.

The sentence 10.100a may be true and b false even though the components 'Punakha is in Nepal' and 'Paris is in Japan' are both false. It's as if the subordinate clause (the belief context) is a walled-off, opaque domain, as far as the truth value of the main sentence is concerned. It seems that in such examples we need access to the content of the subject's belief, necessitating an extra level of sense, or in a more recent terminology, intension. The notion was developed formally by Richard Montague (1974); see Dowty (1979) for discussion.

The challenge for formal semantics is to develop the semantic model to reflect the interpretation and calculation that is so central to language. One strategy has been to enrich the formal devices in certain areas where intensionality seems most clearly exhibited in natural languages. Such areas include **modality, tense, aspect** and **verbs of propositional attitude**. In each of these areas there has been research into formal semantic accounts. We cannot go into these developments in any detail here; instead we are pausing merely to sketch some of the main areas of focus and to refer the reader to the relevant literature.

10.8.2 Modality

As we saw in chapter 5, modality is often described in terms of two related aspects of meaning. The first, **epistemic** modality, concerns the resources available to the speaker to express judgement of fact versus possibility. The second, **deontic** modality, allows the expression of obligation and permission, often in terms of morality and law. All languages allow speakers a range of positions in both of these aspects. If we take epistemic modality, for example, we can quote Allan's scale of modality in 10.101 below (1986: 2. 289–90), which he views as a scale of implicatures such that each is stronger than the next about the fact of **p**:

10.101 a. I know that **p**.
     b. I am absolutely certain that **p**.
     c. I am almost certain that **p**.
     d. I believe that **p**.
     e. I am pretty certain that **p**.
     f. I think that **p**.
     g. I think/believe that **p** is probable.
     h. I think/believe that perhaps **p**.
     i. Possibly **p**.
     j. I suppose it is possible that **p**.
     k. It is not impossible that **p**.
     l. It is not necessarily impossible that **p**.
     m. It is unlikely that **p**.
     n. It is very unlikely that **p**.
     o. It is almost impossible that **p**.
     p. It is impossible that **p**.
     q. It is not the case that **p**.
     r. It is absolutely certain that not-**p**.

Even if we don't agree with Allan's selection or the ordering in this list, it is clear that there is a large range of options available to the speaker. Some of these choices of degree of commitment to the truth of **p** derive from the meaning of verbs like *believe, know,* etc.; others from negation; or from adjectives and adverbs like *possible* and *possibly.* The use of different intonation patterns can add further distinctions. In response to these facts about modality, **modal logics** were developed. The simplest approach employs a twofold division of epistemic modality into **fact** versus **possibility**, or 'situation as is' versus 'situation as may be'. One way of discussing this distinction between the actual and the non-actual is to talk of **possible worlds,** a phrase derived from Leibniz and formally developed by Kripke (see for example Kripke 1980). This is a difficult and controversial area in the philosophical literature but the notion has been important in formal semantics (see for example Lewis 1973, 1986). We can recognize the idea that a speaker, in moving away from certainty, can envisage two or more possible scenarios. So if we say *Fritz may be on the last train,* we entertain two situations: one where Fritz is on the train and another where he is not. Thus we imagine one situation where the statement *Fritz is on the last train* is true and another, where it is not. One way of dealing with this is to see truth as being relativized to possible situations, or possible worlds, to use this terminology.[15]

To reflect this, logicians introduce two logical operators $\lozenge$ 'it is possible that' and $\square$ 'it is necessary that'. These can be put in front of any formula of the predicate logic, i.e.

10.102 $\lozenge\phi =$ it is possible that ϕ
               $\square\phi =$ it is necessary that ϕ

The semantic definition of these relies on this new ontology of possible worlds: $\square$ means 'true in all possible worlds' (i.e. no alternatives are envisaged by the speaker) and $\lozenge$ means 'true in some possible worlds' (i.e. the speaker does envisage alternative scenarios). The formal implication of this is that truth must be relativized not to one situation but to one amongst a series of possible situations (worlds), including the actual situation (world). This means that our model must be expanded to include this multiplicity of situations, i.e. now $M = \{W, U, F\}$ where, as before, $U =$ the domain of individuals in a situation, F is the denotation assignment function, and the new element W is a set of possible worlds.

Relativizing truth to possible worlds enables one to adopt extensionally defined versions of Frege's notion of **sense** (*Sinn*), distinguished from **reference** (*Bedeutung*), as discussed in chapter 2. Using the term **intension** for sense, we can say that in this approach the intension of an expression is a function from possible worlds to its extension. In other words the function will give us the denotation of a particular linguistic expression in possible circumstances. Thus the intensions of nominals (NP), informally viewed as individual concepts, can now be viewed as functions from possible worlds to individuals; the intensions of predicates (VP), characterized as properties, can be viewed as functions from possible worlds to sets of individuals; and the intensions of sentences (S), characterized by Frege as the thoughts expressed by sentences, i.e. propositions, can be viewed as functions from worlds to truth values. See Chierchia and McConnell-Ginet (2000: 257–328) for discussion.

This approach raises interesting issues: for example, how many possible situations are relevant to a specific utterance? How are the possible situations ranked, by a combination of the linguistic expressions and background knowledge, so that some are more probable than others? We cannot pursue these issues any further here; readers are referred to Allwood et al. (1977: 108–24), Cann (1993: 263–81) and Chierchia and McConnell-Ginet (2000: 257–328) for introductory discussions.

The second type of modality, deontic modality, has been treated in a similar way: as a projection from the world as it is to the world as it should be under some moral or legal code, i.e. as the speaker entertaining an idealized world. Deontic modal operators have been suggested for logic, including Oφ 'obligatorily that φ' and Pφ 'permitted that φ'. The former can be interpreted denotationally as 'true in all morally or legally ideal worlds' and the latter as 'true in some morally or legally ideal worlds'. Again see Allwood et al. (1977: 108–24) for discussion.

10.8.3 Tense and aspect

These two further important intensional categories are, as discussed in chapter 5, related to the speaker's view of time. We need not review our earlier discussion here but in denotational terms, the speaker's ability to view propositions as timeless and eternal as in sentences like *All men are mortal*, or as fixed in relation to the time of utterance, or some other point identified in the metaphorical flow of time, clearly has truth-conditional implications. Take for example the sentences in 10.103 below:

10.103   a. The Irish punt will be replaced by the euro.
          b. The Irish punt was replaced by the euro.

These sentences differ in truth value being read by you today rather than say, in January 2002, and the only difference between them is their tense. We saw that an utterance can only be given a truth value relative to a situation: it seems that part of the character of situations may be their location in time.

One response has been to incorporate time into model-theoretic semantics. One way to do this is to include tense operators, similar to the modal operators we have just mentioned. We might for example include three operators: **Past**(φ), **Present**(φ) and **Future**(φ). This would allow formulae like 10.104 below:

Figure 10.1   Instants in the flow of time

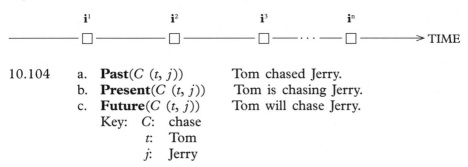

10.104   a. **Past**(C (t, j))   Tom chased Jerry.
          b. **Present**(C (t, j))   Tom is chasing Jerry.
          c. **Future**(C (t, j))   Tom will chase Jerry.
              Key: C: chase
                    t: Tom
                    j: Jerry

Such tense operators rely upon a division of the flow of time into a series of ordered instants, as in 10.105 below, where i = instant and < = before:

10.105 $i^1 < i^2 < i^3 \ldots < i^n$

or alternatively as in figure 10.1. If we select instant i^3 in figure 10.1 as **now**, then the evaluation procedure for the formula **Past**(C (t, j)) in 10.104a above will state that it is true if C (t, j) is true at time i^n, where $i^n < i^3$; that is, if it is true at a time before now. In other words the model will relativize formulae to both a situation and a time, so that our model is now $M = <W$, U, F, I, $<$ >, where I are the instants in time and < is the ordering relation 'before'. See Gamut (1991, vol 2: 32–44) and Cann (1993: 233–51) for introductory discussions of tense logics.

We saw in chapter 5 that tense is inextricably linked to **aspect**, a speaker's choice of viewing a situation as complete or incomplete, stretched over time or punctal, depending on the aspectual parameters of the language. When we come to consider the distribution of an activity or state over time, one useful modification to our simple model of time is to allow **intervals** of time in addition to just points or instants. Intervals can be defined in terms of instants: thus we can have an interval **k** which will be a continuous series of instants stretching between an initial and final instant, say i^3 to i^7. We can represent this as **k** = [i^3, i^7]. Intervals can be ordered with respect to other intervals in various ways, some of which we can show in diagram form in figure 10.2. Here interval **j** precedes interval **k**; interval **l** overlaps **k**; and **m** is contained within **k**. This treatment of intervals might allow description of stretches of time, and interrelations between times, like those in 10.106 below:

10.106   a. I studied Hausa for three years, then gave it up.
           b. She was ill all last week, when the interviews took place.

Formal approaches have to cope with the various aspectual and situation-type distinctions we looked at in chapter 5. Cann (1993: 251ff.) proposes, for example, a perfective aspect operator **Perf** and an imperfective operator

Figure 10.2   Intervals of time

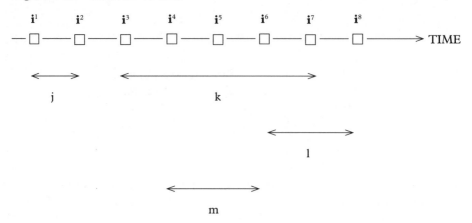

Impf for predicate logic, which will further relativize the truth of logical formulae. These operators rely on the idea of intervals of time. Without giving the formal definitions, a perfective formula will be true if both the start and end instants are included before the reference time point,[16] thus reflecting the complete interpretation of the perfective aspect. An imperfective formula, on the other hand, will be true if the activity overflows the time interval that is being interpreted. Thus our sentence 10.104a above, repeated as 10.107a below, can be given the simple perfective interpretation as in 10.107b:

10.107   a.   Tom chased Jerry.
           b.   **Past(Perf(***C*** (*t, j*)))**

The evaluation procedures for this formula will state that it is only true if the action of chasing is complete before the time of utterance. We can compare this with the imperfective clause in 10.108a below, represented in the formula in 10.108b:

10.108   a.   Tom was chasing Jerry (when I opened the door).
           b.   **(Past(Impf(***C*** (*t, j*))))**

Here the evaluation procedure will require that for 10.108b to be true the time interval for the chasing activity (*C*) should overlap the door-opening event.

   These are of course only preliminary sketches of the task facing formal semanticists: to model formally the tense and aspect distinctions found in languages, some of which we saw in chapter 5. See Cann (1993: 251–62) for further discussion.

   In the next section we discuss attempts to model formally the dynamism and context-dependence of language use.

10.9   Dynamic Approaches to Discourse

Our discussion of formal semantics so far has been concerned with the analysis of individual sentences. However, as we discussed in chapter 7, sentences are uttered in a context of discourse and many features of language reveal speakers' efforts to package their messages against the current context, in particular to take account of their hearers' knowledge and interpretive task. There have been a number of proposals to model formally the influence of discourse context on meaning, including File Change Semantics (Heim 1983, 1989) which uses the metaphor of files for information states in discourse and Dynamic Semantics (Groenendijk and Stokhof 1991, Groenendijk et al. 1996), where meaning is viewed as the potential to change information states. In this section we focus on one further approach, Discourse Representation Theory (DRT) (Kamp and Reyle 1993) and look briefly at how it attempts to model context dependency. From a wide range of issues discussed in this theory we shall select just one: discourse anaphora. Our account will be an informal one; the technical details can be found in Kamp and Reyle (1993). We begin by sketching in the background.

10.9.1   Anaphora in and across sentences

In chapter 7 we discussed the anaphoric use of pronouns. Traditionally the pronoun *himself* in 10.109 below is said to gain its denotation indirectly through coreference with the preceding nominal, *James*. They are said to be coreferential, i.e. denote the same entity in the situation described. As shown in a below, this can be reflected by attaching referential subscript indices; and as b shows, in predicate logic this relationship can be represented by giving each nominal the same individual constant:

10.109   a.   James$_i$ mistrusts himself$_i$.
           b. $M(j, j)$

Since quantified nominals don't directly denote an individual, sentences like 10.110a below are given a representation like 10.110b in predicate logic, where the pronoun is treated as a variable bound by a quantifier:

10.110   a.   Every thief mistrusts himself.
           b. $(\forall x\colon T(x))\ M(x, x)$

We also discussed in chapter 7 how new entities are often introduced into a discourse by an indefinite noun phrase and thereafter referred to by a range of definite nominals varying in their informational status, including pronouns. Once again, in an example like 10.111 below, the pronoun is said to be anaphorically related to the preceding indefinite NP:

10.111   Joan bought a car$_i$ and it$_i$ doesn't start.

In predicate logic this use of indefinite nominals can be treated as a kind of existential assertion and the pronoun again treated as a variable bound by the quantifying expression, as shown below:

10.112 $(\exists x: C(x))\ B(j, x) \wedge \neg S(x)$
           Paraphrase: There is car such that Joan bought it and it doesn't start.

This parallel between indefinite NPs and quantifiers breaks down in cross-sentential anaphora. For quantifiers the representation correctly predicts that anaphoric pronouns cannot occur outside the scope of the quantifier, such as in a following sentence. See the example below, where we assume the two sentences are spoken in sequence by the same speaker:

10.113   a. Every girl$_i$ came to the dance.
                $(\forall x: G(x))\ C(x, d)$
           b. ?She$_i$ met Alexander.
                $M(x, a)$

In the logical form in b the variable x is not bound by the quantifier in the preceding sentence and is therefore uninterpretable. This correctly predicts the fact that the pronoun *she* in b cannot refer back to *every girl* in a.
     However, indefinite NPs do allow cross-sentential anaphora; see for example:

10.114   a. A girl$_i$ came to the dance. She$_i$ met Alexander.

One way of reflecting this behaviour of indefinite nominals is to recognize that a discourse has a level of structure above the individual sentences and to view the role of indefinite nominals as introducing entities into this discourse structure. These are called **discourse referents** (Karttunen 1976) and the idea is that they have a lifespan in the discourse during which they can be referred to by pronouns. This lifespan can be limited by semantic operators such as negation. For example a discourse referent set up by an indefinite NP under negation has its lifespan limited to the scope of that negation. See the following example, where we assume the a and b sentences are uttered in succession by the same speaker:

10.115   a. Joan can't [afford a Ferrari$_i$].
           b. ?She likes it$_i$ though.

Here the pronoun *it* cannot refer back to the indefinite NP *a Ferrari* because the latter's lifespan as a discourse referent is limited by the scope of *not*, shown by square brackets. As we shall see, Discourse Representation Theory is one way of formalizing such a notion of discourse referents.

10.9.2 Donkey sentences

Even within a single sentence there are examples where anaphora between indefinite NPs and pronouns causes problems for a quantifier-variable binding account. If we take sentence 10.116a below we can represent it in standard predicate logic as 10.116b:

10.116   a.   If Joan owns a Ferrari she is rich.
           b. $(\exists x \ (F(x) \wedge O(j, x))) \rightarrow R(j)$

However, applying the same translation procedure to 10.117a gives us 10.117b:

10.117   a.   If a teenager owns a Ferrari he races it.
           b. $(\exists x \exists y \ (T(x) \wedge F(y) \wedge O(x, y))) \rightarrow R(x, y)$

Though these two sentences seem to have the same syntactic structure, 117b is not a legal formula because the variables in the consequent of the implication are not correctly bound by the relevant existential quantifiers. To capture the meaning of 10.117a in a well-formed formula we have to use something like 10.118 below:

10.118   a. $\forall x \forall y \ ((T(x) \wedge F(y) \wedge O(x, y))) \rightarrow R(x, y))$
           b.   Paraphrase: For all x, all y: if x is a teenager, y is a Ferrari, and x owns y, then x races y

This does capture the fact that the preferred interpretation of 10.117 has universal force, i.e. that all teenagers who have Ferraris race them. However the problem here is that we have translated the indefinite nominal *a Ferrari* by a universal quantifier expression in 10.118a and by an existential quantifier expression in 10.117b. This is a threat to the notion of compositionality and is another version of our isomorphism problem earlier. It seems unsatisfactory that an indefinite NP is sometimes treated as an existential quantifier and at other times as a universal quantifier, the deciding factor apparently being the presence of an anaphoric pronoun.

    Examples like 10.117a are known as **donkey sentences** after Geach's (1962) discussion of this problem using examples like *If a farmer owns a donkey, he beats it* and *Every farmer who owns a donkey beats it*. In essence, the problem with the pronoun *it* in these examples is that it cannot be a referring expression, since there is no specific donkey it denotes. However, as we have seen, treating *it* as a bound variable leads to other problems.[17]

10.9.3 DRT and discourse anaphora

Discourse Representation Theory (DRT) formalizes a level of discourse structure which is updated by successive sentences and forms a representation of the discourse referents introduced so far. The discourse referents form an intermediate level between the nominals and the real individuals in the situation described. The main form of representation is a Discourse Representation Structure (DRS), usually presented in a box format, as shown below. These DRSs are built up by construction rules from the linguistic input, sentence by sentence. If we take the sentences in 10.119 below as uttered in sequence, the first sentence will trigger the construction of the DRS in 10.120:

10.119   a.   Alexander met a girl$_i$.
           b.   She$_i$ smiled.

10.120

$$
\boxed{
\begin{array}{l}
\text{x \quad y} \\
\hline
\text{Alexander (x)} \\
\text{Girl (y)} \\
\text{met (x, y)}
\end{array}
}
$$

The discourse referents are given in the top line of the DRS, called the universe of the DRS, and below them are conditions giving the properties of the discourse referents. These conditions govern whether the DRS can be embedded into the model of the current state of the discourse. A DRS is true if all of the discourse referents can be mapped to individuals in the situation described in such a way that the conditions are met. A name like *Alexander* in 10.119 denotes an individual, while an indefinite NP like *a girl* will be satisfied by any individual meeting the property of being a girl. The third condition is the relation *met* (x, y). We can see that the truth conditions for sentence 10.119a are given here by a combination of the discourse referents and the conditions. The sentence will be true of a situation if it contains two individuals; one named Alexander, the other a girl, and if the first met the second. An important point here is that in an example like this the introduction of a discourse referent into a DRS carries an existential commitment. Thus the indefinite NP *a girl* is treated as having existential force, though there are other ways of introducing indefinite nominals which do not have this existential commitment, as we shall see below. The initial DRS is labelled K_0, the next K_1 and so on. The latest K acts as the context against which a new sentence in the discourse is interpreted.

The second sentence in 10.119 updates the discourse and adds another discourse referent, *she*. The embedding rule for pronouns will say that we must find an accessible antecedent for it. In this case gender is a factor since *she* must find a feminine antecedent. If the correct antecedent for the pronoun is identified, the result is the extended version below of the original DRS with a new reference marker and a new condition:

10.121

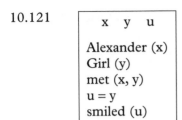

A negative sentence like 10.122 below will be assigned the DRS in 10.123:

10.122   Joan does not own a Ferrari.

10.123

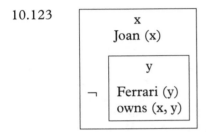

Here the DRS contains one discourse referent and two conditions: the first is the usual naming relation, Joan (x); and the second is a second DRS embedded in the first and marked by the logical negation sign ¬. The satisfaction of this second condition is that there is not a Ferrari such that Joan owns it. This contained DRS is said to be **subordinate** to the containing DRS and is triggered by the construction rules for negation. This subordination has two effects on any discourse referents within the embedded DRS. The first, as suggested by our characterization of how the condition in 10.123 is satisfied, is that there is no existential interpretation for discourse referents in this type of subordinate DRS. Thus there is no existential commitment with the indefinite NP *a Ferrari* in this sentence, unlike *a girl* in 10.119.

The second effect follows from the existence of **accessibility rules** in DRT. Briefly, proper nouns (names) are always accessible in the subsequent discourse, i.e. once introduced can always be referred to by an anaphoric pronoun. The accessibility of other nominals depends on the structure of the DRSs they occur in. For negatives, the rule is that discourse referents introduced within a subordinate DRS under the scope of negation are inaccessible to pronouns in subsequent stages of the DRS.[18] This means that the discourse referent y (i.e. *a Ferrari*) in 10.123 is inaccessible to subsequent pronouns. We can look at our earlier example 10.115, repeated below, to show this.

10.124   a. Joan can't afford a Ferrari$_i$.
          b. ?She likes it$_i$ though.

We can suggest 10.125 below as a DRS after the two sentences in 10.124:

10.125

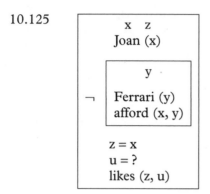

The pronoun *she* in the second sentence is successfully interpreted as anaphoric with *Joan* in the first sentence, and hence $z = x$ in the DRS conditions. However, we have written a question mark in the identification of an antecedent for u (i.e. *it*) because the only possible antecedent for y (i.e. *a Ferrari*) is not accessible since it occurs in the subordinate DRS box under negation. This explains the semantic anomaly of 10.124 above and provides a formalization of one aspect of the notion of discourse referent lifespan mentioned in section 10.9.1.

Sentences with conditionals are also represented with subordinate DRSs as conditions. The construction rules for these embed two DRSs linked by a connector ⇒, which parallels the material implication in predicate logic. The first DRS represents the antecedent and the second the consequent. Our earlier example *If Joan owns a Ferrari she is rich* would be given the complex DRS below (assuming an integration into a preceding empty DRS):

10.126

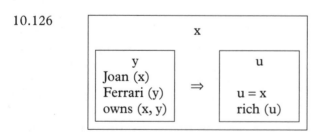

In this DRS the accessibility rule for names (that they are accessible to the whole of the subsequent discourse or have an 'eternal' lifespan, so to speak) is reflected by the discourse referent x (for *Joan*) being represented in the containing DRS, outside the subordinate boxes for the antecedent and consequent.

A donkey sentence like 10.117 earlier *If a teenager owns a Ferrari he races it* would be given a DRS like the following:

10.127

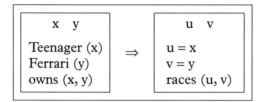

The accessibility rules for conditional sentences state that the antecedent discourse referents are accessible from the consequent but not vice versa, i.e. anaphora can reach 'up and back' but not 'down and forward'. This means that the pronoun *it* can refer anaphorically to *a Ferrari* in 10.117 because the discourse referent in the antecedent is accessible to the pronoun in the consequent. On the other hand, a sentence like *?If a teenager$_i$ owns it$_k$ he$_i$ races a Ferrari$_k$* is anomalous because the indefinite nominal in the consequent is not accessible to *it* in the antecedent.

Sentences with universal quantifiers are given a representation like conditionals; 10.128 below can be given the DRS in 10.129:

10.128   Every teenager who owns a Ferrari is rich.

10.129

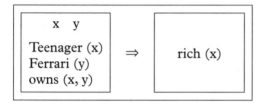

A donkey sentence with *every* like 10.130 below is therefore given the DRS 10.131, which we can compare with 10.127 above:

10.130   Every teenager who owns a Ferrari races it.

10.131

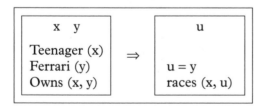

This representation brings together the two forms of donkey sentences into a structurally similar representation.

All of these conditional DRSs share an accessibility rule: any discourse referent introduced in a subordinate DRS is inaccessible to pronouns in a condition outside the subordinate DRS. This explains the impossible anaphora in 10.132 below, which would have the DRS 10.133:

10.132   Every student reads [a book on semantics]$_i$. ?It$_i$ is heavy.

10.133

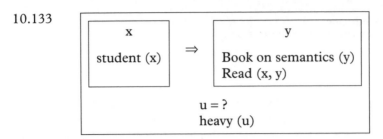

In 10.133 we again use a question mark to show that the pronoun *it* in the second sentence cannot be anaphorically related to any antecedent nominal. The discourse referent *book on semantics* is not accessible to the pronoun because it is in a subordinate DRS while the pronoun is in the superordinate DRS. This accessibility constraint explains the difference between indefinite nominals and quantified nominals in licensing a subsequent pronoun. Compare 10.132 above with 10.134 below:

10.134   A student read [a book on semantics]$_i$. It$_i$ was heavy.

In 10.134 the pronoun can be anaphorically related to the indefinite NP *a book on semantics* because the structure of the DRS involves no subordination.
    We leave our brief review of DRT at this point. Our discussion has revealed that the theory has a number of advantages in the description of discourse anaphora. The theory formalizes the notion of discourse referents and provides a unified explanation for the lifespan in the discourse of different nominals. In particular we saw that DRT distinguishes between names, which are always available for subsequent anaphoric pronouns, and indefinite NPs, whose lifespan depends on the type of sentence they occur in, for example: positive assertions, negative sentences, conditional sentences, and universally quantified sentences. The theory brings out the similarity between conditional and universally quantified donkey sentences and collapses the treatment of indefinite nominals in donkey sentences to the general cases. Finally DRT's view of an incrementally adjusted discourse structure seems very appealing in the light of our discussion in chapter 7. This structure can be viewed as one facet of the kind of knowledge representation that we described in chapter 7 as being cooperatively managed by participants in discourse.

10.10 Summary

In this chapter we have attempted an outline of how a formal semantic analysis might proceed. We have looked at how English sentences might be translated into a logical metalanguage, the predicate logic, and how this logic can be given a denotational semantics via model theory. We began with the translation and interpretation of simple statements. We then looked at quantification by discussing sentences with the universal quantifier $\forall$ and the existential quantifier $\exists$, and looked at compound sentences, using the example of the connective $\wedge$ 'and'. We then turned briefly to word meaning in this approach. Having sketched in this basic formal model, we began to look at how it has been extended to reflect important features of natural language semantics. We began by looking at how the treatment of quantifiers in first-order predicate logic has to be extended to reflect natural language quantifiers. We saw how the notion of generalized quantifiers has been applied to solve descriptive problems in English quantifiers. We turned then to the treatment of pronominal anaphora and looked at how Discourse Representation Theory models anaphora within and between sentences by establishing a dynamic model of discourse structure.

In the simple model M_1 we concentrated on the extensions of expressions like nominals, predicates and sentences. We have seen, however, that in a number of different ways we need to expand such a model to take account of intensional features of language. The developments we have touched on – possible worlds, models of time and aspect – are mechanisms introduced to reflect this intensionality. It is at this point – intensions – that we can perhaps see denotational approaches coming into contact with representational approaches. For the latter will ask the essentially psychological question about intensions: how is it that speakers identify a relationship between a word and its extension? If we look back to our model M_1 we can see that we used a function F_1 to return the denotations of constants and predicates in the situation. It is this function, relating the logical translation of nouns like *cat* and *dog* to the entities in the situation, for which representational approaches will seek a psychological explanation. It might thus be possible to view the different traditions of denotational and representational semantics as complementary lines of enquiry, concerning themselves with two related aspects of meaning.

FURTHER READING

There are several very good introductions to logic and the choice depends on the reader's taste. Allwood et al. (1977) and McCawley (1981) are intended for a linguistics audience. Other more general introductions are Guttenplan (1986) and McKay (1989).

There are a number of good introductions to formal semantics: Chierchia and McConnnell-Ginet (2000) and Cann (1993) both provide in-depth descriptions of the kind of model-theoretic semantics outlined in this chapter. De Swart (1998) is a concise and accessible introduction. Lappin (1996) is a comprehensive collection of papers which review topics of contemporary research in formal semantics. Gamut

(1991) consists of two volumes: the first is an introduction to logic; the second deals with intensional logics and formal semantics, and includes an introduction to Montague Grammar. The basic reference for Discourse Representation Theory is Kamp and Reyle (1993).

EXERCISES

10.1   Translate the following sentences into predicate logic. For compound sentences use the truth-functional connectives we employed in this chapter. Some symbols are provided for your use:

[Symbols: a = Arthur, m = Merlin, g = Guinevere, l = Lancelot, e = the sword Excalibur, $K(x)$ = x was a king, $Q(x)$ = x was a queen, $W(x)$ = x was a wizard, $A(x, y)$ = x advised y, $P(x, y)$ = x possessed y, $L(x, y)$ = x loved y]

   a.   Arthur was a king and Merlin was a wizard.
   b.   If Arthur was a king, then Guinevere was a queen.
   c.   Arthur, who was a king, possessed the sword Excalibur.
   d.   Merlin did not advise Lancelot.
   e.   Either Lancelot loved Guinevere or Guinevere loved Lancelot.
   f.   Merlin was a wizard who advised Arthur.

10.2   Translate the following sentences into predicate logic, using the restricted format for $\exists$ and $\forall$, the existential and universal quantifiers, as necessary. Note which sentences, if any, allow two interpretations.

[Symbols: l = Lancelot, h = the Holy Grail, $D(x)$ = x is a dragon, $N(x, y)$ = x was nervous of y, $K(x, y)$ = x was keen on y, $H(x, y)$ = x hated y, $S(x, y)$ = x searched for y]

   a.   Lancelot hated all dragons.
   b.   Every dragon was nervous of Lancelot.
   c.   One dragon was nervous of everyone.
   d.   Someone searched for the Holy Grail.
   e.   Every dragon wasn't keen on maidens.
   f.   Every dragon who was keen on maidens was nervous of Lancelot.
   g.   Not everyone searched for the Holy Grail.
   h.   No dragon searched for Lancelot.

10.3   For the following exercise, assume the model M_3 specified below:

U_3 = {Lancelot, Gawaine, Elaine, Igraine, dragon}
$F_3(l)$ = Lancelot, $F_3(g)$ = Gawaine, $F_3(e)$ = Elaine, $F_3(i)$ = Igraine, $F_3(d)$ = dragon
$F_3(M)$ = was a maiden = {<Elaine>, <Igraine>}
$F_3(K)$ = was a knight = {<Lancelot>, <Gawaine>}
$F_3(D)$ = was a dragon = {<dragon>}
$F_3(L)$ = loved = {<Elaine, Lancelot>, <Igraine, Gawaine>, <Gawaine, Igraine>}
$F_3(C)$ = captured = {<dragon, Elaine>, <dragon, Igraine>}
$F_3(S)$ = slew = {<Lancelot, dragon>}
$F_3(F)$ = freed = {<Lancelot, Elaine>, <Lancelot, Igraine>}

Calculate the truth value of the following sentences with respect to M_3:

a. $L(g, i)$
b. $C(d, l)$
c. $(\forall x: M(x))\ L(x, g)$
d. $(\exists x: M(x))\ L(x, g)$
e. $S(l, d) \land \neg(\exists x: K(x))\ L(x, e)$
f. $(\forall x: D(x))\ S(l, x) \land (\forall y: M(y))\ F(l, y)$

10.4 Assuming the truth tables for the connectives given in 1a–c below, evaluate the truth of the sentences in 2 with respect to the same model M_3 above:

1 a.

p	**q**	**p ∨ q**
T	T	T
T	F	T
F	T	T
F	F	F

b.

p	**q**	**p ∨ₑ q**
T	T	F
T	F	T
F	T	T
F	F	F

c.

p	**q**	**p → q**
T	T	T
T	F	F
F	T	T
F	F	T

2 a. $F(l, e) \vee F(l, i)$
   b. $F(l, e) \vee_e F(l, i)$
   c. $S(l, d) \rightarrow F(l, e)$
   d. $L(g, i) \rightarrow F(g, i)$

10.5 Use the formulae of meaning postulates to represent the semantic relations between the following pairs of words:

> sweater/jumper
> true/false
> gun/weapon
> open/shut (of a door)
> uppercut/punch (in boxing)
> car/automobile

10.6 In section 10.7.3 we discussed the symmetry of quantifiers. For each of the quantifiers below decide whether it is symmetrical or asymmetrical:

   a. many (in its cardinal use)
   b. few (in its cardinal use)
   c. every
   d. (at least) four

10.7 In section 10.7.4 we gave as examples of negative polarity items the words *any*, *ever* and *yet*. Decide which elements in the following sentences are also good candidates for negative polarity items.

   a. She seldom lifted a finger to help.
   b. I never touch a drop of alcohol.
   c. He rarely contributes a lot of money.
   d. He was so scared he couldn't budge an inch.
   e. They never uttered so much as a word of thanks.
   f. I don't care a fig for her opinion.

10.8 In section 10.7.4 we discussed the monotonicity of quantifiers. Assuming a generalized quantifier format, for each of the quantifiers below use your own examples to decide whether they are (a) upward or downward entailing in the left argument and (b) upward or downward entailing in the right argument:

   a. most
   b. many
   c. (exactly) two

10.9   Below is a mini-discourse of two sentences. Assume that there is no preceding context. Give a DRT Discourse Representation Structure (DRS) for the first sentence and a second updated DRS after the second is embedded:

A man bought a donkey. He fed it.

10.10   Discuss which NPs in the following sentences introduce discourse referents that are accessible for coreference with pronouns in subsequent sentences.

a.   If Carl drinks a beer he is happy.
b.   Maura does not own a scanner.
c.   Every student who does an exercise enjoys it.

NOTES

1   This term describes the studies in formal semantics which have followed the work of Richard Montague. As mentioned in chapter 4, Montague hypothesized that the methods of logic could be used to analyse the semantics of English and other natural languages: 'There is in my opinion no important theoretical difference between natural languages and the artificial languages of logicians: indeed, I consider it possible to comprehend the syntax and semantics of both kinds of language within a single, natural and mathematically precise theory' (Montague 1974: 222, cited in Cann 1993: 2). For introductions to Montague semantics see Dowty et al. (1981) and Cann (1993).

2   This quotation refers to **possible states of affairs**. This is another way of referring to the notion of **possible worlds**. We met this notion briefly in chapter 5 when we discussed modality; we come back to it again later in this chapter.

3   See Haack (1978) for an accessible description of the development of modern logic, and its philosophical background.

4   For an introductory discussion of animal communication systems, see Akmajian et al. (1984: 9–45).

5   For a modern translation of Frege's work into English, see Frege (1980). Frege's work on the logic of quantifiers seems to have been independently paralleled in the investigations of the logician Charles Sanders Peirce. See Haack (1978: 39ff.).

6   For example, we shall not deal with the fundamental relationship between syntactic rules and semantic rules that is characteristic of Montague Grammar.

7   Note that though the universal quantifier sets up a range of applicability for the generalization, it does not carry any existential commitment. Our expression in 10.23 is equivalent to saying that if there were students, then they wrote a paper (or more opaquely, perhaps, there is no such thing as a student who didn't write a paper). Because of the truth behaviour of material implication, discussed in chapter 4, if there are no students, then our sentence is vacuously true. So, rather counter-intuitively, *Every student wrote a paper* is held to be true

when there are no students. We can show this with the following truth table (based on the table for → described in 4.28 in chapter 4):

	Sx	$W(x, p)$	$(Sx \rightarrow W(x, p))$
1	T	T	T
2	T	F	F
3	F	T	T
4	F	F	T

If there are no students (no thing is a student) then lines 3 and 4 of this table apply and in both the whole expression is true. Clearly, though, it would be very odd to say *Every student wrote a paper* when there were no students and therefore no papers. One way of explaining this is to say that it is because the universal quantifier is quantifying over the universe of individuals, whether they are students or not. In section 10.7.1 below we discuss proposals to restrict the range of the quantifier to the type of things named by the nominal, here students. The existential quantifier ∃ described below in the text does carry an existential commitment.

8   As we noted earlier, some predicates only require one argument, e.g. *Fred smokes S(f)*, others two, *Pat resembles Beethoven R(p, b)*, or three *Giovanni gave the cello to Mike G(g, c, m)*. In logic any number of arguments is theoretically possible; in English, of course, the normal requirements for a verb would be one, two or three arguments (with a few verbs like *bet* having four).

9   We will assume the following set theory notion and representations:

1   A **set** {..}, which can be identified by listing the members, e.g. {Mercury, Mars, Earth, ...} or by describing an attribute of the members, e.g. {x: x is a planet in the solar system}.

2   **Set membership, x ∈ A**, e.g. Mercury ∈ {x: x is a planet in the solar system}.

3   **Subset, A ⊆ B**, where every member of **A** is a member of **B**, e.g. {Venus, Jupiter} ⊆ {x: x is a planet in the solar system}.

4   **Intersection** of sets, **A ∩ B**, which is the set consisting of the elements which are members of both **A** and **B**, e.g. {Venus, Mars, Jupiter, Saturn} ∩ {Mars, Jupiter, Uranus, Pluto} = {Mars, Jupiter}.

5   **Ordered pair, <a, b>**, where the ordering is significant, e.g. <Mercury, Venus> ≠ <Venus, Mercury>.

6   **Ordered n-tuple, $<a_1, a_2, a_3 \ldots a_n>$**, e.g. the 4-tuple <Mercury, Venus, Earth, Mars>.

7   **Cardinality** of **A**, |**A**|, which is the number of members in **A**.

8 |**A**| = five, the cardinality of **A** is five, i.e. **A** has five members.

9 |**A**| > |**B**|, the cardinality of **A** is greater than **B**; i.e. **A** has more members than B.

10 |**A**| ≥ |**B**|, the cardinality of **A** is greater than or equal to **B**; i.e. **A** has the same or more members than B.

11   **A − B, A minus B**, the set of members of A that are not also members of B.

12   Ø is the empty set.

10   We ignore here the logic possibility but murine improbability that Jerry hunts himself.

11   Of course, in our informal presentation here we necessarily take on trust these advantages of formality and explicitness: we have not investigated the formal nature of sets, functions, relations and the logics. For an excellent introduction to the mathematical foundations of these notions, see Partee et al. (1990).

12   Note that since meaning postulates express relationships between the **extensions** of linguistic expressions, they constitute knowledge about the world rather than about words.

13   This formulation is described as the **relational** view of quantifying determiners since it treats the determiner as a two-place predicate taking sets as arguments, i.e. as denoting a relation between sets. An alternative is the **functional** view where the determiner is a function that maps a common noun denotation onto a noun phrase, which is the generalized quantifier. The generalized quantifier then takes a VP denotation as an argument to build propositions. See Keenan (1996) for discussion and Chierchia and McConnell-Ginet (2000: 501f.) for an introductory description.

14   This existential *there* construction must be distinguished from other sentences beginning with *there*, for example the use of *there* to introduce lists, as in A: *Which paintings do you have left?* B: *Well, there's the Picasso, the Rembrandt and the Klee.* This construction behaves differently, allowing for example: *There's most of the Impressionists, and there's both Kandinskys.*

15   For a discussion of the application of possible-world semantics to the issue of fictional entities and worlds that we discussed in chapter 2, see Lewis (1978).

16   As we saw in chapter 5, the reference time point may be the time of utterance as in the perfective in 1 below; or a time in the future or past of the time of utterance, as in the perfectives in 2 and 3:

1   He has served three presidents.
2   By next year, he will have served three presidents.
3   By 1992, he had served three presidents.

17   Seuren (1994: 1060) points out another problem for a bound variable analysis: that is, that our translation via the universal quantifier $\forall$ in 10.116 lacks generality because a similar scope problem occurs in sentences like *If it's a good thing that Smith owns a donkey, it's a bad thing that he beats it* and *Either Smith no longer owns a donkey or he still beats it.* For discussion of donkey sentences see Kamp (1981), Reinhart (1986), Heim (1990) and Seuren (1994).

18   For a discussion of counterexamples to this generalization, and a proposal for a solution, see Krahmer (1998: 65f.).

chapter 11

Cognitive Semantics

11.1 Introduction

In this chapter we look at semantics within the approach known as *cognitive semantics*. As is often the case with labels for theories,[1] this may be objected to as being rather uninformative: in this instance because, as we have seen, in many semantic approaches it is assumed that language is a mental faculty and that linguistic abilities are supported by special forms of knowledge. Hence for many linguists semantics is necessarily a part of the inquiry into cognition. However, as we shall see, writers in the general approach called *cognitive linguistics*, and other scholars who are broadly in sympathy with them, share a particular view of linguistic knowledge. This view is that there is no separation of linguistic knowledge from general thinking or cognition. Contrary to the influential views of the philosopher Jerry Fodor or of Noam Chomsky,[2] these scholars see linguistic behaviour as another part of the general cognitive abilities which allow learning, reasoning, etc. So perhaps we can take the label *cognitive linguistics* as representing the slogan 'linguistic knowledge is part of general cognition'. As we shall see, this slogan does fit work in semantics in this approach.

We can begin by outlining some of the main principles behind this general approach. Cognitive linguists often point to a division between **formal** and **functional** approaches to language. Formal approaches, such as **generative**

grammar (Chomsky 1988), are often associated with a certain view of language and cognition: that knowledge of linguistic structures and rules forms an autonomous module (or faculty), independent of other mental processes of attention, memory and reasoning. This external view of an independent linguistic module is often combined with a view of internal modularity: that different levels of linguistic analysis, such as phonology, syntax and semantics, form independent modules. In this view, the difference between modules is one of kind: thus externally, it is good practice to investigate linguistic principles without reference to other mental faculties; and internally, to investigate, say, syntactic principles without reference to semantic content. This characterization of formal approaches concentrates on its epistemological implications. Formalism also implies the desirability and possibility of stating the autonomous principles in ways that are formally elegant, conceptually simple, and mathematically well-formed.[3]

Functionalism, with which cognitive linguists identify themselves, implies a quite different view of language: that externally, principles of language use embody more general cognitive principles; and internally, that explanation must cross boundaries between levels of analysis. In this view the difference between language and other mental processes is possibly one of degree but is not one of kind. Thus it makes sense to look for principles shared across a range of cognitive domains. Similarly, it is argued that no adequate account of grammatical rules is possible without taking the meaning of elements into account.

This general difference of approach underlies specific positions taken by cognitive linguists on a number of issues: in each case their approach seeks to break down the abstractions and specializations characteristic of formalism, many of which we have met in earlier chapters. Thus studies in cognitive semantics have tended to blur, if not ignore, the commonly made distinctions between linguistic knowledge and encyclopaedic, real-world knowledge – a topic we touched on earlier; and between literal and figurative language, as we shall see. Similarly cognitive linguists share the functionalist view that distinguishing linguistic levels of analysis, while a useful ploy for practical description, is potentially harmful to our conceptions of language, since syntax, for example, can never be autonomous from semantics or pragmatics. Ultimately, this view goes, the explanation of grammatical patterns cannot be given in terms of abstract syntactic principles but only in terms of the speaker's intended meaning in particular contexts of language use.

A further distinction that is reassessed in this framework is the traditional structuralist division between, to use Ferdinand de Saussure's (1974) terms, **diachronic** (or historical) linguistics and **synchronic** linguistics. In his foundational lectures, de Saussure, attempting to free linguistics from etymological explanation, proposed his famous abstraction: a **synchronic** linguistics, where considerations of historical change might be ignored, as if in describing a language we could factor out or 'freeze' time.[4] Such an idealization has been accepted in many linguistic theories, but is currently questioned in functional approaches. Linguistic structures, in a functionalist perspective, have evolved through long periods of use and the processes of change are evident in and relevant to an understanding of the current use of the language. Thus processes of **grammaticalization**, for example, where lexical categories may over time develop into functional categories and independent words become inflections, can provide evidence of general linguistic and cognitive principles, as discussed by Heine et al. (1991) and Hopper and Traugott (1993).[5]

If we turn to meaning, a defining characteristic of cognitive semantics is the rejection of what is termed **objectivist semantics**. George Lakoff (1988: 123–4), for example, assigns to objectivism the basic metaphysical belief that categories exist in objective reality, together with their properties and relations, independently of consciousness. Associated with this is the view that the symbols of language are meaningful because they are associated with these objective categories. This gives rise to a particular approach to semantics which Lakoff characterizes under three 'doctrines':

11.1   Objectivist semantics (adapted from Lakoff 1988: 125–6)
      a.   The doctrine of truth-conditional meaning: Meaning is based on reference and truth.
      b.   The 'correspondence theory' of truth: Truth consists in the correspondence between symbols and states of affairs in the world.
      c.   The doctrine of objective reference: There is an 'objectively correct' way to associate symbols with things in the world.

In rejecting these views, cognitive semanticists place themselves in opposition to the formal semantics approach described in chapter 10. Cognitive semanticists take the view that we have no access to a reality independent of human categorization and that therefore the structure of reality as reflected in language is a product of the human mind. Consequently they reject the **correspondence theory of truth**, discussed in chapters 4 and 10. For these writers, linguistic truth and falsity must be relative to the way an observer construes a situation, based on his or her conceptual framework.[6] The real focus of investigation should, in this view, be these conceptual frameworks and how language use reflects them. In the rest of this chapter we examine this line of inquiry; we might begin here by asking of this approach our deceptively simple question: what is meaning?

One answer in the cognitive semantics literature is that meaning is based on conventionalized conceptual structures. Thus semantic structure, along with other cognitive domains, reflects the mental categories which people have formed from their experience of growing up and acting in the world. A number of conceptual structures and processes are identified in this literature but special attention is often given to **metaphor**. Cognitive linguists agree with the proposal by George Lakoff and Johnson (1980), Lakoff (1987) and Mark Johnson (1987) that metaphor is an essential element in our categorization of the world and our thinking processes. As we shall see, metaphor is seen as related to other fundamental structures such as **image schemas**, which provide a kind of basic conceptual framework derived from perception and bodily experience and Fauconnier's (1985, 1994) notion of **mental spaces**, which are mental structures which speakers set up to manipulate reference to entities. Cognitive linguists also investigate the conceptual processes which reveal the importance of the speaker's construal of a scene: processes such as **viewpoint shifting, figure-ground shifting** and **profiling**. We look at these structures and processes in successive sections later.

A consequence of the view of language we have briefly outlined is that the study of semantics, and linguistics, must be an interdisciplinary activity. One result is that scholars working within this and related frameworks tend to stray across intra- and interdisciplinary boundaries more easily than most. The approach to metaphor we discuss in the next section has, for example, been applied not only to the study of grammar and semantics, but also to historical linguistics (Sweetser 1990), categories of thought (George Lakoff 1987), poetic language (Lakoff and Turner 1989), rhetoric (Turner 1987) and ethics (Mark Johnson 1993), amongst other areas. In our discussion, we concentrate on semantic issues and we begin with metaphor in section 11.2.

11.2   Metaphor

11.2.1   Introduction

Metaphor has traditionally been viewed as the most important form of **figurative** language use, and is usually seen as reaching its most sophisticated forms in literary or poetic language. We can, however, take a couple of examples from journalism to begin our discussion. Both are from reports on the 2002 Hollywood film awards, the 'Oscars':

11.2   Movie studios love a good fight, and a bad one too. But the Oscar battles have become trench warfare and dirty tricks.

11.3   . . . a best actress race that has taken on heat as longtime prohibitive favourite Sissy Spacek has suddenly caught a glimpse of Halle Berry in her rear view mirror.[7]

As we can see, in 11.2 the awards competition is portrayed in terms of warfare, while in 11.3 the image is of a car race. There are many explanations of how metaphors work but a common idea is that metaphor is somewhat like **simile** (e.g. *Reading that essay was like wading through mud*) in that it involves the identification of resemblances, but that metaphor goes further by causing a transference, where properties are transferred from one concept to another. This transference has some interesting properties, as we will see later.

Before we go on, let's introduce some terminology. The two concepts involved in a metaphor are referred to in various ways in the literature. We can select two: the starting-point or described concept (in our examples above, the Oscar awards) is often called the **target** domain, while the comparison concept or the analogy (in our two examples, war and car racing) is called the **source** domain. In I. A. Richards' (1936) terminology the former is called the **tenor** and the latter, the **vehicle**. Both sets of terms are commonly used in the literature; we will adopt the former: target and source.

There are two traditional positions on the role of metaphor in language. The first, often called the **classical** view since it can be traced back to Aristotle's writings on metaphor, sees metaphor as a kind of decorative addition to ordinary plain language; a rhetorical device to be used at certain times to gain certain effects. This view portrays metaphor as something outside normal language and which requires special forms of interpretation from listeners or readers. A version of this approach is often adopted in the **literal language theory** we described in chapter 1. In this view metaphor is often seen as a departure from literal language, detected as anomalous by the hearer, who then has to employ some strategies to construct the speaker's intended meaning. We can take as an example of this general approach Searle (1979: 114), who describes the start of the process thus (where a contextual assumption is that Sam is a person):

11.4   Suppose he hears the utterance, 'Sam is a pig.' He knows that cannot be literally true, that the utterance, if he tries to take it literally, is radically defective. And, indeed, such defectiveness is a feature of nearly all the examples that we have considered so far. The defects which cue the hearer may be obvious falsehood, semantic nonsense, violations of the rules of speech acts, or violations of conversational principles of communication. This suggests a strategy that underlies the first step: *Where the utterance is defective if taken literally, look for an utterance meaning that differs from sentence meaning* [author's italics].

We won't go into details of the various proposals that have been made for the next steps that the hearer uses to repair the 'defective' utterance; see Ortony (1979) for some proposals.

The second traditional approach to metaphor, often called the **Romantic** view since it is associated with eighteenth- and nineteenth-century Romantic views of the imagination, takes a very different view of metaphor. In this view metaphor is integral to language and thought as a way of experiencing the world. It is evidence of the role of the imagination in conceptualizing and reasoning and it follows that all language is metaphorical. In particular, there is no distinction between literal and figurative language.[8]

11.2.2   Metaphor in cognitive semantics

An important characteristic of cognitive semantics is the central role in thought and language assigned to metaphor. Given the classical/Romantic opposition we have described, the cognitive semantics approach can be seen as an extension of the Romantic view.[9] Cognitivists argue that metaphor is ubiquitous in ordinary language, though they pull back a little from the strong Romantic position that all language is metaphorical. While metaphor is seen as a very important mode of thinking and talking about the world, it is accepted that there are also non-metaphorical concepts:

11.5   Metaphors allow us to understand one domain of experience in terms of another. To serve this function, there must be some grounding, some concepts that are not completely understood via metaphor to serve as source domains.   (Lakoff and Turner 1989: 135)

In emphasizing the important role of metaphor in ordinary language, Lakoff and his colleagues have identified a large number of common metaphors. One group, for example, they describe as **spatial** metaphors, for example the many metaphors associated with an UP-DOWN orientation. These include the following, where we select a few of their examples (Lakoff and Johnson 1980: 14–21):

11.6   a.   HAPPY IS UP; SAD IS DOWN
              I'm feeling *up*. My spirits *rose*. You're in *high* spirits. I'm feeling *down*. I'm *depressed*. He's really *low* these days. My spirits *sank*.
         b.   CONSCIOUS IS UP; UNCONSCIOUS IS DOWN
              Wake *up*. He *fell* asleep. He *dropped* off to sleep. He's *under* hypnosis. He *sank* into a coma.
         c.   HEALTH AND LIFE ARE UP; SICKNESS AND DEATH ARE DOWN
              He's at the *peak* of health. He's in *top* shape. He *fell* ill. He's *sinking* fast. He came *down* with the flu. His health is *declining*.
         d.   HAVING CONTROL OR FORCE IS UP; BEING SUBJECT TO CONTROL OR FORCE IS DOWN
              I have control *over* her. He's at the *height* of his powers. He's in a *superior* position. He ranks *above* me in strength. He is *under* my control. He *fell* from power. He is my social *inferior*.
         e.   GOOD IS UP; BAD IS DOWN
              Things are looking *up*. We hit a *peak* last year, but it's been *downhill* ever since. Things are at an all-time *low*. He does *high*-quality work.
         f.   VIRTUE IS UP; DEPRAVITY IS DOWN
              He is *high*-minded. She has *high* standards. She is an *upstanding* citizen. That was a *low* trick. Don't be *underhanded*. I wouldn't *stoop* to that. That was a *low-down* thing to do.

As the authors point out, these metaphors seem to be based on our bodily experiences of lying down and getting up and their associations with consciousness, health and power, i.e. of verticality in human experience. We will discuss this experiential basis in section 11.4 below, when we discuss image schemas. For now we can see that Lakoff and Johnson's point is that in using language like this, speakers are not adding rhetorical or poetical flourishes to their language: this is how we conceive of happiness, health, etc. As a result metaphors are conceptual structures which pervade ordinary language. In section 11.2.3 we look at some of the features of metaphor identified in this approach.

11.2.3   Features of metaphor

Cognitive semanticists argue that, far from being idiosyncratic anomalies, metaphors exhibit characteristic and systematic features. We can look at some of these characteristics under the headings of conventionality, systematicity, asymmetry and abstraction. The first, **conventionality**, raises the issue of the novelty of the metaphor: clearly the first of our two examples in 11.2 and 11.3 is less novel than the second. As we discussed in chapter 1, some writers would claim that some metaphors have become fossilized or **dead** metaphors. In the literal language theory this means that they have ceased to be metaphors and have passed into literal language, as suggested by Searle (1979: 122):

11.7   *Dead metaphor.* The original sentence meaning is bypassed and the sentence acquires a new literal meaning identical with the former metaphorical meaning. This is a shift from the metaphorical utterance . . . to the literal utterance.

Cognitive semanticists argue against this approach, pointing out that even familiar metaphors can be given new life, thus showing that they retain their metaphorical status. If we take, for example the UP-DOWN metaphor, we might consider an instance like *My spirits rose* to be a dead metaphor, yet this general metaphor is continually being extended: it is no accident in this view that stimulant recreational drugs were called *uppers* and tranquillizers, *downers*.

The second feature, **systematicity**, refers to the way that a metaphor does not just set up a single point of comparison: features of the source and target domain are joined so that the metaphor may be extended, or have its own internal logic. We can take an example from a *Science* magazine article about the sun, where the development of suns is metaphorically viewed as children growing up:

11.8   A nursery of unruly stars in the Orion Nebula has yielded the best look at our sun's baby album . . .[10]

This metaphor is part of an extended metaphorical structure which surfaces through the rest of this report; see the following extracts which extend the mapping between suns and children:

11.9   a.   Based on data from NASA's orbiting Chandra X-ray Observatory, it appears that the sun threw more tantrums than expected, in the form of powerful x-ray flares . . .

         b.   More than 4.5 billion years of evolution have erased all traces of the sun's youth . . .

This systematicity has been an important focus in cognitive semantic views of metaphor: Lakoff and Turner (1989) identify, for example, a metaphor LIFE IS A JOURNEY, which pervades our ordinary way of talking. Thus birth is often described as arrival as in *The baby is due next week*, or *She has a baby on the way*; and death is viewed as a departure as in *She passed away this morning* or *He's gone*. Lakoff and Turner (1989: 3–4) identify a systematicity in this mapping between the two concepts:

11.10   LIFE IS A JOURNEY
–The person leading a life is a traveller.
–His purposes are destinations.
–The means for achieving purposes are routes.
–Difficulties in life are impediments to travel.
–Counsellors are guides.
–Progress is the distance travelled.
–Things you gauge your progress by are landmarks.
–Material resources and talents are provisions.

Their point is that we use this mapping every day in ordinary speech as when we use expressions like: *Giving the children a good start in life*; *He's over the hill*; *I was bogged down in a dead-end job*; *Her career is at a standstill*; *They're embarking on a new career*; *He's gone off the rails*; *Are you at a cross-roads in your life?*; *I'm past it* (= *I'm too old*); *He's getting on* (= *he's ageing*), etc.

Another example comes from the role of metaphor in the creation of new vocabulary: the coining of the term *computer virus* for a specific type of harmful program; see Fauconnier (1997: 19ff.) for discussion. This coining is based on a conceptual model of biological viruses which is generalized or schematized away from the biological details:

11.11   Biological virus schema (Fauconnier 1997: 19)
        a. x is present, but unwanted; it comes in, or is put in, from the outside; it does not naturally belong;
        b. x is able to replicate; new tokens of x appear that have the same undesirable properties as the original x;
        c. x disrupts the 'standard' function of the system;
        d.   the system should be protected against x; this might be achieved if the system were such that x could not come into

it, or if other elements were added to the system that would counteract the effects of *x*, or eject *x*, or destroy *x*.

This schema is transferred to the general aspects of the computer situation; it provides a way of characterizing the new domain. The schema in 11.11 is itself based on lower-level schemas like image schemas of container, path (discussed later in this chapter) and force dynamics: entry, resistance etc. (Talmy 2000 1: 409–69).

This metaphorical mapping between a health schema and a computer domain can be viewed as a form of **analogical mapping** (Gentner 1983; Holyoak and Thagard 1995). It licenses a whole system of lexical innovations so that the anti-virus programs can be called things like 'Dr Solomon's'; they are said to 'disinfect' programs, files can be said to be 'infected', and the program places them in special areas of memory called 'quarantine'.

The importance of the process of metaphorical extension of the vocabulary can be seen from the following list of conventionalized mappings from parts of the human body:

11.12   Conventionalized metaphors of body parts in English (Ungerer and Schmid 1996: 117)

head	of department, of state, of government, of a page, of a queue, of a flower, of a beer, of stairs, of a bed, of a tape recorder, of a syntactic construction
face	of a mountain, of a building, of a watch
eye	of a potato, of a needle, of a hurricane, of a butterfly, in a flower, hooks and eyes
mouth	of a hole, of a tunnel, of a cave, of a river
lip	of a cup, of a jug, of a crater, of a plate
nose	of an aircraft, of a tool, of a gun
neck	of land, of the woods, of a shirt, bottle-neck
shoulder	of a hill or mountain, of a bottle, of a road, of a jacket
arm	of a chair, of the sea, of a tree, of a coat or jacket, of a record player
hands	of a watch, of an altimeter/speedometer

Our third feature, **asymmetry**, refers to the way that metaphors are **directional**. They do not set up a symmetrical comparison between two concepts, establishing points of similarity. Instead they provoke the listener to transfer features from the source to the target. We can take the metaphor LIFE IS A JOURNEY as an example: this metaphor is asymmetrical and the mapping does not work the other way around. We do not conventionally describe journeys in terms of life, so that it sounds odd to say *Our flight was born (i.e. arrived) a few minutes early* or *By the time we got there, the boat had died (i.e. gone)*. Even if we are able to set up such a metaphor, it is clear that the meaning would be different from that of the original structure.

Our final feature, **abstraction,** is related to this asymmetry. It has often been noted that a typical metaphor uses a more concrete source to describe a more abstract target. Again the LIFE IS A JOURNEY metaphor exhibits this feature: the common, everyday experience of physically moving about the earth is used to characterize the mysterious (and unreported) processes of birth and death, and the perhaps equally mysterious processes of ageing, organizing a career, etc. This is not a necessary feature of metaphors: the source and target may be equally concrete or abstract, but as we shall see, this typical viewing of the abstract through the concrete is seen in cognitive semantics as allowing metaphor its central role in the categorizing of new concepts, and in the organization of experience.

11.2.4   The influence of metaphor

Cognitivists argue that because of their presence in speakers' minds, metaphors exert influence over a wide range of linguistic behaviours. Sweetser (1990), for example, identifies a cross-linguistic metaphor MIND-AS-BODY, as when in English we speak of *grasping* an idea or *holding* a thought. She identifies this metaphorical viewing of the mental in terms of the physical as an important influence in the historical development of **polysemy** and of cognate words in related languages. Thus in English the verb *see* has two meanings: the basic physical one of 'perceiving with the eyes' and the metaphorically extended one of 'understanding' as in *I see what you mean.* Sweetser discusses how over time verbs of sense perception in Indo-European languages have shown a consistent and widespread tendency to shift from the physical to the mental domain. Her claim is that this basic underlying metaphor underlies the paths of semantic change in many languages so that words of seeing come to mean understanding, words of hearing to mean obeying, and words of tasting to mean choosing, deciding or expressing personal preferences. Some of her examples are given below (1990: 32ff.):

11.13   a.   seeing → understanding
                Indo-European root *weid- 'see':[11]
                Greek *eîdon* 'see', perfective *oîdoa* 'know' (> English *idea*)
                English *wise, wit*
                Latin *video* 'see'
                Irish *fios* 'knowledge'
           b.   hearing → paying attention to, obeying
                Indo-European root *k'leu-s-* 'hear, listen'
                English *listen*
                Danish *lystre* 'obey'
           c.   tasting → choosing, expressing preferences
                possible Indo-European root *g'eus* 'taste'

Greek *geúomai* 'taste'
Latin *gustare* 'taste'
Gothic *kiusan* 'try'
Old English *ceosan* 'choose'
Sanskrit *jus-* 'enjoy'[12]

Sweetser's point is that historical semantic change is not random but is influenced by such metaphors as MIND-AS-BODY. Thus metaphor, as one type of cognitive structuring, is seen to drive lexical change in a motivated way, and provides a key to understanding the creation of polysemy and the phenomenon of semantic shift. See also Heine et al. (1991), who provide a wide range of examples to support their own version of the same thesis: that metaphor underlies historical change. We will look at explanations of polysemy again in section 11.5.

In this section we have looked briefly at cognitivist investigations of the role of metaphor in language. Next we turn to a related process: metonymy.

11.3 Metonymy

We discussed metonymy in chapter 7 as a referential strategy, describing it in traditional terms as identifying a referent by something associated with it. This reflects the traditional definition in terms of **contiguity**. For cognitive semanticists metonymy shows many of the same features as metaphor: they are both conceptual processes; both may be conventionalized; both are used to create new lexical resources in language and both show the same dependence on real-world knowledge or cognitive frames. The distinction between them is made in this literature (Lakoff and Johnson 1980; Lakoff 1987; Lakoff and Turner 1989) in terms of these cognitive frames. Metaphor is viewed as a mapping across conceptual domains, for example disease and computers in our example above of *computer virus*. Metonymy establishes a connection within a single domain.

Various taxonomies of metonymic relations have been proposed, including those by Lakoff and Johnson (1980), Fass (1991), Nunberg (1995) and Kövecses and Radden (1998). We give some typical strategies below, with examples (and traditional terms in parentheses):

11.14   Types of metonymic relation
          PART FOR WHOLE (synecdoche)
          All hands on deck
          WHOLE FOR PART (synecdoche)
          Brazil won the world cup.
          CONTAINER FOR CONTENT
          I don't drink more than two bottles.
          MATERIAL FOR OBJECT

She needs a glass.
PRODUCER FOR PRODUCT
I'll buy you that Rembrandt.
PLACE FOR INSTITUTION
Downing Street has made no comment.
INSTITUTION FOR PEOPLE
The Senate isn't happy with this bill.
PLACE FOR EVENT
Hiroshima changed our view of war.
CONTROLLED FOR CONTROLLER
All the hospitals are on strike.
CAUSE FOR EFFECT
His native tongue is Hausa.

As with metaphor, metonymy is a productive way of creating new vocabulary. We can give just two conventionalized examples from the PRODUCER FOR PRODUCT relation: *shrapnel* from the English general who invented the type of shell, and *silhouette* from the French finance minister who designed the technique.

There have been attempts to account for the particular choice of metonymic reference points. Some choices seem more common and natural than others, for example to use *tongue* for *language* rather than *throat*, or *head* for a person rather than, say *waist*. Langacker (1993: 30) suggested a general notion of salience, where items are graded for relative salience, for example (where > = more salient): human > non-human, whole > part, visible > non-visible, and concrete > abstract. Kövecses and Radden (1998) develop this idea further, appealing to experiential and in particular perceptual motivation for principles governing the choice of metonymic reference point.

We have now seen something of the related processes of metaphor and metonymy. In section 11.4 we move on to consider the experientialist basis of metaphors, when we look at another, more basic cognitive structure proposed in this approach: **image schemas**.

11.4 Image Schemas

Image schemas are an important form of conceptual structure in the cognitive semantics literature. The basic idea is that because of our physical experience of being and acting in the world – of perceiving the environment, moving our bodies, exerting and experiencing force, etc. – we form basic conceptual structures which we then use to organize thought across a range of more abstract domains. In Mark Johnson (1987), whose proposals we will examine in this section, these image schemas are proposed as a more primitive level of cognitive structure underlying metaphor and which provide a link between bodily experience and higher cognitive domains such as language. We can look at some examples of image schemas, beginning with the **Containment** schema.

11.4.1 Containment schema

Mark Johnson (1987: 21ff.) gives the example of the schema of **Containment**, which derives from our experience of the human body itself as a container; from experience of being physically located ourselves within bounded locations like rooms, beds, etc.; and also of putting objects into containers. The result is an abstract schema, of physical containment, which can be represented by a very simple image like figure 11.1, representing an entity within a bounded location.

Such a schema has certain experientially based characteristics: it has a kind of natural logic, including for example the 'rules' in 11.15:

11.15   a.   Containers are a kind of disjunction: elements are either inside or outside the container.

         b.   Containment is typically transitive: if the container is placed in another container the entity is within both, as Johnson says: 'If I am *in* bed, and my bed is *in* my room, then I am *in* my room'.

The schema is also associated with a group of implications, which can be seen as natural inferences about containment. Johnson calls these 'entailments' and gives examples like the following (adapted from Johnson 1987: 22):

11.16   a.   Experience of containment typically involves protection from outside forces.

         b.   Containment limits forces, such as movement, within the container.

         c.   The contained entity experiences relative fixity of location.

         d.   The containment affects an observer's view of the contained entity, either improving such a view or blocking it (containers may hide or display).

Figure 11.1 Containment

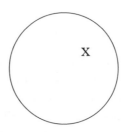

Source: Mark Johnson (1987: 23)

The fact that a schema has parts which 'hang together' in a way that is motivated by experience leads Johnson to call them **gestalt structures** (1987: 44):

11.17   I am using the term 'gestalt structure' to mean an organised, unified whole within our experience and understanding that manifests a repeatable pattern or structure. Some people use the term 'gestalt' to mean a mere form or shape with no internal structure. In contrast to such a view, my entire project rests on showing that experiential gestalts have internal structure that connects up aspects of our experience and leads to inferences in our conceptual structure.

Though we have represented this schema in a static image like figure 11.1, it is important to remember that these schemas are in essence neither static nor restricted to images. The schema may be dynamic, as we shall see shortly with path and force schemas, which involve movement and change.

    This schema of containment can be extended by a process of metaphorical extension into abstract domains. Lakoff and Johnson (1980) identify CONTAINER as one of a group of **ontological** metaphors, where our experience of non-physical phenomena is described in terms of simple physical objects like substances and containers. For example the visual field is often conceived as a container, as in examples like: *The ship is coming into view*; *He's out of sight now*; *There's nothing in sight* (p. 30). Similarly, activities can be viewed as containers: *I put a lot of energy into washing the windows*; *He's out of the race* (p. 31), *She's deep in thought*. States can be viewed in the same way: *He's in love*; *He's coming out of the coma now* (p. 32), *She got into a rage*, *We stood in silence*. For Lakoff and Johnson these examples are typical and reveal the important role of metaphor in allowing us to conceptualize experience.

    Some other schemas identified by Mark Johnson (1987) include *Path*, *Links*, *Forces*, *Balance*, *Up-Down*, *Front-Back*, *Part-Whole* and *Centre-Periphery*. We might briefly look at the **Path** schema, and some of his examples of **Force** schemas, since these have been used in a number of linguistic studies.

11.4.2   Path schema

The **Path** schema is shown in figure 11.2. Johnson claims that this schema reflects our everyday experience of moving around the world and experiencing the movements of other entities. Our journeys typically have a beginning and an end, a sequence of places on the way and direction. Other movements may include projected paths, like the flight of a stone thrown through the air. Based on such experiences the path schema contains a starting point (marked A in figure 11.2), an end point (marked B), and a sequence of

Figure 11.2 Path schema

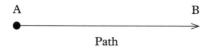

Path

Source: Mark Johnson (1987: 114)

contiguous locations connecting them (marked by the arrow). This schema has a number of associated implications, as listed in 11.18:

11.18   a.   Since A and B are connected by a series of contiguous loca-
              tions, getting from A to B implies passing through the inter-
              mediate points.
         b.   Paths tend to be associated with directional movement along
              them, say from A to B.
         c.   There is an association with time. Since a person traversing
              a path takes time to do so, points on the path are readily
              associated with temporal sequence. Thus an implication is
              that the further along the path an entity is, the more time has
              elapsed.

These implications are evidenced in the metaphorical extension of this schema into abstract domains: we talk, for example, of achieving purposes as paths, as in 11.19 below:

11.19   a.   He's writing a PhD thesis and he's nearly there.
         b.   I meant to finish painting it yesterday, but I got side-tracked.

and we saw examples in the last section of the related, more elaborated metaphor of LIFE IS A JOURNEY, which derives from this schema.

11.4.3   Force schemas

The **Force** schemas include the basic force schema of **Compulsion**, as shown in figure 11.3, where a force vector **F** acts on an entity u. In this diagram the essential element is movement along a trajectory: the dashed line represents the fact that the force may be blocked or may continue.

In figure 11.4 we see the more specific schema of **Blockage**, where a force meets an obstruction and acts in various ways: being diverted, or continuing on by moving the obstacle or passing through it.

Figure 11.3 Compulsion

Figure 11.4   Blockage

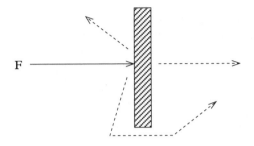

Figure 11.5   Removal of restraint

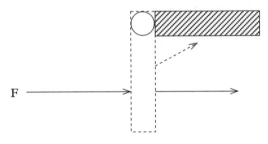

Source: Adapted from Mark Johnson (1987: 47)

Figure 11.5 shows the related schemas of **Removal of Restraint**, where the removal (by another cause) of a blockage allows an exertion of force to continue along a trajectory.

These force schemas, like other image schemas, are held to arise from our everyday experiences as we grew as children, of moving around our environment and interacting with animate and inanimate entities. As with other image schemas they are held to be pre-linguistic and to shape the form of our linguistic categories. In the next section we discuss an important application of schemas: to describe polysemy.

11.5   Polysemy

Image schemas and their extension by metaphor have been used to describe a number of areas of language which display **polysemy**: the phenomenon discussed in chapter 3 where we find a group of related but distinct meanings attached to a word. G. Lakoff (1987) uses the term **radial category** for the characteristic pattern produced by the metaphorical extension of meanings from a central origin. We can look at two examples of this phenomenon from English: prepositions and modal verbs.

11.5.1   Prepositions

The schema of **Containment** has been used to investigate the semantics of
spatial prepositions in a number of languages including the Cora language
of Mexico (Langacker and Cassad 1985), English (Herkovits 1986) and
French (Vandeloise 1991). These studies use schemas to explore the typical
polysemy of prepositions: the fact that we can, for example, use the English
preposition *in* in a number of related but distinct ways, as in the examples
below given by Herkovits (1986):

11.20   a.   the water in the vase
           b.   the crack in the vase
           c.   the crack in the surface
           d.   the bird in the tree
           e.   the chair in the corner
           f.   the nail in the box
           g.   the muscles in his leg
           h.   the pear in the bowl
           i.   the block in the box
           j.   the block in the rectangular area
           k.   the gap in the border
           l.   the bird in the field

It is easy to see the different relationships between the entity and the container in these examples. The water is likely to be entirely contained in the
vase in 11.20a but the pear in 11.20h could easily be sitting on top of a pile
of fruit and thus protrude beyond the top edge of the bowl. Similarly the
bird in 11.20d might be inside a hole in the tree-trunk but, equally, might
be sitting on a branch which if 'inside' anything is inside our projection of
the tree's shape. Meanwhile in 11.21 the bird might be flying or hovering
several feet above the field. Herkovits's point is that such extended uses are
typical and regular, i.e. not idiomatic. This seems to be supported by the
fact that the studies of other languages mentioned above come up with
similar examples. Herkovits claims that these uses are most satisfactorily
described by viewing them as extensions from a central, ideal containment
schema which she describes in words as 'the inclusion of a geometric construct in a one-, two-, or three-dimensional geometric construct'.

   There are two important points to make about this polysemy from a
cognitive semantics perspective: the first is that the various and varying real-
world situations are described in language in a way that is essentially metaphorical in nature, relating them all to an underlying schema of containment.
The second is that the relationship between the various senses is not arbitrary
but systematic and natural. We can see the latter point if we look briefly at
Brugman and Lakoff's (1988) description of the preposition *over*. They
argue that the polysemous nature of this and other prepositions cannot be
accurately described using semantic features or definitions but instead requires

an essentially topographical approach, i.e. a description employing spatial models. They claim (1988: 479):

11.21   Topological concepts are needed in order to account for how prepositions can be used to characterize an infinity of visual scenes.

The polysemous nature of *over* can be shown, as we did for *in* earlier, by a set of examples (Brugman and Lakoff 1988):

11.22   a. The plane is flying over the hill. *→ above across sense*
         b. Sam walked over the hill. *adding Information (1st. type)*
         c. The bird flew over the yard. *from above across sense*
         d. The bird flew over the wall.
         e. Sam lives over the hill.
         f. The painting is over the mantel. *→ above sense (not path, not restrict... ÷ TR - LM*
         g. The board is over the hole. *→ covering sense*
         h. She spread the tablecloth over the table. *covering sense with path element*
         i. The city clouded over.
         j. The guards were posted all over the hill. *Covering sense with quantifier.*
         k. Harry still hasn't gotten over his divorce. *Metaphorical (above/across)*

Brugman and Lakoff propose a complex structure for the meanings of *over*: the preposition has a number of related senses, of which we can select three, termed the **above-across** sense, the **above** sense and the **covering** sense. Each of these senses is then structured as a radial category with extensions from a central prototype. Let us take the **above-across** sense first. This sense of *over* is described in terms of a **Path** image schema, using the terms **trajector** (TR) for a moving entity and **landmark** (LM) for the background against which movement occurs.[13] Brugman and Lakoff represent this in a schema like figure 11.6. This schema would fit for example 11.22a, *The plane is flying over the hill*. In this approach several other senses of *over* can be systematically related to this central schema by a number of basic processes, for example by adding information to the schema or by metaphor. In the first type of process the central schema may alter along a number of parameters: for example there may be contact between the trajector and the landmark as in 11.22b *Sam walked over the hill*, shown schematically in figure 11.7. Other information may be added about the landmark, which may be viewed as different geometric shapes: as an extended area as in 11.22c; or as a vertical form as in 11.22d. Alternatively the focus may be on the end-point of the path as in 11.22e. In the second type of process the preposition can be used metaphorically, where it interacts with the metaphorical structures available to the language users. Thus in 11.22k we see a version of the LIFE AS A JOURNEY metaphor we discussed earlier, where problems are seen as obstacles.

A second major sense of *over* is the **above** sense, as in 11.22f above: *The painting is over the mantel*. This sense is stative and has no path element. It

Figure 11.6   Prototypical **above-across** sense of *over*

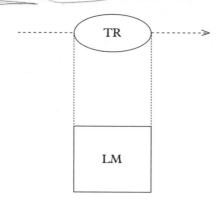

Source: Brugman and Lakoff (1988: 482)

Figure 11.7   Sam walked over the hill

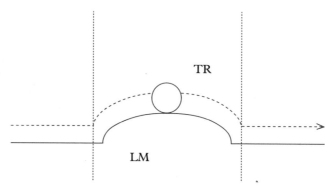

Source: Brugman and Lakoff (1988: 483)

can be represented by the schema in figure 11.8. Since this schema does not include a path element it has no meaning of **across**. It also differs from the first sense in that there are no restrictions on the shape of the landmark, nor can there be contact between trajector and landmark. If there is contact we are more likely to use another preposition, such as *on* as in *The painting is on the mantel*.

Our third sense, or group of senses, of *over* is the **covering** sense which can be represented in figure 11.9. The schema in this figure corresponds to sentence 11.22g above: *The board is over the hole*. This schema may have a path element depicting the motion of the trajector into its position over the landmark as in 11.22h *She spread the tablecloth over the table* or 11.22i *The city clouded over*. In this schema the use of a quantifier like *all* changes the nature of the trajector, as for example in sentence 11.22j: *The guards*

Figure 11.8   The above sense of *over*

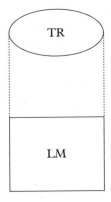

Source: Brugman and Lakoff (1988: 487)

Figure 11.9   The covering sense of *over*

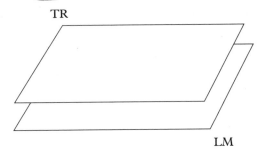

Source: Brugman and Lakoff (1988: 489)

were posted all over the hill. Here the trajector is what Brugman and Lakoff call a **multiplex** trajector, made up of many individual elements. This is schematically represented as in figure 11.10.

We have looked at three of the major sense groups of *over* identified in this analysis. In each sense group there is a prototypical schema which is related to a number of extended senses, thus exhibiting the radial category structure we mentioned earlier. This prototypicality also extends to the relationship between the sense groups: see Brugman and Lakoff (1988) for arguments that our first sense group, the **above-across** sense, is the pro- totypical group for *over*.

An important element of this analysis is the claim that the processes which extend senses from a central prototype to form a radial category are systematic and widespread. Brugman and Lakoff (1988) claim, for example, that any path schema will allow a focus on the end-point, as we saw for *over* in 11.22e. We can see this with the prepositions in 11.23–5 below:

Figure 11.10   Multiplex version of the **covering** sense of *over*

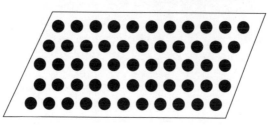

Source: Brugman and Lakoff (1988: 490)

11.23   a.   He walked across the road.
           b.   He works across the road.

11.24   a.   You go around the corner.
           b.   She lives around the corner.

11.25   a.   Walk through the atrium and turn to the left.
           b.   His office is through the atrium and to the left.

Each of the prepositions in 11.23–5 shows this ability to support a motion variant in the a sentence and a stative variant in the b sentence, where the latter identifies the end-point or destination of the path.

11.5.2   Modal verbs

Force schemas have been used to describe polysemy in modal verbs. As we saw in chapter 5, modal verbs like English *may* and *can* typically have both **deontic** and **epistemic** senses. Talmy (1985, 1988), for example, uses force schemas to analyse modal verbs like *must, may* and *can* in their deontic uses: for example *must* used to express obligation as in 11.26a below, *may* used for permission as in 11.26b and *can* used for ability as in 11.26c:

11.26   a.   You *must* hand in your term essay before the end of this week.
           b.   You *may* enter the studio when the light goes out.
           c.   She *can* swim much better than me.

Talmy analyses these deontic uses in terms of forces and barriers. He proposes, for example, that a typical use of *may* as permission is an example of removing a barrier or keeping back a potential but absent barrier. Thus in 11.26b some potential barrier to entering the studio is identified as being negated.

Sweetser (1990) adopts and extends this analysis of *may*. She observes that the normal use of *may* is when the barrier is a social one (deriving from authority). The verb *let* is used in a similar way, as in 11.27a below, but, as

Sweetser notes, with this verb there are physical analogues to this removal of a potential barrier as in 11.27b:

11.27   a. I'll *let* you smoke in the car, but just for today.
         b. The hole in the roof *let* the rain in.

In this approach, the other deontic modals can also be given a force schema analysis: for example, the use of *must* for obligation is an example of the Compulsion Force schema. In 11.26a above the force is the teacher's authority but it can also be a moral or religious force as in *You must respect your parents* or *You must pray five times a day*. The idea seems to be that there is a conceptual link between someone physically pushing you in a direction and a moral force impelling you to act in a certain way. Both are forces which can be resisted or acceded to; in this approach a common conceptual schema unites the characterization of the two situations.

Sweetser (1990) analyses the **epistemic** use of modals as a metaphorical extension of these deontic uses. We can take the examples of *must* and *may*. In its epistemic use *must* can express a reasonable conclusion as in 11.28a and b:

11.28   a. It's dead. The battery *must* have run down.
         b. You've travelled all day. You *must* be tired.

The epistemic use of *may* expresses possibility as in 11.29:

11.29   a. You *may* feel a bit sick when we take off.
         b. He *may not* last out the whole game.

Sweetser argues that such uses of modals for rational argument and judgement are derived from their uses for the real world of social obligation and permission. This derivation follows the usual metaphorical extension from the external concrete world to the internal world of cognition and emotion. Thus to take the example of *may*, the epistemic use is again taken to represent a lack of barrier. Here, though, the barrier is to the line of reasoning leading to the conclusion expressed. Thus a sentence like 11.30a below can be paraphrased as 11.30b:

11.30   a. You may be right.
         b. There is no evidence preventing the conclusion that you are right.

Thus an overt parallel is drawn in this account between barriers in social action and barriers in mental reasoning.

In a similar way epistemic *must* is interpreted as the Compulsion Force schema extended to the domain of reasoning. So 11.31a below is paraphrased as 11.31b:

11.31   a.   You must have driven too fast.
          b.   The evidence forces my conclusion that you drove too fast.

Thus Sweetser is arguing that evidence is conceptualized as a force analog-
ous to social pressure and laws, moving a person's judgement in a certain
direction.

   This type of analysis is extended to other modals but we need not follow
the analysis further: we can identify from these few examples her claim that
the relationship between the deontic and epistemic use of each modal is not
accidental but a further example of polysemy: i.e. the different uses are
semantically related. What relates them, in this view, is the metaphorical
extension of the force and barriers schemas from the social world to our
inner reasoning.

   So, to conclude this section, we have seen that image schemas are proposed as experientially based conceptual constructs by which we characterize, for example, spatial relations, and which can be metaphorically
extended across a range of domains, typically shifting from the external and
concrete to the internal and abstract. Such schemas are seen as the building
blocks of metaphor, allowing us to conceive of emotional states as containers (*She's in love*), evidence as compulsion (*He must be guilty*), or purposes
as paths (A: *Have you finished the book?* B: *I'm getting there*). Polysemy is the
result of this extension of schemas to form radial categories and is seen as
a natural and ubiquitous phenomenon in language. In the next section we
look at another form of conceptual structure identified in this approach:
mental spaces.

11.6   Mental Spaces

Mental spaces are conceptual structures, originally proposed by Gilles
Fauconnier (1985, 1994), to describe how language users assign and manipulate reference, including the use of names, definite descriptions and
pronouns. Fauconnier's structures are set up in the light of a particular view
of meaning: that when we study linguistic meaning we are studying the way
that language provides a patchy and partial trigger for a series of complex
cognitive procedures. In this view meaning is not 'in' language; rather,
language is like a recipe for constructing meaning, a recipe which relies on
a lot of independent cognitive activity. Moreover this process of meaning
construction is a discourse-based process, implying that typically a single
sentence is only a step in the recipe and cannot be clearly analysed without
recognizing its relationship to and dependency on earlier sentences.

   So Fauconnier's focus is on the cognitive processes triggered during discourse by linguistic structures. Within this, a particular topic of investigation
has been the management of reference: the issue of how speakers and
hearers keep track of the entities referred to in the language. The central

idea is that when we are involved in using language, for example in conversation, we are continually constructing domains, so that if we talk about, say, Shakespeare's play *Julius Caesar*, we might maintain several relevant domains, or mental spaces. One domain is the world of the play, while another might be the real world, where Julius Caesar is a historical figure. Our referential practices make use of such divisions into domains so that we can use the same name *Julius Caesar* to talk about the historical person and the character in the play. Between our different uses of the name there are nevertheless links: we might want to say, for example, that Shakespeare's character is meant to describe the historical figure. Such processes can be quite complicated: we might go to see a performance of the play and afterwards say *Julius Caesar was too young*, referring now to the actor playing the part. Or if we saw some children running off with the foyer's life-size figure of the actor in costume, we might say *Hey, they're stealing Julius Caesar*. So we can use the same name to refer to a historical person, a role in a play written about him, an actor playing that role and a figure of that actor playing the role. Fauconnier's point is that such flexibility is inherent in our use of referring expressions: his mental spaces are an attempt to explain such behaviour.

Mental spaces can be seen as a cognitive parallel to the notion of possible worlds in formal semantics, as discussed in chapter 10, since it is assumed that speakers can partition off and hold separate domains of reference. Some of these might be very complex: we might, for example, be talking of the world of Charles Dickens's *A Tale of Two Cities* and refer to individuals in that novel, like *Charles Dornay* and *Sydney Carton*. Or the domain might be very sparsely furnished, provoked just by a counterfactual as in *If I were you, I'd go on a diet*, where once the shift from the real to the non-real domain is made in the first clause, the *I* in the second clause identifies not the speaker but the addressee. Here, however, any further implications of this domain, or mental space, are not explored and it remains a local, minimal space.

11.6.1 Connections between spaces

One important issue is what links there might be between mental spaces. What, for example, allows us to use the name *Julius Caesar* as we did, for a historical person, a role in a play, an actor, etc.? Fauconnier (1994), building on work by Jackendoff (1975) and Nunburg (1978, 1979) discusses the way that speakers can make reference to entities by a number of indirect strategies. We can for example refer to a representation of someone by their name: so that looking at a photograph of a friend I might say *Graham looks really young*, where *Graham* refers to the picture of Graham (who in reality might look far from young). Fauconnier uses the terms **trigger** and **target** here: the name of the real Graham is the trigger and the target (what I want to describe) is the image. Clearly photographs and the

Figure 11.11   Person–image connector

| Trigger | IMAGE (connector) | Target |
| a: person | ⎯⎯⎯⎯⎯⎯⎯⎯⎯⎯⟶ | b: image |

girl with blue eyes   girl with green eyes

Source: Based on Fauconnier (1994)

people in them are related by the viewer's recognition of resemblance, but similar strategies are widespread. We can refer, for example, to a book or books by the author's name and say sentences like *Shakespeare's on the top shelf*. Similarly, a nurse might say *The gall bladder in the end bed is awake*; or in a favourite type of example in this literature, a waiter might say *The ham omelette wants his bill*. In chapter 7 we called this phenomenon **metonymy**. Fauconnier employs an **identification principle** which allows speakers to use such referential shifts; one version is in 11.32 below (1994: 3):

11.32   If two objects (in the most general sense), *a* and *b*, are linked by a pragmatic function *F* (*b* = *F*(*a*)), a description of *a*, d_a, may be used to identify its counterpart *b*.

So since in our photograph example real Graham (*a*) and photo Graham (*b*) are linked by the pragmatic function IMAGE, a description of real Graham (his name, d_a) can be used to identify his photographic image (*b*). It is assumed that there might be a number of such pragmatic functions, as we shall see.

We can look at some more complicated examples of this referential shifting by looking at Fauconnier's account of Jackendoff's (1975) example in 11.33 below:

11.33   In Len's painting, the girl with blue eyes has green eyes.

Let us take as an interpretation of this sentence the situation where the speaker knows the identity of the artist's model, knows that she has blue eyes and is pointing out that the painter has decided to give her green eyes in the picture. The proposal is that here two mental spaces are set up: one is the real world (as the speaker knows it) which has in it a girl with blue eyes; the other the space of the painting which has a girl with green eyes. The sentence 11.33 explicitly connects these two girls, saying in effect they are in the image–person relationship we discussed for our hypothetical friend Graham earlier. This can be represented in figure 11.11, which shows the connection (our image relationship) as an arrow.

Fauconnier, following Jackendoff (1975), makes the point that this can be likened to the relationship between beliefs and reality: thus, paralleling 11.33 above we can say 11.34 and 11.35 below:

Figure 11.12   World–mind connector

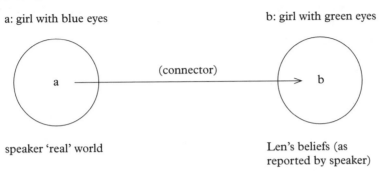

a: girl with blue eyes   b: girl with green eyes

(connector)

speaker 'real' world   Len's beliefs (as
                                             reported by speaker)

Source: Based on Fauconnier (1994)

Figure 11.13   Image–person connector

Trigger   IMAGE (connector)   Target
a: image   b: person

girl with brown eyes   girl with blue eyes

Source: Based on Fauconnier (1994)

11.34   Len believes that the girl with blue eyes has green eyes.

11.35   Len wants the girl with blue eyes to have green eyes.

Here Len's belief and wish are at odds with reality as known by the speaker.
In the semantics literature such examples are often described as instances
of **belief contexts**. In this theory they are viewed as a mental parallel to the
image relation, and are represented by similar diagrams, using a belief or
MIND connector, as in figure 11.12. As Fauconnier points out, the speaker
can work such relationships in the other direction. Taking the image relationship as an example, a speaker might say, looking at a picture: *In reality,
the girl with brown eyes has blue eyes.* Here the trigger is the image and the
target is the real girl, as shown in figure 11.13.
   These examples are of mental spaces created by talking of paintings and
a person's beliefs and wishes. There are in fact a whole range of linguistic
elements which serve as triggers for setting up mental spaces, which
Fauconnier calls **spacebuilders**. These include adverbials of location and
time like *in Joan's novel, in Peter's painting, when she was a child, after we find
the crash site,* etc. They also include adverbs like *possibly* and *really*; connectives like *if . . . then*; and certain verbs like *believe, hope* and *imagine*. The context in which a sentence is uttered will provide the anchoring or background
mental space. Where spaces are stacked inside one another, the including

space is referred to as the **parent** space. Often, of course, the default (unmarked) highest parent space will be reality, or more accurately the current speaker's assessment of reality. Take, for example, a speaker uttering the sentences in 11.36 below:

11.36   Barry's in the pub. His wife thinks he's in the office.

Here the initial space is the speaker's reality (R) where Barry is in the pub, then the phrase *his wife thinks* sets up a new mental space (M) in which his counterpart Barry$_2$ is in the office. The speaker can then develop either space, talking about what Barry$_1$ is doing in R or what Barry$_2$ is (supposedly) doing in M.

11.6.2   Referential opacity

One important advantage to this idea of mental spaces and links between them is that it can be used to explain the phenomenon of **referential opacity**. This is the traditionally problematic area where, as we discussed in chapter 2, knowledge interacts with reference. Let's take, for example, sentence 11.37 below to be true of a policeman called Jones:

11.37   Jones believes that the leader of the Black Gulch Gang is a sociopath.

If Jones does not know that his wife is the leader of the Black Gulch Gang we can also take the sentence 11.38 below to be true at the same time:

11.38   Jones doesn't believe his wife is a sociopath.

Because of what Jones knows, we are not ascribing contradictory beliefs to him, even though the nominals *his wife* and *the leader of the Black Gulch Gang* denote the same individual. This is a typical effect of belief contexts and in chapter 2 we saw that such examples have been used to argue that there must be more to meaning than simply denotation.

   As we discussed in chapter 10, sentences like 11.37 are described as **opaque contexts**. In this type of example the opacity is associated with embedded clauses under verbs of propositional attitudes like *believe, want, suspect, hope,* etc. To give another example, a sentence like 11.39 below can have two distinct interpretations:

11.39   The Captain suspects that a detective in the squad is taking bribes.

If we take 11.39 to mean that the Captain suspects a particular detective, this is called the **specific** or **transparent** reading. If, on the other hand, we take 11.39 to mean that the Captain suspects that one of the detectives is

Figure 11.14   First interpretation of *In the film, Michelle is a witch*

m1: Michelle   m2: witch

ACTOR

m1   m2

R   F

involved but doesn't know which one, this is called the **non-specific** or
opaque reading. In another terminology used in logic, the transparent reading
(the captain knows which individual) is given the Latin label the *de re*
interpretation (meaning roughly 'of the thing') while the opaque reading is
called the *de dicto* interpretation (roughly 'of what is said').

In the mental spaces approach these two interpretations do not arise from
any ambiguity in the sentence but from two different space-connecting strategies that hearers may use. Nor are opaque contexts restricted to verbs of
propositional attitude: they are a regular consequence of referential strategies. To show this, we might go back to an example of identifying actors and
parts. Suppose for example a speaker says 11.40 below:

11.40   In the film, Michelle is a witch.

This sentence sets up two spaces which we can identify as speaker's reality
(*R*) and the film (*F*). The name *Michelle* can be used to refer in two ways.
In the first there is the kind of referential shifting we described earlier:
Michelle is the name of a person in *R*, but the speaker uses her name to
describe the film images of her acting the role of a witch (here of course the
film images may or may not resemble real-life Michelle). We could call this
connector ACTOR. We can represent this interpretation in figure 11.14. We
can roughly describe this as: real-life Michelle plays the film part of a witch.
In the second interpretation there is no referential shifting between the two
mental spaces: *Michelle* is the name of a character in the film space and we
predicate of this character that she is a witch. This interpretation can be
represented in figure 11.15. We can roughly describe this as: in the film the
character Michelle is a witch.

These two interpretations are predicted to be regular options whenever
two spaces are set up like this and this same behaviour is used to explain
the examples of referential opacity we have been looking at. If we go back
to example 11.37 *Jones believes that the leader of the Black Gulch Gang is a
sociopath*, the verb *believe* is a spacebuilder which adds the space of Jones's
belief (call it space *B*) to the parent space, which we can take to be the
speaker's reality (call this space *R*), although of course our sentence could

Figure 11.15   Second interpretation of *In the film, Michelle is a witch*

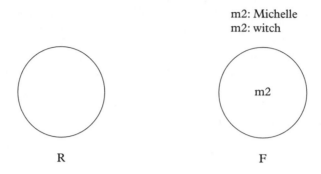

m2: Michelle
m2: witch

R   F

Figure 11.16   Transparent reading of example 11.37

g1: gangleader   g2: sociopath

R   B

easily be embedded in a story or someone else's belief. The transparent
reading of this sentence will be where Jones knows the identity of the
gangleader in reality and sets up a belief space where he describes the gangleader as a sociopath. There is therefore a referential link between the
gangleader in reality and the gangleader in Jones' belief, shown by the
connector arrow in figure 11.16. We can roughly describe this as: Jones
know the identity of the gangleader in *R* and in his belief space *B* the
gangleader is a sociopath.

   The opaque reading of this sentence will be where Jones doesn't know the
identity of the gangleader in *R* but has a belief about this person in *B*: here
there is no referential link between the reality space and the belief space, as
we show in figure 11.17. We can roughly describe this as: Jones doesn't
know the identity of the gangleader in reality but in his belief the gangleader
is a sociopath.

   In this approach any spacebuilder can trigger such ambiguities of interpretation so that a time adverbial like *in 1966* can trigger two readings for
the sentence 11.41 below:

11.41   In 1966 my wife was very young.

Figure 11.17   Opaque reading of example 11.37

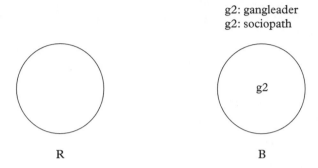

g2: gangleader
g2: sociopath

R   B

Here two time spaces are established: the 'now' of the speaker and the time
1966. The reference to the nominal *my wife* can be interpreted in two ways.
The first simply identifies a wife in the 1966 time space and is consistent
with the speaker either having the same wife in the 'now' space or not. The
second interpretation is that the person who is the speaker's wife now was
not his wife in 1966, but is referred to as *my wife* by a shift linking the
mental spaces. On this type of reading there is nothing odd about the
sentence *In 1966 my wife was a baby*. As Fauconnier points out, this ability
to connect or not connect spaces allows the transparent non-contradictory
readings for his examples in 11.42 and 11.43 below:

11.42   In Canadian football, the 50-yard line is 55 yards away.

11.43   In this new Californian religion, the devil is an angel.

   In this approach, then, the regular system of establishing mental spaces
predicts these types of referential flexibility and the prediction naturally
includes referential opacity. The advantage over traditional accounts, perhaps,
is that this approach moves the phenomenon centre-stage, so to speak, in
the study of reference and predicts that such ambiguities are very widespread and regular.

11.6.3   Presupposition

One further advantage of the mental spaces approach is that it unifies the
account of referential opacity with an analysis of **presupposition**. In our
discussion of presupposition in chapter 4 we saw that one of the problematic features is the defeasibility or cancellability of presuppositions. Thus, for
example, sentence 11.44a below has the presupposition 11.44b, but this is
cancelled in 11.44c by the added clause:

11.44   a. John hasn't stopped smoking.
         b. John used to smoke.
         c. John hasn't stopped smoking, because he never smoked.

We saw that presuppositions can be cancelled by various kinds of contextual information, including general background knowledge. We used examples like 11.45 and 11.46 below, where the presupposition trigger *before* in 11.45a produces the presupposition in 11.45b, while in 11.46 no such presupposition is produced because of what we know about death:

11.45   a. Aunt Lola drank the whole bottle of wine before she finished
             the meal.
         b. Aunt Lola finished the meal.

11.46   Aunt Lola dropped dead before she finished the meal.

We won't go into very much detail of the analysis here but the mental spaces approach explains the cancellation phenomenon by viewing presuppositions as moving ('floating' in Fauconnier's term) from space to space unless blocked by contradiction with the entities and relations (essentially the facts) identified in a space.

We can take the well-worn example of *the king of France* as an example. Fauconnier (1994: 101) discusses the example in 11.47 below:

11.47   Luke believes that it is probable that the king of France is bald,
         even though in fact there is no king of France.

Here we have three mental spaces: we begin with the first parent space of the speaker's reality R; then *believe* sets up a space of Luke's belief B; and *probable* sets up another space P. The presupposition *There is a king of France* originates in P from the sentence *The king of France is bald* and is thus a presupposition of *It is probable that the king of France is bald*. It then 'floats' up to the encompassing parent space B and thus becomes a presupposition of *Luke believes that it is probable that the king of France is bald*. However, the presupposition is blocked from floating into the space R by the explicit clause *in fact there is no king of France*. The advantage of this analysis is that though the presupposition is blocked in R and therefore for the sentence as a whole, the analysis shows how it remains associated with parts of the sentence which relate to other spaces.

The floating or sharing of presuppositions between spaces is possible because of a general similarity principle, or laziness principle, of space creation, which Fauconnier calls optimization, as defined below:

11.48   Optimization (Fauconnier 1994: 91)
         When a daughter space M is set up within a parent space R,
         structure M implicitly so as to maximize similarity with R. In

particular, in the absence of explicit contrary stipulation, assume that

a. elements in R have counterparts in M,
b. the relations holding in R hold for the counterparts in M, and
c. background assumptions in R hold in M.

Though this is only an initial stab at such a principle, we can see that it must operate in all space building and thus not only explains the sharing of presuppositions across mental spaces but also explains why in counterfactuals like 11.49 below:

11.49   If I were rich, I'd move from Ireland to a Caribbean island.

we assume in the hypothetical space that the world is pretty much the same as in reality except for the speaker's increased wealth. We don't assume, for example, that Caribbean islands change to acquire Ireland's climate.[14]

Given such a principle and the mechanism of presupposition floating, it is a straightforward prediction of this approach that all kinds of knowledge about a parent space, say reality, can cancel an incompatible presupposition.

11.6.4   Section summary

At this point we must leave our discussion of mental spaces. From our brief view of this theory, we can see that in proposing these mental structures, Fauconnier is creating a procedural view of the creation of meaning, where very simple processes of space formation and linking are triggered by the linguistic input and combine to allow the participants considerable flexibility in the manipulation of reference and knowledge about domains. The circle diagrams we have seen in this section are a form of notation which helps us to view these various referential strategies as a unified phenomenon. As such, of course, these are still linguistic tools, which presumably must be translated into realistic psychological models. As we have seen, one advantage of this approach is that it firmly situates referential opacity and belief contexts in a family of regular linguistic processes. Thus they are not seen as irregular or exceptional features of languages but as part of the wonderful referential flexibility allowed to speakers by the semantic structures of their languages. The theory has been applied to a variety of other areas including tense, mood and counterfactuals; see Fauconnier (1997) for details. One area of recent interest is **conceptual blending**, where two mental spaces are brought together to produce a third, novel space which inherits some features of the input spaces. One use of this process is in counterfactuals like Fauconnier's (1997) example *In France, Watergate wouldn't have done Nixon any harm*, where aspects of the French and American political systems are yoked together for a comparison which reflects back on them both. This can be seen as another form of analogical process. In the next section we look briefly at Ronald W. Langacker's theory of Cognitive Grammar, which identifies a range of other cognitive processes important in language.

11.7   Langacker's Cognitive Grammar

Ronald W. Langacker (especially 1987, 1991) has proposed a theory called Cognitive Grammar that has been very influential in the development of the cognitive linguistics approach. As we have noted at several points, this theory makes no distinction between grammar and semantics. The lexicon, morphology and syntax are all seen as symbolic systems. A linguistic sign is in this view a mapping or correspondence between a semantic structure and a phonological structure. This is a familiar view of lexical items but Langacker views grammar in the same light. Grammatical categories and constructions are also symbols. This may sound no different from the basic assumption of all linguists who rely on the notion of compositionality: sentences are articulated groupings of words, which are sound-meaning mappings. However, Langacker is quite radical, especially viewed against the structuralist and formalist grammatical traditions, in viewing larger structures as directly symbolic in the same way as words. In this view constructions have meanings in and of themselves.[15] Moreover, in a departure from the traditional view of levels of analysis, items at all levels of the grammar are characterized in the same conceptual terms.

   We can outline some important features of this approach, beginning by looking at how the categories of noun and verb are characterized in semantic/conceptual terms, and related to a cognitive account of clause structure. Thereafter we move on to look at the importance of construal in this theory.

11.7.1   Nouns, verbs and clauses

In this theory linguistic categories reflect conceptual models, such as the idealized cognitive models (ICMs) we discussed in chapter 2. Amongst such models Langacker identifies a naïve world-view that he calls the billiard-ball model. This is a view or theory of reality that incorporates concepts of space, time, energy and matter. He describes it as follows:

11.50   These elements are conceived as constituting a world in which discrete objects move around in space, make contact with one another, and participate in energy interactions. Conceptually, objects and interactions present a maximal contrast, having opposite values for such properties as domain of instantiation (space vs. time), essential constituent (substance vs. energy transfer), and the possibility of conceptualizing one independently of the other (autonomous vs. dependent). Physical objects and energetic inter-

Figure 11.18 Prototypical event scheme

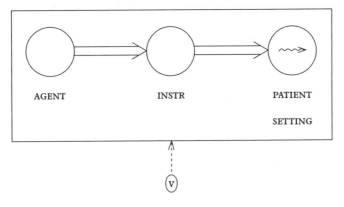

Source: Based on Langacker (1990: 209ff.)

> actions provide the respective prototypes for the noun and verb
> categories, which likewise represent a polar opposition among the
> basic grammatical classes.   (Langacker 1991: 283)

Thus the linguistic categories of noun and verb are characterized in terms
of a cognitive model, a conceptual partitioning of reality. Though the quotation above identifies physical objects as the prototypical nouns, the crucial
cognitive process is the bounding of a portion of experience to create a thing
distinct from its surroundings. So nouns may describe time-stable states and
of course may describe processes or 'interactions' normally identified by
verbs, as in *his arrival among us* or *dieting is bad for you*. This characterization
emphasizes that the conditions for something being a noun are not objectively
out in the world but a product of cognitive processes and a communicative
decision.

The model in 11.50 extends naturally to the characterization of the prototypical transitive clause. Langacker describes this from the viewpoint of a
speaker wanting to communicate a description of an event or scene. The
initial identification of a scene is described (1987: 6) as the 'chunking into
discrete events of temporally contiguous clusters of interactions observed
within a setting'. The tasks of a describer in this account include distinguishing between the occurrence and the setting; establishing a vantage
point; determining what types of entities are to be interpreted as participants
and identifying their forms of interaction. A schema of a canonical transitive
event is given in figure 11.18.

In this schema the viewer, shown as V, is outside the setting and thus is
not a participant, making this a third-person report of an event. The viewer
identifies three elements in an **action chain**: an asymmetrical relationship
where energy is transmitted from one entity to a second entity, and in this
case on to a third. In figure 11.18 the energy transfer is shown as a double-
shafted arrow, and the wavy arrow in the PATIENT represents the change of

state within this entity caused by the interaction. This schema describes a prototypical case where energy originates with an AGENT and ends with a PATIENT, via an intermediate entity the INSTRUMENT.

Thereafter, in choosing to talk about this scene the speaker is faced with a number of choices. An important emphasis in this theory is on the speaker's active characterization of scenes, employing the conventional conceptualizations of language and a range of cognitive processes. A general term for these processes is **construal**: as we mentioned earlier, a basic tenet of cognitive linguistics is that speakers can construe a scene in alternative ways. We discuss some aspects of this choice of construal in the next section.

11.7.2   Construal

One type of construal discussed by Langacker is **profiling**: within the action chain the speaker can choose to profile certain segments of the chain. Some possibilities are schematically shown in figure 11.19. We can use Langacker's example of *Floyd broke the glass with a hammer* to illustrate the possibilities in figure 11.19, where profiled chain a corresponds to sentence 11.60a below; chain b to 11.60b; and chain c to 11.60c:

11.51   a.   Floyd broke the glass with a hammer.
           b.   The hammer broke the glass.
           c.   The glass broke.

Figure 11.19   Profiling within the action chain

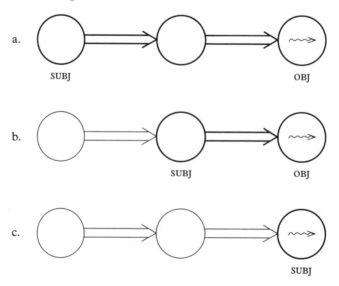

Source: Langacker (1990)

We can see here Langacker proposing his own version of the mapping hierarchies we saw in chapter 6, proposed by Dowty (1991) to relate thematic roles, grammatical relations and syntactic structure. Langacker gives a version of the universal subject hierarchies we discussed there, in terms of action chains (1990: 217):

11.52   The subject is consistently the 'head' of the PROFILED portion of the action chain, i.e. the participant that is farthest 'upstream' with respect to the energy flow. By contrast the object is the 'tail' of the profiled portion of the action chain: the participant distinct from the subject that lies the farthest 'downstream' in the flow of the energy.

For further details of this view of argument structure in terms of action chains and flows of energy, the reader is referred to Langacker (1991: 282–377).

Another important notion is **perspective**, which in Langacker (1987) is taken to include the notions of **viewpoint** and **focus**. This notion of perspective is a reflection of the importance that cognitivists attach to the role of the observer in scenes: in particular, the selection of the observer's viewpoint and the choice of elements to focus on. We can take as a simple example of the former the choice between external and internal viewpoints of a container, as reflected in the two interpretations of the preposition *around* in sentence 11.53 below:

11.53   The children ran around the house.

If we choose an external viewpoint of the house as a container, this sentence describes a scene where the children's motion circles the outside of the house, whereas if we choose an internal viewpoint, the children are moving around within the house's internal space.

We saw something of the linguistic implications of focus in chapter 7 and again in chapter 9, when we discussed Leonard Talmy's analysis of motion events into features including **Figure** and **Ground**, as in, for example, Talmy (1975, 1985). We saw there that the Figure (as we have seen, also called the **trajector**) is an entity chosen to stand out in some way from the background, the Ground (also called the **landmark**). In the case of motion events, the entity which is moving with respect to stationary surroundings tends to be chosen as the Figure. The choice to focus on either Figure or Ground in a scene can have lexical significance: Talmy (1985) describes the choice in English between the verbs *emanate* and *emit* in 11.54 and 11.55 below:

11.54   The light emanated from a beacon.

11.55   The beacon emitted light.

The verb *emanate* requires the Figure as subject; while *emit* requires the Ground as subject. Talmy argues therefore that choosing the former reflects a choice of focus on the Figure; and the latter, focus on the Ground. As we saw in earlier chapters, sometimes the choice of focus involves not separate verbs but different argument structures for the same verb, as in the pairs below:

11.56   a.   The bees swarmed in the field.
          b.   The field swarmed with bees.

11.57   a.   The ice glistened in the moonlight.
          b.   The moonlight glistened on the ice.

There are other related processes of construal proposed in this theory, for example **scanning** (Langacker 1987: 101–5), by which speakers are able to structure a scene in order to form a description. Langacker makes a distinction between **sequential** and **summary** scanning. These are different ways that a reporter may construe a scene. Sequential scanning is a way of viewing a process as a sequence of component sub-events. Summary scanning is a way of viewing a process as a complete unit where all its sub-events are viewed as an integrated whole. Langacker proposes that this difference is reflected in grammar in a number of ways including a speaker's decision to use a noun or a verb to describe an event. So someone going into a room or falling off a cliff can be viewed in sequential mode and described verbally as in the a sentences in 11.58–9 below, or be viewed in summary mode and described with nominals as in the b versions (Langacker 1991: 283):

11.58   a.   Keegan entered the room.
          b.   Keegan's entrance into the room

11.59   a.   Wheeler fell off the cliff.
          b.   Wheeler's fall from the cliff

Langacker uses an analogy to bring out the difference between these modes: sequential scanning is like viewing a motion picture sequence while summary scanning is like viewing a still photograph.

These examples of viewpoint, focusing, profiling and scanning reveal the importance attached in this theory, and in cognitive linguistics generally, to the role of the speaker's construal of a situation in determining meaning.

11.8 Summary

In this chapter we have reviewed the approach known as cognitive semantics. We have seen that a distinctive feature of the approach is its attempt to form an experientialist basis for meaning. Cognitive semanticists propose that the common human experience of maturing and interacting in society motivates basic conceptual structures which make understanding and language possible. In Mark Johnson's (1987) approach, these conceptual structures include pre-linguistic **image schemas**. These image schemas form more abstract cognitive models by processes of **metaphor** and **metonymy**. We saw the importance in Langacker's Cognitive Grammar of the cognitive processes which underpin the speaker's construal of a scene, for example by determining **perspective**, selecting **viewpoint**, **Figure–Ground focus**, **profiling** and **scanning**. We also saw in Fauconnier's theory of **mental models** a mechanism for explaining how participants in a discourse maintain referential links, set up referential domains and regulate knowledge sharing between them.

In earlier chapters we discussed the claim that semantic representations have to be grounded in some way, if semantic analysis is not just to be simply a form of translation. In chapter 10 we saw that in formal semantics this is done by establishing denotational links with the external non-linguistic world. In this chapter we have seen that in cognitive semantics a similar grounding is sought not directly in reality (which in this view is not directly accessible) but in conceptual structures derived from the experience of having human bodies and of sharing in social conventions, and all that this implies.

FURTHER READING

A comprehensive introduction to cognitive semantics is George Lakoff (1987), which includes detailed discussions of the conceptual structures we have discussed. Mark Johnson (1987) investigates the experiential basis of these constructs, while Fauconnier (1994, 1997) describes his work on mental spaces. An encyclopaedic review of the relations between semantics and grammar in cognitive linguistics is given in two books by Langacker, (1987) and (1991). An accessible introduction to cognitive linguistics is Ungerer and Schmid (1996).

At a more specific level, volume 6 (1995) of the journal *Cognitive Linguistics* is a special issue dedicated to articles on spatial language and cognition, several of which deal with prepositions in various languages.

EXERCISES

11.1   Give example sentences in English, and any other language you know, of the metaphors ARGUMENTS ARE BUILDINGS and IDEAS ARE OBJECTS.

11.2   For any two languages you know, discuss similarities and differences in conventionalized metaphors of body parts (e.g. head of a beer, hand of a watch).

11.3   Provide your own examples of the following metonymic strategies:

CONTAINER FOR CONTENTS
WHOLE FOR PART
PART FOR WHOLE
CONTROLLER FOR CONTROLLED
OBJECT USED FOR USER

11.4   In this chapter we discussed the tendency for prepositions to exhibit **polysemy**. As we saw, within cognitive semantics this is described in terms of extension from a prototypical image schema. Below we give examples of three English prepositions: *on, under* and *over*. For each set of examples discuss any differences you detect in how the preposition leads you to conceive of the spatial relations. Discuss how you could informally capture the shared meaning. Then try to use schemas like the diagrams we saw in section 11.4 to capture the distinctions you identify. (Similar examples are discussed in Lakoff 1987, Brugman 1988 and Vandeloise 1991.)

   a.   *on*
        The cup is on the table.
        The fly is on the ceiling.
        The painting is on the wall.
        The shoe is on my foot.
        The leaves are on the tree.
        The house is on fire.

   b.   *under*
        The mechanic is under the car.
        Under the wallpaper the plaster is very damp.
        Our next goal is to explore under the oceans.
        It can breathe under water.
        We have the house under surveillance.
        Try looking under 'Crime Novels'.

   c.   *over*
        The horse jumped over the fence.
        The boys walked over the hill.
        The hawk hovered over the field.
        The bridge stretches over the highway.
        The runner looked over her shoulder at the following group.
        He's over the worst.

11.5 Clearly different prepositions allow different characterizations of spatial relations. However, if we compare two prepositions, say English *on* and *in*, we may find different conceptualizations chosen between individual speakers or between dialects. For example in Irish English, some people, speaking of an item of news, might say *It was **on** the newspaper yesterday*, while others might say ***in** the newspaper*. How would you describe the two different metaphorical strategies in this example? Below are pairs of sentences differing only in the choice of *on* and *in*. Discuss the meaning relationship between the sentences in each pair. Once again discuss whether diagrammatic schemas would help your analysis.

1   a.   I heard it on the radio.
    b.   I heard it in the radio.

2   a.   I heard it on the news.
    b.   I heard it in the news.

3   a.   He lay on his bed.
    b.   He lay in his bed.

4   a.   He lay on his deathbed.
    b.   He lay in his deathbed.

5   a.   I put a new engine on the car.
    b.   I put a new engine in the car.

6   a.   I put a new set of tyres on the car.
    b.   I put a new set of tyres in the car.

7   a.   The children on the bus need to be counted.
    b.   The children in the bus need to be counted.

11.6 We saw how within the **mental spaces** theory, there are pragmatic functions that allow referential connections between mental spaces. One such function was called **Image**, as in examples like *In this painting Napoleon is smiling*. Here the real person (the model) acts as a trigger for the target image (the representation), and thus we can naturally call the image *Napoleon*. This can be abbreviated as:

Image: (connector: model → representation).

We also saw examples of the following pragmatic functions:

Author: (connector: writers → books)
Drama: (connector: characters → actors)

In the examples below, assume a reading which involves such referential shifts. For each sentence, describe a context and invent a label for the pragmatic function involved.

  a.   The BMW is waiting for his ticket.
  b.   I'm the last office on the corridor.
  c.   The liposuction is not pleased.
  d.   Law are moving off campus.
  e.   It's time to give Napoleon his medication.
  f.   The cheeseburger didn't order onions.

Discuss whether there is likely to be a finite set of such functions.

11.7   Using the theory of **mental spaces, spacebuilders** and **referential connectors** outlined in this chapter, discuss the referential interpretations of the sentences below:

  a.   In the novel, Hitler wins World War II.
  b.   Next year this hotel will be a car park.
  c.   Joan wants to marry a millionaire.
  d.   Usually this bus is crowded.
  e.   In 1947 the president was a child.
  f.   Maybe your car isn't your car.

NOTES

1   The label *cognitive* is used in this approach in a number of related ways. Ronald W. Langacker uses the term *cognitive grammar* to describe his own and close colleagues' work, in for example Langacker (1987, 1990). George Lakoff (1988) uses *cognitive semantics* as a cover term for the work of a number of scholars including Langacker, Lakoff himself, Claudia Brugman, Mark Johnson, Gilles Fauconnier, Leonard Talmy and Eve Sweetser, amongst others. References to work by these authors can be found in our References section. As we note, this is a very varied group of scholars, working on different topics and not always sharing the same interests. However, there are unifying factors: there is an International Cognitive Linguistics Association, which publishes a journal *Cognitive Linguistics*, holds an annual conference, and links researchers who share the basic outlook we describe here. In this chapter we will use the term

cognitive semantics in the spirit of Lakoff (1988) as a loose, inclusive term for scholars who, while they may not form a tight, coherent school of thought, do share some basic assumptions about the direction a semantic theory must take.

2 For such views see J. A. Fodor (1983) and Chomsky (1988).

3 For discussion of these aims, and a rejection of them as premature for linguistics, see Fauconnier (1994: xxviii–xlvi).

4 See de Saussure (1974) for discussion.

5 Heine et al. (1991) discuss examples of such processes of grammaticalization. These include full lexical nouns becoming pronouns, e.g. (p. 35) 'Latin *homo* "person, man" to French *on* (impersonal subject pronoun), German *Mann* "man" to *man* (impersonal subject pronoun), and Latin *persona* "person" to French *personne* (negative pronoun, negation marker).' Another example (p. 131) is of nouns for parts of the body becoming spatial adverbs and prepositions, as in the example of Swahili, where what was historically a noun **mbele* 'breast' became a noun *mbele* 'front' and then an adverb 'in front' as shown below:

> Gari liko mbele
> car is front
> 'The car is in front, ahead.'

Similar processes have been identified for a number of African languages; see Heine et al. (1991) for discussion.

6 This of course leaves open the question of the 'fit' between human categorization and what is really out there in the world. The cognitivist position is consistent with a range of views. The point perhaps is that from a linguistic perspective, it is the mapping between language and conceptual structure that is crucial. Clearly conceptual structure is intimately related to perception: for example, we don't have words in our ordinary vocabulary for the light wavelengths we cannot see as colour, or to describe the sound waves we cannot hear. The perceptual and experiential basis of conceptual categories is an important topic of inquiry in cognitive semantics. See the relations identified in Mark Johnson (1987), for example, which we discuss in section 11.3.

7 Example 11.2 is from the article 'Inside the Oscar Wars' in *Time* magazine, 25 March 2002 (p. 56). Example 11.3 is from the article 'This Glorious Mess' in the British newspaper *The Guardian*, Friday 22 March 2002 (Review section, p. 2).

8 For a discussion of this distinction between classical and Romantic views of metaphor, see the accessible overview in Hawkes (1972), and the more extended discussions in Black (1962), Ortony (1979) and Kittay (1987).

9 Given what we have already said about the cognitivist rejection of objectivist semantics, it is interesting to read the remarks of the English Romantic poet Samuel Taylor Coleridge in a letter to James Gillman, written in 1827 (cited in Hawkes 1972: 54–5):

> It is the fundamental mistake of grammarians and writers on the philosophy of grammar and language to suppose that words and their syntax are the immediate representatives of *things*, or that they correspond to *things*. Words correspond to thoughts, and the legitimate order and connection of words to the *laws* of thinking and to the acts and affections of the thinker's mind.

10 From *Science* magazine, volume 295, no. 5561 (p. 1813), 8 March 2002.

11   The symbol * is used in example 11.13, as in historical linguistics, to identify a hypothetical reconstructed form.
12   We could, of course, add modern Indo-European examples like French *goûter* 'taste', Spanish *gustar* 'please', *gustarse* 'like', etc.
13   These are equivalent to the terms **Figure** and **Ground** we met in chapter 9 in our discussion of Leonard Talmy's description of motion events (e.g. Talmy 1985).
14   This principle can be seen as a cognitive parallel to the notion in formal semantics of **resemblance** or **similarity** between possible worlds; see Stalnaker (1968) and Lewis (1973) for discussion.
15   See Goldberg (1995) for a related view of grammatical constructions as cognitive schemas.

References

Akindele, Femi 1990: A sociolinguistic analysis of Yoruba greetings. *African Languages and Cultures* 3.1: 1–14.

Akmajian, A., R. A. Demers and R. M. Harnish 1984: *Linguistics*, second edition. Cambridge, MA: MIT Press.

Allan, Keith 1986: *Linguistic Meaning*, 2 vols. London: Routledge & Kegan Paul.

Allan, Keith 2001: *Natural Language Semantics*. Oxford: Blackwell.

Allen, Woody 1983: *Four Films of Woody Allen: Annie Hall, Interiors, Manhattan, Stardust Memories*. London: Faber.

Allwood, J., L.-G. Andersson and O. Dahl 1977: *Logic in Linguistics*. Cambridge: Cambridge University Press.

Alsina, Alex 1999: On the representation of event structure. In T. Mohanan and L. Wee (eds) *Grammatical Semantics: Evidence for Structure in Meaning*, 77–122. Stanford and National University of Singapore: Center for the Study of Language and Information.

Anderson, J. R. 1976: *Language, Memory and Thought*. Hillsdale, NJ: Lawrence Erlbaum.

Anderson, R. C., R. E. Reynolds, D. L. Schallert and E. T. Goetz 1977: Frameworks for comprehending discourse. *American Educational Research Journal* 14: 367–81.

Anderson, Stephen R. 1971: On the role of deep structure in semantic interpretation. *Foundations of Language* 7: 387–96.

Anderson, Stephen R. 1976: On the notion of subject in ergative languages. In Charles Li (ed.) *Subject and Topic*. New York: Academic Press, 1–24.

Anderson, Stephen R. and Edward L. Keenan 1985: Deixis. In Timothy Shopen (ed.) *Language Typology and Syntactic Description*, vol. III: *Grammatical Categories and the Lexicon*, 259–308. Cambridge: Cambridge University Press.

Andrews, A. 1985: The major functions of the noun phrase. In Timothy Shopen (ed.) *Language Typology and Syntactic Description*, vol. I: *Clause Structure*, 2–154. Cambridge: Cambridge University Press.

Anttila, Raimo 1989: *Historical and Comparative Linguistics*. Amsterdam: John Benjamins.

Ariel, M. 1988: Referring and accessibility. *Journal of Linguistics* 24: 67–87.

Atkinson, J. Maxwell and John Heritage (eds) 1984: *Structures of Social Action*. Cambridge: Cambridge University Press.

Austin, J. L. 1975: *How to Do Things with Words*, second edition. Oxford: Clarendon Press. (First published 1962.)

Avramides, Anita 1989: *Meaning and Mind*. Cambridge, MA: MIT Press.

Ayer, A. J. (ed.) 1959: *Logical Positivism*. New York: Free Press.

Bach, Emmon 1986: The algebra of events. *Linguistics and Philosophy* 9: 5–16.

Bach, K. and R. M. Harnish 1979: *Linguistic Communication and Speech Acts*. Cambridge, MA: MIT Press.

Bakker, E. 1994: Voice, aspect and aktionsart: middle and passive in Ancient Greek. In Barbara Fox and Paul J. Hopper (eds) *Voice: Form and Function*, 23–48. Amsterdam: John Benjamins.

Barber, E. J. A. 1975: Voice: beyond the passive. *Berkeley Linguistics Society* 1: 16–23.

Barwise, Jon 1988: On the circumstantial relation between meaning and content. In Umberto Eco, Marco Santambrogio and Patrizia Violi (eds) *Meaning and Mental Representations*, 23–40. Bloomington and Indianapolis: Indiana University Press.

Barwise, Jon and Robin Cooper 1981: Generalized quantifiers and natural language. *Linguistics and Philosophy* 4: 159–219.

Barwise, Jon and John Perry 1983: *Situations and Attitudes*. Cambridge, MA: MIT Press.

Beaver, David 1997: Presupposition. In Johan van Bentham and Alice ter Meulen (eds), *Handbook of Logic and Language*, 939–1008. Amsterdam: Elsevier.

Berlin, Brent and Paul Kay 1969: *Basic Color Terms: Their Universality and Evolution*. Berkeley, CA: University of California Press.

Berlin, Brent, Dennis E. Breedlove and Peter H. Raven 1974: *Principles of Tzeltal Plant Classification*. New York: Academic Press.

Binnick, Robert I. 1991: *Time and the Verb: A Guide to Tense and Aspect*. Oxford: Oxford University Press.

Black, Max 1962: *Models and Metaphors*. Ithaca, NY: Cornell University Press.

Blake, B. 1990: *Relational Grammar*. London: Routledge & Kegan Paul.

Blakemore, Diane 1992: *Understanding Utterances: An Introduction to Pragmatics*. Oxford: Blackwell.

Bloomfield, Leonard 1984: *Language*. Chicago: University of Chicago Press. (Originally published 1933.)

Blum-Kulka, S. 1983: Interpreting and performing speech acts in a second language: a cross-cultural study of Hebrew and English. In N. Wolfson and E. Judd (eds), *Sociolinguistics and Language Acquisition*, 36–55. Rowley, MA: Newbury House.

Blum-Kulka, S. 1987: Indirectness and politeness in requests: same or different? *Journal of Pragmatics* 11: 131–46.

Blum-Kulka, S., J. House, and G. Kasper (eds) 1989: *Cross-Cultural Pragmatics: Requests and Apologies*. Norwood, NJ: Ablex.

Boas, Franz 1966: *Introduction to the Handbook of American Indian Languages*, vol. 1. Washington, DC: Smithsonian Institution. (First published 1911.)

Boer, Steven E. and William G. Lycan 1976: *The Myth of Semantic Presupposition*. Bloomington, IN: Indiana University Linguistics Club.

Bowers, J. W. 1982: Does a duck have antlers? Some pragmatics of 'transparent questions'. *Communication Monographs* 42: 63–9.

Bradley, Raymond and Norman Swartz 1979: *Possible World: an Introduction to Logic and Its Philosophy*. Oxford: Blackwell.

Bresnan, Joan 1994: Locative inversion and the architecture of universal grammar. *Language* 70: 72–131.

Brown, Cecil H. 1984: *Language and Living Things*. New Brunswick, NJ: Rutgers University Press.

Brown, G. and G. Yule 1983: *Discourse Analysis*. Cambridge: Cambridge University Press.

Brown, Penelope and Stephen C. Levinson 1978: Universals in language usage: politeness phenomena. In Esther N. Goody (ed.) *Questions and Politeness: Strategies in Social Interaction*, 56–310. Cambridge: Cambridge University Press.

Brown, Penelope and Stephen C. Levinson 1987: *Politeness: Some Universals in Language Usage*. Cambridge: Cambridge University Press.

Brugman, Claudia 1988: *The Story of Over: Polysemy, Semantics and the Structure of the Lexicon*. New York: Garland.

Brugman, Claudia and George Lakoff 1988: Cognitive topology and lexical networks. In S. Small, G. Cottrell and M. Tanenhaus (eds) *Lexical Ambiguity Resolution: Perspectives from Psycholinguistics, Neuropsychology and Artificial Intelligence*, 477–508. San Mateo, CA: Morgan Kaufmann.

Butt, John and Carmen Benjamin 1994: *A New Reference Grammar of Modern Spanish*, second edition. London: Edward Arnold.

Bybee, Joan 1985: *Morphology*. Amsterdam: Benjamins.

Bybee, Joan, Revere Perkins and William Pagliuca 1994: *The Evolution of Grammar: Tense, Aspect, and Modality in the Languages of the World*. Chicago, IL: University of Chicago Press.

Bybee, Joan and Suzanne Fleischman (eds) 1995: *Modality in Grammar and Discourse*. Amsterdam: John Benjamins.

Cann, Ronnie 1993: *Formal Semantics*. Cambridge: Cambridge University Press.

Carnap, Rudolf 1942: *Introduction to Semantics*. Cambridge, MA: Harvard University Press.

Carnap, Rudolf 1952: Meaning postulates. *Philosophical Studies* 3: 65–73.

Carnap, Rudolf 1956: *Meaning and Necessity: a Study in Semantics and Modal Logic*, second edition. Chicago, IL: University of Chicago Press.

le Carré, John 1993: *The Night Manager*. London: Hodder and Stoughton.

Carroll, D. W. 1986: *Psychology of Language*. Monterey, CA: Brooks/Cole.

Carstairs-McCarthy, Andrew 1992: *Current Morphology*. London: Routledge & Kegan Paul.

Chafe, Wallace 1976: Givenness, contrastiveness, definiteness, subjects, topics, and points of view. In C. N. Li (ed.) *Subject and Topic*, 25–55. New York: Academic Press.

Chafe, Wallace 1986: Evidentiality in English conversation and academic writing. In Wallace Chafe and Johanna Nichols (eds) *Evidentiality: the Linguistic Coding of Epistemology*, 261–72. Norwood, NJ: Ablex.

Chafe, Wallace and Johanna Nichols (eds) 1986: *Evidentiality: the Linguistic Coding of Epistemology*. Norwood, NJ: Ablex.

Chierchia, G. and S. McConnell-Ginet 1990/2000: *Meaning and Grammar: an Introduction to Semantics*, second edition. Cambridge, MA: MIT Press. (First edition 1990.)

Choi, Soonja and Melissa Bowerman 1992: Learning to express motion events in English and Korean: the influence of language-specific lexicalization patterns. In Beth Levin and Steven Pinker (eds) *Lexical and Conceptual Semantics*, 83–121. Oxford: Blackwell.

Chomsky, Noam 1957: *Syntactic Structures*. The Hague: Mouton.

Chomsky, Noam 1965: *Aspects of the Theory of Syntax*. Cambridge, MA: MIT Press.

Chomsky, Noam 1987: Language in a psychological setting. *Sophia Linguistica* (Tokyo) 22: 1–73.

Chomsky, Noam 1988: *Language and Problems of Knowledge. The Managua Lectures*. Cambridge, MA: MIT Press.

Chung, Sandra and Alan Timberlake 1985: Tense, aspect and mood. In Timothy Shopen (ed.) *Language Typology and Syntactic Description*, vol. III: *Grammatical Categories and the Lexicon*, 202–58. Cambridge: Cambridge University Press.

Churchland, Paul 1985: Conceptual progress and word/world relations: in search of the essence of natural kinds. *Canadian Journal of Philosophy* 15: 1, 1–17.

Clark, E. V. 1983: Meanings and concepts. In J. H. Flavell and E. M. Markman (eds) *Cognitive Development*, vol. III of P. H. Mussen (ed.) *Handbook of Child Psychology*, fourth edition. New York: Wiley, 787–840.

Clark, H. H. 1977: Bridging. In P. N. Johnson-Laird and P. C. Wason (eds) *Thinking: Readings in Cognitive Science*, 411–20. Cambridge: Cambridge University Press.

Clark, H. H. 1978: Inferring what is meant. In W. J. M. Levelt and G. B. Flores dArcais (eds) *Studies in the Perception of Language*, 295–322. Chichester: Wiley.

Clark, H. H. 1994: Discourse in production. In Morton A. Gernsbacher (ed.) *Handbook of Psycholinguistics*, 985–1021. San Diego: Academic Press.

Clark, H. H. and P. Lucy 1975: Understanding what is meant from what is said: a study in conversationally conveyed requests. *Journal of Verbal Learning and Verbal Behaviour* 14: 56–72.

Clark, H. H. and D. H. Schunk 1980: Polite responses to polite requests. *Cognition* 8: 111–43.

Cole, Peter (ed.) 1978: *Syntax and Semantics*, vol. 9: *Pragmatics*. New York: Academic Press.

Cole, Peter and Jerry Morgan (eds) 1975: *Syntax and Semantics*, vol. 3: *Speech Acts*. New York: Academic Press.

Collins, A. M. and M. R. Quillian 1969: Retrieval time from semantic memory. *Journal of Verbal Learning and Verbal Behavior* 8: 240–8.

Comrie, B. 1976: *Aspect*. Cambridge: Cambridge University Press.

Comrie, B. 1981: *Language Universals and Linguistic Typology*. Oxford: Blackwell.

Comrie, B. 1985: *Tense*. Cambridge: Cambridge University Press.

Conklin, H. 1964: Hanunoo color categories. In D. Hymes (ed.) *Language in Culture and Society: A Reader in Linguistics and Anthropology*, 189–92. New York: Harper and Row.

Cook, Vivian and Mark Newson 1995: *Chomsky's Universal Grammar*, second edition. Oxford: Blackwell.

Couper-Kuhlen, E. 1979: *The Prepositional Passive in English*. Tübingen: Niemeyer.

Croft, William 1990: *Typology and Universals*. Cambridge: Cambridge University Press.

Croft, William 1991a: Possible verbs and the structure of events. In S. L. Tsohahatzidis (ed.) *Meanings and Prototypes: Studies on Linguistic Categorization*. London: Routledge & Kegan Paul.

Croft, William 1991b: *Syntactic Categories and Grammatical Relations*. Chicago, IL: University of Chicago Press.

Cruse, D. A. 1986: *Lexical Semantics*. Cambridge: Cambridge University Press.

Culicover, Peter and Louise McNally 1998: *Syntax and Semantics 29: The Limits of Syntax*. New York: Academic Press.

Cullingford, R. 1978: Script application: computer understanding of newspaper stories. PhD thesis, Yale University.

Cummings, E. E. 1944: *1 × 1*. New York: Harcourt Brace Jovanovich.

Cureton, R. 1979: The exceptions to passive in English: a pragmatic hypothesis. *Studies in the Linguistic Sciences* 9.2: 39–53.

Dahl, Östen 1985: *Tense and Aspect Systems*. Oxford: Blackwell.

Davidson, Donald 1967: Truth and meaning. *Synthese* 17: 304–23. Reprinted in A. Martinich (ed.) 1985: *The Philosophy of Language*. Cambridge, MA: MIT Press.

Davidson, Donald 1980: *Essays on Actions and Events*. Oxford: Clarendon.

Davidson, Donald 1984: *Inquiries into Truth and Interpretation*. Oxford: Oxford University Press.

Dawson, Les 1979: *The Les Dawson Joke Book*. London: Arrow Books.

Dennett, Daniel C. 1987: *The Intentional Stance*. Cambridge, MA: MIT Press.

Devitt, Michael and Kim Sterelny 1987: *Language and Reality: an Introduction to the Philosophy of Language*. Oxford: Blackwell.

Dixon, R. M. W. 1979: Ergativity. *Language* 55.1: 59–138.

Dixon, R. M. W. 1991: *A New Approach to English Grammar on Semantic Principles*. Oxford: Oxford University Press.

Donnellan, Keith S. 1972: Proper names and identifying descriptions. In Donald Davidson and Gilbert Harmon (eds) *Semantics of Natural Language*, 356–79. Dordrecht: Reidel.

Downing, P. 1977: On 'basic levels' and the categorisation of objects in English discourse. *Proceedings of the Berkeley Linguistics Society* 3: 475–87.

Dowty, David R. 1979: *Word Meaning and Montague Grammar*. Dordrecht: Reidel.

Dowty, David R. 1986: Thematic roles and semantics. *Berkeley Linguistics Society* 12: 340–54.

Dowty, David R. 1989: On the semantic content of the notion 'thematic role'. In B. Partee, G. Chierchia and R. Turner (eds) *Properties, Types and Meanings*, vol. 2, 69–130. Dordrecht: Kluwer.

Dowty, David R. 1991: Thematic proto-roles and argument selection. *Language* 67: 574–619.

Dowty, David, Robert E. Wall and Stanley Peters 1981: *Introduction to Montague Semantics*. Dordrecht: Reidel.

Dryer, Matthew S. 1996: Focus, pragmatic presupposition, and activated propositions. *Journal of Pragmatics* 26: 475–523.

Dummett, M. 1981: *Frege: Philosophy of Language*, second edition. London: Duckworth.

Eco, Umberto 1976: *A Theory of Semiotics*. Bloomington, IN: Indiana University Press.

Eco, Umberto, Marco Santambrogio and Patrizia Violi (eds) 1988: *Meaning and Mental Representations*. Bloomington and Indianapolis: Indiana University Press.

Emonds, J. 1985: *A Unified Theory of Syntactic Categories*. Dordrecht: Foris.

Ervin-Tripp, Susan 1976: Is Sybil there? The structure of some American English directives. *Language in Society* 5: 25–66.

Evens, Martha Walton (ed.) 1988: *Relational Models of the Lexicon: Representing Knowledge in Semantic Networks.* Cambridge: Cambridge University Press.

Eysenck, Michael W. and Mark T. Keane 2000: *Cognitive Psychology: a Student's Handbook,* fourth edition. Hove: Psychology Press.

Fass, Dan 1991: met*: A method for discriminating metonymy and metaphor by computer. *Computational Linguistics* 17(1): 49–90.

Fass, Dan 1997: *Processing Metonymy and Metaphor.* Greenwich, CT: Ablex.

Fauconnier, Gilles 1985: *Mental Spaces.* Cambridge, MA: MIT Press.

Fauconnier, Gilles 1988: Quantification, roles and domains. In Umberto Eco, Marco Santambrogio and Patrizia Violi (eds) *Meaning and Mental Representations,* 61–80. Bloomington and Indianapolis: Indiana University Press.

Fauconnier, Gilles 1994: *Mental Spaces: Aspects of Meaning Construction in Natural Language.* Cambridge: Cambridge University Press.

Fauconnier, Gilles 1997: *Mappings in Thought and Language.* Cambridge: Cambridge University Press.

Fillmore, Charles J. 1968: The case for Case. In E. Bach and R. Harms (eds) *Universals in Linguistic Theory,* 1–88. New York: Holt, Rinehart & Winston.

Fillmore, Charles J. 1982a: Towards a descriptive framework for spatial deixis. In R. J. Jarvell and W. Klein (eds) *Speech, Place and Action: Studies in Deixis and Related Topics,* 31–59. London: Wiley.

Fillmore, Charles J. 1982b: Frame semantics. In Linguistic Society of Korea (ed.), *Linguistics in the Morning Calm,* 111–38. Seoul: Hanshin.

Fillmore, Charles J. 1997: *Lectures on Deixis.* Stanford: Center for the Study of Language and Information.

Firth, J. R. 1957: Modes of meaning. In J. R. Firth, *Papers in Linguistics 1934–1951.* London: Oxford University Press.

Fleischman, Suzanne 1982: The past and future: Are they *coming* or *going? Proceedings of the Eighth Annual Meeting of the Berkeley Linguistics Society,* 322–4.

Fleischman, Suzanne 1989: Temporal distance: a basic linguistic metaphor. *Studies in Language* 13.1: 1–50.

Fodor, J. A. 1970: Three reasons for not deriving 'kill' from 'cause to die'. *Linguistic Inquiry* 1: 429–38.

Fodor, J. A. 1975: *The Language of Thought.* New York: Thomas Crowell.

Fodor, J. A. 1980: Fixation of belief and concept acquisition. In M. Piatelli-Palmarini (ed.) *Language and Learning.* Cambridge, MA: Harvard University Press.

Fodor, J. A. 1981a: Methodological solipsism considered as a research strategy. In J. A. Fodor, *Representations: Philosophical Essays on the Foundations of Cognitive Science,* 225–53. Cambridge, MA: MIT Press, Bradford Books.

Fodor, J. A. 1981b: The present status of the innateness controversy. In J. A. Fodor, *Representations: Philosophical Essays on the Foundations of Cognitive Science,* 257–316. Cambridge, MA: MIT Press, Bradford Books.

Fodor, J. A. 1983: *The Modularity of Mind.* Cambridge, MA: MIT Press.

Fodor, J. A. 1987: *Psychosemantics: The Problem of Meaning in the Philosophy of Mind.* Cambridge, MA: MIT Press.

Fodor, J. A., M. Garrett, E. Walker, and C. Parkes 1980: Against definitions. *Cognition* 8: 263–367.

Fodor, J. D. 1979: The King of France is false. In C.-K. Oh and D. A. Dinneen (eds) *Syntax and Semantics 11: Presupposition,* 200–20. New York: Academic Press.

Fodor, J. D. 1983: *Semantics: Theories of Meaning in Generative Grammar.* Brighton: Harvester.

Fodor, J. D., J. A. Fodor and M. Garrett 1975: The psychological unreality of semantic representations. *Linguistic Inquiry* 6: 515–32.

Foley, W. 1997: *Anthropological Linguistics*. Oxford: Blackwell.

Foley, William and Robert Van Valin 1984: *Functional Syntax and Universal Grammar*. Cambridge: Cambridge University Press.

Fox, Barbara and Paul J. Hopper (eds) 1994: *Voice: Form and Function*. Amsterdam: John Benjamins.

Fraser, Bruce 1975: Hedged performatives. In Peter Cole and Jerry Morgan (eds) *Syntax and Semantics*, vol. 3: *Speech Acts*, 187–210. New York: Academic Press.

Frawley, William 1992: *Linguistic Semantics*. Hillsdale, NJ: Lawrence Erlbaum.

Frege, Gottlob 1980: *Translations from the Philosophical Writings of Gottlob Frege*, edited by Peter Geach and Max Black. Oxford: Blackwell.

Gamut, L. T. F. 1991: *Logic, Language, and Meaning*, 2 vols. Chicago, IL: University of Chicago Press.

Gazdar, Gerald 1979: *Pragmatics: Implicature, Presupposition, and Logical Form*. New York: Academic Press.

Gazdar, Gerald 1981: Speech act assignment. In A. K. Joshi, B. L. Webber and I. A. Sag (eds) *Elements of Discourse Understanding*. Cambridge: Cambridge University Press.

Gazdar, Gerald, Ewan Klein, Geofrey Pullum and Ivan Sag 1985: *Generalized Phrase Structure Grammar*. Oxford: Blackwell.

Geach, P. T. 1962: *Reference and Generality*. Ithaca, NY: Cornell.

Geiger, R. A. and B. Rudzka-Ostyn (eds) 1993: *Conceptualizations and Mental Processing in Language*. Berlin: Mouton de Gruyter.

Gentner, D. 1975: Evidence for the psychological reality of semantic components: the verbs of possession. In D. A. Norman and D. E. Rumelhart (eds) *Explorations in Cognition*. San Francisco: Freeman.

Gentner, D. 1981: Verb structures in memory for sentences: evidence for componential representation. *Cognitive Psychology* 13: 56–83.

Gentner, D. 1983: Structure-mapping: a theoretical framework for analogy. *Cognitive Science* 7: 155–70.

Gibbs, R. W. 1987: Mutual knowledge and the psychology of conversational inference. *Journal of Pragmatics* 11: 561–88.

Givón, T. 1984a: Direct object and dative shifting: semantic and pragmatic case. In Frans Plank (ed.) *Objects: Towards a Theory of Grammatical Relations*, 151–82. London: Academic Press.

Givón, T. 1984b: *Syntax: a Functional-Typological Introduction*, vol. 1. Amsterdam: John Benjamins.

Givón, T. 1990: *Syntax: a Functional-Typological Introduction*, vol. 2. Amsterdam: John Benjamins.

Givón, T. (ed.) 1983: *Topic Continuity in Discourse: a Quantitative Cross-Language Study*. Amsterdam: John Benjamins.

Givón, T. (ed.) 1994: *The Pragmatics of Voice: Inverse, Passive, Antipassive*. Amsterdam: John Benjamins.

Givón, T. and L. Yang 1994: The rise of the English GET-passive. In Barbara Fox and Paul J. Hopper (eds) *Voice: Form and Function*, 120–49. Amsterdam: John Benjamins.

Gleason, H. A. 1955: *An Introduction to Descriptive Linguistics*. New York: Holt, Rinehart & Winston.

Goddard, Cliff 2001: Lexico-semantic universals: a critical overview. *Linguistic Typology* 5.1: 1–65.

Goddard, Cliff and Anna Wierzbicka (eds) 1994: *Semantic and Lexical Universals*. Amsterdam: John Benjamins.

Goffman, Erving 1967: *Interaction Ritual: Essays in Face-to-Face Behavior*. Garden City, NY: Anchor Books.

Goffman, Erving 1971: *Relations in Public*. New York: Basic Books.

Goffman, Erving 1981: *Forms of Talk*. Philadelphia: University of Pennsylvania Press.

Goldberg, A. 1995: *Constructions: A Construction Grammar Approach to Argument Structure*. Chicago, IL: University of Chicago Press.

Goodenough, Ward 1970: *Description and Comparison in Cultural Anthropology*. Chicago, IL: Aldine.

Goodwin, C. 1979: *Conversation Organization*. New York: Academic Press.

Gordon David and George Lakoff 1975: Conversational postulates. In Peter Cole and Jerry Morgan (eds) *Syntax and Semantics*, vol. 3: *Speech Acts*, 83–106. New York: Academic Press.

Grayling, A. C. 1982: *An Introduction to Philosophical Logic*. Brighton: Harvester Press.

Green, G. 1974: *Semantic and Syntactic Regularity*. Bloomington, IL: Indiana University Press.

Greene, Judith 1986: *Language Understanding: a Cognitive Approach*. Open Guides to Psychology. Milton Keynes: Open University Press.

Grice, H. Paul 1975: Logic and conversation. In Peter Cole and Jerry Morgan (eds) *Syntax and Semantics*, vol. 3: *Speech Acts*, 43–58. New York: Academic Press.

Grice, H. Paul 1978: Further notes on logic and conversation. In Peter Cole (ed.) *Syntax and Semantics*, vol. 9: *Pragmatics*, 113–28. New York: Academic Press.

Grimshaw, Jane 1990: *Argument Structure*. Cambridge, MA: MIT Press.

Grimshaw, Jane 1994: Semantic content and semantic structure. Ms. Rutgers University, New Brunswick, New Jersey.

Groenendijk, Jeroen, and Martin Stokhof 1991: Dynamic predicate logic. *Linguistics and Philosophy* 14: 39–100.

Groenendijk, Jeroen, Martin Stokhof and Frank Veltman 1996: Coreference and modality. In Shalom Lappin (ed.) *The Handbook of Contemporary Semantic Theory*, 179–213. Oxford: Blackwell.

Gropen, Jess, Steven Pinker, Michelle Hollander and Richard Goldberg 1991: Affectedness and direct objects: the role of lexical semantics in the acquisition of verb argument structure. In Beth Levin and Steven Pinker (eds) *Lexical and Conceptual Semantics*, 153–95. Oxford: Blackwell.

Gruber, J. S. 1965: Studies in lexical relations. PhD dissertation, MIT, Cambridge, MA: Reprinted by Indiana University Linguistics Club, Bloomington, Indiana.

Gruber, J. S. 1976: *Lexical Structure in Syntax and Semantics*. Amsterdam: North-Holland.

Gu, Y. 1990: Politeness phenomena in Modern Chinese. *Journal of Pragmatics* 14: 237–57.

Gumperz, John J. and Dell Hymes (eds) 1972: *Directions in Sociolinguistics: The Ethnography of Communication*. New York: Holt, Rinehart & Winston.

Gumperz, John J. and Stephen C. Levinson (eds) 1996: *Rethinking Linguistic Relativity*. Cambridge: Cambridge University Press.

Gundel, Jeanette K., Nancy Hedberg and Ron Zacharski 1993: Cognitive status and the form of referring expressions in discourse. *Language* 69: 274–307.

Gundel, Jeanette K., Nancy Hedberg and Ron Zacharski 2000: Status cognitif et forme des anaphoriques indirects. *Verbum* 22: 79–102.

Guttenplan, S. 1986: *The Languages of Logic*. Oxford: Blackwell.

Haack, Susan 1978: *Philosophy of Logics*. Cambridge: Cambridge University Press.

Haegeman, Liliane 1994: *Introduction to Government and Binding Theory*, second edition. Oxford: Blackwell.

Haiman, John 1985: *Iconicity in Syntax*. Amsterdam: John Benjamins.

Halliday, M. A. K. 1966: Lexis as a linguistic level. In C. E. Bazell, J. C. Catford, M. A. K. Halliday and R. H. Robins (eds) *In Memory of J. R. Firth*. London: Longman.

Halliday, M. A. K. and R. Hasan 1976: *Cohesion in English*. London: Longman.

Halliday, M. A. K. 1994: *An Introduction to Functional Grammar*. London: Edward Arnold.

Hammer, A. E. 1991: *Hammer's German Grammar and Usage*, second edition revised by Martin Durrell. London: Edward Arnold.

Hancher, M. 1979: The classification of illocutionary acts. *Language in Society* 8.1: 1–14.

Hardman, Martha James 1986: Data-source marking in the Jaqi languages. In Wallace Chafe and Johanna Nichols (eds) *Evidentiality: the Linguistic Coding of Epistemology*, 113–36. Norwood, NJ: Ablex.

Harris, R. J. 1977: Comprehension of pragmatic implications in advertising. *Journal of Applied Psychology* 62: 603–8.

Hawkes, Terence 1972: *Metaphor*. London: Methuen.

Hayward, R. J. 1990: Notes on the Zayse language. In R. J. Hayward (ed.) *Omotic Linguistics*. London: School of Oriental and African Studies.

Heider, E. 1971: Focal color areas and the development of color names. *Developmental Psychology* 4: 447–55.

Heider, E. 1972a: Probabilities, sampling, and the ethnographic method: the case of Dani colour names. *Man* 7.3: 448–66.

Heider, E. 1972b: Universals in color naming and memory. *Journal of Experimental Psychology* 93.1: 10–20.

Heim, Irene 1983: On the projection problem for presupposition. In M. Barlow, D. P. Flickinger and M. T. Westcoat (eds) *Proceedings of the West Coast Conference on Formal Linguistics*, vol. 2. Stanford: Stanford Linguistics Association.

Heim, Irene 1989: *The Semantics of Definite and Indefinite NPs*. New York: Garland Press.

Heim, Irene 1990: E-type pronouns and the donkey anaphora. *Linguistics and Philosophy* 13: 137–77.

Heim, Irene 1992: Presupposition projection and the semantics of attitude verbs. *Journal of Semantics* 9: 183–221.

Heim, Irene and Angelika Kratzer 1998: *Semantics in Generative Grammar*. Oxford: Blackwell.

Heine, Bernd, Ulrike Claudi and Friederike Hünnemeyer 1991: *Grammaticalization: a Conceptual Framework*. Chicago: University of Chicago Press.

Herkovits, Annette 1986: *Language and Spatial Cognition: an Interdisciplinary Study of the Prepositions in English*. Cambridge: Cambridge University Press.

Hockett, Charles F. 1958: *A Course in Modern Linguistics*. New York: Macmillan.

Holyoak, K. and P. Thagard 1995: *Mental Leaps: Analogy in Creative Thought*. Cambridge, MA: MIT Press.

Hopper, Paul J. and Sandra A. Thompson 1980: Transitivity in grammar and discourse. *Language* 56: 251–399.

Hopper, Paul J. and Elizabeth Closs Traugott 1993: *Grammaticalization*. Cambridge: Cambridge University Press.

Horn, L. R. 1984: Towards a new taxonomy for pragmatic inference: Q- and R-based implicature. In D. Schiffrin (ed.) *Meaning, Form and Use in Context*, 11–42. Washington DC: Georgetown University Press.

Horn, L. R. 1989: *A Natural History of Negation*. Chicago: University of Chicago.

Horn, L. R. 1996: Presupposition and implicature. In Shalom Lappin (ed.) *The Handbook of Contemporary Semantic Theory*, 299–320. Oxford: Blackwell.

House, J. and G. Kasper 1981: Politeness markers in English and German. In F. Coulmas (ed.) *Conversational Routine: Explorations in Standardized Communication Situations and Prepatterned Speech*, 157–85. The Hague: Mouton.

Huddleston, Rodney 1984: *Introduction to the Grammar of English*. Cambridge: Cambridge University Press.

Hunn, Eugene S. 1977: *Tzeltal Folk Zoology: The Classification of Discontinuities in Nature*. New York: Academic Press.

Hwang, J. 1990: 'Deference' versus 'politeness' in Korean speech. *International Journal of the Sociology of Language* 82: 41–55.

Jackendoff, R. 1972: *Semantic Interpretation in Generative Grammar*. Cambridge, MA: MIT Press.

Jackendoff, R. 1975: On belief contexts. *Linguistic Inquiry* 6.1: 53–93.

Jackendoff, R. 1983: *Semantics and Cognition*. Cambridge, MA: MIT Press.

Jackendoff, R. 1987: *Consciousness and the Computational Mind*. Cambridge, MA: MIT Press.

Jackendoff, R. 1990: *Semantic Structures*. Cambridge, MA: MIT Press.

Jackendoff, R. 1992: Parts and boundaries. In Beth Levin and Steven Pinker (eds) *Lexical and Conceptual Semantics*, 9–45. Oxford: Blackwell.

Jacobsen, William H. Jr. 1986: The heterogeneity of evidentials in Makah. In Wallace Chafe and Johanna Nichols (eds) *Evidentiality: the Linguistic Coding of Epistemology*, 3–28. Norwood, NJ: Ablex.

Jaggar, Philip J. 2001: *Hausa*. London Oriental and African Language Library. Amsterdam: John Benjamins.

Jaggar, Philip J. and Malami Buba 1994: The space and time adverbials NAN/CAN in Hausa: cracking the deictic code. *Language Sciences* 16: 387–421.

Jakobson, R. 1968: *Child Language, Aphasia and Linguistic Universals*. The Hague: Mouton.

Jeffries, L. and P. Willis 1984: A return to the spray paint issue. *Journal of Pragmatics* 8: 715–29.

Jespersen, Otto 1931: *A Modern English Grammar on Historical Principles*. 4 vols. London: George Allen & Unwin.

Johnson, Mark 1987: *The Body in the Mind: The Bodily Basis of Meaning, Imagination, and Reason*. Chicago: University of Chicago Press.

Johnson, Mark 1993: *Moral Imagination: Implications of Cognitive Science for Ethics*. Chicago: University of Chicago Press.

Johnson, M. K., J. D. Bransford and S. Solomon 1973: Memory for tacit implications of sentences. *Journal of Experimental Psychology* 98: 203–5.

Johnson, Samuel 1983: *A Dictionary of the English Language*. London: Times Books. (First published 1755.)

Johnson-Laird, P. N. 1983: *Mental Models: Towards a Cognitive Science of Language, Inference, and Consciousness*. Cambridge: Cambridge University Press.

Johnson-Laird, P. N. and P. C. Wason 1977: *Thinking: Readings in Cognitive Science*. Cambridge: Cambridge University Press.

Jolley, Nicholas (ed.) 1995: *The Cambridge Companion to Leibniz*. Cambridge: Cambridge University Press.

Jones, D. 1976: *The Phoneme: its Nature and Use*, third edition. Cambridge: Cambridge University Press.

de Jong, F. 1987: The compositional nature of (in)definiteness. In E. Reuland and A. ter Meulen (eds) *The Representation of (In)definiteness*, 170–85. Cambridge, MA: MIT Press.

Judge, Ann and F. G. Healey 1985: *A Reference Grammar of Modern French*. London: Edward Arnold.

Kamp, Hans 1981: A theory of truth and semantic representation. In J. Groenendijk et al. (eds) *Formal Methods in the Study of Language*, 277–322. Amsterdam: Mathematisch Centrum.

Kamp, Hans and Uwe Reyle 1993: *From Discourse to Logic: Introduction to Modeltheoretic Semantics of Natural Language, Formal Logic and Discourse Representation Theory*. Dordrecht: Kluwer.

Kant, Immanuel 1993: *Critique of Pure Reason*. Revised and expanded translation by Vasilis Politis. London: Everyman. (First published 1781.)

Karttunen, L. 1976: Discourse referents. In J. D. McCawley (ed.) *Syntax and Semantics*, vol. 7, 363–85. New York: Academic Press.

Katz, J. J. 1972: *Semantic Theory*. New York: Harper and Row.

Katz, J. J. 1987: Common sense in semantics. In E. Lepore (ed.) *New Directions in Semantics*, 157–233. New York: Academic Press.

Katz, J. J. and J. A. Fodor 1963: The structure of a semantic theory. *Language* 39: 170–210.

Katz, J. J. and P. M. Postal 1964: *An Integrated Theory of Linguistic Descriptions*. Cambridge, MA: MIT Press.

Kay, Paul and Chad McDaniel 1978: The linguistic significance of the meanings of basic color terms. *Language* 54.3: 610–46.

Kay, Paul and Willett Kempton 1984: What is the Sapir–Whorf hypothesis? *American Anthropologist* 86.1: 65–79.

Kay, Paul, Brent Berlin, Luisa Maffi and William Merrifield 1997: Color naming across languages. In C. Hardin and L. Maffi (eds) *Color Categories in Thought and Language*. Cambridge: Cambridge University Press.

Keenan, Edward L. 1985: Passive in the world's languages. In Timothy Shopen (ed.) *Language Typology and Syntactic Description*, vol. 1, 243–81. Cambridge: Cambridge University Press.

Keenan, Edward L. 1987: A semantic definition of 'indefinite NP'. In E. Reuland and A. ter Meulen (eds) *The Representation of (In)definiteness*, 286–317. Cambridge, MA: MIT Press.

Keenan, Edward L. 1996: The semantics of determiners. In Shalom Lappin (ed.) *The Handbook of Contemporary Semantic Theory*, 41–63. Oxford: Blackwell.

Keil, Frank C. 1987: Conceptual development and category structure. In Ulric Neisser (ed.) *Concepts Reconsidered: the Ecological and Intellectual Bases of Categorization*, 175–200. Cambridge: Cambridge University Press.

Keil, Frank C. 1989: *Concepts, Kinds and Conceptual Development*. Cambridge, MA: MIT Press.

Kemmer, Suzanne 1994: Middle voice, transitivity, and the elaboration of events. In Barbara Fox and Paul J. Hopper (eds) *Voice: Form and Function*, 179–230. Amsterdam: John Benjamins.

Kempson, Ruth M. 1975: *Presupposition and the Delimitation of Semantics*. Cambridge: Cambridge University Press.

Kempson, Ruth M. 1977: *Semantic Theory*. Cambridge: Cambridge University Press.

Kempson, Ruth M. 1988a: Grammar and conversational principles. In Frederick J. Newmeyer (ed.) *Linguistics: The Cambridge Survey*, vol. 2, 139–63. Cambridge: Cambridge University Press.

Kempson, Ruth M. 1988b: Logical form: the grammar–cognition interface. *Journal of Linguistics* 24: 393–431.

Kempson, Ruth M. (ed.) 1988: *Mental Representations: the Interface between Language and Reality*. Cambridge: Cambridge University Press.

Kenny, Anthony 1995: *Frege*. London: Penguin Books.

Kess, J. F. and R. A. Hoppe 1985: Bias, individual preferences and 'shared knowledge' in ambiguity. *Journal of Pragmatics* 9: 21–39.

Kintsch, W. 1974: *The Representation of Meaning in Memory*. Hillsdale, NJ: Lawrence Erlbaum.

Kirsner, Robert S. 1976: On the subjectless 'pseudo-passive' in Dutch and the semantics of background agents. In Charles N. Li (ed.) *Subject and Topic*, 385–415. New York: Academic Press.

Kittay, E. F. 1987: *Metaphor: its Cognitive Force and Linguistic Structure*. New York: Oxford University Press.

Klaiman, M. H. 1991: *Grammatical Voice*. Cambridge: Cambridge University Press.

Kövecses, Zoltán and Günter Radden 1998: Metonymy: developing a cognitive linguistic view. *Cognitive Linguistics* 9.1: 37–77.

Krahmer, Emiel 1998: *Presupposition and Anaphora*. Stanford: Center for the Study of Language and Information.

Kripke, Saul 1971: Identity and necessity. In M. Munitiz (ed.) *Identity and Individuation*, 135–64. New York: New York University Press.

Kripke, Saul 1979: Speaker's reference and semantic reference. In P. French, T. E. Uehling Jr. and H. K. Wettstein (eds) *Contemporary Perspectives in the Philosophy of Language*, 6–27. Minneapolis: University of Minnesota Press.

Kripke, Saul 1980: *Naming and Necessity*. Oxford: Blackwell.

Kuno, Susumu 1973: *The Structure of the Japanese Language*. Cambridge, MA: MIT Press.

Kuno, Susumu 1987: *Functional Syntax: Anaphora, Discourse and Empathy*. Chicago: University of Chicago Press.

Labov, W. 1973: The boundaries of words and their meanings. In C.-J. N. Bailey and R. W. Shuy (eds) *New Ways of Analysing Variation in English*, 340–73. Washington, DC: Georgetown University Press.

Laduslaw, William A. 1979: Polarity sensitivity as inherent scope relations. Ph.D. dissertation, University of Texas at Austin.

Laduslaw, William A. 1996: Negation and polarity items. In Shalom Lappin (ed.) *The Handbook of Contemporary Semantic Theory*, 321–41. Oxford: Blackwell.

Laduslaw, William A. and David R. Dowty 1988: Toward a nongrammatical account of thematic roles. In W. Wilkins (ed.) *Syntax and Semantics*, vol. 21: *Thematic Relations*, 61–73. New York: Academic Press.

Lakoff, George 1987: *Women, Fire and Dangerous Things: What Categories Reveal about the Mind*. Chicago: University of Chicago Press.

Lakoff, George 1988: Cognitive semantics. In Umberto Eco, Marco Santambrogio and Patrizia Violi (eds) *Meaning and Mental Representations*, 119–54. Bloomington and Indianapolis: Indiana University Press.

Lakoff, George and Mark Johnson 1980: *Metaphors We Live By*. Chicago: University of Chicago Press.

Lakoff, George and Mark Turner 1989: *More than Cool Reason: a Field Guide to Poetic Metaphor*. Chicago: University of Chicago Press.

Lakoff, R. T. 1968: *Abstract Syntax and Latin Complementation*. Cambridge, MA: MIT Press.

Lakoff, R. T. 1971: Passive resistance. *CLS* 7, University of Chicago, Chicago Linguistics Society.

Langacker, Ronald W. 1987: *Foundations of Cognitive Grammar*, vol. 1. Stanford, CA: Stanford University Press.

Langacker, Ronald W. 1990: *Concept, Image and Symbol: the Cognitive Basis of Grammar*. Berlin: Mouton de Gruyter.

Langacker, Ronald W. 1991: *Foundations of Cognitive Grammar*, vol. 2: *Descriptive Applications*. Stanford, CA: Stanford University Press.

Langacker, Ronald W. 1993: Reference-point constructions. *Cognitive Linguistics* 4: 1–38.

Langacker, Ronald W. and Eugene H. Cassad 1985: 'Inside' and 'outside' in Cora grammar. *International Journal of American Linguistics* 51: 247–81. Reprinted in Ronald W. Langacker 1990: *Concept, Image and Symbol: the Cognitive Basis of Grammar*, 33–57. Berlin: Mouton de Gruyter.

Lappin, Shalom (ed.) 1996: *The Handbook of Contemporary Semantic Theory*. Oxford: Blackwell.

Lee, Penny. 1996: *The Whorf Theory Complex: A Critical Reconstruction*. Amsterdam: John Benjamins.

Leech, Geoffrey N. 1971: *Meaning and the English Verb*. London: Longman.

Leech, Geoffrey N. 1981: *Semantics*, second edition. Harmondsworth: Penguin.

Leech, Geoffrey N. 1983: *Principles of Pragmatics*. London: Longman.

Lehrer, Adrienne 1974: *Semantic Fields and Lexical Structure*. Amsterdam: North-Holland.

Lehrer, Adrienne and Eva Feder (eds) 1992: *Frames, Fields and Contrasts: New Essays in Semantic and Lexical Organization*. Hillsdale, NJ: Lawrence Erlbaum.

Leibniz, Gottfried Wilhelm 1981: *New Essays Concerning Human Understanding*. Translated and edited by Peter Remnant and Jonathan Bennett. Cambridge: Cambridge University Press. (First published 1765.)

Lepschy, Guilio C. 1982: *A Survey of Structural Linguistics*, new edition. London: André Deutsch.

Levin, Beth 1993: *English Verb Classes and Alternations*. Chicago: University of Chicago Press.

Levin, Beth and Steven Pinker (eds) 1992: *Lexical and Conceptual Semantics*. Oxford: Blackwell.

Levin, Beth and Malka Rappaport Hovav 1991: Wiping the slate clean: a lexical semantic exploration. In Beth Levin and Steven Pinker (eds) *Lexical and Conceptual Semantics*, 123–51. Oxford: Blackwell.

Levin, Beth and Malka Rappaport Hovav 1995: *Unaccusativity: At the Syntax–Lexical Semantics Interface*. Cambridge, MA: MIT Press.

Levinson, Stephen C. 1983: *Pragmatics*. Cambridge: Cambridge University Press.

Levinson, Stephen C. 1991: Pragmatic revision of the binding conditions revisited. *Journal of Linguistics* 27: 107–61.

Levinson, Stephen C. 2000: *Presumptive Meanings: The Theory of Generalized Conversational Implicature*. Cambridge, MA: MIT Press.

Lewis, David K. 1972: General semantics. In D. Davidson and G. Harman (eds) *Semantics for Natural Languages*, 169–218. Dordrecht: Reidel.

Lewis, David K. 1973: *Counterfactuals*. Oxford: Blackwell.

Lewis, David K. 1978: Truth in fiction. *American Philosophical Quarterly* 15: 37–46.

Lewis, David K. 1979: Scorekeeping in a language game. *Journal of Philosophical Logic* 8: 339–59.

Lewis, David K. 1986: *The Plurality of Worlds*. Oxford: Blackwell.

Li, Charles N. (ed.) 1976: *Subject and Topic*. New York: Academic Press.

Li, Charles N. and Sandra A. Thompson 1976: Subject and topic: a new typology of language. In C. N. Li (ed.) *Subject and Topic*, 457–89. New York: Academic Press.

Locke, John 1959: *An Essay Concerning Human Understanding*, edited by A. C. Fraser. New York: Dover. (First published 1690.)

Lounsbury, Floyd 1964: A formal account of the Crow- and Omaha-type kinship terminologies. In W. H. Goodenough (ed.) *Explorations in Cultural Anthropology*, 351–94. New York: McGraw-Hill. Reprinted in Stephen A. Tyler (ed.) 1969: *Cognitive Anthropology*, 212–45. New York: Holt, Rinehart & Winston.

Loux, Michael J. (ed.) 1979: *The Possible and the Actual: Readings in the Metaphysics of Modality*. Ithaca, NY: Cornell University Press.

Lucy, John A. 1992a: *Grammatical Categories and Cognition: A Case Study of the Linguistic Relativity Hypothesis*. Cambridge: Cambridge University Press.

Lucy, John A. 1992b: *Language Diversity and Cognitive Development: A Reformulation of the Linguistic Relativity Hypothesis*. Cambridge: Cambridge University Press.

Lucy, John A. 1997: The linguistics of 'color'. In C. Hardin and L. Maffi (eds) *Color Categories in Thought and Language*, 320–46. Cambridge: Cambridge University Press.

Lyons, John 1963: *Structural Semantics*. Oxford: Blackwell.

Lyons, John 1968: *Introduction to Theoretical Linguistics*. Cambridge: Cambridge University Press.

Lyons, John 1977: *Semantics*, 2 volumes. Cambridge: Cambridge University Press.

Lyons, John 1981: *Language, Meaning and Context*. London: Fontana.

Lyons, John (ed.) 1970: *New Horizons in Linguistics*. Harmondsworth: Penguin.

MacCormac, Earl R. 1985: *A Cognitive Theory of Metaphor*. Cambridge, MA: MIT Press.

MacKenzie, I. E. 1997: *Introduction to Linguistic Philosophy*. London: Sage.

Macnamara, John 1982: *Names for Things: A Study of Human Learning*. Cambridge, MA: MIT Press.

McCawley, James D. 1981: *Everything that Linguists have Always Wanted to Know about Logic**. Oxford: Blackwell.

McCulloch, G. 1989: *The Game of the Name*. Oxford: Clarendon Press.

McKay, Thomas J. 1989: *Modern Formal Logic*. Basingstoke: Palgrave Macmillan.

Malkiel, Y. 1959: Studies in irreversible binomials. *Lingua* 8: 113–60.

Markman, E. M. 1989: *Categorization and Naming in Children*. Cambridge, MA: MIT Press.

Martin, R. M. 1987: *The Meaning of Language*. Cambridge, MA: MIT Press.

Martinich, A. (ed.) 1985: *The Philosophy of Language*. Oxford: Oxford University Press.

Matsumoto, Y. 1988: Reexamination of the universality of face: politeness phenomena in Japanese. *Journal of Pragmatics* 12: 403–26.

Matsumoto, Y. 1989: Politeness and conversational universals: observations from Japanese. *Multilingua* 8: 207–21.

Matthews, P. H. 1974: *Morphology*. Cambridge: Cambridge University Press.

Matthews, P. H. 1993: *Grammatical Theory in the United States from Bloomfield to Chomsky*. Cambridge: Cambridge University Press.

Medin, Douglas L. and Brian H. Ross 1992: *Cognitive Psychology*. San Diego, CA: Harcourt Brace Jovanovich.

Mel'čuk, Igor and Alexander Zholkovsky 1988: The explanatory combinatorial dictionary. In Martha Walton Evens (ed.) *Relational Models of the Lexicon: Representing Knowledge in Semantic Networks*, 41–74. Cambridge: Cambridge University Press.

Mervis, Carolyn 1987: Child-basic object categories and early lexical development. In Ulric Neisser (ed.) *Concepts Reconsidered: the Ecological and Intellectual Bases of Categorization*, 201–33. Cambridge: Cambridge University Press.

Mey, Jacob L. 2001: *Pragmatics: An Introduction*, second edition. Oxford: Blackwell.

Mill, John Stuart 1961: *A System of Logic*, eighth edition. London: Longman. (First published 1867.)

Miller, George A. and Philip N. Johnson-Laird 1976: *Language and Perception*. Cambridge, MA: Harrard/Belknap.

Milsark, G. 1977: Toward an explanation of certain peculiarities of the existential construction in English. *Linguistic Analysis* 3: 1–29.

Minsky, Marvin L. 1977: Frame-system theory. In P. N. Johnson-Laird and P. C. Wason (eds) *Thinking: Readings in Cognitive Science*. Cambridge: Cambridge University Press.

Mithun, Marianne 1991: Active/agentive case marking and its motivations. *Language* 67.3: 510–46.

Mohanan, Tara and K. P. Mohanan 1999: On representations in grammatical semantics. In Tara Mohanan and Lionel Wee (eds) *Grammatical Semantics: Evidence for Structure in Meaning*, 23–75. Stanford and National University of Singapore: Center for the Study of Language and Information.

Mohanan, Tara and Lionel Wee (eds) 1999: *Grammatical Semantics: Evidence for Structure in Meaning*. Stanford and National University of Singapore: Center for the Study of Language and Information.

Montague, Richard 1969: On the nature of certain philosophical entities. *The Monist* 53: 159–94. Reprinted in Richard Montague (1974), *Formal Philosophy: Selected Papers of Richard Montague*, 119–47. New Haven, CT: Yale University Press.

Montague, Richard 1974: *Formal Philosophy: Selected Papers of Richard Montague*. Edited and with an introduction by Richmond H. Thomason. New Haven, CT: Yale University Press.

Morris, Charles 1938: *Foundations of the Theory of Signs*. International Encyclopedia of Unified Science, vol. 1, no. 2. Chicago: University of Chicago Press.

Morris, Charles 1955: *Signs, Language and Behavior*. New York: George Braziller. (First published by Prentice-Hall in 1946.)

Munitiz, M. (ed.) 1971: *Identity and Individuation*. New York: New York University Press.

Murphy, G. L. and D. L. Medin 1985: The role of theories in conceptual coherence. *Psychological Review* 92: 289–316.

Neisser, Ulric (ed.) 1987: *Concepts Reconsidered: the Ecological and Intellectual Bases of Categorization*. Cambridge: Cambridge University Press.

Nichols, Johanna 1992: *Linguistic Diversity in Space and Time*. Chicago: University of Chicago Press.

Nofsinger, R. E. 1976: Answering questions indirectly. *Human Communication Research* 2: 171–81.

Noonan, Michael 1994: A tale of two passives in Irish. In Barbara Fox and Paul J. Hopper (eds) *Voice: Form and Function*, 279–311. Amsterdam: John Benjamins.

Nunberg, G. 1978: The pragmatics of reference. Bloomington, IN: Indiana University Linguistics Club.

Nunberg, G. 1979: The non-uniqueness of semantic solutions: polysemy. *Linguistics and Philosophy* 3.2: 143–84.

Nunberg, G. 1995: Transfers of meaning. *Journal of Semantics* 12.2: 109–32.

O'Brien, Flann 1967: *At-Swim-Two-Birds*. London: Penguin Books.

O'Faolain, Sean 1972: *And Again?* London: Penguin Books.

Ogihara, Toshi 1989: Temporal reference in English and Japanese. PhD. dissertation, University of Texas at Austin. (Distributed by Indiana University Linguistics Club, 1992.)

Oh, C.-K. and D. A. Dinneen (eds) 1979: *Syntax and Semantics 11: Presupposition*. New York: Academic Press.

Ortony, Andrew (ed.) 1979: *Metaphor and Thought*. Cambridge: Cambridge University Press.

Palmer, F. R. 1981: *Semantics*, second edition. Cambridge: Cambridge University Press.

Palmer, F. R. 1986: *Mood and Modality*. Cambridge: Cambridge University Press.

Palmer, F. R. 1994: *Grammatical Roles and Relations*. Cambridge: Cambridge University Press.

Partee, Barbara H., Alice ter Meulen and Robert E. Wall 1990: *Mathematical Models in Linguistics*. Dordrecht: Kluwer.

Pearce, W. B. and F. Conklin 1979: A model of hierarchical meaning in coherent conversation and a study of 'indirect responses'. *Communication Monographs* 46: 75–87.

Perkins, Michael R. 1983: *Modal Expressions in English*. London: Frances Pinter.

Perlmutter, David M. 1978: Impersonal passives and the unaccusative hypothesis. *Berkeley Linguistics Society* 4: 157–89.

Perlmutter, David M. and Paul M. Postal 1984: Impersonal passives and some relational laws. In David M. Perlmutter and Carl G. Rosen (eds) *Studies in Relational Grammar*, vol. 2, 126–70. Chicago: University of Chicago Press.

Pinker, Steven 1989: *Learnability and Cognition: The Acquisition of Argument Structure*. Cambridge, MA: MIT Press.

Pinker, Steven 1994: *The Language Instinct*. London: Penguin Books.

Pollard, Carl and Ivan A. Sag 1987: *Information-Based Syntax and Semantics*, vol. 1: *Fundamentals*. Stanford, CA: Center for the Study of Language and Information.

Prince, E. F. 1981: Towards a taxonomy of given-new information. In P. Cole (ed.) *Radical Pragmatics*, 223–55. New York: Academic Press.

Prince, E. F. 1985: Fancy syntax and 'shared knowledge'. *Journal of Pragmatics* 9: 65–81.

Prince, E. F. 1992: The ZPG letter: subjects, definiteness, and information-status. In W. C. Mann and S. A. Thompson (eds) *Discourse Description: Diverse Linguistic Analyses of a Fund-Raising Text*. Amsterdam: John Benjamins.

Pulman, S. G. 1983: *Word Meaning and Belief*. London: Croom Helm.

Pustejovsky, James 1992: The syntax of event structure. In Beth Levin and Steven Pinker (eds) *Lexical and Conceptual Semantics*, 47–81. Oxford: Blackwell.

Pustejovsky, James 1995: *The Generative Lexicon*. Cambridge, MA: MIT Press.

Pustejovsky, James (ed.) 1993: *Semantics and the Lexicon*. Dordrecht: Kluwer.

Pustejovsky, James and Branimir Boguraev (eds) 1996: *Lexical Semantics: the Problem of Polysemy*. Oxford: Clarendon Press.

Putnam, Hilary 1962: It ain't necessarily so. *Journal of Philosophy* 59, 22: 658–71.

Putnam, Hilary 1975: The meaning of *meaning*. In K. Gunderson (ed.) *Language, Mind and Knowledge*, 131–93. Minneapolis: University of Minnesota Press.

Quine, W. V. 1953: *From a Logical Point of View*. Cambridge, MA: Harvard University Press.

Quine, W. V. 1960: *Word and Object*. Cambridge, MA: MIT Press.

Quine, W. V. 1976: *The Ways of Paradox and Other Essays*. Cambridge, MA: Harvard University Press.

Quine, W. V. 1980: *Elementary Logic*, revised edition. Cambridge, MA: MIT Press.

Quirk, Randolph, Sidney Greenbaum, Geoffrey Leech and Jan Svartvik 1985: *A Comprehensive Grammar of the English Language*. London: Longman.

Radford, A. 1988: *Transformational Grammar*. Cambridge: Cambridge University Press.

Rand, Sharon R. 1993: *The French Imparfait and Passé Simple in Discourse*. Arlington, TX: Summer Institute of Linguistics and the University of Texas at Arlington.

Rappaport, Malka and Beth Levin 1985: A case study in lexical analysis: the locative alternation. Unpublished manuscript: MIT Center for Cognitive Science.

Rappaport, Malka and Beth Levin 1988: What to do with theta-roles. In W. Wilkins (ed.) *Syntax and Semantics*, vol. 21: *Thematic Relations*, 7–36. New York: Academic Press.

Rauh, G. (ed.) 1983: *Essays on Deixis*. Tubingen: Narr.

Ravin, Y. and C. Leacock (eds) 2000: *Polysemy: Theoretical and Computational Approaches*. Oxford: Oxford University Press.

Reinhart, Tanya 1986: On the interpretation of 'donkey' sentences. In E. C. Traugott et al. (eds) *On Conditionals*, 103–22. Cambridge: Cambridge University Press.

Richards, I. A. 1936: *The Philosophy of Rhetoric*. London: Oxford University Press.

Robins, R. H. 1990: *A Short History of Linguistics*, third edition. London: Longman.

Roca, I. M. (ed.) 1992: *Thematic Structure: Its Role in Grammar*. Berlin: Mouton de Gruyter.

Rosch, Eleanor 1973a: On the internal structure of perceptual and semantic categories. In Timothy Moore (ed.) *Cognitive Development and the Acquisition of Language*, 111–44. New York: Academic Press.

Rosch, Eleanor 1973b: Natural categories. *Cognitive Psychology* 4, 328–50.

Rosch, Eleanor 1975: Cognitive reference points. *Cognitive Psychology* 7, 532–47.

Rosch, Eleanor 1977: Linguistic relativity. In P. N. Johnson-Laird and P. C. Wason (eds) *Thinking: Readings in Cognitive Science*, 501–22. Cambridge: Cambridge University Press.

Rosch, Eleanor and Carolyn Mervis 1975: Family resemblances: studies in the internal structure of categories. *Cognitive Psychology* 7, 573–605.

Rosch, Eleanor, Carolyn Mervis, Wayne Gray, David Johnson and Penny Boyes-Braem 1976: Basic objects in natural categories. *Cognitive Psychology* 8: 382–439.

Rudzka-Ostyn, B. 1993: Introduction. In R. A. Geiger and B. Rudzka-Ostyn (eds) *Conceptualizations and Mental Processing in Language*, 1–20. Berlin: Mouton de Gruyter.

Russell, Bertrand 1905: On denoting. *Mind* 14: 479–93.

Russell, Bertrand 1967: *The Problems of Philosophy*. London: Oxford Paperbacks. (First published 1917.)

Sadock, Jerrold M. 1974: *Towards a Linguistic Theory of Speech Acts*. New York: Academic Press.

Sadock, Jerrold M. 1978: On testing for conversational implicature. In Peter Cole (ed.) *Syntax and Semantics*, vol. 9: *Pragmatics*, 281–97. New York: Academic Press.

Sadock, Jerrold M. and Arnold M. Zwicky 1985: Speech act distinctions in syntax. In Timothy Shopen (ed.) *Language Typology and Syntactic Description*, vol. 1, 155–96. Cambridge: Cambridge University Press.

Saeed, John Ibrahim 1984: *The Syntax of Focus and Topic in Somali.* Hamburg: Helmut Buske.

Saeed, John Ibrahim 1993: *Somali Reference Grammar,* second edition. Kensington, MD: Dunwoody Press.

Saeed, John Ibrahim 1995: The semantics of middle voice in Somali. *African Languages and Cultures* 8.1: 61–85.

Saeed, John Ibrahim 1999: *Somali.* London Oriental and African Language Library. Amsterdam: John Benjamins.

Saeed, John Ibrahim 2000: The functions of focus in Somali. *Lingua Posnaniensis* XLII: 133–43.

Sag, Ivan A. and Thomas Wasow 1999: *Syntactic Theory: A Formal Introduction.* Stanford, CA: Center for the Study of Language and Information.

Sahlins, M. 1976: Colors and cultures. *Semiotica* 16: 1–22.

Samet, Jerry and Owen Flanagan 1989: Innate representations. In Stuart Silvers (ed.) *Representation: Readings in the Philosophy of Mental Representation,* 189–210. Dordrecht: Kluwer.

Sapir, Edward 1949a: *Language: an Introduction to the Study of Speech.* New York: Harcourt Brace. (First published 1921.)

Sapir, Edward 1949b: *Selected Writings in Language, Culture and Personality.* Edited by D. G. Mandelbaum. Berkeley, CA: University of California Press.

Sapir, Edward 1956: *Culture, Language and Society: Selected Essays.* Edited by D. G. Mandelbaum. Berkeley, CA: University of California Press.

de Saussure, Ferdinand 1974: *Course in General Linguistics.* Edited by Charles Bally and Albert Sechehaye, translation by Wade Baskin. Glasgow: Fontana/Collins. (First published 1915 as *Cours de Linguistique Générale.* Paris: Pyot.)

Saville-Troike, Muriel 1989: *The Ethnography of Communication: an Introduction,* second edition. Oxford: Blackwell.

Schank, R. C. and R. P. Abelson 1977: *Scripts, Plans, Goals and Understanding.* Hillsdale, NJ: Lawrence Erlbaum.

Schank, Roger and Alex Kass 1988: Knowledge representation in people and machines. In Umberto Eco, Marco Santambrogio and Patrizia Violi (eds) *Meaning and Mental Representations,* 181–200. Bloomington and Indianapolis: Indiana University Press.

Schegloff, Emanuel A. 1972: Sequencing in conversational openings. In J. Gumpertz and D. Hymes (eds) *Directions in Sociolinguistics,* 346–80. New York: Holt, Rinehart & Winston.

Schegloff, Emanuel A. 1979: The relevance of repair to syntax-for-conversation. In T. Givón (ed.) *Syntax and Semantics, 12: Discourse and Syntax,* 261–88. New York: Academic Press.

Schegloff, Emanuel A. and Harvey Sacks 1973: Opening up closings. *Semiotica* 7: 289–327.

Schiffer, S. 1972 *Meaning.* Oxford: Oxford University Press.

Schiffrin, Deborah 1981: Tense variations in narration. *Language* 57: 45–62.

Schiffrin, Deborah 1994: *Approaches to Discourse.* Oxford: Blackwell.

Schwartz, Stephen 1979: Natural kind terms. *Cognition* 7: 301–15.

Schwartz, Stephen 1980: Natural kinds and nominal kinds. *Mind* 89: 182–95.

Schwarz, David 1979: *Naming and Referring.* Berlin: Mouton de Gruyter.

Searle, J. R. 1958: Proper names. *Mind* 67: 166–73.

Searle, J. R. 1969: *Speech Acts.* Cambridge: Cambridge University Press.

Searle, J. R. 1975: Indirect speech acts. In Peter Cole and Jerry Morgan (eds) *Syntax and Semantics,* vol. 3: *Speech Acts,* 59–82. New York: Academic Press.

Searle, J. R. 1976: The classification of illocutionary acts. *Language in Society* 5: 1–23. Reprinted in J. R. Searle, *Expression and Meaning: Studies in the Theory of Speech Acts*, 1979. Cambridge: Cambridge University Press, 1–29.

Searle, J. R. 1979: Metaphor. In Andrew Ortony (ed.) *Metaphor and Thought*, 92–123. Cambridge: Cambridge University Press.

Sebeok, Thomas A. 1994: *An Introduction to Semiotics*. London: Pinter.

Seuren, Peter A. M. 1994: Donkey sentences. In R. Asher (ed.) *Encyclopedia of Language and Linguistics*, vol. 2, 1059–60. Oxford: Pergamon Press.

Shopen, Timothy (ed.) 1985: *Language Typology and Syntactic Description*, 3 vols. Cambridge: Cambridge University Press.

Sifianou, Maria 1992: *Politeness Phenomena in England and Greece: a Cross-Cultural Perspective*. Oxford: Clarendon Press.

Silvers, Stuart (ed.) 1989: *Representation: Readings in the Philosophy of Mental Representation*. Dordrecht: Kluwer.

Smith, Carlotta S. 1991: *The Parameter of Aspect*. Dordrecht: Kluwer.

Smith, Edward E. and Douglas L. Medin 1981: *Categories and Concepts*. Cambridge, MA: Harvard University Press.

Smith, N. V. and D. Wilson 1979: *Modern Linguistics*. Harmondsworth: Penguin.

Smith, N. V. (ed.) 1982: *Mutual Knowledge*. London: Academic Press.

Spencer, Andrew 1991: *Morphological Theory*. Oxford: Blackwell.

Sperber, D. and D. Wilson 1995: *Relevance: Communication and Cognition*, second edition. Oxford: Blackwell.

Stalnaker, R. 1968: A theory of conditionals. In N. Rescher (ed.) *Studies in Logical Theory*. Oxford: Blackwell.

Stalnaker, R. 1974: Pragmatic presuppositions. In M. Munitz and P. Unger (eds) *Semantics and Philosophy*, 197–213. New York: New York University Press.

Stalnaker, R. 1984: *Inquiry*. Cambridge, MA: MIT Press.

Stillings, N. A., S. E. Weisler, C. H. Chase, M. H. Feinstein, J. L. Garfield and E. L. Rissland 1995: *Cognitive Science: an Introduction*. Cambridge, MA: MIT Press.

Stockwell, R. P., P. Schachter and B. H. Partee 1973: *The Major Syntactic Structures of English*. New York: Holt, Rinehart & Winston.

Strawson, P. F. 1950: On referring. *Mind* 59: 320–44.

Svensén, Bo 1993: *Practical Lexicography*. Oxford: Oxford University Press.

Swadesh, Morris 1972: What is glottochronology? In Morris Swadesh, *The Origin and Diversification of Languages*, 271–84, edited by Joel Sherzer. London: Routledge and Kegan Paul. (Article originally published in 1960.)

de Swart, Henriëtte 1998: *Introduction to Natural Language Semantics*. Stanford, CA: Center for the Study of Language and Information.

Sweetser, Eve E. 1990: *From Etymology to Pragmatics*. Cambridge: Cambridge University Press.

Talmy, Leonard 1975: Semantics and syntax of motion. In J. P. Kimball (ed.) *Syntax and Semantics*, vol. 4, 181–238. London: Academic Press.

Talmy, Leonard 1983: How language structures space. In Herbert Pick and Linda Acredolo (eds), *Spatial Orientation: Theory, Research, and Application*, 225–82. New York: Plenum Press.

Talmy, Leonard 1985: Lexicalization patterns: semantic structure in lexical forms. In Timothy Shopen (ed.) *Language Typology and Syntactic Description*, vol. 3: 57–149. Cambridge: Cambridge University Press.

Talmy, Leonard 1988: Force dynamics in language and cognition. *Cognitive Science* 12: 49–100.

Talmy, Leonard 2000: *Toward a Cognitive Semantics*. Two volumes. Cambridge, MA: MIT Press.

Tanaka, J. W. and M. Taylor 1991: Object categories and expertise: is the basic level in the eye of the beholder? *Cognitive Psychology* 23: 457–82.

Tannen, D. 1984: *Conversational Style: Analyzing Talk Among Friends*. Norwood, NJ: Ablex.

Tannen, D. 1986: *That's Not What I Meant: How Conversational Style Makes or Breaks Your Relations with Others*. New York: W. Morrow.

Tannen, D. 1990: *You Just Don't Understand: Men and Women in Conversation*. New York: W. Morrow.

Tarski, Alfred 1944: The semantic conception of truth. *Philosophy and Phenomenological Research* 4: 341–75. Reprinted in A. Martinich (ed.) 1985: *The Philosophy of Language*. Oxford: Oxford University Press.

Tarski, Alfred 1956: *Logic, Semantics, Metamathematics, Papers from 1923 to 1938*. Translated by J. H. Woodger. Oxford: Oxford University Press.

Taylor, John R. 1989: *Linguistic Categorization: Prototypes in Linguistic Theory*. Oxford: Oxford University Press.

Tenny, Carol and James Pustejovsky (eds) 2000: *Events as Grammatical Objects: The Converging Perspectives of Lexical Semantics and Syntax*. Stanford, CA: Centre for the Study of Language and Information.

Thomas, J. 1983: Cross-cultural pragmatic failure. *Applied Linguistics* 4: 91–112.

Tiee, Henry Hung-Yeh 1986: *A Reference Grammar of Chinese with Exercises*. Tucson: University of Arizona Press.

Trask, R. L. 1996: *Historical Linguistics*. London: Arnold.

Treffry, Diane (ed.) 2000: *Collins English Dictionary*, fifth edition. London and Glasgow: HarperCollins Publishers.

Turner, Mark 1987: *Death is the Mother of Beauty: Mind, Metaphor, Criticism*. Chicago: University of Chicago Press.

Tyler, Stephen A. (ed.) 1969: *Cognitive Anthropology*. New York: Holt, Rinehart & Winston.

Unger, Peter 1983: The causal theory of reference. *Philosophical Studies* 43: 1–45.

Ungerer, Friedrich and Hans-Jörg Schmid 1996: *An Introduction to Cognitive Linguistics*. London: Longman.

Vallduví, Enric and Elisabet Engdahl 1996: The linguistic realization of information packaging. *Linguistics* 34: 459–519.

Vandeloise, Claude 1991: *Spatial Prepositions: a Case Study from French*. Chicago: University of Chicago Press.

Vanderveken, Daniel 1990: *Meaning and Speech Acts*, 2 vols. Cambridge: Cambridge University Press.

Van Valin, Robert D. and Randy J. LaPolla 1997: *Syntax: Structure, Meaning and Function*. Cambridge: Cambridge University Press.

Vendler, Z. 1957: Verbs and times. *The Philosophical Review* 66: 143–60.

Vendler, Z. 1967: *Linguistics in Philosophy*. Ithaca, NY: Cornell University Press.

Verkuyl, H. J. 1993: *A Theory of Aspectuality: the Interaction betweeen Temporal and Atemporal Structure*. Cambridge: Cambridge University Press.

Vlach, Frank 1981: The semantics of the progressive. In P. Tedeschi and A. Zaenen (eds) *Tense and Aspect. Syntax and Semantics*, vol. 14: 271–92. New York: Academic Press.

van Voorst, Jan 1988: *Event Semantics*. Amsterdam: John Benjamins.

Weiner, E. Judith and William Labov 1983: Constraints on the agentless passive. *Journal of Linguistics* 19: 29–58.

Whitney, W. D. 1867: *Language and the Study of Language*. London and New York: Charles Scribner & Sons. Extracted in M. Silverstein (ed.) 1971: *Whitney on Language*, 7–110. Cambridge, MA: MIT Press.

Whorf, Benjamin Lee 1956: *Language, Thought, and Reality: Selected Writings of Benjamin Lee Whorf*. Edited by John B. Carroll. Cambridge, MA: MIT Press.

Wierzbicka, Anna 1980: *Lingua Mentalis: the Semantics of Natural Language*. New York: Academic Press.

Wierzbicka, Anna 1985: Different cultures, different languages, different speech acts: Polish vs. English. *Journal of Pragmatics* 9: 145–78.

Wierzbicka, Anna 1990: The meaning of color terms: semantics, culture and cognition. *Cognitive Linguistics* 1: 99–150.

Wierzbicka, Anna 1992: *Semantics, Culture, and Cognition: Universal Concepts in Culture-Specific Configurations*. Oxford: Oxford University Press.

Wierzbicka, Anna 1996: *Semantics: Primes and Universals*. Oxford: Oxford University Press.

Wilkins, W. (ed.) 1988: *Syntax and Semantics*, vol. 21: *Thematic Relations*. New York: Academic Press.

Williams, Edwin 1981: Argument structure and morphology. *The Linguistic Review* 1.1: 81–114.

Williams, Edwin 1994: *Thematic Structure in Syntax*. Cambridge, MA: MIT Press.

Wilson, D. 1975: *Presupposition and Non-Truth Conditional Semantics*. New York: Academic Press.

Wilson, D. and D. Sperber 1979: Ordered entailments: an alternative to presuppositional theories. In C.-K. Oh and D. A. Dinneen (eds) *Syntax and Semantics 11, Presupposition*, 299–323. New York: Academic Press.

Wilson, N. L. 1967: Linguistic butter and philosophical parsnips. *The Journal of Philosophy* 64: 55–67.

van der Wouden, A. 1997: *Negative Contexts: Collocation, Polarity and Multiple Negation*. London: Routledge.

Wunderlich, Dieter 1997: Cause and the structure of verbs. *Linguistic Inquiry* 28: 27–68.

Zwicky, A. 1971: In a manner of speaking. *Linguistic Inquiry* 2: 223–33.

Index